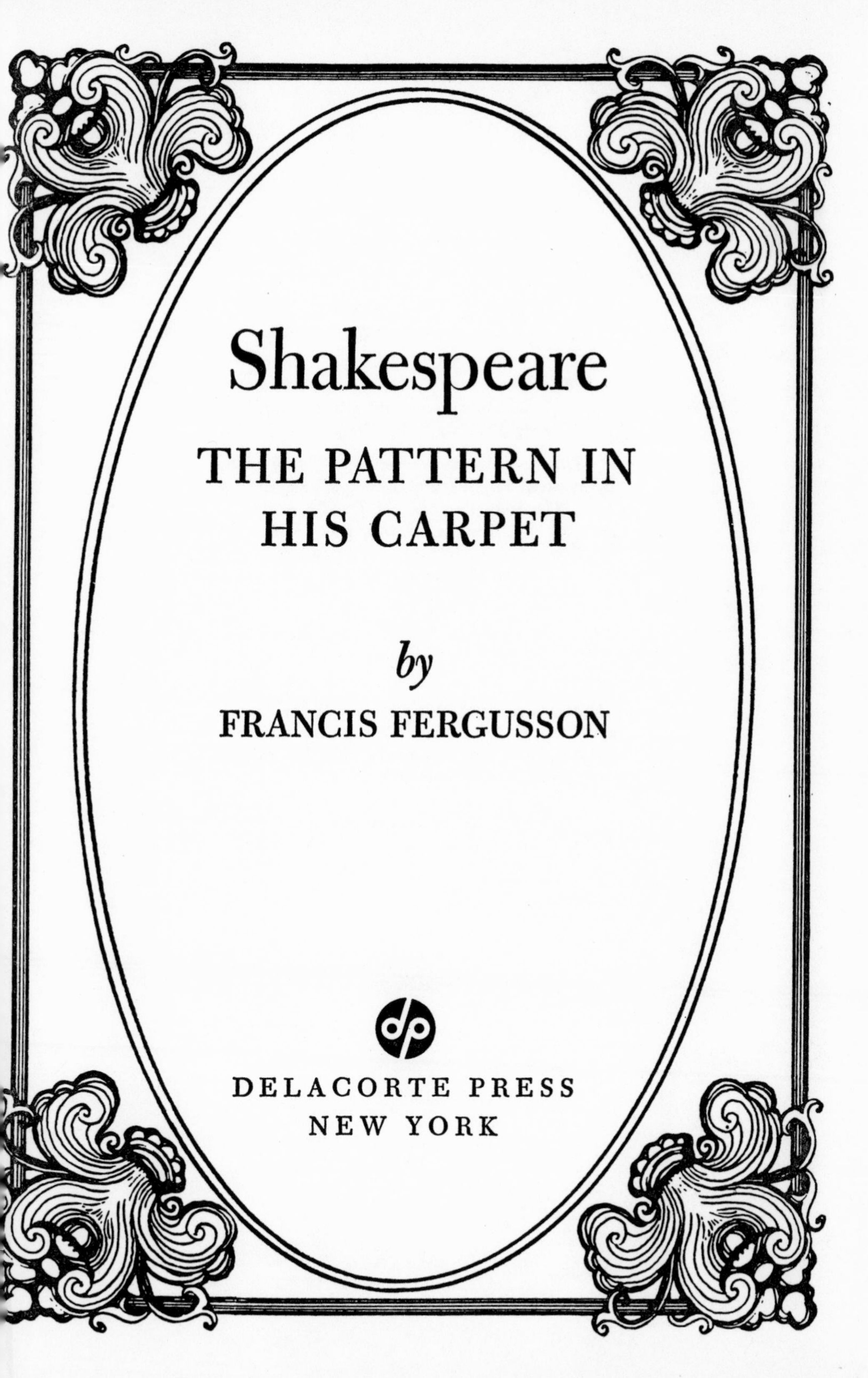

Shakespeare

THE PATTERN IN HIS CARPET

by

FRANCIS FERGUSSON

DELACORTE PRESS
NEW YORK

Printed in the United States of America
Library of Congress Catalog Card Number: 71-102803
First printing

Contents

PART FOUR: 1608–1616

Preface

This book contains all of the essays that were written in the course of about eleven years to introduce the plays in the Laurel Shakespeare series. They are reprinted here with only minor changes, but I have arranged them chronologically according to the four main parts of Shakespeare's career. I have also added five general essays, one on my aims and methods ("On Reading Shakespeare") and four others on Shakespeare's recurrent themes as they appear, in various ways, in the four stages of his development. The book is thus a reading of Shakespeare's whole theater; but it is not a paraphrase, or any sort of substitute for direct familiarity with the plays themselves. I hope it may lead to fresh readings of Shakespeare's own inexhaustible work.

I wish to offer my special thanks to my collaborators in the Laurel series, beginning with the late Charles Jasper Sisson, the textual editor and scholarly adviser for the whole series. Each of the following connoisseurs of Shakespeare generously contributed a commentary to one of the volumes in the series: W. H. Auden, C. L. Barber, Eric Berry, the late R. P. Blackmur, E. Martin Browne, J. A. Bryant, Jr., Kenneth Burke, Morris Carnovsky, Robert H. Chapman, Eame Church, J. V. Cunningham, Alan S. Downer, the late Elizabeth Drew, Maurice Evans, Dudley Fitts, Sir Tyrone Guthrie, John Houseman, Dorothy Jeakins, Lincoln Kirstein, Philip Lawrence, R. W. B. Lewis, Frederic McConnell, Howard Nemerov, Joseph Papp, Sir Ralph Richardson, Flora Robson, Jean Rosenthal, James Sandoe, Douglas Seale, Charles H. Shattuck, Monroe K. Spears, D. A. Traversi, Virgil Thompson, the late William Troy, Stuart Vaughan, and Dame Margaret Webster. I have often tacitly learned from them.

It was Mr. Frank Taylor who first planned the Laurel Shakespeare, and Mr. Richard Fisher, and then Mr. Ross Claiborne, who as editors-in-chief brought the series to completion. I am most grateful to them for their ideas and their warm and unfailing support.

F. F.

Kingston
June, 1968

Shakespeare

THE PATTERN IN HIS CARPET

PRELIMINARY CONSIDERATIONS

On Reading Shakespeare

> We do not understand Shakespeare from a single reading, and certainly not from a single play. There is a relation between the various plays of Shakespeare, taken in order; and it is a work of years to venture even one individual interpretation of the pattern in Shakespeare's carpet.
>
> T. S. ELIOT (from *Dante,* 1929)

The aim of this "reading" of Shakespeare is to seek out his poetic intention in each play, and then (mulling over the whole sequence from *The Comedy of Errors* through *The Tempest*) to bring out the recurrent themes which indicate basic elements in his vision of human life. Needless to say, such a reading cannot be either final or complete. But I hope it may serve as a prolegomenon, and an invitation to other readers to continue the perennial exploration.

In working through the plays one after the other I assumed that Shakespeare did have a very conscious intention in making each one. Fifty or sixty years ago that assumption might have been questioned, for the old notion of Shakespeare as the "untutored genius" had not yet been thoroughly discredited; but now most serious readers assume that he knew just what he was doing. It is the safest assumption: necessary if one is to learn from his craft as poet of the theater instead of judging it in advance, and necessary also if one is to avoid such suggestive but a priori and partial labels as "existentialist," "mannerist" and the like. In short, one should, I think, read Shakespeare as a master; one, moreover, who is capable of rewarding our attention in new ways.

In spite of this quality, it was never his own intention to be original: "I tell you what mine authors say," as old Gower, the Chorus of *Pericles, Prince of Tyre,* puts it. All but two of Shakespeare's plays (*Love's Labour's Lost* and *The Tempest*) are based on more or less familiar narratives from the vast Renaissance heritage of legend, fiction, history, and folktale. Moreover, in reworking his sources for the theater he always understood them in the light of his own ancient classical and Biblical tradition. One might say of him, as Ezra Pound (in *The Spirit of Romance*) said of Dante, that he was *diablement dans les idées reçues,* "devilishly conventional." The quality of freshness and vitality that subsequent generations have always felt in his plays is the by-product of his zeal for truth and his sophisticated respect for the wisdom of the race.

Hamlet's famous charge to the Players very briefly indicates what Shakespeare's own purpose must have been in preparing his old stories for the stage:

> to hold as 'twere the mirror up to nature; to show virtue her own feature, scorn her own image, and the very age and body of the time his form and pressure.
>
> (Act III, scene 2)

His primary aim was to make theater poetry as that art has been practiced (with varying success) since the Greeks. When Hamlet says the purpose of their art is to hold the mirror up to nature he endorses Aristotle's indispensable definition of drama as "the imitation of an action." In each play one may learn to see the one underlying action, or "motive," which Shakespeare imitates by means of his plot-making, his character-drawing, and his wonderfully flexible language. The more one studies the play in this way, the better one understands its careful art, and the more immediately living it appears, for Shakespeare sensed human motive with uncanny accuracy. In the readings of the plays, however, I have refrained from detailed technical analysis of this kind, partly because I have had so much to say on this matter in other places, partly because I wanted to leave room to consider the customs, symbols, and implicit beliefs that Shakespeare mirrors, for without taking account of them one can hardly understand the action itself. One cannot, for example, understand the motivation of the history plays without some knowledge of what the sacred crown meant in Shakespeare's time.

Shakespeare's first concern was usually to make his stories credible: "Think ye see/ The very persons of our noble story/ As they were living," we are told in the Prologue to *Henry VIII*. He greatly improved the verisimilitude of his sources, for, as he re-imagined his old stories, he fed them from his own observation and experience. But his realism is not that of the "fourth wall," like the photographic style of the nineteenth-century theater: it is the religious realism which has been explained to us by Erich Auerbach and other students of the Middle Ages. That "realism" is based ultimately on the faith that God Himself speaks through the visible world and all that occurs there. The poet's task, therefore, is first of all to reflect God's world with pious accuracy, and then to interpret correctly the meaning—God's truth—which it embodies. Whatever Shakespeare's formal belief may have been, he inherited from the Middle Ages this conception of poetry, and the medieval habits of allegorical interpretation that go with it. When Hamlet tells the players that they must show "virtue her own feature, scorn her own image," he refers to the moral meaning of the action they are mirroring, the "trope" as it was traditionally called. When he adds, "the very age and body of the time his form and pressure," he refers to the religious meaning, the so-called *allegoria:* "what you must believe" —in this case the medieval faith, culminating in the Creed, that "the time" does have a form and meaning because God speaks through the events of history. Everyone remembers how important that was for Hamlet himself, who believed that Claudius had thrown the times out of joint, and that he was born to set them right by bringing out their true, if hellish, meaning.

In dramatizing his old stories Shakespeare took full responsibility for embodying their true moral and religious meanings. In *The Merchant of Venice, Measure for Measure,* and *The Tempest,* that is obvious, because Portia, the Duke of Vienna, and Prospero have explicit didactic aims, and demonstrate the traditional meanings of conduct in several ways. But Shakespeare more or less tacitly places each of his stories, infinitely various as they are, by means of these two coordinates, reasoned ethics and faith, and one must be aware of that, if one is to understand his intention. For him, however, "meaning" was not a matter of abstract doctrine.

Eliot once wrote that Dante had a philosophy while Shakespeare did not. It would be more accurate to say that both had a *vision* of man and his destiny rather than an abstract philosophy—and a vision, moreover, formed in each case by the central classical-Biblical tradition. When they looked at the sky they saw the same Ptolemaic order in the stars, combined with the same mythic figures of ancient lineage, the setting that Shakespeare's symbolic stage represented. When they looked at man trying to find his way between earth and heaven—as they saw him in the flesh or read about him in history and legend—they deciphered the meanings of his strange doings by placing them in the timeless context of Greek ethics, and also by analogy with the timeless *and* historic drama of Redemption as summarized in the Christian Creed, which gave everything men did its significant place in history. That, of course, was the accepted "world-picture" as Tillyard rightly called it, available to any poet of the time. But as far as I know, only Dante, the lean, visionary prophet of the Renaissance, and Shakespeare, its enormously wealthy heir, were able to use it in all its harmonious complexity to mirror earthly life. Perhaps that is what Eliot meant when he said that Shakespeare and Dante "share the modern world between them; there is no third."

The analogies between the two masters become still clearer (and still more useful) as one proceeds from Shakespeare's individual plays toward a "reading" of the whole sequence. Everyone knows that Shakespeare's theater is the most varied or "myriad-minded" in existence. He was able to move with speed and apparent ease from history to fairy tale, from contemporary fiction to ancient parable, always sensing the action, whether foolish or evil or merely dreamy, with full sympathy, and instantly adjusting his style and attitude so as to present the story just seriously (or just lightly) enough. Such imaginative wealth seems trackless; but one gradually sees that certain themes recur through most of Shakespeare's career: that of the monarch as earthly "figure" of God; that of romantic love with its magical potentialities both deathly and life-giving; that of lethal treachery and its counterpart, fidelity. And if one happens to be reading Dante concurrently one sees that these are Dante's basic themes also, in that part of the *Commedia* (between the bottom of hell and the visionary garden of Eden) where he presents man's earthly life precariously guided (as it must be on earth) by reason and faith. These themes come, in both Dante and Shakespeare, from the common, underlying vision of human nature and its destiny. If Shakespeare could turn so easily from one theme to another, from one imagined world of experience to an entirely different one, it is because for him they all had a kind of objective existence within the capacious "world-picture." He did not so much invent them as perceive them freshly, moving from one to another as though from room to room in some vast old house. That is why the first two *cantiche* of the *Commedia* provide the best clue to a reading of Shakespeare's theater as a whole: "Our knowledge of Dante and Shakespeare interacts," as Ezra Pound wrote in 1910.

I find no evidence that Shakespeare ever rejected, or even altered, this great underlying vision of man's life on earth, but of course he did not realize it fully until experience and thought had ripened it for him. And in the course of his career different aspects of it preoccupied him: in his youth, its promises of felicity; in the middle of the journey, its dark and terrifying depths; near the end of his career, its ancient signs of the natural sequence from cradle to grave. Hence the arrangement of this book. The plays are grouped chronologically, according to the four main parts of Shakespeare's career, and within each part according to the recurrent themes that indicate his constant, but deepening vision.

The Chronology of Shakespeare's Career

We know far too little about Shakespeare's life to trace his development as man and poet with certainty, or in satisfying detail. But the few undisputed facts we do have, together with the order in which he wrote his plays (now fairly well established by the patient labors of generations of scholars), suffice to reveal at least the main phases of his career, and that is the chronological scheme followed in this book. I summarize it here, before proceeding to the plays themselves, which are, and must remain, the chief source of our understanding of Shakespeare.

William Shakespeare was christened in Stratford on April twenty-sixth, 1564. The exact date of his birth is unknown, but it is traditionally celebrated on the twenty-third, because that is Saint George's Day, and Saint George is England's patron saint.

The Shakespeares were a prosperous and locally prominent family. William was the oldest of six children. His father, John Shakespeare, the son of a tenant farmer, had moved to Stratford as a young man, and there built for himself a successful business career as a glover and a dealer in wool, timber, and other commodities. John also held office as justice of the peace and high bailiff (mayor); and late in life he was granted a coat of arms, which made him a "gentleman." Shakespeare's mother, Mary Arden, a member of a family of small landowners, must have brought her husband both social standing and land.

Stratford, about a hundred miles northwest of London, was a prosperous market town, one of the largest in Warwickshire. A great deal is known about Stratford, which enables us to understand something of Shakespeare's boyhood there. The town supported a grammar school which was free to the sons of burgesses, of whom Shakespeare was one. Grammar schools were designed to prepare their students for one of the universities, and in Stratford the masters were university graduates. The education they gave was narrow but thorough. It included some history and religious instruction, but was based chiefly on Latin and the arts of language: grammar, logic, rhetoric, and what we call "public speaking." Shakespeare read a number of Latin authors, including Ovid and probably Plautus, whose comedies he imitated when he started to write for the stage. The children went to school on weekdays, summer and winter, from seven in the morning until five in the afternoon, with two hours off for dinner. Shakespeare must have started this strict routine as soon as he knew his catechism.

During his boyhood Stratford was regularly visited by touring players, including the best companies in England. The plays they brought were moralizing works on Biblical or classical themes, very wooden compared with what Shakespeare himself would write. But his future profession was highly esteemed; the players were received in the guildhall by leading citizens, including no doubt Shakespeare's father. For the rest, we may safely imagine Shakespeare as engaged in the usual activities of a boy in a country town, acquiring the intimate knowledge of the countryside and its rural types which is reflected in his plays.

We do not know what Shakespeare did between the time he left school and his departure for London. Some of the stories about him—that he was for a time a country schoolmaster, that he got into trouble for poaching deer—are possible, but unproved. We do know that he married Ann Hathaway, daughter of a yeoman farmer, in 1582, when he was eighteen and she was twenty-three. Their first child, Susan, was baptized six months later. Perhaps the Shakespeares were "betrothed"—which, by the custom of the time, would have made them legally married—some months before the recorded church ceremony. They had two more children—the twins, Hamnet and Judith—who were christened in 1585. Shakespeare departed for London very soon after that. He did not take his family with him, for he occupied bachelor's lodgings in London for most of the rest of his life. But he was also a householder in Stratford, and apparently continued to think of himself as a resident.

London, when Shakespeare went there as a young man, in about 1586, was enjoying the great years of Queen Elizabeth's reign. She had ascended the throne in 1558; in 1588 her navy had its famous victory over the Spanish Armada, which marked England's emergence as a great sea-power and symbolized the national rebirth. The city of London had its ancient mercantile traditions, its bourgeois freedoms, and, among the city officials, a certain puritanical spirit of its own. But the city had spread far beyond the medieval walls, and Renaissance London contained between 100,000 and 200,000 inhabitants. As the seat of Elizabeth's court it was the unrivaled center of English politics and culture. It was a university town, for the Inns of Court, resident law-schools for young gentlemen of wealth, were there; and it was full of foreigners from the continent of Europe. As a great port it was in touch with the Indies, the Mediterranean, and the Americas. Shakespeare never went to a university, but London was admirably fitted to complete his education in Italian and French, in history and literature, in the great professions, and to give him direct experience of the ways of men at an exciting moment in history. The theater was near the center of life in Renaissance London, and Shakespeare must have been close to many of the great figures and great events of his time.

Much is known about London and about the theaters where Shakespeare worked, but little is known directly about his own doings. Contemporary comments on him, and on his plays, suggest that most of his great vitality went straight into his work for the theater. Legal and business documents, church records, and the like enable the experts to fix a few important dates in his personal and professional life. And the dates of his plays, though disputed in detail, are well enough established to give us the approximate sequence. It is convenient (following Professor Peter Alexander and others) to distinguish four main periods in Shakespeare's career:

i. Apprenticeship to the London Theater: From Shakespeare's arrival in London (circa 1586) until he joined the Lord Chamberlain's Men, in 1594.

Shakespeare entered the theater as an actor when he first went to London, or as soon thereafter as he had acquired the necessary training. He was to be an actor and actor-manager for the rest of his life, and in that capacity, rather than as a playwright, he made a very good living. Playwrights received a smaller share of the theater's revenue then than they do now. They sold their scripts outright, for very small sums, to the actors, who then divided the receipts among themselves. Shakespeare, however, began to write at once. By 1594 he had completed the following list: *Titus Andronicus; Henry VI,* Parts 1, 2, and 3; *The Comedy of Errors; Two Gentlemen of Verona; The Taming of the Shrew; Richard III; Love's Labour's Lost;* and probably *King John.*

As though all this were not enough, the young Shakespeare spent part of the years 1592–1594, when the plague made one of its descents upon London and the theaters were closed, writing his narrative poems, *Venus and Adonis, The Rape of Lucrece,* and *The Phoenix and the Turtle,* and perhaps some of the sonnets too. He dedicated *Venus and Adonis* to Southampton, the famous patron of the arts. It was immediately successful, and it made Shakespeare's reputation as a writer in circles where the theater was not considered polite literature.

ii. Growing Mastery: From 1594, when Shakespeare joined the Lord Chamberlain's Men, to 1599, when the Globe Theatre opened.

The Lord Chamberlain's Men, which Shakespeare joined in 1594, was the company of actor-managers with whom he was to work for the rest of his life. It was the best company in London, including Richard Burbage, soon to be recognized as England's leading actor; Heminge and Condell, who were to publish the First Folio of Shakespeare's plays after his death; and Will Kempe, the renowned comedian. Their patron, the Lord Chamberlain (Lord Hunsdon), was a member of the Queen's privy council, in charge of her household and all the entertainments. He did not support his players; their income came mostly from their large public audiences. But he lent them the prestige of the crown, defended them from the officials of the city of London (who had a bourgeois and puritanical mistrust of the theater), and arranged for their frequent and well-paid appearances at court. In addition to regular performances in the public theaters and at court, the Lord Chamberlain's Men toured the provinces in the summer, and sometimes at other seasons also, when the plague forced the closing of the city theaters.

In 1595 Shakespeare's only son, Hamnet, died in Stratford at the age of eleven. In 1597 he bought New Place, the largest house in Stratford, evidence that he was making a good living, and also that he continued to think of himself as a resident of his native town.

He wrote the following plays in approximately this period: *Romeo and Juliet; Richard II; Henry IV*, Parts 1 and 2; *The Merchant of Venice; A Midsummer Night's Dream; The Merry Wives of Windsor; Much Ado About Nothing; Henry V; As You Like It;* and perhaps *Twelfth Night.*

These are the plays of the most popular playwright of the day: Shakespeare was giving his public what it wanted. But he was also unfolding, through the popular tales he dramatized, his own intimate sense of human life. The plays may be classified as comedies, histories, and tragedies, but each one is unique. They owe more to Shakespeare's own flexible art than they do to the theatrical conventions he inherited.

iii. Maturity: The years of the great tragedies, from the acquisition of the Globe Theatre in 1599 to the acquisition of the Blackfriars' Theatre in 1608.

In 1599, the Lord Chamberlain's Men acquired the illustrious Globe Theatre, which they were to occupy for the rest of Shakespeare's life. Elizabeth died in 1603, and James I ascended the throne. Fortunately James was as fond of the theater as Elizabeth had been. He made the Lord Chamberlain's Men "the King's Men," thus taking Shakespeare's company under his royal patronage, and recognizing it as the finest in London. The King's Men seem to have enjoyed almost unbroken success, for they played often at court and continued to attract large audiences at the Globe.

Shakespeare wrote the following plays in this period of eight or nine years: *Julius Caesar; Hamlet; All's Well That Ends Well; Troilus and Cressida; Measure for Measure; Othello; King Lear; Macbeth; Antony and Cleopatra; Timon of Athens; Coriolanus.*

The list looks to succeeding generations like a unique but natural miracle, a sequoia forest of the human spirit; but Shakespeare completed the great labors of his maturity in undiminished strength. Then he went on to digest the tragic vision in its turn, placing it in the serener perspective of the end of his life in the theater.

iv. The Final Retrospect: From the acquisition of the Blackfriars' Theatre in 1608 to Shakespeare's death in Stratford in 1616.

The King's Men bought the Blackfriars' Theatre in 1608, and thereafter used it regularly, in bad weather, in addition to their Globe Theatre. Blackfriars' was so called because it was in one of the monasteries which had been taken over by the crown under Henry VIII. It was an indoor theater and had been used for some years by a company of boy-actors. The influence of its indoor stage can be seen in Shakespeare's last plays; and the increasing use of indoor stages from this time onward prepared the evolution of the modern theater. The "inn-yard theaters," like the Globe, for which most of Shakespeare's plays were written, were soon to disappear.

The purchase of Blackfriars' is one of several signs that Shakespeare was ending his theatrical career in comfort and prosperity. Some time after 1610 he began, probably gradually, to retire from active work in the theater, and his last days were spent in his house, New Place, in Stratford. His bequests, including the famous one of his "second-best bed" to his wife, reveal a very substantial citizen of his native town. His small legacies to fellow members of the King's Men show his respect and affection for his lifelong colleagues; and the preface which Heminge and Condell wrote for their First Folio of his plays shows that they continued to revere him eight years after his death. Shakespeare's company must have possessed some rare virtues in addition to their talent, for the King's Men lasted longer than any theater group in the English-speaking world, before or since. And Shakespeare's art owes a great deal to the acting ensemble for which he wrote.

He completed the following plays in this period: *Pericles, Cymbeline, The Winter's Tale, The Tempest,* and *Henry VIII.*

Shakespeare did not impress his contemporaries as a spectacular personality, though many of them knew he was the foremost dramatist of that, or perhaps any, age. Ben Jonson, in the verses he wrote to go with the portrait in the First Folio, speaks for all who attempt to picture Shakespeare:

TO THE READER

This Figure, that thou seest put,
It was for gentle Shakespeare cut:
Wherein the Graver had a strife
with Nature, to out doo the life:
O, could he but have drawne his wit
As well in brasse, as he hath hit
His face, the Print would then surpasse
All, that was ever writ in brasse.
But, since he cannot, Reader, looke
Not on his Picture, but his Booke.

Shakespeare died in Stratford in 1616, at the unbelievably early age of fifty-two.

Shakespeare's Theater

Shakespeare wrote most of his plays for the Globe Theatre. He wrote also for the court, the Inns of Court, and, toward the end of his career, for the indoor stage of the Blackfriars' Theatre. But it was the Globe, its permanent acting-company, and its large public audiences, which chiefly determined the style of Shakespeare's dramaturgy. That theater was Shakespeare's instrument, as important for his art as the orchestra available to a composer is for the music he writes.

Most of our knowledge of the Globe is derived from the contemporary sketch of the Swan—like the Globe, one of the "public theaters"—which is reproduced on page 15. Recent students of Shakespeare's theater have made far more elaborate, and largely conjectural, reconstructions of the Globe. The following simplified description refers to the accompanying sketch.

In the center, the stage-house, where the actors dressed and stored their costumes and properties, rises to a height of three stories, and is topped by the "hut," where the flag flies. In front of it the platform (five or six feet above the ground) projects into the "yard" where the groundlings stood. The yard is encircled by three roofed balconies, and there the richer members of the audience sat on cushioned seats. The yard and part of the platform are open to the sky. The facade of the stage-house has large double doors on either side, and the Globe had also a central opening (not shown in the sketch) equipped with curtains which could be closed, or opened to reveal an inner room. There is a large balcony at the second-story level; and the hut could be used for musicians, sound effects, and machinery. A roof, called "the heavens," supported on tall, ornate pillars, covers the upper stage; and there was a trapdoor in the platform leading down to the cellar or "hell," which could also be entered from inside the stage-house.

This theater may strike us as primitive, but Shakespeare's contemporaries thought it rich and splendid. The interior was elaborately carved and painted, in a style like that of the allegorical archways erected in the London streets for James I's coronation. For performances the stage would be hung with banners and tapestries, or, for a tragedy, with black. The actors were gorgeously and expensively costumed, and they used elaborate properties, not only "hand-props" like weapons and torches, but portable thrones, altars, and the like. They made frequent use of sound effects for thunder or the noise of battle. Music, a widely cultivated art at the time, was important. In Shakespeare's plays it was an essential element of his theatrical "orchestration." He used it to change the mood, to stress a rhythm, or to punctuate the movement of the story.

The stage of the Globe, complicated as it was, was a permanent setting entirely unlike the modern "picture-frame" stage. Realistic or illusory settings of the kind we know were impossible, and the permanently visible structure could not be changed. The light came from the sky, and the resources of modern lighting were undreamed of. The effect was to focus attention upon the actors and what they said. The Globe could accommodate two thousand spectators or more, but packed closely around three sides of the stage, they could follow the subtleties of the playing like audiences in our "arena" theaters. The audience looked, perforce, to the actors, not only to create the characters, but also to build imaginatively, in word and deed, the changing scenes of the story.

There is every reason to believe that the actors in Shakespeare's company were up to their great task. The arts of language both written and spoken were carefully cultivated, in the schools and pulpits as well as in the theater. Actors were expected not only to command the language, but to dance, sing, play musical instruments, and fence well enough to please the connoisseurs. Women's parts were taken by boys, also highly trained. They had often been choristers, accustomed to singing good and difficult music, or members of one of the children's theaters. According to some contemporary testimony, they were better than the actresses on the Continent. The art of acting, indeed—as distinguished from type-casting or the exploitation of the actor's sex or personality—was apparently well understood. The actors were used to playing a great variety of roles, often several parts in one production. The great Burbage played such varied characters as Hamlet, Macbeth, and Othello. Shakespeare himself must have chosen him for these roles, or written the roles for him, which strongly suggests that he was an artist with a very flexible and reliable technique. Shakespeare himself was an actor, and the art of acting is at the very root of his whole playwrighting art. We must think of that company, not like the cast of a Broadway show, hastily assembled for four weeks' rehearsal, but as resembling one of the highly trained companies of modern Europe. It must have been, in short, an accomplished and experienced ensemble.

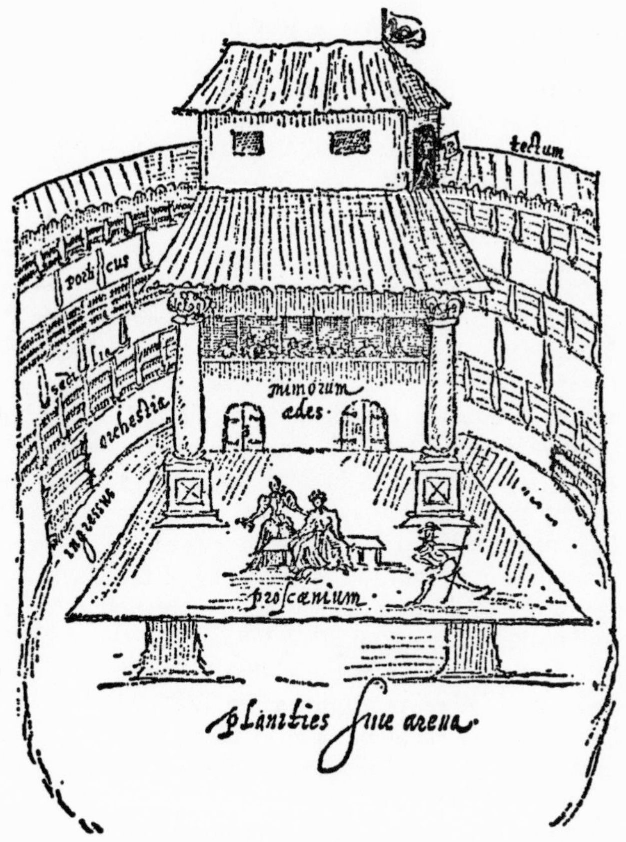

The Swan Theatre. Based on a drawing by Johannes de Witt in Arend van Buchell's commonplace book.

Shakespeare's unrealistic or make-believe theater, with the skilled player on the nearly empty platform, gave the dramatic poet great imaginative freedom. Modern playwrights often envy this freedom, and seek it on the arena stage or on the bare stage. Thornton Wilder's *Our Town,* for instance, counts entirely on the actors and the willing audience to establish the scenes of the play. But Shakespeare's theater, in its very structure, placed the poet and actors in the center, and so determined the style we know. In the opening scene of *Hamlet,* Shakespeare, with the aid of two players, creates the night on the parapet in a matter of seconds:

BARNARDO
'Tis now struck twelve, get thee to bed, Francisco.
FRANCISCO
For this relief much thanks, 'tis better cold,
And I am sick at heart.
BARNARDO
Have you had quiet guard?
FRANCISCO
Not a mouse stirring.

Much of the sweep of Shakespeare's poetry, its power to evoke scenes of many kinds and moods, is based on the collaboration between poet, actor, and audience in a theater where literal realism was impossible.

On that stage, moreover, Shakespeare was not limited to a realistic time-scheme, or to detailed specifications of place. He used both time and place, not for documentation, but as means of conveying the action of the story. It is a mistake to inquire (as many students have felt obliged to do) just how many days or weeks Hamlet spent in England, or just which room in the palace Cleopatra occupies at the moment; such information is irrelevant to the unfolding of the play.

The stage of the Globe was, however, an extremely flexible instrument for suggesting changes of place where that was essential. The main playing-area was no doubt the platform, but the stage-house facade offered many other possibilities for the make-believe of the players. The big doors could be opened for the entrance of military processions, funerals, or royal progresses. The balcony could represent a castle parapet, or Cleopatra's monument, or Juliet's bedroom window. The central opening might be used as an inner room, or its curtains might be suddenly opened to reveal a special effect, a prepared "set-piece" like the armed head, bloody child, and endless row of kings with which the Witches startle Macbeth. Careful studies of recent years have shown us how flexible that stage was. The clarity and theatrical effectiveness of Shakespeare's plays are evident as soon as one understands the stage for which he wrote them.

The traditional divisions of Shakespeare's plays into acts and scenes, with indications of place for every scene, were added by the long sequence of editors of the texts. The plays were originally played straight through, with no intermissions, and with only such suggestions of place as emerged from the play itself. The traditional labels of act, scene, and place are retained in this series to assist the reader (who does not have the benefit of Shakespeare's stage) to get his bearings. But to sense the rhythm which Shakespeare intended, one should think of the play as unfolding without a break from beginning to end.

One should also know something about what the theater meant to Shakespeare's Londoners, for a theater is partly the creation of its audience. The theater was the Londoner's chief form of amusement, rivaled only by the bawdy-houses and the savage sport of bear-baiting. Everyone went to the theater: the much-maligned groundlings who could stand in the yard and watch the show for a penny; law students, by all accounts a lively and intelligent group; the nobles and rich merchants, with their ladies; the "prentices," who have been described as clerks and young business people; in short, a cross-section of that great generation. They did not have our newspapers, magazines, movies, radio, or television. Even books were much rarer and harder to get than they are now. The London theater was a chief medium of public communication and an important instrument in the building of the common picture of man and his society. Holinshed and other recent chroniclers were interpreting English history as leading up to Elizabeth's beloved reign; Roman history, Italian and French fiction, and old stories and legends of many kinds were widely read; and narratives from all these sources were made to live again in the performances of the players. Hamlet must have expressed the common feeling when he called the players "abstracts and brief chronicles of the time." His definition of the purpose of playing suggests what the theater meant then: "To hold, as 'twere, the mirror up to nature; to show virtue her own feature, scorn her own image, and the very age and body of the time his form and pressure."

The proud device which Shakespeare's company adopted for their Globe Theatre was Hercules lifting the sphere of the earth. There are many indications in Shakespeare's plays that he thought of his theater's "wooden O" as a microcosm, a symbolic representation of man's world as that age conceived it. Burbage, playing Hamlet, could point to the platform on which he stood as "this goodly frame, the earth," which seemed to him, in his melancholy, "a sterile promontory." When he spoke of the heavens as "this majestical roof fretted with golden fire" he had the actual roof far above his head, which was in fact painted, probably with stars, signs of the zodiac, or allegorical figures. When he heard his father's ghost the sound came from the cellarage or "hell" under the platform. Thus Shakespeare used his stage, not only to present the immediate events of the story, but also the cosmic setting where man, crawling between heaven and earth, met his mysterious fate. The modern reader can enter the world of Shakespeare's poetry more easily, and with fuller understanding, if he remembers that the symbolic stage itself was a basis for it.

PART ONE

TO 1594

Apprenticeship to the London Theater

Every writer for the theater must find common ground with his audience if he is to practice his art at all. A politician has to acquire a constituency before he can cultivate the arts of the statesman, and a playwright, however deep or subtle he may aspire to be, must have a live audience to play their essential part in the making of the show. Shakespeare seems to have known that from the first, if one may judge by his earliest plays. He apprenticed himself to the theater as he found it, and rapidly secured his hold on audiences in London by demonstrating his mastery of several accepted forms.

It would be a mistake to look for the insight and poetic scope of Shakespeare's maturity in these early plays, but they all fulfilled his modest intention: if properly performed they can hold an audience even now. They are better on the stage than they are in a book, but they are interesting to read, too, as Shakespeare's beginnings; and one may appreciate his sheer theatrical dexterity more easily in them, where his own unique vision is at a minimum, than in his later and richer works.

They show, among other things, that even as a beginner he could hold an audience in more ways than one, by lending his talents to various forms and conventions. In the course of about eight years he wrote, as though to the manner born, at least four different kinds of plays: the farce-comedies, the histories, and two plays that refuse to fit neatly into any category: *Titus Andronicus* and *Love's Labour's Lost*.

In *Titus* he must have set out deliberately, and probably with tongue in cheek, to hit the popular taste for theatrical horrors. He did hit it—and incidentally anticipated a vogue of our own, which goes under such labels as "theater of cruelty" and "theater of the absurd." *Love's Labour's Lost* is at the opposite pole from *Titus* both in its aim and in its dramaturgic style. It is a polite, leisurely comic parable of Shakespeare's own devising, addressed to a select, sophisticated group instead of the wide popular audience he had in mind in making *Titus*. It mockingly pictures the Italian humanism, with its self-conscious refinements and Latin pedantries, which was then the vogue in cultivated circles all over Europe. As in his early sonnets and his narrative poems, *Venus and Adonis* and *The Rape of Lucrece,* the young Shakespeare was widening his audience to include highbrow circles that tended to scorn the popular theater. He was never to write another play quite like this one, but thenceforth he could picture the cultivated upper classes whenever it suited his larger purposes—as one may see, for instance, in *Hamlet* and in *Much Ado About Nothing.*

The other three comedies—or farces, as they should rather be called —*The Comedy of Errors, The Taming of the Shrew,* and *Two Gentlemen of Verona,* are popular in aim. They have none of the literary Latinity that gives *Love's Labour's Lost* its special flavor, but they too reflect the current interest in the classics, for they are all based, in various ways, upon the Latin theatrical tradition of comedy, then flourishing in the vaudeville-like *commedia dell'arte,* and (especially in Italy) in very knowing imitations, adaptations, and translations of Roman comedy. This is the most unbroken and the most reliable tradition of the European theater, destined to have its perfect flowering fifty years later in the theater of Molière. Shakespeare acquired its secrets quite naturally, for like Molière he had been brought up on Plautus in school, and he must have seen the players of the *commedia* in London. His maiden effort in comedy, *The Comedy of Errors,* shows a mastery of the essentials of this theater: its conventionalized but sharply defined characters; its appeal to the shrewd mind rather than the emotions; its reliance upon a wittily intricate plot. This play and *The Taming of the Shrew* are perennially popular, and even *Two Gentlemen of Verona,* less purely Latin in inspiration and put together with less sureness of touch, can still work on the stage.

Shakespeare never forgot the mastery of plot-making which he first acquired in these comedies. And from time to time, when he needed it, he briefly resumed the ironic detachment of classic comedy. But after his apprenticeship he completely lost interest in the genre itself. The comedy of his next phase is quite different: much more English, much more his own unique creation. The romantic motive which then interested him transformed his basic conception of the comic art itself.

The history plays of Shakespeare's apprenticeship, on the other hand, were to prove to be the root of his mature conception of all serious drama. He found the history play as one of the regnant forms of popular theater when he first went to London, and proceeded forthwith to make it his own. Unlike Latinate comedy, the history play was a native growth, sustained by the fervent English faith in their monarchy, which was then represented by the great Elizabeth. It was based on medieval custom and belief, and at the same time upon the current life of the realm and its exciting political affairs.

More than thirty years ago E. M. W. Tillyard explained (in his *Shakespeare's History Plays*) how the Tudor chroniclers, especially Hall, Holinshed, and More, made the theme of English history available to the poets and playwrights. The chroniclers shared the all but universal belief of the time that only a monarch could establish the order of justice and defend the realm from its enemies at home and abroad, and that a benevolent Providence, therefore, must eventually provide their country with the proper ruler. It was in this faith that they interpreted the long history of England, with its many internal and external struggles. They saw in the success of the Tudors, which finally ended the destructive Wars of the Roses, the predestined happy ending of England's time of troubles. Before Shakespeare began writing his histories Samuel Daniell had written a long narrative poem, *The Civille Wars,* on this theme—that of "the Tudor epic," as Tillyard called it. A number of lesser playwrights had dramatized parts of the story for the popular stage, and Shakespeare made full use of their work as well as that of the chroniclers when he came to write his own histories.

He was to return to English history again and again through the first two phases of his career, a period of about fourteen years. He apparently did not plan all of the histories in advance, for they were not composed in chronological order. The following table shows the relation of the historic sequence to the order of Shakespeare's compositions:

The Kings and Their Dates	*Dates of the Plays*	
King John, 1167–1216	1594 or later	
King Richard II, 1347–1400	1595–1597	written during Shakespeare's second phase
King Henry IV, Parts 1, 2, 1367–1413	1596–1597	
King Henry V, 1387–1422	1599	
King Henry VI, Parts 1, 2, 3, 1421–1471	1588–1592	
King Richard III, 1452–1485	1592	
King Henry VIII, 1491–1547	1613 Shakespeare's last play	

As the table shows, he wrote the end of the "Tudor epic" first: the Henry VI plays and *Richard III;* next *King John,* which is outside the main historic sequence; and then, in his second period, *Richard II* and the Henry IV plays, which recount the beginnings of the civil wars. *Henry V* appears to have been an afterthought; and *Henry VIII*, an occasional piece, has little if any relation to the others.

The history play as Shakespeare found it was a rather crude form, owing its popular appeal to patriotic fervor, hero-worship, fast-moving narrative, and the perennial fascination of mischief in high places. In his first efforts, the Henry VI plays, Shakespeare is careful to respect these basic requirements of the genre, but one can find in them some signs of his unique genius. The most striking is his prowess in sheer theatrical story-telling, his inborn ability to keep several narratives going at once, without confusion, and in fugue-like rhythm that moves us naturally to the end. But in *Richard III* and *King John* the "Shakespearean" qualities are also evident in brilliant characterization, like that of Richard himself, and in the more rich and varied language.

In both of these plays, moreover, Shakespeare begins to realize the wonderful possibilities in the form itself, based as it is on the man who holds the throne, symbolic center of the common life. Thus in *Richard III* it is Richard who sets the cruel rules of the game, and the other characters are compelled to adopt some of his frank and ruthless modes of action, with the result that the play as a whole acquires a poetic and moral unity of tone undreamed-of by Shakespeare's simpleminded predecessors. In *King John* the faithlessness of the King and the selfishness of all the powers at home and abroad who have a stake in the rule of England divide the country into smaller and smaller, and more and more savage, factions. It is a question whether this play succeeds, and whether it can be made to work on the modern stage, but it is extremely interesting as a very early version of Shakespeare's vision of the anarchy which must ensue when the wrong man wears the crown. The theme is developed in this play with greater power and imaginative unity than in *Henry VI;* it even foretells, though dimly, the great tragedies of monarchy, *Hamlet, Macbeth,* and *Lear.*

It took Shakespeare an amazingly short time to learn how to use the popular history play for his own deeper purposes. One may, if one prefers, think of *Richard III* and *King John* as belonging to the next phase of his career, when his mastery, and therefore his originality, are unmistakable. His development was swift and continuous, and dividing it up according to the date is bound to be rather arbitrary. But, in general, one may say that he began the exploitation of the history play in his apprenticeship, completed it in the next phase, and used it, when he had reached full maturity, as the foundation of his tragedy.

The Plays in Chronological Order

TITUS ANDRONICUS

Titus Andronicus, written in the late 1580's, may be Shakespeare's first work for the professional stage. It is a gory and sensational tale of crimes in high places, recounted in the rapid, boyish style of certain popular plays of the time, and it has few of the qualities for which Shakespeare's later plays are admired. But it proves to have plenty of theatrical vitality now, if well produced, for it speaks to some kinds of contemporary taste also. Moreover, it has certain elements of structure and character which Shakespeare was to use again and again in his later plays.

Shakespeare's exact source has never been found, but experts in the period believe that the story was familiar, for it was frequently mentioned, and it exists in a prose chapbook published in the eighteenth century. It seems to have been a medieval tale, for though it is ostensibly about Rome it has no relation to specific facts of Roman history. It reflects a general impression of Rome as a city of incredible cruelty and corruption, such as one may get from a reading of the Latin historians of the decadence: a setting as promising as "Machiavellian" Italy for an Elizabethan "revenge play" or a dark, savage chronicle a la Seneca. To fill out the story with learned or grisly detail Shakespeare drew on the Latin literature he had so lately read in school, especially his favorite *Metamorphoses* of Ovid. But in every case he went beyond his models, confecting his horror story knowingly and with apparent gusto. It will not do to excuse *Titus* on the ground of young Shakespeare's supposed naïveté: he was quite clear about what he meant to do.

He gets the story under way with dexterity and speed by using his "symbolic stage" to make the situation in Rome clear visually, almost before the actors begin to speak:

Rome. Before the Capitol; a tomb below.

Flourish. Enter MARCUS, TRIBUNE *and* SENATE *above. Enter below,* SATURNINUS *with* SOLDIERS *at one door,* BASSIANUS *with* SOLDIERS *at the other, and* ROMANS. *Drums and trumpets.*

On the floor of the stage the two sons of the late Emperor, Saturninus and Bassianus, rivals for the crown, confront each other; above (on the open balcony of the stage-house) the Senate and the Tribune represent the supreme authority of the Roman people. The tomb is that of Titus' family, the Andronici, sign of the grandeur and the glum Roman piety of that proud tribe. When Marcus the Tribune announces that the aged conqueror Titus has been chosen Emperor, the rivals rather sourly accept the verdict, and retire with their troops, and then the Captain proclaims that Titus himself, returning from his latest victory, is about to make his triumphal entry into Rome:

Drums and trumpets sound. Enter in procession MARTIUS and MUTIUS, two SOLDIERS bearing a coffin covered in black, LUCIUS and QUINTUS, then TITUS followed by TAMORA, her three SONS, AARON, and others as prisoners. The SOLDIERS set the coffin down.

The pompous procession displays not only Titus' last success, but the sinister elements that will soon prove his undoing: his sons' black coffin; the Gothic Queen Tamora, with her three dreadful boys and her lover, Aaron the Moor, who is as black as a vice in one of the old morality plays.

Titus loses no time in putting his dead sons into the family tomb, and sacrificing Tamora's eldest son there, according to the cruel Roman religious custom, so that *his* sons' ghosts may rest in peace. Thus he instantly makes Tamora his deadly enemy, and when he bestows his crown on Saturninus, pleading (like Lear) his age and weariness, he makes himself another even more powerful enemy. Saturninus soon proves to be exactly as saturnine as his name; he cannot tolerate anyone with Titus' prestige. His first act is to ask for the hand of Titus' daughter, Lavinia, and the flattered old man consents, forgetting or disregarding the fact that Lavinia is betrothed to Bassianus. Bassianus, with the aid of Titus' own sons, seizes her, and in the scuffle Titus kills his son Mutius. In the meantime Saturninus has noted Tamora's charms; he decides to make her his Empress and relinquish Lavinia. It would seem, at this point, that everyone was ready to kill everyone else, but Tamora postpones the carnage by smoothing things over. She has a plan for ruining the Andronici which she hints to Saturninus. As this eventful first act ends, all the enemies agree to a banquet that very night as Saturninus' guests, and a hunting-party the next day as Titus' guests—assuming, apparently, that hatred and mistrust are normal in Rome.

There is only one more important character to be heard from: Aaron the Moor, with whom Tamora is still hopelessly infatuated, in spite of her marriage to the Emperor. At the beginning of Act II Aaron cheerfully and frankly explains himself to the audience:

> Now climbeth Tamora Olympus' top,
> Safe out of fortune's shot, and sits aloft . . .
>
> Then, Aaron, arm thy heart, and fit thy thoughts,
> To mount aloft with thy imperial mistress,
> And mount her pitch, whom thou in triumph long
> Hast prisoner held . . .

It is Aaron who will engineer the ruin of Titus and his whole family, and he finds, at once, the opportunity to start this mischief, which he enjoys even more than he does Tamora. Her two sons, Chiron and Demetrius, enter, quarreling over Lavinia, whom they both want; and Aaron persuades them that it would be more sensible for them to combine forces so that they can both rape her; and he outlines a plan for accomplishing that during the morrow's hunting-party. The rest of Act II shows the amazing success of this plan. Tamora's boys murder Bassianus and toss him into a pit, then duly rape Lavinia and cut off her tongue and hands to prevent her from identifying her assailants. Aaron lures Titus' sons, Quintus and Martius, to the lonely spot, and tricks them into falling into the pit where Bassianus' corpse lies. He then brings both the Emperor's party and Titus' to the scene and persuades everyone that Quintus and Martius, trapped with the body, had committed the murder.

Act III shows Titus at the lowest point in his unfortunate career. Two of his sons are in prison for murder, and he beseeches the Senators in vain to save them. Lucius (his third and last son) is banished, and Titus, in despair, urges him to go: "Rome," he remarks, "is but a wilderness of tigers"—and his audience must agree. Marcus then appears with the mute and mutilated Lavinia, the most painful evidence of Aaron's enterprise. He comes himself, ostensibly to offer Titus help: the Emperor has agreed to save the imprisoned boys if Titus, or his brother, or Lucius, will chop off a hand and send it to him by Aaron. Titus is almost tearfully grateful; he chops off his right hand and gives it to Aaron, who disappears with it. But in a few minutes he sends it back with the heads of the two boys—a joke very characteristic of that humorous villain, and indeed of the whole sardonic fable.

In Act IV Titus' fortunes improve somewhat, and his enemies begin to run into trouble. Lavinia manages to write her story by gripping a pen in her teeth and guiding it with the stumps of her hands. Tamora gives birth to Aaron's black baby, awkwardly unmistakable evidence of her adultery. Aaron unexpectedly proves to be a doting parent, and he flees with his infant to the Goths. There, however, he meets the banished Lucius, now general of the Gothic army, and is taken prisoner.

There is no need to summarize all of the final intricate maneuvers. Titus murders Tamora's two sons with the clumsy but enthusiastic assistance of Lavinia, makes a pie out of them with his own hands, and serves it to Tamora coquettishly dressed as a chef. By the end of Act V all of the principal dramatis personae have been slaughtered except Marcus the Tribune and Lucius. It is Lucius who inherits the crown and the dismaying job of pacifying what is left of Rome (Act V, scene 3):

> You sad-faced men, people and sons of Rome,
> By uproars severed, as a flight of fowl
> Scattered by winds and high tempestuous gusts,
> O let me teach you how to knit again
> This scattered corn into one mutual sheaf,
> These broken limbs again into one body.

The restoration of order in the state ends this bloody tale, just as it ends the stories of Shakespeare's great histories and tragedies. But we have seen no harmony in Titus' Rome all evening, no basis for a humane order, and Lucius' soothing rhythms are too sudden, too unprepared, to be credible. The ending has a purely formal, theatrical effect, like that of the sentimental song with which popular comedy so often ends after an evening of broad farce.

Compared with any of Shakespeare's later plays, *Titus* is extremely crude. Most of its critics so describe it, and some of them have even tried to maintain that Shakespeare didn't really write it. But the study of the theater for which Shakespeare was writing has made his first play more understandable: he was not trying to write tragedy as he learned to understand it in later years, but to hit the popular taste, and that he accomplished with dexterity. The popular forms most frequently mentioned as his models are the "revenge play" of the type of Kyd's *Spanish Tragedy*, Seneca's tragedies, and the morality plays.

The notion of revenge hardly accounts for the carnage, or the ostensible motivation, of this play. When Titus starts things off by slaughtering Tamora's eldest son, he seeks to appease his own sons' restless ghosts, according to a cruel Roman religious custom. He is surprised when Tamora (who is unimpressed by Roman rites) resents the murder. It is true that she craves revenge; but most of the damage is done by her two surviving sons, who merely want to satisfy their depraved lust, and by Aaron, who enjoys mischief of all kinds for its own sweet sake. The revenge plays, however, do appeal to the appetite for evil-doing on the stage, and so helped establish the taste that Shakespeare was appealing to. The same is true of Seneca's coldly sensational tragedies: they gave a classic sanction to the taste for violence. Shakespeare may have remembered the cannibal banquet in Seneca's *Thyestes*, but his own version, with Titus apologizing, like any anxious housewife, for his humble home-cooking, is much more intriguing. He also improves on Ovid's account of the rape of Procne, the ultimate source of Lavinia's story, by giving poor Lavinia *two* ravishers, and lopping off her hands as well as her tongue.

The morality plays, which were beginning to be old-fashioned at the time, offer the best clue to the two-dimensional, boldly theatrical style of *Titus*. In the moralities the dramatis personae—Covetousness, Mischief, Mercy, and the like—were not conceived as human individuals in the round, but as flat, recognizable images of moral concepts, and the characters in *Titus* are presented in a similar way. Saturninus is simply saturnine, Tamora and her sons, who pretend to be, respectively, Revenge, Rape, and Murder in the absurd masquerade in Act V, are hardly more human than those labels, and Aaron is very much like Mischief, the popular clowning figure, both in his black color and in his confident appeal to his audience's delight in the notion of pure, uninhibited evil. In plays of this kind neither the actors nor the audience believe in the human reality of the characters, or follow their sufferings with sympathy. Old-fashioned melodrama is in this unrealistic convention, and so is classic comedy. In its theatrical style *Titus* is closer to our own "black comedy" than it is to the serious tragedies of Shakespeare's maturity. Some of its effects remind one of the currently fashionable "theater of cruelty" and "theater of the absurd."

If one thinks of *Titus* in relation to Shakespeare's later plays, it appears, I think, that Shakespeare could hardly have thought its sardonic style the only way to present man on the stage. He never lost his taste for "gallows humor," as Falstaff with the corpse of Hotspur, or Hamlet with poor Yorick's skull, clearly shows, but in *Henry IV* and *Hamlet* the ghastly grin alternates with more serious and compassionate attitudes. Moreover, Shakespeare was to return later to several of the themes he first sketched in *Titus*, in order to bring out their serious meanings.

"Rome," for instance, in the three great plays based on Plutarch, *Julius Caesar, Coriolanus,* and *Antony and Cleopatra,* is transformed into the august image, filled with the moral and political significance that the Renaissance saw in the Roman heritage. In *Lear* he returns to a plot based on the ruler's renunciation of the responsibilities of rule, with the chaos that follows in the state. But old Lear's folly is seen, from the beginning, as violating a humane order, and therefore tragic *as well as* absurd. Richard III and Iago are both descended from Aaron, and they have much of his theatrical gusto and verve. But both are much more credible as real men, and are therefore not only fascinating mischief-makers but parts of tragic patterns of true pity and terror. In *Titus* he was not trying for tragic pathos or tragic insight, but the fascination of violence and scandal.

Of course Shakespeare could not have foreseen the great plays of his maturity when he wrote *Titus;* he didn't have them to read as we do. But he already had the histrionic ability to use a theatrical style with conviction, yet without naively losing his heart to it. He seems to have understood what the sardonic-melodramatic style of this play could and could *not* do; that is why, when we read it now, we must be careful not to take it more seriously than he did.

HENRY VI
PARTS 1, 2, AND 3

The three parts of *Henry VI* were written near the beginning of Shakespeare's career, probably between 1588 and 1592. With *Richard III* they constitute the first series of history plays that he wrote. They have less poetic mastery, less depth of thought and feeling, than the later plays, and have been less often performed, but the three together make a coherent sequence of epic sweep, and they can be very effective on the stage.

There are many questions about *Henry VI* which the scholars have not settled to their mutual satisfaction. The exact dates and the order in which the three parts were written are still disputed. It has been maintained that the plays as we have them are Shakespeare's revisions of his own or another's work. But until new evidence is discovered we may assume, I think, that the trilogy is essentially Shakespeare's, if only because he alone could have made a coherent drama out of Henry's disastrous reign, which extended from 1421 to 1471. The chroniclers that Shakespeare used (chiefly Hall and some of Holinshed) recount an endless series of intrigues and battles, among a great many kings, queens, nobles, and prelates, who were taking advantage of Henry's weakness to usurp power. Shakespeare keeps the facts of this stretch of history that seem to him the most significant, but does not hesitate to omit a great deal, to change the chronology, and to introduce episodes of legendary rather than historic value. Fortunately for us, he makes a much simpler and more understandable story than the chroniclers do out of Henry's reign.

The story of the trilogy is not that of Henry himself, but of the sacred crown of England, which he so weakly holds. Shakespeare takes it for granted (as he does in all of the English history plays) that his audiences are primarily concerned with the fate of their beloved country, and have unquestioning faith in the crown, as the one sure means of safeguarding the national peace, order, and honor. But Henry VI was a gentle, timid soul, quite unfit to rule or to defend the royal authority from enemies abroad or ambitious nobles at home, and his "disastrous reign," as it was called, was a black time for the "sceptred isle." In each part, Shakespeare presents a struggle for the crown, which reaches its climax and ends in that part. At the same time he shows the beginnings of a new struggle, which will be the main theme of the next part. Thus each part has its own unity, picturing a phase of England's descent into chaos and tyranny; but the downward movement never ends until the monstrous Richard murders Henry, foretelling his own criminal reign as Richard III.

Part 1 opens with the funeral of Henry V, and Bedford's forebodings:

> Hung be the heavens with black, yield day to night;
> Comets importing change of times and states,
> Brandish your crystal tresses in the sky.

Bedford is remembering that Henry V, by means of his "famous victories," had almost succeeded in making good the ancient claim to the crown of France, and had thereby united England behind him in a frenzy of patriotic feeling. But he had inherited the crown from Henry IV, who got it by murdering Richard II, and only his personal prestige as conquering hero had quieted Richard's disgruntled heirs. With his death, who can keep the proud nobles in order, and who can hold the

French at bay? Henry VI is an infant, and Gloucester, the Lord Protector, rules in his name; but the sinister Bishop of Winchester is already planning to get control of Henry to assure his own power. Soon we shall learn of the growing feud between Somerset, of the House of Lancaster, and York, who regards himself as Richard II's heir. Meanwhile the French are beginning to drive out the English, and the lords of England, divided as they are, must turn their attention to that war.

The main story of *Part 1* is the series of conflicts between Joan of Arc and Talbot, whereby France is lost to the English crown. Talbot is presented as a superb soldier and a lonely survivor of the days of Henry V, when everyone was loyal to the crown—the natural representative of embattled England in this dark time. Shakespeare puts together several of his exploits in battle without much regard for chronology, and adds the gallant episode of the Countess of Auvergne, which shows the hero in a lighter mood. But Talbot is doomed by Joan's witchcraft, and by the feud between Somerset and York, who, to discredit each other, fail to send him the necessary aid. The pathos of his death with his heroic son (Act IV, scenes 5, 6, and 7) is exploited to the full. As for Joan of Arc, Shakespeare simply uses her as a foil for Talbot and a symbol of French perfidy. He presents her at first as an inspired military leader, to account for her victories, and then (Act V, scene 3) as a witch deserted by her demons. In her last appearance she is an ungrateful and lying slut, who deserves to be burned at the stake. Joan was, and still is, a mysterious figure, and some modern scholars connect her with witchcraft rather than orthodox Christian sanctity. But Shakespeare, intent upon the jingoistic theme of the French wars, shows little interest in what Joan herself may have been.

The feuds between Gloucester and the Bishop of Windsor, and between York and Somerset, account for England's loss of France, but also suggest the conflicts which will take the center of the stage in *Part 2*. As Exeter puts it (Act III, scene 1):

> This late dissension grown between the peers
> Burns under feigned ashes of forged love,
> And will at last break out into a flame.

Part 1 ends with Talbot and Joan both dead, and a humiliating peace patched up with France. But we know that the crown is threatened in England itself, and when Suffolk boldly forces Henry to marry the French princess Margaret, Gloucester points out that the marriage also means trouble ahead.

Part 1 must have covered eighteen years—from Henry's infancy to his betrothal to Margaret. Shakespeare makes no attempt to suggest this passage of time. In the whole trilogy his method is to telescope the crucial events of Henry's long reign in order to make a continually developing drama. The whole fifty years is under the sign of "comets importing change of times and states," and as the plays unfold we tell time, not by the calendar, but by the signs of England's worsening state.

Part 2 opens with a long, beautifully built scene in London, which sums up the sad results of *Part 1,* and sets the stage for the struggle in England. Suffolk brings Margaret and the peace treaty to Henry, who is surrounded by the threatening lords whom we met in *Part 1.* When the King, Margaret, and Suffolk leave, Gloucester speaks for them all in bitterly bewailing both marriage and treaty; but as Lord Protector he is bluntly and honestly concerned to defend the royal authority. When he leaves we gradually learn that only the Nevils (Salisbury and Warwick) are prepared to support him for the good of the country. The Bishop of Windsor, now Cardinal Beaufort, Somerset, and York, much as they hate each other, agree to join Suffolk and Margaret against Gloucester. In short, the powerful nobles are postponing their struggle for power only until they can get rid of the Lord Protector, their most formidable obstacle. So the stage is set for the main story of *Part 2:* Gloucester's destruction and the anarchy that immediately follows.

Shakespeare makes Gloucester a noble and doomed representative of the old faithful spirit of England, corresponding to the ill-fated Talbot of *Part 1.* The incident of Peter and Horner (Act I, scene 3) shows him wisely ruling in Henry's name without usurping any power for himself. The incident of Simpcox, the false miracle-man, shows him telling Henry the truth, instead of flattering his sentimental religiosity. When the Cardinal, with the connivance of Margaret and Suffolk, traps Gloucester's ambitious wife Eleanor in a seditious plot, Gloucester is deeply wounded, but never loses his loyalty. His enemies fight unfairly (like the French against Talbot), but they fail to persuade either Henry or the people to turn against him. At last the Cardinal, Margaret, Suffolk, and York decide on his murder, cynically disregarding poor King Henry, and relying on their combined power to quell the disturbances they foresee must follow when the people learn that their beloved Lord Protector has been slaughtered.

The end of Gloucester is the climax and turning point of this play, and also of the trilogy as a whole, for he is the last loyal and legally empowered defender of Henry's crown, and when he is gone there is no central authority in England for the rest of Henry's lifetime. All of Act III is devoted to his passing—a sequence of great power and excitement. It represents his enemies' victory, but also their doom, for the anarchy suggested in Act I, scene 1, quickly overtakes them all. By the time the act is over, Suffolk is banished (shortly to be murdered); York is in Ireland building his seditious army; the Cardinal has died, assured of damnation, and Henry is left to the mercy of his formidable Queen—as helpless a victim as the country he represents.

Most of Act IV is devoted to the rebellion of Cade, who has been encouraged by York. He quickly raises a mob, with the aid of a classic revolutionary creed—the rejection of all authority but his own, a romantic, utopian communism, and a hatred of all learning—which Shakespeare presents as both laughable and sinister. Cade himself, with his enthusiastic butcheries, and his invention of a royal genealogy for himself, reflects the mischief of the peers of England, but he is more likable than they are, being more simpleminded. Behind him is the fickle mob, which lifts him to power and as quickly drops him again. In Shakespeare's political plays the mob (not to be confused with "the people") is the most ominous sign of social disintegration, and its appearance here shows the inevitable and far-reaching results of the murder of the Lord Protector.

This play ends with Margaret in flight with Henry, after the battle of St. Albans, before York and his three sons; the last of Gloucester's enemies bent on each other's destruction, and the royal authority lost to sight between the embittered factions.

Part 3 pictures the final phase of the growing anarchy of Henry's reign. It is usually considered the least successful of the three plays, and the history of that time as recorded in the chronicles, a monotonous series of treacherous intrigues and inconclusive battles, is unpromising material for a dramatist. But Shakespeare contrives to give it dramatic form by focusing on the struggle between Margaret and the House of York, and he keeps us reminded of its meaning: the foreordained end of disloyalty and faithless ambition.

In the first scene he presents York, unscrupulous as he is, as the man best fitted to be king, and therefore England's best hope at that moment. We have heard his legal claim, based on genealogy and history, argued at length in *Part 1* and *Part 2*, and now he forces Henry to acknowledge its justice. We know that he is a soldier, a skilled politician, and a strong man with the talents of the natural ruler, and when he offers to let Henry be king while he lives, provided he bequeaths the crown to the House of York, this compromise seems to promise peace and order at last. It is Margaret who scornfully rejects an arrangement that humiliates her and the King, and disinherits her son, the moment she hears of it; and the fighting resumes more bitterly than ever. When Margaret and her ally Clifford capture York at Butterfield, mock him with a paper crown, then stab and finally behead him (Act I, scene 4), our hatred of the Queen and our sympathy for York are increased. When York's son and heir, Edward, blames Margaret for everything just before the battle of Towton (Act II, scene 2), he is evidently speaking for Shakespeare and his patriotic audience:

For what hath broached this insult but thy pride?
Hadst thou been meek, our title still had slept,
And we in pity of the gentle King,
Had slipped our claim until another age.

Thus in the first part of this play York and his sons (like Talbot and Gloucester in a less desperate time) represent the true royal order—not as it is, but as it might have been. The wistful hope they bring, however, is soon lost.

The turning point comes in Act III, when we see that York's sons, unlike their father, are totally unfit to rule. Edward, who is king at that moment, sends Warwick to ask for the hand of Bona, the sister of the Queen of France. And then, while his brothers Richard and Clarence look on with cynical asides to each other, he makes love to Lady Jane Grey. He thereby makes enemies out of the King of France, Warwick, and eventually Clarence, all of whom join Margaret to dethrone him. The fighting starts again, and now there is nothing to choose between Margaret and the House of York. Shakespeare makes a fast-moving story out of their cruel tussles in Acts IV and V; but with the sacred crown violated by both sides, and the country ripped to pieces, the princes' rivalries, though destructive, are meaningless in themselves.

Shakespeare invites his audience to remember the theme of the trilogy as a whole, and in that light to view the anarchy of Acts IV and V with a certain gloomy detachment. Thus in the middle of the ferocious battle of Towton (Act II, scene 5) he shows us Henry meditating on the poor shepherd who lives his life in peace and in accord with the order of nature—a life denied to the King by treachery and war. Henry then sees the son who has killed his father and the father who has killed his son, epitomes of crime against the natural order; and we realize that the "gentle king" has been voicing the plaint of the whole suffering country. In Act IV, scene 4, when the fortunes of war are shifting back and forth with crazy speed, Edward's Queen, pregnant with that Elizabeth who will one day marry Richmond and so unite York and Lancaster and bring peace at last, flees to sanctuary: "fair hope," she says, "must hinder life's decay." These two choric scenes, interludes in the savage story, remind us that Henry's evil times, long as they are, will not last forever.

The main business of *Part 3*, however, is to trace the crucial events of the end of this reign, and crooked Richard is both the agent and the chief spokesman of the final phase. We have been aware of him since the end of *Part 2* as the strongest and most ominous of York's sons; it is he who opens *Part 3* by slamming Somerset's severed head to the floor; and in Act III, scene 2, he foretells his bloody path to the throne in a long, melodramatic monologue. It is he who finally kills Henry (Act V, scene 6):

> Down, down to hell, and say I sent thee thither,
> (*stabs him again*)
> I that have neither pity, love, nor fear.

Dehumanized in spirit as he is, and distorted in body, he serves at the end, like the final tableau of a Greek tragedy, to make the evil of Henry's disastrous reign concretely visible.

If one comes to *Henry VI* after reading some of the later histories, the characterization, the dramaturgic style, and much of the language must strike one as rather rough-and-ready. The minor characters are often hard to tell apart, and important figures like Talbot, the Lord Protector, Queen Margaret, the Cardinal, and the monstrous Richard, though blocked-in in bold outline and extremely actable within the broad situations of the plot, are not developed with the loving imagination one finds in the great characters of the later Shakespeare. Henry himself has some fine passages of pity and almost saintly detachment, but that side of his character is not very intelligibly related to his cowardly irresponsibility. The language of the plays is very serviceable as a narrative medium, but much of it is so high-pitched that it becomes monotonous, and it is ornamented with too many classical allusions in the pedantic taste of that time. Allegorical scenes, like the picking of the white and the red rose (*Part I*, Act II, scene 4), or Henry's vision of the murdering son and father, with their symmetrical, "ritual" style, are more clumsily related to the story than similar sequences in the later plays. There are, in short, plenty of signs of haste and inexperience in the actual writing of all three parts.

But as I have tried to suggest by pointing out the main structure of each play, there is nothing hasty or ill-digested in the dramatic conception of the trilogy as a whole. In giving theatrical form and meaning to Henry's reign, Shakespeare seems to have had already that philosophy of human society and of history which is the clue to the motivation of the later history plays, and of *Hamlet, Macbeth,* and *Lear.* By placing the sacred crown, ancient and publicly accepted symbol of the true order, at the center, he is enabled to follow the destinies of many different characters, with diverse and often conflicting motives, as variations on a tragic action of more than individual or momentary significance.

THE COMEDY OF ERRORS

This comedy may have been written as early as 1589, but there is nothing about it to suggest the clumsiness of youth. It is an almost perfect farce of a Latin type, and (granted a reasonably good performance) it will produce laughter with the infallibility of a machine. This may not be so evident as one reads it for the first time. Like all comedy in this tradition, *The Comedy of Errors* reveals its true quality only in the theater.

The play is based upon a Roman comedy, Plautus' *Menaechmi,* which in turn was derived from a still older Greek play. Shakespeare must have become familiar with Plautus when he was a boy in Stratford, for that author was read in Latin, and sometimes staged, in the Elizabethan schools. The young Shakespeare was, I suppose, looking for a reliable plot for his maiden effort in comedy, and the *Menaechmi,* whose comic situations were at least two thousand years old, had stood the test of time: Plautus was much relished in Shakespeare's England. In adapting the *Menaechmi,* he may have taken a few ideas from another play of Plautus', the *Amphitruo;* and for the prologue and the dénouement he used the romantic story of old Egeon and his long-lost family, which he had probably read in Gower's *Confessio Amantis.*

The situation on which the farce is based is improbable, simple, and absurd. Identical twins, both named Antipholus, were separated in their infancy when their family was shipwrecked. One was brought up in Ephesus, the other in Syracuse, and when the play opens Antipholus of Syracuse is in Ephesus searching for his long-lost brother. The errors of the title arise when the wife and friends of Antipholus of Ephesus confuse him with his Syracusan brother, of whom they have never heard. All of this is straight from the *Menaechmi;* but Shakespeare outdoes his Latin master by providing the identical Antipholuses with identical twins for servants, the two Dromios. The indistinguishable Dromios multiply the possibilities of error, and of course they make the situation still more wildly improbable. Plautus, with his single set of interchangeable twins, tries to make the coincidences credible, while his two young men keep crossing each other's paths without ever meeting. But Shakespeare has a different attitude. By exaggerating and overdoing coincidence he seems to be inviting us to laugh at the whole silly plot; yet at the same time he exploits each situation as though it were real: makes-believe it with a perfectly straight face. Thereby he makes his play both more elaborate and more lightly agile than Plautus'.

The structure of the plot is much admired by critics, and rightly so. Shakespeare must be given full credit for it, because, though the basic situation and some of the incidents are in Plautus, Shakespeare had to rearrange everything when he added the identical Dromios; and the sequence of incidents that gives the play its form and its ceaseless comic movement is his. He involves the two Antipholuses and the two Dromios as closely as possible in each other's affairs, yet he is obliged to keep the twins from actually meeting, for that would clear up all the errors instantly, and so end the play. The characters in the play must never know, until the end, why they are so frustrated, but the audience must be clear all along which Antipholus and which Dromio they are seeing, if they are to enjoy the mounting bewilderment of the Ephesians.

Every scene in the play (except for the first, a prologue devoted to old father Egeon's misfortunes) is based on a mistake in identity. And yet, on this extremely simple situation, Shakespeare builds mounting excitement, and the appearance of variety, as more and more characters are added to the confusion without ever quite clearing up the error. We watch the fun as we might a juggling act, in which more and more balls are tossed into the air: we know that a single slip will bring the whole effect down with a crash. Or one might compare the structure of the play to a "round," or "catch," which was very popular in Shakespeare's time: the simple device of bringing more and more singers in with the same tune can produce an effect of variety and excitement like that of the play. In the play this comical fugue reaches a climax in Act III, scene 1, when Antipholus of Ephesus and his Dromio are refused admission to their own house, while his brother from Syracuse and his Dromio are feasting within. It reaches a second climax in Act IV, when all the characters have been drawn into a madly deluded chase through the streets of Ephesus; and this chase continues until the dénouement in Act V, when the twins finally meet.

In this play Shakespeare followed Plautus' light, amusing, and superficial style of character-drawing. In classical comedy it is assumed that human nature is incorrigible in its greeds, vices, and follies; that there are only a few human types; and that everyone can recognize them at once. Plautus' Menaechmus (Shakespeare's Antipholus) is simply the standard young citizen with the standard set of associates: scolding wife, grasping courtesan, shameless parasite, impudent servingman, and a few friends, other merchants with whom he has business. Shakespeare slightly changed Plautus' cast for his London audience. He omitted the parasite, presumably because that ubiquitous figure of classical comedy was not labeled as such in London. He added the wife's sister (Luciana) and expanded the part of the wife herself (Adriana). In Plautus the wife is only a tough scold, and the husband treats her and his courtesan with the same frank cynicism. Shakespeare's Antipholus and Adriana are less hard and cold than their Roman forebears; but they too are presented as familiar types, not as individuals whose sufferings we are supposed to understand and share. The fact that Adriana weeps copiously when she is not scolding has led some critics to think Shakespeare meant us to take her seriously. But Luciana is on hand at once (Act II, scene 1) to make us see her as laughably childish: "Fie how impatience lowereth in your face," she says; and at the end (Act V) the Abbess sums her up: "Thy jealous fits/ Hath scared thy husband from the use of wits." In farce of this kind it ruins everything to sympathize with the characters. Adriana is presented as the eternal, incurably discontented wife; we are expected to laugh at her tantrums just as we do at the beatings the Antipholuses administer to their yelling Dromios.

Every situation, ridiculous though it appears to the audience, must be played straight, for if it is not, the whole structure of make-believe collapses: the Ephesians do not know why they are continually frustrated, and do not find their frustrations a bit amusing. The motivation of this play is like that of all classical comedy: everyone is pursuing pleasure and/or money. We must see the Ephesians busy with these serious pursuits when "the boys from Syracuse" come to town, and they must try their best to continue them even when they are involved in the mistakes which the Syracusans so unintentionally produce. Actors who try to be amusing, instead of relying on the situations, make the play intolerably slow, heavy, and "cute."

The Comedy of Errors is the purest—the most consistent—of Shakespeare's farces; and yet he frames it, between the prologue and the dénouement, in the story of old Egeon and his long-lost family, a romantic narrative filled with nostalgia and "sweet sadness." Perhaps he felt the need to soften the impact of the hard old Latin piece, in order to fit the taste of his English popular audience. The formula for our own popular entertainment includes a dose of sentimentality at the end, to top off an evening of broad and bawdy humor. Classical taste prefers the single tone, and from this point of view the framework that Shakespeare added to Plautus' comedy might seem a blemish. But we can see, in the light of Shakespeare's later work, that he was feeling his way toward the more many-sided vision and the subtler art of his maturity, when he learned how to harmonize the laughable and the lyric.

In later years Shakespeare used some of the plot-devices of *The Comedy of Errors* for different and much more "Shakespearean" purposes. In the great comedies of romance, *A Midsummer Night's Dream, As You Like It, Much Ado,* and *Twelfth Night,* he depends on mistaken identity almost as much as he does in this play; but the young lovers in the later plays fall into absurd errors not only because they don't know the facts, but because their visions are distorted by their own green terrors and longings, and must be matured and enlightened before they can see clearly. At the beginning of his final phase Shakespeare returned to the story of Egeon and his lost family, and made out of it that strange play, *Pericles, Prince of Tyre,* which is, among other things, a parable of innocence and experience in the course of a whole generation.

If one remembers these later works one can see more clearly just what Shakespeare's intention was in *The Comedy of Errors*. He sets it all in the streets of Ephesus, a place as public and objective as a baseball diamond or a chess board. There is no need there for psychology or individual portraiture to understand what happens; and because we never share the feelings or emotionally colored perceptions of any of the characters, there is no room for lyric poetry. The characters never learn anything but the facts, never come to understand themselves or each other any better than they did at first; and the audience is not offered any new insights either, but is simply invited to laugh once more at incurable, familiar human folly. Shakespeare accepted the strict limitations of style and of medium that define the convention of classical comedy. And he made not only an indestructible entertainment but (what is less evident at first) an elegant theatrical form.

THE TWO GENTLEMEN OF VERONA

This play was written, probably, by 1590. It does not have a very good reputation among the critics, but that may be partly because they tend to judge it as a romantic comedy, and then find that it lacks both the fine character-drawing and the poetry of *Twelfth Night* or *A Midsummer Night's Dream.* It does have subtle, imaginative touches, but it is, I think, essentially very light entertainment, and like all farce-comedies it reveals its true point and quality only in a lively performance.

Shakespeare, as was his lifelong habit, used old, familiar stories as the basis of the plot. The situation that gives the play its title—that of two sworn friends (Proteus and Valentine) who fall in love with the same girl (Silvia) and so jeopardize their friendship—had been a favorite with Renaissance storytellers since Boccaccio and Chaucer. Shakespeare must have known it in various versions, including those in *The Governour,* by Sir Thomas Elyot (1531), and Lyly's *Euphues* (1579). In the old versions the moral dilemma of the two friends is the center of interest, and the story is made the excuse for leisurely philosophizing on the superiority of rational friendship to irrational love. Shakespeare takes the philosophy for granted, but is much more interested in the absurd situations that the two friends' plight gives rise to. He combines that story with another, which appears in the play as that of Proteus and his faithful Julia. Julia pursues her changeable lover in a page's disguise, when he leaves her, and assists him to woo Valentine's girl, Silvia, when he falls in love with her. This theme was popular too, but it is thought that Shakespeare used the version in *Diana Enamorada* by Jorge de Montemayor (1542). The *Diana* is a long elaborate pastoral romance, with the traditional Golden Age scene: pretty glades, clear springs, nymphs, shepherds, and satyr-like giants. Its daydreamy eroticism leads to doctrines of courtly love, and lots of Neoplatonic philosophizing. From Montemayor's story (if it is indeed his source) Shakespeare takes only the basic plot, and by combining it with the tale of the two friends he makes a fast-moving, "plotty" entertainment similar to his Latin farce.

In scene 1 we meet the two gentlemen in Verona, as Valentine (whose father is sending him to Milan to complete his education) takes leave of his dear friend Proteus. Proteus is staying in Verona to court Julia, and Valentine tells us just what to think of him and all who fall in love:

> Love is your master, for he masters you:
> And he that is so yoked by a fool
> Methinks should not be chronicled for wise.

To emphasize the point, we next see Julia (scene 2) in the charming bit when she tears up Proteus' love letter, and then pieces it together again so she can read it, while her maid Lucetta very gently mocks her. And then (scene 3) when Proteus learns that his father is sending him to Milan too, he briefly laments his separation from Julia:

> O, how this spring of love resembleth
> The uncertain glory of an April day,
> Which now shows all the beauty of the sun,
> And by and by a cloud takes all away.

The melodious fluency with which he brings out this unoriginal thought sets the style for all four silly lovers: the fact that they, and their sentiments, are extremely routine, is the basis of the fun.

In Act II the "plot thickens" very quickly, thanks to the fool, love. In Milan, Valentine is smitten with the Duke's daughter Silvia the instant he sees her, and she with him; their antics are as laughable as Julia's. In Verona Proteus and Julia part with vows of eternal fidelity (scene 2), and the moment Proteus reaches Milan and sees Silvia, he falls in love with *her*. He learns that the Duke wants Silvia to marry Thurio, whom she disdains, and that she has agreed to elope with Valentine that very night. He notes that Silvia has "dazzled my reason's light," and that, unless he recovers, he will have to get her. The long monologue (scene 6) in which he makes up his mind to betray Valentine to the Duke may be described as a farcical variation on the philosophizing about love that goes on at such length in the old romantic stories:

Love bade me swear, and Love bids me forswear.
O sweet-suggesting love, if thou hast sinned,
Teach me, thy templed subject, to excuse it.

Love obliges, providing Proteus with a candid, if unromantic, excuse:

Julia I lose, and Valentine I lose.
If I keep them I needs must lose myself;
If I lose them, thus find I by my loss—
For Valentine, myself; for Julia, Silvia.
I to myself am dearer than a friend

. . .

And Silvia—witness Heaven, that made her fair—
Shows Julia but a swarthy Ethiop.

Love's egoistic rationalization is so neat that we accept Proteus, in spite of his dirty trick, as a most amusing comic—the more so when we see Julia, in the next scene, getting ready to pursue him in her page-disguise.

In Act III Proteus' intricate plot for getting Silvia in spite of Valentine, the Duke, and Thurio seems to be succeeding. He tells the Duke Valentine's exact plan for extracting Silvia by means of a rope ladder. The Duke can then trap Valentine into admitting everything by pretending to ask his advice on the best way for *him* to get a girl whom he is not allowed to see. Poor Valentine tells the Duke just how these things are managed, and generously offers to lend him his own rope ladder. The Duke banishes him, and Valentine takes off for the woods, with the enthusiastic assistance of Proteus. Having got Valentine out of the way, Proteus is able to persuade the grateful Duke to hire him to woo Silvia on behalf of the inept Thurio, and incidentally to poison her mind against his dear friend (scene 2). This is the climax of the play, and the most extravagant result of obeying love the fool.

In Act IV we see all four of love's subjects frustrated and moping. Valentine is captured by Robin Hood-like Outlaws in "A forest near Milan," but is made their king when he pretends to have killed a man (scene 1). Proteus reflects (scene 2) that he has made a hopeless mess, merely antagonizing Silvia by his treachery to Valentine, the Duke, and Thurio, instead of making her love him. Julia reaches Milan in her page-disguise, but only to see her beloved Proteus wooing Silvia with music. When she takes service with Proteus he employs her to fetch Silvia's picture for him. This act is the most "romantic" part of the play, with its music and the laments of the tearful girls for their inaccessible young men. In their lyrical exchanges they make play with "music," "picture," and "shadow"—metaphorical themes that Shakespeare was to employ, with wider and wider meanings, all his life. But these pretty effects are mockingly interrupted (scene 4) when Launce appears to explain *his* unrequited love for his dog, Crab. Crab's misdeeds—stinking up the dining room and pissing against my lady's farthingale—seem more forgivable than those of his human counterpart, Proteus.

In Act V the required happy ending is brought about with dispatch —too much dispatch, according to most critics. Silvia chases Valentine into the forest, the Duke, Proteus, and Thurio chase her, and the Outlaws capture them all. Valentine, as Outlaw-king, can now straighten everything out. Proteus immediately repents his treacheries, and Valentine not only forgives him but offers him Silvia too, to seal their reconciliation—whereupon poor Julia in her page-disguise, seeing Proteus about to elude her after all, falls in a faint. Valentine has been much blamed by the critics for so quickly handing over his beloved Silvia, and there is much speculation about why she herself says nothing. But luckily Proteus decides that he prefers Julia to Silvia after all, and the way is clear for a double marriage. The Duke pardons the Outlaws, and they too join in the general rejoicing. As for the moral of the tale, Julia does her best to find one when she apologizes for her "immodest raiment":

> It is the lesser blot, modesty finds,
> Women to change their shapes than men their minds.

It is certainly a very modest conclusion to emerge from so much intrigue; but in this play the silly intrigue is itself the point, not any deeper moral or psychological meaning.

In this summary I have said nothing about the two servingmen, Speed and Launce, because I wanted to bring out the consistently farcical quality of the plot, which is Shakespeare's chief means of keeping his audience amused. But the plot would perhaps be too slight for an evening's entertainment without the servants, who are used to make joking interludes in the movement of the story. Speed, with his verbal humor in the taste of the time, is likely to prove boring, but Launce is one of Shakespeare's own miraculous clowns. One is tempted to think Shakespeare had a particular actor in mind, a natural comic, and wrote the part for him.

Most of the adverse criticisms of this play are directed against the two gentlemen, who (the critics complain) are no gentlemen at all. Proteus, as his name tells us in advance, is totally unreliable. Valentine abruptly loses his principles when he falls in love with Silvia, but we might put that down to "romantic love" were it not for his equally abrupt shift at the end, when he hands his beloved to Proteus (of all people) without consulting her at all. Such criticisms assume that Shakespeare was trying to write a romantic comedy like *Twelfth Night,* and clumsily failing. It seems to me much more sensible to give him credit for knowing just how silly his gentlemen would appear. In the excellent production of the play for the Shakespeare Festival in Central Park, the audience laughed at them from beginning to end, and it was clear, I thought, that they were taking the play exactly as Shakespeare meant it. He was making fun of youthful infatuation and the conventional notions of eternal friendship and courtly love in order to entertain his popular audience, and his play can still entertain us in the same way.

There are, of course, elements in *Two Gentlemen* that Shakespeare would develop later, in his true romantic comedies, notably the roles of Julia and Silvia, with their rueful constancy and their musical laments. But the pastoral scene of the old romances, which he would use later to make the magic "worlds" of Illyria or Arden, is represented here, very perfunctorily, only by the Outlaws' greenwood. The scene of *Two Gentlemen* is Verona and Milan—the ordinary world, with ordinary love, a familiar disease of youth, like the measles. We are not supposed to identify ourselves with the lovers in order to share their feelings and visions, but to watch them with amusement from the outside.

In recent years it has been pointed out, notably by Professor O. J. Campbell, that *Two Gentlemen,* like its predecessors, *The Comedy of Errors* and *The Taming of the Shrew,* owes a great deal to the commedia dell'arte. The commedia was the "improvised comedy" of the Italian players which was popular all over Europe in Shakespeare's time. Each player was identified with one traditional character, or type, the most important being two old men, Pantalone and the Doctor; two pairs of lovers, elegant, solemn young people equipped with books of poetry or treatises on courtly love; two servingmen, fast-talkers and agile gymnasts; two serving-girls; and the bragging soldier. The players used scenarios derived from Roman comedy, but improvised the acting, the movement, and the dialogue, except for songs and a few set speeches. The scenarios were usually love intrigues, with the young men plotting to get the girls away from the old men (rich fathers or absurd rivals) or from each other.

No one can point to a particular commedia scenario that Shakespeare might have used for this play, and his familiarity with the players cannot be proved except for the evidence in his plays. But it is obvious that both the cast and the plot of *Two Gentlemen* are very much like a typical commedia. So is its style or tone: the characters types rather than individuals, laughable just because they act according to type; the underlying attitude detached and witty rather than lyrical or sentimental. It would seem that, in extracting his plot from his sources, Shakespeare's inspiration was much closer to the commedia than it was to romance. He made a light, firm structure of broadly comic situations, which his actors, with little regard to the subtleties of character or feeling, could use to entertain a popular audience for a couple of hours.

THE TAMING OF THE SHREW

Shakespeare had in all probability written *The Taming of the Shrew* by 1592, when he was twenty-eight. It is one of his earliest surviving plays and (by his standards) the work of a beginner. But he seems to have known, even then, exactly what he wished to do: to make a scenario which the actors could use as the framework for an evening's hilarious entertainment. He succeeded far better than he could have hoped to do. *The Shrew* has held the stage ever since he wrote it. It appears on the contemporary stage frequently, and with success, in productions and adaptations of every description. It is one of the easiest and most "sure-fire" of his plays, for good actors know instinctively how to handle its quick, clear succession of farcical situations, and the reader can enjoy it at once, and interpret it according to his own taste.

Because it is basically so clear and simple, it can be understood and judged in various ways. Those who come to it from a reading of Shakespeare's later comedies sometimes find it lacking in subtlety, even cruel and vulgar. But it is beloved in the theater, and some critics, including Dr. Johnson and Hazlitt, gave it their august approval. Shakespeare made it out of three quite different stories. The central plot is that of Bianca, her rich father, Baptista Minola, and her three suitors. Shakespeare added to this plot the story of "Kate the curst" and her energetic suitor Petruchio by making Kate the elder daughter, who must be married before Bianca. The "Induction," in which the drunken tinker, Christopher Sly, is kidnapped for an evening of luxury and invited to see *The Taming of the Shrew,* is from a third source. In the play as we have it, all these elements fuse naturally together to make an evening's entertainment. But one can understand the possibilities in the script better—and the disagreements of the critics—if one remembers Shakespeare's variegated sources. It was always his custom to use familiar tales for the plots of his plays. In *The Shrew* his characteristic method can be seen more clearly than in the later and more mysterious plays.

We usually assume that the play is simply about Petruchio's violent wooing of Kate—and with good reason, for their affair gives the play its title and attracts the crowd generation after generation. The problem of taming a wife is as old, laughable, and insoluble as death and taxes. It can be found in European literature in many versions, several of which Shakespeare might have known. One of them is a popular tale in doggerel verse called "A Merry Jest of a Shrewd and Curst Wife Lapped in Morel's Skin, for her Good Behaviour." It is very crude, but lively and illuminating as a specimen of uninhibited popular humor shortly before Shakespeare's time. The fun depends almost entirely upon the physical struggles between the man and his domineering wife, and the effect is bawdy and brutal—when the husband finally wins he flays his wife and wraps her in the salted hide of his old horse "Morel." It has been conjectured that this was Shakespeare's immediate source for Katharine and Petruchio; but if so he completely transformed it, shifting the interest to the human relation between the two. Some of the old violence still shows through in unimaginative productions, and Shakespeare no doubt counted on the elementary basis of the squabble to add "salt" and excitement. But his Katharine and Petruchio, though lightly sketched, already suggest his own humane and balanced vision.

Shakespeare sees Katharine and Petruchio as in love, almost from the first meeting. Their fights are partly a flirtatious game, partly a matter of egoism, male and female, with a good deal of bluffing on both sides. Katharine is perhaps testing Petruchio, hoping half-consciously that he will survive her impossible stunts and thereby prove to be the husband she requires. Petruchio accepts the challenge with relish; we feel some love and insight in him even as he roars at the terrible Katharine, starves her, and tramples on her tender vanities. At the end of the play, when both are for the moment exhausted, Katharine gives her famous speech on wifely duty. There is plenty of irony in this speech—which no husband in the audience can miss—but there is gratitude too. Katharine has wakened from her nightmare of the bad little girl; she has grown up; the strenuous game has, for the moment at least, a happy ending.

It has often been pointed out that Katharine and Petruchio foreshadow Beatrice and Benedick in *Much Ado About Nothing,* Shakespeare's final word on the battles of the egoistic young in love. But in that play he lifts the theme to the most poetic high comedy, whereas in *The Shrew* he sticks to the mood and style of farce. The play should be read, as well as performed, with that style in mind. Petruchio, for instance, may be heard roaring offstage, and then appear cracking a ten-foot bullwhip (as he did in the recent production of the American Shakespeare Festival); the effect is hilarious, not brutal, because the style is right. The whip shows (with overemphasis) how Petruchio feels, but it is no more frightening than the firecrackers in the circus that blow the clowns twenty feet in all directions—after which they all get up and run away. Such is the magic of the best popular farce of all ages and countries.

The whole play of *The Shrew* owes a great deal to farce of this kind, which the young Shakespeare knew in Latin, French, and especially Italian plays; much lighter and drier entertainment than native British humor like "A Merry Jest." The main plot, that of Bianca and her suitors, is a typical Latin comedy of "intrigue"—a game for the girl, or the money, or both. The characters are lightly sketched as familiar types; the situations are obvious and universal; the point is neither psychology nor feeling, but wit, and the absurd complexities of the plot. Baptista wants to marry off his daughters as richly and speedily as possible; Lucentio wants Bianca; Hortensio wants her money; and old Gremio wants to warm his old bones with a young wife. On this earthy basis all the arabesques of the intrigue are built, including the improbable disguises of Lucentio and Hortensio as pedants, the exchanges of clothes between master and man, and the rest. Shakespeare took the Bianca story directly or indirectly from Gascoigne's *The Supposes,* a translation of Ariosto's Italian comedy, *Gli Suppositi.* Ariosto in turn had derived his play from two Latin comedies, one by Terence and one by Plautus. Ariosto's play is swifter and more intelligent than his Latin models, and Gascoigne's English version preserves some of its sophistication. It was performed with success for the alert and well-educated young gentlemen-law students at Gray's Inn, and Shakespeare would have known of it as a rather special hit of a past season. When he combined it with the Induction and the Katharine-Petruchio story to make *The Shrew,* he transformed it and made it his

end, and in the text we have, Sly disappears in the first act. Did Shakespeare bring him back in some earlier version, to let us know that the "dream" of the play was over? Or did he rely on Katharine's final monologue to dispel the mood of farce and return us to the sadder and wider human world? A good actress, who felt the new tenderness in Kate's relation to Petruchio, could certainly use that final monologue, ironic as it is, for that purpose. But we cannot be sure what Shakespeare wanted to do with Sly after the first act; and on that unanswered question hang a number of disputed textual problems which are beyond the scope of this introduction.

In *The Taming of the Shrew* we can see Shakespeare, more clearly than in the later plays, as he makes his theater magic: seeing the perennial human meaning in old, familiar stories; weaving them together with his uncanny understanding of his stage, his actors, and his audience. *The Shrew* is put together with far less poetic unity than the comedies of his later phase, but it shows, already, his theatrical mastery.

RICHARD III

Richard III was written about 1592 and was one of Shakespeare's first big successes. Though it has a great deal of political and psychological wisdom, it is essentially a melodrama, full of sardonic humor and of the youthful Shakespeare's delight in thunderous language. It has fascinated audiences since its first appearance on Shakespeare's own stage.

It is the story and the character of Richard himself that give the play its extraordinary theatrical vitality. The Tudor historians had created the popular image of Richard as a heartless villain, and at least two plays had been written about him, before Shakespeare wrote his play. Modern historians criticize the Tudor interpretation of King Richard, but Shakespeare accepted it with gusto, making him a horrible example of mischief in high places. His Richard, when played with the right smiling and demoniac energy, enthralls us still, whether we know anything about English history or not.

Shakespeare's patriotic audience, however, would have found Richard's story absorbing not only because of Richard but because it marks the turning point in the bloody narrative of the English crown. Richard appears at the end of Henry VI's "disastrous reign" as the visible epitome of that savage moment, as his own House of York returns to power. But it is Edward, not Richard, who becomes king:

> Now is the winter of my discontent
> Made glorious summer by this sun of York,

as he sardonically remarks at the beginning of this play. While he lives he will dominate the scene, but everyone in Shakespeare's audience knew that he would be defeated, at last, by Henry Tudor, who would become king as Henry VII, and the grandfather of the great Elizabeth herself.

It is Richard's own relatives that stand in his way, and he proceeds with the greatest enthusiasm and dexterity to get rid of them one by one. The King obligingly dies, but Richard has to arrange the murders of his brother Clarence, of the Queen's kinsmen, of his lukewarm follower Hastings, and finally of the little Princes. He marries Anne to settle the Lancastrian claim to the throne, and he fools and bullies the Londoners into accepting him as king. All of this he accomplishes in the first three acts.

Shakespeare makes Richard understandable as the deformed child who becomes a spiritually distorted man, and takes savage and ironically smiling vengeance upon the world for his misfortune. But he was more interested in the theatrical effectiveness of such a character than in trying to account for him psychologically. His Richard is the heartless villain of Senecan melodrama, who at the same time has the humor and intelligence to see himself as the "Vice" of the old morality plays, a figure traditionally played for laughs. Richard onstage can satisfy our savage instincts, and also our appetite for huge Aristophanic farce.

The princes and nobles around Richard lack his fascination, and they have none of the human depth of Shakespeare's later characters. But there is a great political wisdom in Shakespeare's picture of their dangerous struggle for power. They are always trying to guide their policies according to the party they believe to be the strongest. They make friends solely in order to get ahead, and instantly betray them when it serves their purpose. They are in fact the typical "palace guard" as it appears in every generation around the center of power; but in this case their struggles acquire the cruel color of Richard's personality. They are just what old Margaret calls them: "wrangling pirates."

The central story of the play is of course that of Richard, but Shakespeare does not forget the wider theme which unites *Richard III* with the other histories, that of England and her longed-for peace. The widowed Margaret, the old Duchess of York, Edward's widow, Elizabeth, and Richard's unwilling wife, Anne, are on hand to bewail the bloody treacheries and to pray for England's deliverance. And we are given glimpses of the common people, who know very well that their rulers, as they tear each other to pieces, are also destroying the England of the humble folk. These motifs make a dark background for Richard's impudent successes, and prepare us for the more solemn ending of the play.

We hear the "wailing Queens" for the first time in Act I, scene 3. They return in force at the end of Act IV (scene 4). Old Margaret notes with gusto that her dire predictions are being fulfilled:

> So now prosperity begins to mellow,
> And drop into the rotten mouth of death.

Her longest speech runs to thirty-four lines, and the other wailing Queens are not far behind her. The scenes of women's lamentation strike the modern reader as much too long, and they are always cut in production. They have, like so much of the play, the formality of the "classical" plays which were written in imitation of Seneca. Even the violent disputes are often formal, like Richard's with Anne in Act I, scene 2, or with Elizabeth in Act IV, scene 4. The antagonists have a sharp exchange of single lines, the so-called *stichomythia:*

> RICHARD
> Infer fair England's peace by this alliance.
> ELIZABETH
> Which she shall purchase with still-lasting war.
> RICHARD
> Tell her, the King that may command, entreats.
> ELIZABETH
> That at her hands which the King's King forbids.

Such fights are like operatic duets, and the Queens' prolonged curses are like operatic arias, or Senecan choruses. The Elizabethans apparently relished the form itself, as one may relish the "form" of a good boxer; but to us they are likely to seem merely artificial. That, however, should not obscure the underlying theatrical power of the "wailing" scenes. There is more anger than self-pity in the women's tirades, and the joy of anger is infectious:

> ELIZABETH
> O thou well skilled in curses, stay awhile,

And teach me how to curse mine enemies.

MARGARET

Forbear to sleep the night, and fast the day;
Compare dead happiness with living woe;
Think that thy babes were sweeter than they were.

There is humor here, as well as pathos; part of the fun of the play is in its resounding curses.

The scenes of the common people, contrasting with the Queens' high style, are deflated and realistic. The thug whom Richard has hired to murder brother George of Clarence is bothered by his conscience:

> I'll not meddle with it, it makes a man a coward. A man cannot steal, but it accuseth him. A man cannot swear, but it checks him. A man cannot lie with his neighbour's wife, but it detects him. . . . every man that means to live well endeavours to trust to himself, and to live without it.

The murderer slyly speaks for the audience, who can recognize in what he says their own dealings with their consciences. He also describes the action of the play, in which everyone (reflecting Richard's style) gets rid of his conscience and trusts to himself alone in the struggle for power. The citizens know just what is going on throughout. In Act II, scene 3, after Edward's death, they see clearly what will happen with a child on the throne. In Act III, scene 6, the Scrivener, on his way to post a notice of Hastings' execution, understands that Richard has liquidated another man who stood in his way: "Who is so gross/ That cannot see this palpable device?" Even when the Londoners give Richard the crown they are not really fooled. The common people are close to the meaning of the play as Shakespeare saw it; they express both its sardonic and its serious aspects.

The turning point comes at the end of Act III, when Richard gets the crown. He must now take the consequences of his crimes. His follower, Stanley, looks for a way to leave him; Buckingham, his chief ally, runs away and starts a rebellion; Henry Tudor, Earl of Richmond, approaches from France with an army.

At this point Richard himself changes, as though his inspiration had left him. He does not rejoice in his old devilish way when the Londoners make him king. When he bullies Elizabeth into granting him her daughter's hand he lacks the comic verve he displayed in the similar scene (Act I, scene 2) when he wooed and won the Lady Anne. These scenes are psychologically convincing; Richard's pleasure, we see, was in the savage game of power, and once he has the prize he realizes that, if he is to keep it, he has nothing to look forward to but more crimes.

But this change is hard to put over in performance. The audience misses its evil clown, and Shakespeare is not prepared to show us the depths of Richard's failure. Richard says (Act IV, scene 2):

> But I am in
> So far in blood, that sin will pluck on sin.

We are reminded of Macbeth's terrible line (Act III, scene 4 of that play):

> I am in blood
> Stepped in so far, that should I wade no more,
> Returning were as tedious as go o'er.

Macbeth's words convey the very essence of weariness and stale horror, while what Richard says merely gives us the facts of his situation. When Shakespeare wrote this play he had not yet attained his full poetic power, or his full vision of evil and its effects on the human psyche. Richard, in his fall, does not hold us with the tragic pity and terror of *Macbeth.*

Shakespeare, however, does not expect him to. To carry the end of the play he counts less on Richard than upon the patriotic theme of the whole sequence of histories, and it is, of course, Henry Tudor, Earl of Richmond, who announces the stirring finale. Listen to the military music of his speech (Act V, scene 2):

> Fellows in arms, and my most loving friends,
> Bruised underneath the yoke of tyranny,
> Thus far into the bowels of the land
> Have we marched on without impediment. . . .
>
> The wretched, bloody, and usurping boar,
> That spoiled your summer fields and fruitful vines,
> Swills your warm blood like wash, and makes his trough
> In your embowelled bosoms, this foul swine
> Lies now even in the centre of this isle . . .
>
> In God's name cheerly on, courageous friends,
> To reap the harvest of perpetual peace
> By this one bloody trial of sharp war.

The fifth act is all based on the famous battle of Bosworth Field, which to Shakespeare's audience meant the beginning of England's health and "perpetual peace." It is a formal set-piece, which concludes both this play and the sequence which began with *Henry VI, Part 1.* The feeling is almost religious, and the style is allegorical. The battle–like so many battles in Shakespeare—has some of the meaning of the medieval "ordeal" in which the rival champions, submitting their causes to the "arbitrement of war," fought in order to discover the will of God. Richard sets up his tent on one side of the stage, Richmond sets up his on the other side. On the night before the battle, the ghosts of the Princes whom Richard has murdered come to curse him and foretell his doom, while they give Richmond

> The sweetest sleep, and fairest-boding dreams,
> That ever entered in a drowsy head.

In the morning each champion addresses his soldiers. Richmond invokes God and England's patron saint, Saint George, while Richard appeals to fear, hatred, and the joys of fighting. The old Richard flashes forth here at the end, and when he yells the famous line, "My kingdom for a horse!" we sympathize even as we rejoice in his death. So Shakespeare ends his story, absorbing it into the wider theme of England triumphant.

Richard III is a masterpiece of Shakespeare's youth. It does not have the depth or the haunting poetry of *Macbeth,* but we feel in it the great tragedies to come. Some of it is too elaborately rhetorical for our taste; yet the theatrical power of its fierce humor is irresistible, and its political wisdom applies to our own or any time.

LOVE'S LABOUR'S LOST

Shakespeare's early plays were usually written for the popular theater, but *Love's Labour's Lost* (1592) is evidently intended as an entertainment for a special, highly educated audience, probably the court of Queen Elizabeth. The popular theater was looked down upon at that time by the connoisseurs of literature, and it has been conjectured that Shakespeare, who was then known simply as an actor and journeyman-playwright, wanted to prove that he could address the cultivated classes in their own terms. He certainly does so, in this play, with complete mastery: it is a gently mocking picture of the poses and the fads, especially that for absurdly overrefined language, which then were characteristic of the intellectual circles.

Dr. Johnson reported that "all the editors have concurred to censure" the play, and "some have rejected it as unworthy of our poet." They objected to its bawdy passages (so much more cheerful than our dank pornography) and to its intolerably affected language. Many critics since then agree in censuring its artificial language, as though Shakespeare himself were infatuated with it. We now see that he was ridiculing the language of his characters, and that much of the interest of the play lies in his extremely sophisticated mockery of the far-fetched puns, rhetorical figures, elaborate conceits, and pedantic allusions to classical literature current in that highbrow circle. Moreover, each character has his own style, which exactly reflects his own fond picture of himself. Shakespeare even at the beginning of his career was a completely conscious craftsman of language.

The central story of the play is soon told. Ferdinand, King of Navarre, and his three friends swear to renounce the pleasures of the world for three years, especially women, in order to devote themselves to art and learning—and find themselves forsworn the moment the Princess of France and her attendant ladies invade their bachelor domain. Shakespeare seems to have invented this slender fable himself. No doubt he learned something about sophisticated comedy from Lyly's polite court plays, and from the refined comedy of the Italian humanists. But the types and customs of leisured society itself, rather than any previous plays or stories, seem to have been the "source" of *Love's Labour's Lost.*

Because the play so obviously reflects contemporary manners, many scholarly efforts have been made to identify Ferdinand's circle with a particular group. The visit of the Princess of France to Navarre recalls a visit by Marguerite de Valois to her husband, Henri IV, in 1578; but though Shakespeare uses French names for his leading characters he shows no interest in the facts of that historic event. To some students, the characters in the play suggest well-known figures in England; but the fact is that Shakespeare might have known or heard about more than one "Academe" like Ferdinand's serious little group. Castiglione's book, *The Courtier,* which was used in England as a kind of handbook for polite society, describes a little Italian court in which highbrow conversation is the favorite parlor game. The "Academe" or imitation Platonic Academy was a well-known toy, and Shakespeare's educated audience would have understood what Ferdinand was trying to do, even though his attempt to do without women was a heresy from the point of view of Castiglione's ideal court, where the ladies ruled in the tradition of courtly love.

In planning the Princess's visit to Ferdinand's court, Shakespeare must have been thinking of one of Queen Elizabeth's "Progresses." The Queen liked to travel through her realm with a great retinue, stopping on her way at the castles of the great nobles. The lucky (or unlucky) host whom she thus honored was expected not only to feed and lodge her whole train, but to divert her with games, masques, and pageants. The Princess of France has the right to expect such festivals when she comes to Navarre. She finds, instead, the cold comfort of the womanless court, until the last act, when the King, vanquished by love, belatedly tries to entertain her properly. But the whole play is conceived as a masque or a pageant, rather than as a conventional comedy with a fast-moving story. Queen Elizabeth (if she was indeed in the first audience) would have seen a leisurely procession of contrasting characters: the rude King and his friends in scholarly black; her stage-counterpart, the Princess and her retinue, in gorgeous finery; the Pedant, the Curate, and Don Armado, recalling in their costumes traditional figures of the commedia dell'arte; the country bumpkins, redolent of Shakespeare's hometown. Each character presents himself in his own remarkable language, poetic, or pedantic, or pompous. In a good production, like that of Stratford, Ontario, in 1961, the masque-like quality of the play, heightened by the use of music and carefully designed movement, is very clear.

The title of the play accurately defines the action of the little story: the futile efforts of the bookish Ferdinand and his friends, when they have been overcome by love, to woo their ladies. It is clear in the first scene that the four gentlemen will try to woo the four ladies, impeded though they are by their oath and by their literary affectations. As they endeavor to extricate themselves the ladies merrily laugh them out of countenance. Don Armado, the elegant but penniless Spanish gentleman who loves the country wench Jaquenetta, and vainly woos her in learned language, provides an amusing and touching variation on the main theme.

The protagonist of the main story is the King's friend Berowne, a vigorous and witty young man rather like Benedick in *Much Ado About Nothing*. Though he whimsically takes the oath of abstinence along with the rest, he knows that they are defying both nature and the traditional cult of courtly love, and he points out, in the first scene, that the visit of the Princess of France on an important diplomatic mission will force them to break their oaths at once. When the ladies arrive

(Act II) he instantly starts a battle of wits with two of the masked beauties, in the affected style of fashionable flirtation. But left alone (Act III) he confesses in very plain language that love has vanquished him:

> Well, I will love, write, sigh, pray, sue, and groan.
> Some men must love my lady, and some Joan.

Berowne is the center of the comic turning point and recognition (Act IV, scene 3), a sequence of multiple eavesdropping and neat, predictable surprises, as artificially symmetrical as classical ballet. He hears the King, Dumaine, and Longaville dolefully confess their loves, and then he, in turn, is caught by them. When all have confessed to each other, Berowne's friends beseech him to rationalize their plight: to "prove/ Our loving lawful and our faith not torn." He responds in the famous monologue on love as wisdom, a virtuoso bit for a good actor.

Because Berowne is the most free-spirited and intelligent of the characters, we look to him throughout to explain the action of the play. It is love that moves all the characters, behind their silly poses, and Berowne in his various speeches shows us, I think, the young Shakespeare's own many-sided conception of that passion. Berowne describes love with no nonsense when he first decides he must have Rosaline: "Dread prince of plackets, king of codpieces." But he also fully accepts the vision of love's possible meanings embodied in the tradition of romance and courtly love. In the triumphant apologia for love that he offers the King and his friends in Act IV, he says,

> From women's eyes this doctrine I derive.
> They sparkle still the right Promethean fire;
> They are the books, the arts, the academes,
> That show, contain and nourish all the world.

Three hundred years before Shakespeare, Dante had written, "My lady carries love in her eyes." The notion that the love that appears in a woman's eyes is, if properly interpreted, a kind of revelation, a source of inspiration and insight, is one of the great themes of romance. Berowne, at this comic moment, is being witty and humorously eloquent, but he feels that what he says is true.

The relations of Don Armado with his beloved Jaquenetta and her solid country swain Costard make an amusing series of interludes in the unhurried progress of the main story. Don Armado is called "the Braggart" in early editions of the play, for he is based on the commedia dell'arte figure of the boastful, hollowly ferocious soldier. Shakespeare, however, endowed the traditional type with a new meaning and a subtle individual character. Don Armado loves old-fashioned military finery, but nothing is left of his boastfulness but harmless pleasure in rhetorical flourishes. He loves not only Jaquenetta but the wit of Moth, his small pert page, and everything that is honorable, learned, and romantic. He is an authentically Spanish type, a wistful but gallant soul of childlike purity, a relative of the great Don Quixote himself.

Holofernes, the pedantic schoolmaster, and Sir Nathaniel, the Curate, his zealous understudy in elaborate verbosity, have even less to do with the main story than Don Armado does. The theatrical inspiration for these two is also a commedia character: the Doctor of Bologna, who usually does very little but waddle onto the stage in his academic shovel-hat, black robe, and enormous belly, to bore everyone with a flood of incomprehensible dog-Latin. In the same way, Holofernes and Sir Nathaniel are brought on spinning their verbal ingenuities, ravishing each other with majestic absurdities and resonant Latin platitudes: they are amusing enough just as they are, without any story. But Shakespeare gives them an individual touch too; he makes them types of the English countryside, part of the rural setting of Ferdinand's court.

In the last act all of the characters assemble to offer the Princess some diversions of their own devising, the proper way to entertain a royal visitor. The King and his friends present their elaborate, clumsy, and transparent Muscovite masquerade. Holofernes, the Curate, Don Armado, and Costard collaborate on an ambitiously learned pageant, showing "Nine Worthies," i.e., famous heroes of history and legend. One can imagine that Shakespeare, the professional theater man from London, must have seen many such homemade shows with a mixture of amusement and sympathy. At this point in the play they serve—when both rather pathetically fail—to bring the main story to an end. The Princess and her ladies laugh their suitors' masquerade out of countenance, and then the King and his friends unkindly heckle the Nine Worthies. Costard, defending the Curate, who played Alexander the Great, offers the perfect apologia for the whole show: "He is a marvellous good neighbor, faith, and a very good bowler: but for Alisander, alas, you see how 'tis, a little o'erparted." We are made to feel here (Act V, scene 2) that love's labor has been lost indeed. The bookish subtleties, the artificial ingenuities of rhetoric, and the flirtatious game of wit have all failed, and reduced the fond lovers to a point of childish frustration.

But this impression is brief: Shakespeare never ends his comedies on a sour note. He changes the mood in several steps. First he brings on Marcade with the not unexpected news of the death of the Princess's father. That breaks up all pretense of festivity, for the Princess must prepare to leave at once. The King and his friends at last plainly and seriously propose marriage to their ladies, and the ladies condescend to answer seriously. It is "a time methinks too short," the Princess says, "to make a world-without-end bargain in," but she and her ladies give their suitors some hope. If they will spend a year in abstinence, silence, and good works, thereby expiating their broken oath and proving their sincerity, the ladies will again listen to their protestations of love.

Don Armado officiates at the play's finale. He too will do penance for love's sake: "I have vowed to Jaquenetta to hold the plough for her sweet sake three years." He offers the company the little Masque of Spring and Winter. Perhaps it is arranged so that all may take part; however it is staged it must make us feel that all are "at one," if not in actual marriage, at least in a common feeling of humanity. The wonderful songs, "When daisies pied and violets blue" for spring, and "When icicles hang by the wall" for winter completely dispel the artificial verbosities, the vain labors of love, which we have heard all evening. They are as simple and magical as nursery rhymes, and they restore us to the world of nature where all must feel the passage of spring and winter, love and death, with no words at all.

Love's Labour's Lost is not very seductive at first, for much of the language has lost its point for us, and must be deciphered with the aid of the glossary. But one can learn to relish it as soon as one sees how we are meant to take it. It is a unique kind of entertainment, more like a leisured pageant than an agile farce. It is not "colored as love wills," and it does not end in marriage, like the romantic comedies, for love is absurdly hampered by pedantic postures until the very end. Yet all the characters are fond, even in their vanities, and Shakespeare manages to make us feel his highbrow courtiers, pompous gentlemen, and verbose pedagogues as gentle, childlike creatures under the surface. It is marvelous that, at the beginning of his career, he could fix that subtle vision, and then find the verbal and theatrical means to realize it so exactly.

KING JOHN

This play was written, most probably, between 1594 and 1596, in the years when Shakespeare was writing his other histories. It does not, however, form part of the connected series that recounts the vicissitudes of the English crown from the dethronement of Richard II to the dethronement of Richard III by Elizabeth's grandfather. John's reign, some two hundred years earlier than Richard II's, was a series of disasters, and Shakespeare does not make him the "hero." For that reason many critics find that the play lacks dramatic unity, and they are puzzled about the meaning that Shakespeare saw in this grisly bit of history. Yet it is generally agreed that the play is full of life, and that it has much fine verse in Shakespeare's early manner.

We are likely to remember John, if at all, as the king who was forced by his rebellious Barons to grant them the Magna Charta, a document that the historians of the last century regarded as a landmark in the struggle for civil liberty. But the chroniclers whom Shakespeare read pay little attention to the Magna Charta. They saw John, in spite of his crimes and follies, as analogous to their own great Elizabeth in his struggle against the traditional enemies of the crown: the jealous nobles at home, and France and the Pope abroad. Shakespeare's most direct source was a chronicle play, *The Troublesome Raigne of King John,* which presents John's reign from that point of view. In making his own play Shakespeare further emphasizes the welfare of England, embodied in the monarchy, as the center of interest for his patriotic audience. He reduces the old play, which is in two parts, to about half its length, and gives it the same kind of dramatic structure that one finds in his other serious plays.

In John's time, less than a hundred and fifty years after the Norman Conquest, France and England were struggling to define their separate nationalities, and their kings were disputing the right to the crown, or crowns. In the opening scene (all of Act I) we see how the dynastic and family squabble brings war between the two countries. King Philip of France demands that John surrender his crown to his nephew Arthur.

The formidable dowager Queen Elinor, who is the mother of John and Richard Coeur de Lion, and the grandmother of Arthur, supports John, though she cynically reminds him that he owes his crown to "strong possession" and not "right." They are joined by Coeur de Lion's bastard son, Philip, who turns out to be John's strongest supporter. Arthur's mother, Constance, of course passionately backs King Philip of France.

In Act II the warring Kings with their relatives, followers, and allies are encamped for a parley before Angiers. That town refuses to allow either King to enter, on the ground that they cannot tell which one is their rightful sovereign. The Kings accordingly join battle to decide the point, but fight to a draw, and Angiers still refuses to recognize either. The Bastard then persuades the Kings to reduce Angiers before they settle their own fight; and under that threat the resourceful burghers suggest that the French Dauphin, Louis, marry John's niece, Blanche of Spain. This arrangement for patching up a peace is accepted, though it cynically ignores Arthur's claims, ostensibly the cause of the war in the first place.

Act III opens with the marriage proceeding as planned, while Constance loudly protests the betrayal of her son. At that point the Pope's legate, Pandulph, arrives to demand that Stephen Langton, whom the Pope had appointed Archbishop of Canterbury and John had fired, be reinstated. When John angrily refuses, Pandulph excommunicates him, and then persuades King Philip to declare war on him as a heretic. By this time the nature of John's complex struggle with his two foreign enemies is clear. It reaches its climax and turning point in the battle in which the English capture Arthur and return to England, and it looks as though John had saved his crown and his country. But Shakespeare is careful to make the meaning of this victory very dubious. Pandulph accurately prophesies the troubles in store for John at home, and the French, with his encouragement, recover their appetite for war.

In Act IV we see how John and all England suffer the results of his faithless operations. It is from this point onward that Shakespeare most radically changes the plot of *The Troublesome Raigne.* He makes Act IV, as in his other plays, the Pathos which follows the climactic fight of Act III. Arthur's death makes the Barons rebel and then desert to the French who, we hear, have landed an army under the Dauphin on English soil. John is left to face these calamities with little support except that of the loyal Bastard.

In Act V Shakespeare telescopes a large part of *The Troublesome Raigne* in order to present, with almost farcical speed, the incredible treacheries of the four fighting factions, the King, the Barons, France, and the Pope. England is providentially saved when Pandulph, having secured John's dishonest submission, calls off the French; John dies, poisoned by a monk, and Prince Henry, sign of a new phase in England's history, ascends the throne.

Shakespeare's changes in the plot serve to make the myopic irresponsibility of the fighting rulers, and its all but fatal results for England, much clearer than they were in the more simpleminded *Troublesome Raigne*. His portrayal of the characters has the same effect. The characters in *The Troublesome Raigne* are nonentities: the interest is not in human motivation but (as in a boy's adventure story) only in what happened and who won the fight. Shakespeare does not bother to re-create most of the important historic characters. We understand what the English and French leaders are up to in each of the rapidly shifting situations, but we do not know them well enough to get their points of view, or follow their troubles with sympathy. John has at least two very fine scenes: his sly incitement of Hubert to murder Arthur (Act III, scene 3), and his death in the last scene, when his physical pains are made very real. But we never get inside him or feel with him as we do with other criminal kings, even Richard III; his doings, and the messes he makes, are coldly seen from without. But Shakespeare did endow several of the less important characters with individuality and depth of feeling, as only he could do. The Bastard, Constance, Arthur, Hubert, and (in another way) Pandulph are real to us, as individuals. They are strategically placed where they can both see and suffer, though not control, the events, and we instinctively look to them for understanding. Through their reactions Shakespeare reveals the form and meaning he sees in John's reign.

The Bastard is much the most important of these "choric" characters. Both by his character and by his situation he is admirably fitted to make this sordid bit of history acceptable to the nationalistic English. His situation is analogous to John's: John is the actual, but illegitimate king; the Bastard is the actual but illegitimate son of the great Coeur de Lion, king and national hero. Both represent England in the struggle, but John's motive is purely selfish, whereas the Bastard, who has the spirit but not the letter of royalty, gradually shows, beneath his sarcastic impudence, his total commitment to the good of the country. At the end of Act I, as he congratulates his mother on her adulterous affair with Coeur de Lion, he seems to be making a subtle apologia for himself also, and even for John:

Some sins do bear their privilege on earth,
And so doth yours. Your fault was not your folly.
Needs must you lay your heart at his dispose,
Subjected tribute to commanding love.

He means, literally, that Coeur de Lion was irresistible as a man, but I think he also suggests that as king he might command love of another kind: the loyalty the subject owes his sovereign. The symbolic figure of the king was supposed to represent God in earthly government; and the love of God was regarded as a deeper guide to human conduct than justice, or any reasoned moral code. The conflict between rational conduct and loyalty to king and country—whether merely passionate or divine—runs through all of Shakespeare's histories.

Shakespeare endows the Bastard with a combination of unusual vitality and poetic insight, and both qualities are needed to carry off the embarrassing situation of England under John. When he first appears he reminds one of Edmund, in *King Lear*, who was also proud of his father's act of love because it gave him his "fierce quality" without benefit of clergy. Later on, he more closely resembles Prince Hal in *Henry IV*, who also conceals his love for the royal order of England with witty mockery of the King himself. He represents the spirit of England—and its big bones and muscles—as a fighting animal; but at the same time sees what its true welfare would be. He can enthusiastically participate in John's fights, and still see them with relentless clarity.

By the end of Act II the action of the play is well under way, and in the monologue that ends the act the Bastard tells us what it is, and what we are to think of it:

Mad world, mad kings, mad composition!
John, to stop Arthur's title in the whole,
Hath willingly departed with a part;
And France, whose armour conscience buckled on,
Whom zeal and charity brought to the field,
As God's own soldier. . . .
[has now been diverted by Commodity, and] Commodity
Hath drawn him from his own determined aid,
From a resolved and honourable war,
To a most base and vile-concluded peace.

The monologue expresses the Bastard's anger and frustration, and it comes out with a rush of jumbled syntax; but it is essential for the understanding of the play. France has now been drawn into the power-game as John plays it: with no rules but "commodity": i.e., momentary advantage. The action lacks "all direction, purpose, course, intent," and must therefore shift with each new situation. The Bastard certainly speaks for Shakespeare here; for in replotting the old play he stressed the irresponsible changing of sides; and in characterizing the antagonists he did not endow them with any deeper motives than momentary advantage. Under the pompous facade of royalty they are hardly more than mistrustful animals; and their battles would be merely farcical were it not that England's fate hangs on the issue. For that reason we must do what we can with John; and the Bastard ironically plunges back into the game as defined:

> Since kings break faith upon commodity,
> Gain be my lord, for I will worship thee.

Until Act IV he will be too busy playing the game to make any extended comments on the action.

It is Constance who interprets the action for us in the first part of Act III:

> Gone to be married? Gone to swear a peace?
> False blood to false blood joined! . . .
>
> Believe me, I do not believe thee, man,
> I have a King's oath to the contrary.

She is as tough a fighter as the rest, but at this point, having lost and been pushed aside, she can see the incredible royal wavering with deadly clarity. Shakespeare makes her a very intelligent woman, and a strong one, who can be witty even in her despair. After the battle in which John captures Arthur (scenes 2 and 3), she invokes death (scene 4):

> Death, death, o amiable lovely death,
> Thou odoriferous stench, sound rottenness,
> Arise forth from the couch of lasting night.

Her aria, with its curious variations on death as both horrible and desirable, looks artificial to us, and it is in fact a set-piece in a convention that we have lost. But one must remember that Constance (like the cursing Queens in *Richard III*) has no power to do anything *but* lament; and one feels the true note of grief under the elaboration. It is through Constance that we first see the dark background and the pathetic consequences of the struggle.

At the end of the act, Pandulph takes up the role of chorus or "reflector" of the action. Being less personally involved than Constance, he can remind us that England's fate is involved with Arthur's. The audience would presumably have hated Pandulph, who, on behalf of the Pope, is dictating to an English monarch, but they would have admired and feared his political sagacity. His cynical prophecy, that John would inevitably destroy Arthur and so turn his own countrymen against him, sums up the results of Act III, and prepares us for the long pathos of Act IV.

Act IV is built around young Arthur, the most touching victim of his elders' selfish treacheries, and, as the legitimate king, the visible symbol of all England's helpless suffering. The plot is devised to show how all the divided and sorely puzzled English are just as ineffectual as Arthur. Hubert cannot bring himself to obey his King and kill Arthur, but in the long run fails to save him. John cannot appease the angry Barons, for when they make their protest he wrongly believes that Arthur is dead already. The Barons are thus frustrated also; and diagnosing the situation wrongly, they prepare to make the treasonable pact with the French which they will betray later. Arthur's death, when he jumps off the wall, gives the sharpest impression of the country's painful bewilderment. The Bastard puts it all into words for us in his monologue at the end of the act:

> I am amazed methinks, and lose my way
> Among the thorns and dangers of this world.

He lacks the comic verve, at this point, which serves him so well in fighting; and as Hubert carries off Arthur's body he tries to get his bearings with reference to his deeper motive, his love for England:

> How easy dost thou take all England up!
> From forth this morsel of dead royalty,
> The life, the right, and truth of all this realm
> Is fled to heaven; and England now is left
> To tug and scamble, and to part by th'teeth
> The unowed interest of proud swelling state.

He sees the dog-fight to which England is now reduced against the vision of the divinely sanctioned order of the monarchy as it *should* be. His speech thus recapitulates the symbolic structure of Act IV; and he ends it like a storyteller building suspense:

> A thousand businesses are brief in hand,
> And heaven itself doth frown upon the land.

This is the formula for Act V in this and all of Shakespeare's serious plays: in the foreground the frantic "businesses" of the struggling humans, in the background frowning heaven, or fate, or Providence, which will at last end the action in a way that no one can quite foresee or control.

Shakespeare, as I have pointed out, does indeed show "a thousand businesses" by concentrating much of the narrative in the last act. The effect is to remind us sharply of the Bastard's ironic description of the action at the end of Act II: all direction and purpose gone, the bewildered fighters change sides faster than ever. But he must play the game to the end, and he proves the most agile of all: "Be stirring as the time," he tells the wavering John. We can feel both his pleasure in the dog-fight and his deeper loyalty, when de defies France and the Pope at once at the end of scene 2: "Now hear our English King,/ For thus his royalty doth speak in me." He cannot foresee the harsh decrees of fate, or frowning heaven: the drowning of part of his army, John's submission to the Pope, John's death by poison. But he accepts them all without wavering in his loyalty, and when John dies he says:

> Art thou gone so? I do but stay behind
> To do the office for thee of revenge,
> And then my soul shall wait on thee to heaven,
> As it on earth hath been thy servant still.

He expects to die fighting the Dauphin; but then he learns that Pandulph has called off the French and he is free to offer his services to Prince Henry, "lineal state and glory of the land." Heaven has smiled at last; the mad world of John's time is gone. He gratefully dismisses it in the patriotic speech that ends the play:

> O let us pay the time but needful woe,
> Since it hath been beforehand with our griefs.

Like Shakespeare in his work as playwright, the Bastard has made the best of a bad time, and can now turn soberly toward the future.

As many critics have pointed out, Shakespeare faced new and difficult problems in dramatizing John's reign. He could rely, as always in the histories, upon his audience's passionate faith in the crown, symbol of their country's welfare; and, following the chroniclers, he could bring out the analogies between the perils that threatened it in John's time, and those that Elizabeth herself was facing. But he seems to have decided in advance that John himself could not be made to carry this timeless theme. He was not the legitimate king, like the weak Richard

II, not the born ruler, like the usurper Henry IV, and he was incapable of a sustained evil motive, like Richard III's. Being merely selfish, he lacked the vision of the crown as a sacred trust and could therefore neither defend nor betray it; and Shakespeare accordingly plotted his story as savage farce or childish pathos, meaningless or "mad" in itself. He relies on the Bastard to "redeem the time"—living through its criminal follies with ironic pugnacity, yet emerging at the end, with a reaffirmation of the love of country. This strikes me as a most interesting solution, characteristic of Shakespeare's subtlety, candor, and resourcefulness; but I do not know how successful it can be in the modern theater.

PART TWO

1594–1599

Mastery of the Popular Theater: Romance and English History

In the second phase of his career Shakespeare was the most popular playwright in London, working with the best company of actors, an apprentice no longer, but the master of the theater and its arts. There is no sudden change to mark the beginning of this phase, but the plays clearly show deeper vision, greater technical virtuosity, and the originality which comes from sharper insight combined with more perfect control of the medium. The plays are all aimed at the popular theater, but at the same time they embody Shakespeare's own unique spirit more freely than the plays of his apprenticeship.

His greater freedom is most evident in the fabulous characters that now suddenly people his stage. Falstaff and Harry the Hotspur, Shylock, Beatrice and Benedick, Juliet and her Nurse, have lives of their own, yet each one is unmistakably Shakespeare's creation. His imagination was fed by the lively types swarming around him in London, and probably by the actors he knew in his own company. One can often sense in the many-sided humanity of his characters—their fatness or leanness, their tricks of speech, their life-rhythms expressive of individual temperaments—the presence of flesh-and-blood actors who are to perform them. But only Shakespeare could have brought them all alive on the stage by his incredibly flexible mimetic sympathy.

His ability to appropriate the individual lives around him is cognate with a heightened awareness of the community as a whole and its rich old traditions. He now begins to make fuller use of weddings and funerals, royal pageantry, and folk festivals, both in order to form his plots and to suggest the meanings of his stories. He greatly increases his control of the theatrical possibilities in the symbolic figure of the king. And he takes over new parts of the literary heritage, especially the poetic and narrative tradition of romance, which he uses in all of the plays of this phase except the histories. Romance and history were common resources, available to other poets and playwrights of the time. But only Shakespeare could make use of both, endowing their old themes with fresh theatrical vitality and seeing their meanings more deeply than anyone else.

Comic and Tragic Versions of the Romantic Motive

The tradition of romance had been cultivated for more than four hundred years by the time Shakespeare inherited it, by adepts of courtly love, pastoral storytellers, and various kinds of love poets who were descended more or less remotely from the Provençal troubadours. Shakespeare uses it in his sonnets and narrative poems as well as his plays; he confidently relies on his audience's sophisticated interest in this rather artificial literature. But, like Dante three hundred years earlier, he sees through the conventions of romance to the psychology of infatuation as we recognize it even now, and at the same time suggests the meanings of the mysterious motive by "placing" it in the context of the whole classical-Christian philosophy of love.

The Merchant of Venice is not Shakespeare's most magical romantic comedy, but in it he shows us most clearly, through Portia's father's didactic action in setting up the casket test, and then Portia's in saving her lover in the courtroom scene, where the true romantic commitment belongs in the wider spectrum of loves. The caskets that Portia's lovers must choose from represent three modes of love. The golden one, labeled "what many men desire," represents infatuation with literal beauty, gold as material wealth, or as the wonderful appearance of golden-haired Portia: "love in the eyes," as the Friar will tell Romeo *his* love is. Its meaning, when it is opened, proves to be death. The silver casket promises what the suitor "deserves," thus confusing love with rational justice, and appealing to the suitor's self-love: when opened it shows a "blinking idiot." Shakespeare often brings out the incommensurability of love and justice, and he likes to make fun of clumsy moralists like Malvolio when they blunder into the nonrational world of young love. The leaden casket requires its chooser to "give and hazard all"—and that defines all romantic love whether death-marked or life-giving: an act of faith quite outside reason. That casket, forbidding as it is, proves to contain the picture of Portia, golden hair and all, for she too has "hazarded all" by accepting the test her father set up, just as Bassanio has done.

The same three modes of love (seen now as forms of human conduct in general, rather than merely forms of sexual attachment) make the symbolic structure of the courtroom scene. Bassanio has given and hazarded all for his friend Antonio, who appears to have forfeited his life, and Portia rescues her lover by showing the way through the deceptive appearances of the literal situation, to what everyone justly (because legally) deserves, and thence to the necessary act of faith in the undeserved mercy of God, the supernatural pattern of all true love. The love that Portia demonstrates (though lightly, even playfully presented) is analogous to the love of Beatrice which leads Dante, in the huge scheme of the *Divine Comedy,* out of Hell and up to the purgatorial mountain, where he meets her at last in the terrestrial Paradise. Portia only leads her lover from the money-hell of the Rialto to her "Belmont," but that pretty mountain is made to suggest Eden, earthly felicity, the visionary goal of the love motive in all the romantic comedies.

Romeo and Juliet is Shakespeare's only play about "death-marked" romantic love. The love-death motif was one of the strands in the romance tradition, and Shakespeare carefully echoes it, thus giving his play a poetic resonance which his source, Bandello's novella, entirely lacks. At the same time he both portrays the young lovers with scrupulous realism, and places their motive in the context of traditional wisdom, chiefly by means of the Friar. The Friar tries to make their love lead to earthly felicity, but he fails, partly because Romeo is too impatient to obey anything but "love in the eyes," partly because of the situation in Verona. Romeo dies while he is still like a boy who, as the Friar puts it, "reads by rote and cannot spell." The parallel between Romeo and Juliet and Dante's Paolo and Francesca is evident at once, and the more one explores it the more striking it becomes: the two poets were looking at the same perennial human experience and understanding its meaning in the same way.

In the most beautiful romantic comedies, *A Midsummer Night's Dream, Much Ado About Nothing, As You Like It,* and *Twelfth Night,* Shakespeare is both indulging his audiences and gently mocking them. "If music be the food of love, play on," says Orsino; and in each of these plays the verse-music creates for us a world "colored as love wills": the enchanted Athenian woods, Illyria, the Forest of Arden, or even the perpetual house party in Leonato's Messina; but romantic love is seen, in its perilously deluded course and its ultimate meaning, on the same principle as it was in the more didactic *Merchant of Venice.* The longing young are looking for "true love" just as Bassanio and Portia are. When their quest ends happily (as comedy must) we see that it is not because they knew what they were doing, but because their faith in love itself has survived the absurd complications of the plot, and the bewildering images of joy or sadness which their amorous passions have begotten on their uneducated imaginations. Shakespeare's touch in these comedies is feather-light, but he is careful, as always, to recognize what "truth" there may be in the experience he is presenting.

The formula for these romantic but not meaningless comedies is to be found at the beginning of Act V of *A Midsummer Night's Dream.* Theseus explains to Hippolyta that he simply cannot take seriously "the lunatic, the lover, and the poet," whose imaginations, inspired by their emotions, "give to airy nothing/ A local habitation and a name." He is referring to the enchanted play in the midnight woods which we have just seen; and he adds, "I never may believe/ These antique fables nor these fairy toys." Hippolyta replies:

> But all the story of the night told over,
> And all their minds transfigured so together,
> More witnesseth than fancy's images,
> And grows to something of great constancy.

In other words, the course of the action as a whole, the laughable insistence on true love, is more significant than the music and the jokes and the dreams that constitute the texture of the lovers' search. The material is the "antique fables" of romance, but these fables are interwoven and plotted so as to show a love-quest which mysteriously (and with little relation to what the lovers morally deserve) reaches mutual enlightenment, "something of great constancy."

Hippolyta's formula, which applies to all four of the comedies we are considering, shows how basically Shakespeare's romance differs from the Latinate farce of his apprenticeship. Even when he uses a similar plot device, such as mistaken identity, which he built to such absurd heights in *The Comedy of Errors,* he uses it to produce entirely different effects. That is because the romantic motive, which now interests him, transforms everything. These young lovers could never be straightened out by a mere fact as the twins in *The Comedy of Errors* are. Demanding nothing less than true love, they must have a change of heart to clear their visions before they can see what they are looking for. That is why, in replotting the old stories, Shakespeare so constantly resorted to ritual forms of all kinds, from the folk rites of May Day or Midsummer Eve (which he uses in *A Midsummer Night's Dream*) to the extravagant servitude which the *donna* of the courtly love tradition imposes on her lover-vassal (absurdly adopted by Beatrice in the last part of *Much Ado*). Such rituals are not taken seriously in the comedies, but they are appropriate theatrical devices for presenting a love-quest which proceeds more by faith than by reason.

It is when the bewildering scene of love's ordeals dissolves, day dawns, and reason and common sense return, that we glimpse Hippolyta's "something of great constancy." The lovers who were ready to fight or weep all evening now greet each other with heavenly smiles, and their love, having lost its blinders, spreads out to encompass the whole menagerie of the play—"Noah's Ark," as Touchstone puts it. For a moment we see the world itself in that peaceable light, which does not seem illusory; but the vision is soon gone, and as the play ends (often with music) we say good-bye to it as to something familiar. Shakespeare saw the meaning of this wonderful moment in the context of his classical-Christian scheme. It represents earthly felicity, which, as Dante pointed out, is "figured" both by the classical Golden Age and the Biblical Eden. The ends of these comedies (like the end of the *Purgatorio*) are filled with allusions to both mystic versions of man's earthly goal: God and man, man and woman, earth and heaven, pagan antiquity and the Christian saeculum momentarily and improbably at one. I suppose it was because Shakespeare had meditated on the psychological import of the august old myths that he could make the obligatory happy endings so much happier than those of most comedies. But he gives no indication that his lovers will "live happily ever after." It was believed that fallen man can never again permanently inhabit Eden, and Hippolyta's "something of great constancy" is only the *vision* which comes briefly when human love is, for the moment, rightly oriented. It is "constant" because it is glimpsed in every generation, not because we can hold on to it. Shakespeare's sense of all this partly accounts for the shimmering quality of his style in his romantic entertainments: an effect of longing behind the fun.

The Merry Wives of Windsor, the other comedy written in this period, seems at first glance to be made, like the others, of romantic materials. Both the story of Anne Fenton and her suitors, and the midnight masquerade in the woods with Falstaff as the ancient folk hero, Hern the Hunter, might have been handled romantically. But the romantic motive that lifts the others to poetry is lacking: even Anne, young as she is, hardly feels it, and Falstaff's frustrated affair with the middle-aged wives, though good farce when well acted, is no more romantic than the gambits of the farmyard.

After *Twelfth Night* Shakespeare abandoned romance and all comedy, except the most astringent, while he explored the great tragic vision that possessed him for eight years. He was to return to romance with *Pericles, Prince of Tyre,* at the beginning of his final phase, but by that time he was seeing all his themes together, in the tranquil light of retrospect. It is the histories he wrote at this time that lead straight into his mature art of tragedy.

The Ruler of England as the Center of the Pattern

By the time Shakespeare came to write the histories of this phase he saw that he could use the popular genre to present his deepest insights into the life of the political animal. That was because the monarchy embodied symbolically so much of the ancient wisdom which the Renaissance had inherited from the Middle Ages. The monarch was the center of the life of England: not only the legitimate head of government but the "father of his people" and the "earthly figure of God's majesty." In the dramas reflecting the changing life of England it was natural to compose the picture around the de facto ruler, good or bad, for he was both the center of motivation and the clue to the moral climate of his time. This was perhaps implicit from the first in the "history play," but now Shakespeare exploits the possibilities with more dramaturgic virtuosity and more political sophistication.

The accepted philosophy of the monarchy had two main components: the classical Greek theory of government based largely on Aristotle's *Politics,* and a religious component derived ultimately from Biblical notions of history as a sign (when properly interpreted) of God's will for man. The Greek theory pictures the healthy state on the analogy of the human individual. The parts of society fulfill themselves by performing their proper functions, and thereby contribute to the common life, as the limbs, organs, senses, and emotional and rational faculties of the human being do. The monarch, like reason in the individual, must safeguard this natural order: i.e., rule in accordance with "justice." The microcosm of human society, reflecting the nature of man, was also compared again and again to the macrocosm of Ptolemaic astronomy, in which the sun is "king." Shakespeare takes these standard analogies as axiomatic; he often refers to them in his histories of Christian England, and he elaborates them through the Roman Menenius, in *Coriolanus,* and the Greek Ulysses, in *Troilus and Cressida.*

The religious component of this theory in Christian Europe, the belief that the monarch is divinely designated to "figure" God on earth, is much harder for us to sympathize with in our time than the common-sense classical picture of society, but it was crucial for Shakespeare and most of his contemporaries. In the centuries when Europe was emerging from the dark ages and endeavoring to set up a stable order of society, men of goodwill could easily accept the necessity of a ruler, armed with final authority and sustained by the religious loyalty of his subjects. Greek political theory might be in a sense "true" for all time and rationally demonstrable, but the jealous, squabbling feudal barons did not accept the authority of reason, and reason without history could not determine who was the rightful king. When Shakespeare wrote the passionate defenses of the sacred crown in his histories, he was expressing the prevailing fear of civil war and the almost instinctive reverence for the venerable royal symbol of unity. He was also aware of a very sophisticated political doctrine of monarchy which philosophers and theologians had been discussing for centuries.

The monarchical faith was not only faith in that form of government, but faith in the person of the rightful king. A real live man is required to make the order of justice actual here and now; and if so, it would be impious to doubt that God would somehow provide him. If one is to discover God's will in this matter—the legitimate, the rightful, the divinely sanctioned king—one must read history in the Biblical faith that God speaks through it. That is what Dante did in *De Monarchia,* arguing that the success of Rome in pacifying the world must show that God had chosen that city for the task of rule. The chroniclers that Shakespeare used were in that tradition when they interpreted English history as a divinely guided "epic," culminating in the Tudor regime. Providence itself was supposed to have brought that stable dynasty out of the anarchy of civil war, and the great Elizabeth was revered accordingly, very human woman though she was known to be.

As "figure of God's majesty" the king stood for the moral and religious values upon which society was built; but as he filled that office well or ill he made the good or evil "age and body of the time, his form and pressure." Ideally he would "redeem the time" by making God's timeless truth visible in it; but being only a man, subject to the weakness, evil, and folly of the species, he might darken it instead. These perils, inherent in the religiously sanctioned monarchy, had been often experienced, and were therefore well understood when Shakespeare wrote. In exploring them in his English history plays he was not trying to offer new ideas, but rather to make the old commonplaces shine more vividly, and with deeper implications, than before.

The tragic possibilities of monarchy are particularly clear in *Richard II.* Superficially the play resembles the Henry VI sequence: the reign of a weak king leads to civil war. But in *Richard II* our attention is focused not on the excitement of battles and intrigues, but on the painful moral and religious issues that divide the country and everyone in it. Everyone wants the King to make their England "this other Eden, demi-Paradise," as Gaunt says, for it is the monarch's duty to lead his people back to the mythic state of earthly felicity. But when Bolingbroke dethrones Richard he has reason and justice on his side, while Richard, as the rightful monarch, retains the "divinity" of his sacred office. Everyone (including Bolingbroke) knows that to violate the crown is to destroy the bonds of faith and loyalty that hold the country together; yet no one can pretend that Richard is endeavoring to represent the justice and mercy of God. The whole play may be read as a many-sided debate on this insoluble dilemma; but Richard is the protagonist as well as the de facto ruler, and both the agony and (eventually) the understanding of the painful situation are concentrated in him. As he suffers the results of his irresponsibility he slowly learns to understand both his own vain, childish character and the kingly role (ideally modeled on Christ, the Head of Humanity) which he had failed to play: "I wasted time, and now doth time waste me." *Richard II* is a slight play by Shakespeare's later standards, but it already shows the fundamentals of his vision of the society he knew most intimately, his favorite setting for serious drama.

The two plays named for Henry IV immediately follow *Richard II,* but Henry is not the protagonist of either one. Perhaps Shakespeare felt he had already told Henry's story when he showed, in *Richard II,* how as Bolingbroke he gradually and guiltily usurped the crown; and he apparently did not find Henry's character very interesting in itself. In these plays Henry is the de facto but not the "true" king, even in his own eyes; and Shakespeare presents his reign as a kind of interregnum, or holding operation, a pause in the exciting epic movement toward the predestined Tudor triumph. Henry seems to do well enough with the daily chores of rule, and the only serious threat to his regime is Hotspur's rebellion, which Prince Hal handles almost as a sporting event. But he lacks the ultimate sanction, the blessing of God, which would unite his subjects in faith; and the longer he lives the more impatiently everyone longs for Prince Hal to inherit the crown and usher in a new time.

Henry IV does little; but the plays are properly named for him because his anomalous, frustrated efforts to be the king determine the quality of life in England under his reign. Shakespeare most carefully creates the mood of the faithless time, and builds therein a huge comic picture of the life of the monarchy, in sharpest contrast to the lyric and tragic *Richard II.* The Prince, a playful pre-king, and Falstaff, the universal anti-king, Lord of Misrule and comic Vice, are at the center of the picture. Falstaff is carefully associated with the always popular figure (represented in several ancient folk-rites) who makes a mockery of the official regime, and so he speaks for all who cannot take any order, moral or political, seriously. It is a question how seriously we are to take *him*—but he certainly foretells the bitterer comedy of Shakespeare's tragic period, when he was more deeply concerned with anarchy.

Each of the Henry IV plays presents a different phase of the demoralized, but passing, time. In *Part 1* the Prince and Falstaff can mock the worried regime with gusto, to our perennial delight; but in *Part 2* everyone is older. The Prince has tired of his playboy role and of his huge playmate; Falstaff, feeling unloved, has grown even more shameless; and the King, like his unsponsored reign, has lasted too long. In these two plays Shakespeare displays an almost Chekhovian sense of the importance of time's passage, both in the life of the individual and in the life of the community. In them one may study his uncanny skill in using the character of the reigning monarch to compose a wide, populous, and shifting picture of a whole society—or rather a series of pictures, each one accurately tinted with the mood of its moment of time.

Henry V is the protagonist of his play even more than Richard is of his. Being the national hero, "warlike Harry," the play named for him can only be a series of stirring episodes from his more or less legendary career, with the awkward facts of that stretch of history omitted. Instead of the tragic dialectic of *Richard II,* or the rich diversity of character and motive of *Henry IV,* Parts 1 and 2, Shakespeare shows the English focused upon a single motive: victory under their soldier-king. *Henry V* is the only play Shakespeare ever wrote with that single-minded action, and it is interesting as still another example of his virtuosity with the symbolic figure of the king. But in spite of some magnificent passages the play as a whole is not satisfying, and it is probable that when Shakespeare wrote it, for professional reasons, his interest had already turned from English history to the wider themes of his next phase.

These plays on the themes of romance and the English crown are as a group the most confident, even joyful, that Shakespeare ever wrote. Two of them end unhappily for their protagonists, *Romeo and Juliet* and *Richard II,* but they are lyrical and pathetic rather than truly tragic, as Shakespeare will make us understand tragedy in his next phase. We pity Richard, at the end of the play, because of the childishly literal conception of the royal role that led to his downfall, but at that moment he himself reaffirms the divine harmonies he had failed to apprehend soon enough. We weep for Romeo and Juliet when death overtakes them before they learned to read the full meaning of their love, but this effect depends upon our sharpened sense of what it *did* mean. All the other plays end happily, at least by implication; and in general Shakespeare makes us feel, in this phase, that the ancient dream of earthly felicity represents a true promise for the romantic lovers and for those whose faith is in the sacred crown of England.

In the symbolic scheme of life on earth that Shakespeare inherited, both the commitment of romantic love—"giving and hazarding all"—and faith in the divinely sanctioned ruler, represented ways to Eden, provided that the two "figures" of faith, the beautiful mistress and the monarch, were properly interpreted by all concerned. They correspond to the two guides who lead Dante up the Mount of Purgatory to the terrestrial Paradise: Virgil, who represents the historic, divinely sanctioned Roman Empire and the timeless truths of classical moral and political philosophy, and Beatrice, who stands for the extrarational wisdom of love. It would be natural for Shakespeare to turn back and forth between these two chief "figures" of faith, as he did in these five years, if his own experience were promising. Perhaps something in the public mood of the time, or Shakespeare's own success in the theater, partly accounts for his strong mood of hope. But of course the plays show that he was all the while aware of other possibilities in the human situation, those represented by "hell" where the way is utterly lost; and that is what he will explore in the great plays of his maturity.

The Plays in Chronological Order

ROMEO AND JULIET

Shakespeare wrote his play about youthful love and death in 1594 or 1595, when he himself was only about thirty years old. At about the same time he was writing some of his sonnets, the melodious fairy tale, *A Midsummer Night's Dream,* and *Richard II,* the most lyrical of his histories. He was learning to lift whole plays to the level of poetry while increasing their theatrical power. *Romeo and Juliet* tells a swift story, and it is full of rich characterization and sharp, bawdy humor. At the same time the sequence of its contrasting scenes, and the sound and imagery of its verse, affect us like music.

The story of the doomed young lovers is very old. Shakespeare's immediate source was a narrative poem by Arthur Brooke, *The Tragicall History of Romeus and Juliet* (1562). Brooke had it from the French of Boaistuau, who had it from the Italian of Bandello, who had it from Luigi Da Porto. Beyond that it may be traced back to such classical myths as that of Hero and Leander. The medieval narrative of Tristan and Isolde, familiar to us in Wagner's opera, is on a related theme. Shakespeare used Brooke for his plot and for sketches of some of the characters. But, as usual, he transformed his sources. Brooke's galloping narrative is still readable, and the Italian versions are good of their kind. But Shakespeare seems to have seen the full meaning and pathos of the story for the first time.

He saw it as a tale of the passions of youth. His lovers are very young and innocent when love overwhelms them. So are the bored young men, loafing about town, in whom the passions of the feuding Capulets and Montagues explode so fatally. The old Capulets and Montagues and the worried Prince of Verona feel partly responsible for the feud, and try to control it. The Friar, when Romeo and Juliet confide in him, does his best to guide their love to life and safety. But the moving force which Shakespeare saw in the old story is that glamorous and dangerous passion that everyone feels in youth, and no one fully understands at any age.

He presents this many-sided theme with humor and clarity in Act I, scene 1. A silly squabble between servingmen of the feuding houses starts, out of sheer boredom and animal spirits, when they meet in the street. It builds suddenly from bawdy insults to blows, and from blows to a full-scale brawl which the Prince himself is obliged to quell. The moment the stage is cleared, Benvolio reports to the elder Montagues about their son Romeo, who sighs in the orchard early in the morning: love's helpless victim already, though at the moment he longs for Rosaline, not Juliet. The music of Benvolio's tale of Romeo contrasts with the clatter of the fight, but we already sense that the pugnacious and erotic feelings stirring the young come from the same moody source. And when Romeo wanders on and sees the signs of the brawl, he tells us so:

> Here's much to do with hate, but more with love.
> When then, O brawling love, O loving hate,
> O any thing of nothing first create!

We are already in the "world" of the play, sharing the moods of the troubled young people; we are ready for the story, which begins at the Capulet party, the last scene of Act I. All the dangerous elements of the plot are brought together against the background of music, masks, and summer night. Romeo and Juliet bashfully recognize the love which is their fate, while Juliet's savage cousin Tybalt recognizes Romeo as a Montague and vows to kill him.

Act I, which prepares everything, is marked off by the Chorus who speaks at the beginning and the end of the act. The Chorus, speaking in sonnet form, is the impersonal, musing voice of the storyteller:

> From forth the fatal loins of these two foes,
> A pair of star-crossed lovers take their life.

That famous melody removes us to a distance from the scene, and reminds us that we are watching not only the immediate crisis in Verona but the return of a very old story. The change in point of view may be very effective in the theater. It produces a sense of fate behind what the characters do and say, increases the suspense, and prepares for the poetic scope of the poetry to come.

With the first scene of Act II we are back in the rush of events, which never stops until all is over. In Brooke the story takes months, while Shakespeare concentrates it into about five days. By that means alone he achieves the rhythm of youth, when patience is unknown and every experience of joy or pain is met headlong, for the first time. By means of his setting, Verona in the dog-days, he sharpens all the feelings. Scenes in the still, sunny streets, where the feud breeds in the hot blood of Tybalt and Mercutio, alternate with scenes of starry night or earliest dawn when the lovers steal their moments of "extreme sweet." During Acts II and III the passion of the lovers and the passions of the feud seem to be racing. Meanwhile we learn that Count Paris is pressing for Juliet's hand, and that the Friar is trying to devise a way to save the situation.

In Act II the lovers seem to be winning. The Friar marries them secretly, and Romeo, with that arranged, has his one moment of carefree kidding with his friends Mercutio and Benvolio. But in Act III, scene 1, the feud overtakes them. Tybalt kills Mercutio in the street, and then Romeo kills Tybalt. At almost the same time Paris gets old Capulet's consent to marry Juliet on "Thursday next." Against the background of these misfortunes—accidental, yet all too probable in that risky situation—the lovers have their one night together. We see their parting when the birds wake them at dawn; Romeo flees to Mantua, and Juliet is told that she must marry Paris the next day—Wednesday—for the impatient Capulet has advanced the date. This is the climax and turning point: the lovers' night coincides with the fatality that dooms them.

In Act IV fate, or chance, catches up with the Friar also. He is obliged to arrange Paris' marriage to Juliet, but desperately tries to prevent it by giving Juliet the sleeping-potion. Juliet, when she drinks it alone, must face the thought of death. Next morning Paris and the Capulets must see their wedding celebration turn into a funeral. The complicated effect of wedding-as-funeral and funeral-as-wedding dominates Act IV. It must have pleased Shakespeare, for he used it for a similar purpose in *Much Ado.* It expresses, in theatrical terms, both the pathos and the irony of the situation.

Romeo does not appear in Act IV, but in Act V, scene 1, we see him in Mantua. He has had a dream with some of the ambiguity of Juliet's wedding-funeral:

> I dreamt my lady came and found me dead—
> Strange dream that gives a dead man leave to think—
> And breathed such life with kisses in my lips,
> That I revived and was an emperor.

He has not received the Friar's messages; instead he gets the false news of Juliet's death. He is resolved at once:

> Is it even so? Then I defy you, stars.

This moment corresponds to Juliet's when she drinks the potion; both lovers find the courage to do what love seems to demand. Romeo turns from the Friar, who he thinks has failed him, to the Apothecary, whose poison is sure. In some early versions of the story the Friar himself is suspected of "black magic" but Shakespeare reserves that sinister art for the Apothecary. His Friar, whom we first see at dawn, rejoicing in the beauty of nature, has "white magic." He knows the natural properties of plants, minerals, and human love. The Apothecary is his dark opposite; he knows how to use minerals and plants against nature, to produce death. Armed with his poison, young Romeo races to Juliet's tomb. He outruns the Friar who, with his reverence for life, arrives too late to save the lovers.

The final scene (Act V, scene 3) brings the end which we have felt was "on the cards" all along. The rhythm of the play—that of the heedless, "accident-prone" young—is speeded up for the final crash. Romeo's fight with Paris; the lovers' farewells; the Friar's belated arrival and confused retreat, follow swiftly. With Romeo and Juliet lying dead in the tomb, the churchyard (downstage, no doubt) fills with officers, citizens, Capulets, Montagues, and the Prince. We are reminded of the street brawl that opened the play; of the fight where Tybalt and Mercutio were killed, and of poor Paris' wedding morning with Juliet lying in the semblance of death: the older generation is again mistaken and too late. In the final sequence the Friar and Romeo's and Paris' servingmen explain everything to the Prince. This part of the scene often seems too long to the modern producer, and it is usually cut in performance. But after the confusion of fights, cries, torches, and running people, Shakespeare felt the need of a quieter moment. He wants the audience to reflect on the form and meaning of the swift events they have just seen. By means of the Friar's sad testimony, Shakespeare modulates once more into the detached point of view of the storyteller. "For I will raise her statue in pure gold," says Romeo's father; and old Capulet chimes in:

> As rich shall Romeo's by his lady's lie,
> Poor sacrifices of our enmity.

The final words of the Prince echo the music of the Chorus which we heard at the beginning of the play:

> For never was a story of more woe
> Than this of Juliet and her Romeo.

The plot, or rather the form, that Shakespeare gave the old story holds one completely. The swift yet dreamy alternation of dawn, noon, and starlight seems right, and in reading, or watching a good performance, we do not stop to inquire what day of the week it is. But if, on thinking it over, we do inquire, we find certain inconsistencies in the calendar of the play. The main events seem to occur as follows:

Sunday: The street fight, the Capulet's party (Act I) and the balcony scene (Act II).

Monday: Romeo and Juliet are married (Act II); Tybalt is killed, Romeo is banished; Paris' wedding day is set, and the lovers have their one night together (Act III).

Tuesday: The lovers part at dawn, Romeo flees to Mantua, and Juliet learns she must marry Paris the next day (Act III). The wedding preparations are begun, and Juliet drinks the potion (Act IV).

Wednesday: The wedding party discovers Juliet apparently dead (Act IV).

Thursday: The race for the tomb. The final scene lasts through Thursday night to Friday morning.

The inconsistencies appear in certain references to the time which has elapsed. For instance, in Act II, scene 4, the Nurse tells Romeo, "I anger her sometimes and tell her Paris is the properer man." She seems to imply that weeks, rather than hours, have elapsed since Juliet met Romeo. There is also some trouble about the time when Juliet comes out of her coma, for the Friar has said she would sleep longer than she does according to the calendar. Such inconsistencies probably show that Shakespeare was careless. They also show that he was, as usual, using time only for poetic and dramatic effect, knowing that his audience would never demand scientific accuracy. In studying the time-scheme of the play one must, as always, remember the theater for which Shakespeare wrote. On the permanent setting, in daylight, the scenes follow one another with no intermissions and no pauses for change of setting. The place, the time of day, and the atmosphere of each scene are conveyed imaginatively by what the actors do and say. If one imagines the play performed in that way one can see that Shakespeare used time with great theatrical mastery to speed up, or to slow the action; to give us, not clock-chronology, but the rhythm of the life he was portraying.

Much of the touching quality of the play is due to the setting Shakespeare gave it in the town of Verona. Ostensibly Verona, with its ancient feud, is Italian. But it must have seemed familiar to his English audience, and it seems oddly familiar to us, in spite of its daggers and ruffs and poisons. The Capulets are such parents as we all know: doting, apprehensive, always doing the wrong thing with the best intentions. They are not great nobles, but provincial gentry from Shakespeare's hometown of Stratford. Old Capulet bothers the cook; his lady (like our ambitious mamas) is impressed with Paris' money and social position. The Nurse is practically a member of the family, and can indulge in her impudent garrulity while Lady Capulet merely groans and bites her lip. The Capulets' parties are the kind that our wistful parents give for their marriageable daughters. Romeo and his friends are more elegant than our young men, not in the least embarrassed to wear gorgeous clothes, or to play with poetic and bawdy conceits when they make jokes to kill time. They carry weapons, and their fights (like those Shakespeare must have seen in London streets) are more dangerous than our student riots. But it is not hard to recognize them as youths in the bored, restless period before marriage and settling down. The Friar is perhaps less familiar. He is related to countless intriguing priests in French, Spanish, and Italian plays, but he also expresses much of the wisdom of the play: its delight in the order of nature, and in human love in the natural world.

Romeo and Juliet fit naturally into the life of their town when we first see them. Their adolescence is quieter and moodier than Mercutio's or Benvolio's, but they are not strikingly unusual until love transforms them. Even then Shakespeare keeps us reminded of their extreme youth, and he shows us how their infatuation looks to their friends. When Romeo learns (Act III, scene 3) that he is banished, he has a tantrum in which he sounds more like a child than a hero of tragedy. The Friar scolds him properly:

> Thy tears are womanish, thy wild acts denote
> The unreasonable fury of a beast.

The Nurse is on hand to bring out the comic effect. She has just been through Juliet's hysterics:

> Even so lies she,
> Blubbering and weeping, weeping and blubbering.

Producers are sometimes embarrassed by these tears. They fear that the audience will not be robust enough to see the lovers in this unflattering light and still be moved by their love-death. But the strength of the play is partly in its homey realism, and the love of Romeo and

Juliet is the more touching and frightening for the familiar, domestic scene in which it appears.

The modern producer does, however, have real difficulty with the lovers' tantrums because of the style in which they are written. When the Nurse (Act III, scene 2) cruelly hints at Tybalt's death and Romeo's banishment, Juliet, thinking that Romeo is dead, has a long aria of despair:

> Hath Romeo slain himself? Say thou but ay,
> And that bare vowel I shall poison more
> Than the death-darting eye of cockatrice.
> I am not I, if there be such an I–

and the rest. There is a curious interest, and some psychological subtlety in the puns and conceits, all stemming from "I." But a modern audience cannot accept such dexterity at a moment of high feeling. Shakespeare himself soon learned to rely less on rhetoric and more on his flexible blank verse and his actors' emotion, at moments of this kind. It is in these scenes that we notice Shakespeare's immaturity: he was still experimenting with verse-technique when he wrote this play. The producer is obliged to cut the difficult speeches, but in doing so he must be careful to leave the strong underlying dramatic build intact.

While we see the lovers in the little daylight world of Verona, we are given the scenes that initiate us into the secret, nocturnal world of their love: the Capulets' party, the balcony scene, Juliet's monologue as she waits for night and Romeo; the parting at dawn, and the final scene in the tomb. In these scenes the overpowering sweetness of love is the point, rather than the characters of Romeo and Juliet. When Juliet says (Act II, scene 2)

> My bounty is as boundless as the sea,
> My love as deep,

we ought to feel the love that dwarfs the little girl who speaks, almost forgetting the girl herself. That is why these scenes, miraculous as they are, are not easy to act. The actors should be young enough to charm us in these roles, and at the same time understanding enough to lose their egos in the simplicity of feeling and imagery that Shakespeare provides.

To mark the course of love as Romeo and Juliet follow where it leads, Shakespeare drew on the long tradition of European love-poetry. When they first confess the love that unites them (at the party, Act I, scene 5) they have a delicate duet in the form of a "Petrarchan" sonnet in which religious imagery is half-playfully used to express their human delight:

> If I profane with my unworthiest hand
> This holy shrine, the gentle sin is this,
> My lips two blushing pilgrims ready stand
> To smooth that rough touch with a tender kiss.

While Juliet impatiently waits for Romeo after their secret marriage (Act III, scene 2) she echoes the movement and imagery of the classical epithalamion, or wedding song:

> Gallop apace, you fiery-footed steeds,
> Towards Phoebus' lodging; such a wagoner
> As Phaeton would whip you to the west,
> And bring in cloudy night immediately.

The epithalamion was a joyful song with which the wedding guests were supposed to accompany the ceremonious progress of bride and groom to their nuptial chamber. But Juliet must sing hers alone, in her child's voice; and as we listen we know that her Romeo is banished already. The scene of the lovers' dawn parting is more frightening still (Act III, scene 5). It is based on the "daysong," a form which the twelfth-century troubadors used in the cult of courtly love. No one knows where Shakespeare learned about the daysong, for it was not cultivated in England, but the fact that this scene is based on it was noticed more than a hundred years ago. As in the daysong, the lovers have enjoyed a single night, in secret; day comes too soon, with the voices of the birds; their faithful watcher (the Nurse, in this scene) calls to warn them that they must part. In all of these scenes what the lovers say naturally expresses the way love looks at that moment in the story; and as we read we may not be aware of the old lyric forms that Shakespeare used. But the forms are part of the magic: they suggest, behind Juliet and her Romeo, the mysterious and ancient force of love itself.

There is something sinister about courtly love and its daysongs. In that tradition love is always amoral, all-powerful, and so wonderful that it can be fulfilled only in or through death. The common, daylight world is always love's enemy, the secret night its only friend. It is appropriate that the daysong should be the form of the scene which marks the turning point in the story. In the early parts of the play Romeo and Juliet do not know that their love cannot survive in daytime Verona. But Shakespeare prepares their love-death from the beginning, with his symbolism of day and night. The lovers see each other, again and again, as light which is paradoxically visible only in the dark of night. They see each other that way before they realize what it means. So Romeo sees Juliet when he first spies her at the party:

> O she doth teach the torches to burn bright.
> It seems she hangs upon the cheek of night
> As a rich jewel in an Ethiop's ear.

Shakespeare saw something terrifying, if not in their love itself, at least in their absolute (and too literal and impatient) obedience to it. That is why the end of their story in the dark tomb, surrounded though it is by so many merely chance misfortunes, is the only psychologically and poetically right conclusion.

Shakespeare gives us the full poignancy of Romeo's and Juliet's story, but also the real world of Verona in which it runs its course. He establishes the wider setting before the lovers appear; he makes us aware of it throughout, and he returns to it after their tale is told. He never loses touch with common experience and its sober wisdom, and so he suggests that Romeo and Juliet know love in only one of its forms.

RICHARD II

Richard II, which was written about 1595, is by common consent one of the best of Shakespeare's history plays. It is the first of the series which includes *Henry IV,* Parts 1 and 2, and *Henry V,* but it also stands alone as a complete drama in itself. The story is clear and absorbing, the verse fluent and easy for the modern reader; Richard—a part beloved of actors—is one of Shakespeare's great lyric and dramatic creations.

Richard II, son of Edward the Black Prince, and grandson of Edward III, is acknowledged by everyone, when the play opens, as the true King of England. But he was a weak and irresponsible ruler, and perhaps he had been implicated in the murder of his uncle, Woodstock, Duke of Gloucester. Old John of Gaunt, Duke of Lancaster, and the Duke of York (also his uncles) think him guilty, and so does Bolingbroke, Duke of Hereford and old Gaunt's son and heir. The play shows the painful process whereby Bolingbroke gradually takes power, dethrones Richard, and at last has him murdered. What becomes of the sanctity of the crown, the foundation of all order and loyalty in England, if it can be thus violated by force? Yet how can the country survive when the King himself wastes it like a self-indulgent child? Such is the tragic dilemma which underlies the whole action: everyone seeks (more or less honestly) the welfare of England, but where, in this confusion, is it to be found?

The historic events on which the play is based followed each other swiftly, between April, 1398, and January, 1400, when Richard was murdered in Pomfret Castle. Shakespeare presents the crucial moments with economy, in a few big scenes. In Act I, scene 1, Bolingbroke accuses Mowbray of the murder of the Duke of Gloucester, and Mowbray retorts that Bolingbroke is the traitor. Richard, as king and magistrate, reluctantly agrees to let them resort to the "ordeal of battle" which, according to medieval notions, would reveal the truth, for God would grant victory to the innocent party. But when they meet, with pomp and ceremony, at the lists (Act II, scene 3), Richard stops them before the fight, and then banishes Mowbray forever and Bolingbroke for six years. Was Richard really implicated in the murder as his kinsmen believe, or was he simply afraid of Bolingbroke's growing power and popularity, as he explains to his friends in scene 4? Shakespeare leaves this question open, but when he shows Richard cynically confiscating John of Gaunt's estates the moment he dies, to get money for his Irish wars (Act II, scene 1), we can only sympathize with Richard's enemies. Gaunt's possessions are, of course, rightfully the heritage of his son, Henry Bolingbroke. Before the scene ends we learn that Bolingbroke is already returning from exile to claim them, and his allies hasten to join him. He and his army catch Richard at Flint Castle (Act III, scene 3). Henry Bolingbroke still insists that he only wants his rights and his inheritance, and that he is a loyal subject of King Richard. But he has all the power, and when Richard yields and is taken to London, he is a helpless captive, though still the king in name. This scene marks the climax and the turning point in the queer struggle between Henry Bolingbroke and Richard, whose abdication is now a foregone conclusion. It is staged (Act IV, scene 1) with ceremonious pomp, in Parliament assembled, and in the presence of representatives of the Church and the nobility; and it is in this scene that the political tragedy of Bolingbroke's usurpation, with all the disorder to follow, is felt most sharply. The fifth act is devoted to the pathos of Richard's lonely end, and to images of Bolingbroke, now king as Henry IV, but haunted (as he will be all his life) by his crimes of usurpation and regicide.

The reader can follow the play more easily, I think, if he has this simple narrative in mind to begin with. But the chronicle of fourteenth-century England, exciting as it is, is only the framework of *Richard II.* Shakespeare re-created the characters of history, as was his custom, in order to bring out the meanings he saw in the story. At the center is the painful and puzzling contrast between Richard and Henry Bolingbroke, each with his partisans. Between the main antagonists are such touching figures as York, old John of Gaunt, even the Queen. They can see some wrong on both sides, and they all deeply feel the damage that the struggle between Richard and Bolingbroke is doing to England. And the audience is led to see the unfolding story through the eyes now of one character, now of another.

The followers of Richard and of Bolingbroke are lightly sketched, especially in Acts I and II. They sound very much alike as they speak the fluent verse characteristic of this play; and we cannot make them out as individuals until we see what they do. Richard's friends, Bushy, Bagot, and Green, share Richard's pleasures and encourage him in his irresponsible policies. Through them we get the atmosphere of Richard's court, which was supposed to be the most brilliant in Europe. Bolingbroke's followers, on the other hand, are shrewd and ambitious men of action. Northumberland, Bolingbroke's chief supporter, is recognizably the same tough and treacherous politician whom we meet again in the next play, *Henry IV, Part 1.*

As for Henry Bolingbroke, Shakespeare made him the perfect counterpart to Richard. Strong, able, and very shrewd, he instinctively understands politics as a power-game, in which the laws and loyalties of the monarchy must be respected chiefly because of tradition and public opinion. Through his eyes we see Richard as childish and effeminate, quite out of his element among the quarrelsome dukes and barons who surround the throne. Bolingbroke, a born ruler, inevitably moves toward the crown, and in the first two acts, when Richard proves so inadequate as king, and then (as soon as old Gaunt dies) grabs Bolingbroke's inheritance with the gesture of a spoiled child (Act II, scene 1), our sympathies are all with the usurper. Shakespeare always had great respect for the arts of practical politics. Bolingbroke is a master of that art and its hard necessities, and he dominates the realm of battle and intrigue where the conflicts of the play are decided.

But the characters who do not engage directly in these conflicts—York, and especially old Gaunt and the Queen—are in a position to sense the wider meanings and the more permanent values behind the immediate tussles for power. From time to time the swift movement of the story pauses, as one of these more detached characters takes the stage. The scenes they dominate are essentially lyrical and meditative, like the choruses which, in Greek tragedy, alternate with the high-pitched disputes between the main antagonists.

Thus, for example, old Gaunt on his deathbed (Act II, scene 1) is like "a prophet new inspired." He lifts our thoughts from the exciting events of the moment to the patriotic motive of all the histories, when he utters his famous paean to England, "This royal throne of Kings, this sceptred isle." When he foresees the chaos to come—

> That England that was wont to conquer others,
> Hath made a shameful conquest of itself,

his love, his grief, and his insight dwarf both Richard and Henry. And when he dies we feel that darkness has come: no one is left who can see the true welfare of the country.

The next scene (Act II, scene 2) is dominated by the Queen, who was left to brood when Richard went to Ireland. She has none of Gaunt's intellectual vigor, but (like many sensitive women) she can read the meaning of her *feelings* with frightening honesty. She gives us a more intimate sense than Gaunt did of this moment in the play, which is pregnant with evil to come:

> Some unborn sorrow ripe in fortune's womb
> Is coming towards me, and my inward soul
> With nothing trembles, at something it grieves,
> More than with parting from my lord the King.

Bushy very sensibly tries to explain away her worry:

> Each substance of a grief hath twenty shadows,
> Which shows like grief itself, but is not so.
>
> . . .
>
> So your sweet Majesty,
> Looking awry upon your lord's departure,
> Find shapes of grief more than himself to wail,
> Which looked on as it is, is naught but shadows
> Of what is not.

But the next moment Green arrives to report that Bolingbroke has landed at the head of an army. The Queen was, in her way, "prophetic" too:

> So Green, thou art the midwife to my woe,
> And Bolingbroke my sorrow's dismal heir.
> Now hath my soul brought forth her prodigy,
> And I, a gasping new-delivered mother,
> Have woe to woe, sorrow to sorrow joined.

The whole scene, with its elaborate image of the Queen's terrors as birth pangs, beautifully defines the coming of these choric or prophetic intuitions, which are neither to be dismissed nor completely trusted. We cannot tell, until the actual event, whether they come from "fortune's womb" or only from the womb of one's own grief.

When society is in confusion, as it is in this play, men do not see eye to eye, and it is very hard to tell the difference between the private daydream and the public reality. Richard, for instance, in the first two acts, takes his own greedy feelings as right and true, just as a child does. Old Gaunt tells him (Act II, scene 1),

> A thousand flatterers sit within thy crown,
> Whose compass is no bigger than thy head,
> And yet incaged in so small a verge,
> The waste is no whit lesser than thy land.

At this point not only Gaunt, but Bolingbroke, with his sharp realism, can see much more objectively than Richard. We cannot take the visions in his "head" seriously—except as dangerous to his country. But all of this begins to change in Act III, scene 2, when Richard, landing in his own country after his Irish wars, meets the rude reality of Bolingbroke's armed rebellion. As a man among men he cuts an even sorrier figure than before, with his tears, his vacillations, and his operatic arias. But what he *sees* through his own plight—the crown defied, the sacred order of society violated, the country at war—cuts so deep that he instantly takes the center of the stage. He is like a sensitive child who blurts out the truth with a candor which dismays the adults. Misfortune makes him a kind of naive poet and seer, and he has the power of language to make us feel and see what he does.

The fact is that Richard, trying to understand his sufferings in the rest of the play, expresses the whole subtle, complex medieval conception of the role of the king, the center of the natural (and divinely sanctioned) order of society. This conception underlies all the histories, and Richard, as he brings out its perils and its beauties, becomes by far the most important of those suffering-and-seeing characters who give the play its depth and its emotional impact. But in the last three acts Richard's vision is confirmed by the Queen, and by the Bishop of Carlisle, from their very different points of view.

The Queen sees a bittersweet image of the kingdom of England as it might have been and should have been, when she overhears the moralizing of the Duke of York's old Gardener (Act III, scene 4). The Gardener tells the First Servant to prune the fruit trees,

Which like unruly children make their sire
Stoop with oppression of their prodigal weight.

Puttering about, pulling weeds, supporting weak branches, he ruefully makes believe that the quiet garden is the ideal England at peace and in order, and he the king as the king should be. When he tells his boy that Richard, who did not prune or weed his garden, is about to be deposed, the poor Queen can stand no more, and blames the Gardener for his sad truth:

Thou, old Adam's likeness set to dress this garden,
How dares thy harsh rude tongue sound this unpleasing news?
What Eve, what serpent hath suggested thee
To make a second fall of cursed man?

The whole scene is transparent but intricate allegory, like late medieval paintings and illuminated manuscripts. The pretty figures in the sunlit garden—the Gardener, the flowers—are clear to the eye, but signs, at the same time, of moral and religious doctrine. The Queen sees and understands all too clearly, for (like her premonitions of sorrow in Act II, scene 2) the garden image presents what her own unwelcome feelings tell her.

When Richard first returns from Ireland (Act III, scene 2), he uses a more emotionally colored version of this image of the king as gardener:

As a long-parted mother with her child
Plays fondly with her tears and smiles in meeting;
So weeping, smiling, greet I thee my earth,
And do thee favours with my royal hands.

When he meditates alone just before his death in prison (Act V, scene 5), music which he hears offstage provides him with another metaphor:

How sour sweet music is,
When time is broke, and no proportion kept.
So is it in the music of men's lives.
And here have I the daintiness of ear
To check time broke in a disordered string;
But for the concord of my state and time
Had not an ear to hear my true time broke.
I wasted time, and now doth time waste me.

He sees the king as responsible in his time for harmony, both in his own life and in his state, with its many different lives. His poetic style, expressive as it is of his own remorse, contrasts sharply with the objectivity of the Gardener scene. But it reveals the same medieval ideal of human society, innocent as Eden, harmonious as music.

In the big scene (Act IV, scene 1) when the dignitaries of church and state are gathered in Parliament for the hollow ceremony of Richard's formal abdication, the Bishop of Carlisle strongly presents another aspect of the traditional monarchy:

> What subject can give sentence on his King?
> And who sits here that is not Richard's subject?
>
> . . .
>
> And shall the figure of God's majesty,
> His captain, steward, deputy elect,
> Anointed, crowned, planted many years,
> Be judged by subject and inferior breath,
> And he himself not present?

The Bishop's style is that of political oratory, and he makes an extremely awkward point of constitutional law. He is much more like the political theorists of Shakespeare's own time, who were arguing for the doctrine of "the divine right of kings" for reasons of practical politics, than he is like a medieval saint or poet. But he touches the painful point where the traditional ideal meets Bolingbroke's power, and the actual situation. This is the crux of the tragic dilemma in the play. Shakespeare must have felt that, at that moment of history, *time* was wasting not only Richard but the old order too. Bolingbroke ushers in a new time —closer to Shakespeare's own. In subsequent plays he will present monarchical society from other points of view and in other historical contexts.

Bolingbroke, in his triumph, announces "the wave of the future." We see him in Act V, scenes 3 and 6, as Henry IV, ruling with decision and efficiency but already haunted by his crimes of usurpation and regicide. These scenes relate the play to the epic sequence of the histories. But it is Richard, dominating the finale with his pathos and his growing understanding, who brings *this* play to an end.

Scholars and critics who comment on *Richard II* see many different meanings in it. Is the play primarily a character study of Richard? Or is it, with its melodious verse and elaborately developed metaphors, its poet-king as protagonist, essentially about poetry itself? Or is it a political play arguing for (or against) the traditional beliefs about monarchy? Or is it one of Shakespeare's meditations on appearance and reality, shadow and substance? The answer to all these questions must,

I think, be *yes*. These and other themes may be found in the play. It is of course a history, and recounts one of the struggles for the crown of England. But the struggle is defined in this play by its moment of time—the end of the medieval kingdom of the Plantagenets—and by the contrasting characters who take the stage. Each character sees the mysterious course of history according to his situation, passions, and intelligence. And as we see what they see, one after the other, we make out the story as Shakespeare saw it: in the round, and in many complementary lights.

HENRY IV, PART 1

Henry IV, Part 1, was written in 1596 or 1597. It has been popular since its first appearance, chiefly, perhaps, because of Falstaff, that "huge hill of flesh." For more than two centuries Falstaff so dazzled his audiences that the play itself was neglected. But in recent years we have come to see that the play as a whole is a great masterpiece of the comic imagination, in which Falstaff himself is only one element.

For this play Shakespeare's main sources were Holinshed's *Chronicles*, Samuel Daniell's poem, *The Civille Wars*, and an earlier play, *The Famous Victories of Henry the Fifth*. He accepts the popular, patriotic theme, and then proceeds, as always, to use, or change, the meager facts of history to suit his dramatic purposes. The easiest way to understand the historic events in *Henry IV, Part 1,* is to read its predecessor, *Richard II*. In that play Henry Bolingbroke takes the crown from Richard, the legitimate king but a vain, weak man, and at last has him murdered. When this play opens Bolingbroke is king as Henry IV. He now wants only peace and order, and dreams of a crusade to expiate his crime of regicide. But the Percys, great nobles who had helped Henry against Richard, are chafing under his authority; they point out that their kinsman, Mortimer, had been designated by Richard II as the legitimate heir to the crown. They start a rebellion, led by young Harry Percy, "Hotspur." Shakespeare recognizes the weakness of Henry's position, usurper as he is, but sympathizes with him as the de facto (and very responsible) monarch; and above all as the father of Prince Hal, who, as everyone knew, was to become the national hero, Henry V. The Percys' angry and ill-conceived rebellion, crushed at the battle of Shrewsbury, is the central story of the play.

But the play is much more than an exciting tale of plots and battles. Though it was written just after *Richard II,* it is a far wider canvas, and very different both in theme and tone. *Richard II* is narrowly focused upon the problem of the sanctity of the crown, and owes much of its color to Richard himself, who has a childishly literal belief in the "divine right of kings." Richard's despairing outbursts againt his enemies and his sad, poetic meditations evoke a picture of the kingdom of England like an illumination in a medieval book of hours: a garden which, as he imagines, God had given absolutely to him. Henry IV is, by comparison, a modern monarch, weary now but realistic, and thoroughly trained in practical politics, and his England is that "Merry England" that Shakespeare's audience knew and loved. *Richard II* is consistently lyrical, almost tragic, in feeling, while *Henry IV, Part 1,* shows even the bloody battles of the rebellion with gusto, in a smiling light. And that heroic theme, centering around young Hotspur, is balanced by the profound laughter of Falstaff.

Shakespeare introduces both themes in the first two scenes of the play. First we see the situation as it looks to the King (Act 1, scene 1):

> So shaken as we are, so wan with care,
> Find we a time for frighted peace to pant.

The King has no enthusiasm for more domestic broils, but he sees that Hotspur's rebellion must be dealt with. And he fears that his own Harry will disgrace him: hearing of Hotspur's heroic exploits against the Scots, he says:

> Yea, there thou mak'st me sad, and mak'st me sin
> In envy, that my Lord Northumberland
> Should be the father to so blessed a son . . .
> Whilst I . . .
> See riot and dishonour stain the brow
> Of my young Harry.

For the King, Prince Hal's merry-making is not a joke. But in the very next scene (Act 1, scene 2) we see Hal himself teasing the fabulous Falstaff for his own pleasure and ours. Falstaff is on permanent holiday from the cares of state, and his enjoyment of wit and gluttony is irresistible—even though his very presence is a mockery of the King's high seriousness. But in this scene Shakespeare makes it clear that the

Prince has not forgotten his duty to the crown. In the famous monologue which concludes the scene, Hal explains that he knows his disreputable companions for what they are, that he will assume his princely responsibilities in due time, and that then his apparent irresponsibility will make him seem all the more royal, by contrast:

> I'll so offend, to make offence a skill,
> Redeeming time when men think least I will.

His notion of "redeeming time" suggests religious dedication to his future task as ruler. As heir apparent he represents the patriotic theme of all the histories; he is, in fact, the hero of the play. And through him the anti-heroic Falstaff and the super-heroic Hotspur are related, compared, and played off against each other in many ways. By the end of scene 2 we see already that we must look to the Prince for our understanding of the many-sided action which the play will unroll before us.

During most of the first three acts Prince Hal playfully and ironically explores Falstaff and his low-life companions, while Hotspur in a series of alternating scenes (Act I, scene 3, Act II, scene 3, and Act III, scene 1,) builds up his rebellion. Shakespeare gives the rebels some fine, ringing speeches of defiance in the high style of chivalry, but there is plenty of irony in these scenes too. The weary King is faced with the treacherous Percys, Worcester and Northumberland, as well as the latter's son, Hotspur. They are allied with the "devil" Glendower, a Welshman, a bard and magician as well as a soldier, and the dank, formidable Scot, Douglas. This picturesque gallery is probably intended to suggest the national types which the English monarchy was endeavoring to pacify and unite. But Hotspur is the soul of the rebellion; and through Hotspur's headlong impatience Shakespeare characterizes the rebellion itself. Even uncle Worcester and father Northumberland are powerless to stop Hotspur's wonderful flood of angry blarney:

> By heaven methinks it were an easy leap,
> To pluck bright honour from the pale-faced moon,
> Or dive into the bottom of the deep,
> Where fathom-line could never touch the ground,
> And pluck up drowned honour by the locks,
> So he that doth redeem her thence might wear
> Without corrival all her dignities.
> But out upon this half-faced fellowship!

"He apprehends a world of figures here," remarks Worcester, who has not been able to get in a word, "But not the form of what he should attend."

Hotspur is one of the play's great figures. The historic Hotspur was as old as the King; Shakespeare made him the Prince's age (following Daniel's poem) to fit the crucial role he had designed for him. It is his youth which makes his rebellion at once touching and foolish. His green heroism, his fanatical cult of honor, his scorn for all the lazy pleasures make him fat old Falstaff's counterpart—if anything could counterbalance so vast a mass of sophisticated self-indulgence. And because of his youthful fire and prowess he is the perfect antagonist for the Prince to prove his soldierly metal upon, when he gets ready to assume the martial role. We laugh with him when he mocks the King's emissary (Act 1, scene 3) or Glendower (Act III, scene 1). We laugh at him when his loving wife, her patience exhausted by his egoism, yells in her frustration,

> Out you mad-headed ape, a weasel hath not such a deal of spleen as you are tossed with.

And we are deeply touched when Hal kills him at the end. Only Shakespeare can create, with such apparent ease, a figure to command love, tears, and laughter.

While Hotspur is stirring up trouble in pursuit of honor, Prince Hal is enjoying Falstaff and his low-life companions (Act II, scenes 1, 2, and 4). We are in the tough world of the taverns, where tapsters and coachmen, thieves, bawds, and drunken hangers-on make their headquarters. Their language is full of slang and topical allusions, and the modern reader needs the glossary to understand it—though it is hardly more strange than the lingo of Damon Runyon's Times Square types. The Prince and Poins play upon Falstaff the elaborate practical joke of the Gadshill robbery, a burlesque and colloquial accompaniment to Hotspur's high-style adventures.

Falstaff, of course, dominates these scenes with his bulk and the appalling quantity of shameless humanity that is packed into it. He seems to have appeared full-blown in Shakespeare's imagination, as laughable and inevitable as "the flesh" itself, and just as mysterious. Everyone knows him, like an old friend, the moment he waddles onto the stage, filled with gallons of sack, eggs, and butter, lying cowardice, and unanswerable wit. But Shakespeare himself does not suggest any solemn analysis of his character. Instead he suggests to his audience the deep comic meanings of Falstaff; and that he does through Falstaff's part in the dynamics of the play, and through the comments of the

Prince. In the design of the play Falstaff takes a very old role, which (as recent studies show) Shakespeare's audience would have understood—that of the clown, who had his recognized place in religious and seasonal festivals of England, and in several kinds of plays that grew out of the festivals. When Prince Hal calls him a "reverend Vice" he is thinking of that popular figure in the morality plays who laughs off all virtue, to the delight of the house. When Falstaff, with a straight face, burlesques the King himself (Act II, scene 4), he is playing the part of the Lord of Misrule who, in Christmas ceremonies more ancient than the classic Saturnalia, turned all authority, whether religious, moral, or political, into joyous mockery. One can think of *Henry IV, Part 1*, filled as it is with Elizabethan pride and confidence, as a festive celebration of England. The King and Hotspur proclaim the England of responsible rule, high deeds, and chivalry while Falstaff produces the belly-laugh of the old, unregenerate human who eternally eats and sleeps, indifferent to all the forms of government and morality.

It is the Prince who first reveals his corpulent friend in this mythic light, when we first meet him in Act 1, scene 2:

> FALSTAFF
> Now Hal, what time of day is it lad?
> PRINCE HENRY
> Thou art so fat-witted with drinking of old sack, and unbuttoning thee after supper, and sleeping upon benches after noon, that thou hast forgotten to demand that truly which thou wouldst truly know. What a devil hast thou to do with the time of the day? Unless hours were cups of sack, and minutes capons, and clocks the tongues of bawds, and dials the signs of leaping-houses, and the blessed sun himself a fair hot wench in flame-colored taffeta, I see no reason why thou shouldst be so superfluous to demand the time of the day.

Falstaff reduces time itself to the gaudy procession of fleshly pleasures, and the sun, time-honored symbol of cosmic order, and of the king, the keystone of political and moral order, to a hot wench. Falstaff admits the charge, but elegantly pleads for himself as a nocturnal creature:

> Marry then sweet wag, when thou art King let not us that are squires of the night's body be called thieves of the day's beauty; let us be Diana's foresters, gentlemen of the shade, minions of the moon.

To which the Prince makes a characteristically sobering reply:

> Thou sayest well, and it holds well too, for the fortune of us that are the moon's men doth ebb and flow like the sea, being governed as the sea is by the moon.

In all of this poetic and affectionate fooling, the Prince identifies himself with the marvelous Falstaff, Lord of Misrule, yet never forgets that he must soon play the opposite part in the traditional drama, that of the true king, upholder of order. He makes Falstaff feel it too, and Falstaff is momentarily deflated, like a scolded child: " 'Sblood, I am as melancholy as a gib-cat," he pitifully murmurs, "or a lugged bear."

Many readers have been so charmed by Falstaff that they dislike the Prince for putting him in his place. There is indeed a painful strand in the relationship between the two men; it is felt most strongly at the end of *Henry IV, Part 2,* when Hal, now Henry V, must cut off Falstaff for good. But at this point he shows Hal enjoying his youth and delightedly exploring that unmanageable weight of flesh and anarchic wit. Hal is a farsighted young man, a ruler-in-training, and he plays many roles as he shares the lives of different kinds of men, his future subjects. In this he is akin to Edgar in *King Lear,* who also plays several parts before he comes into his own; or even Hamlet, who assumes his "antic disposition" as a temporary disguise. Like Shakespeare himself the Prince is both inside the play, sustaining its life with sympathy and imagination, and behind the scenes, judging and arranging the characters and their doings. Shakespeare often feels a close analogy between the dramatist, who arranges the creations of his imagination so as to make a coherent and significant play, and the ruler who must try to harmonize the men and motives under him so as to make a community. That is why the Prince, both in his attitudes and his remarks, so often represents the author's point of view, like a chorus.

The Prince's chorus-role is clearest in the great tavern scene (Act II, scene 4), as he takes his ease for the last time before fighting Hotspur. He presents a gallery of the various types he has learned to know, all in the comic spirit which he had learned from Falstaff. He explains to Poins that he has mastered the low-life lingo: "I can drink with any tinker in his own language during my life." He proceeds to demonstrate his skill by teasing the poor stupid drawer, Francis. He caricatures Hotspur, from the point of view of the tavern:

> I am not yet of Percy's mind, the Hotspur of the North, he that kills me some six or seven dozen of Scots at a breakfast, washes his hands, and says to his wife, fie upon this quiet life, I want work. O my sweet Harry, says she, how many hast thou killed to-day? Give my roan horse a drench, says he, and answers, some fourteen an hour after, a trifle, a trifle.

When the news is brought, near the end of the scene, that Hotspur's rebellion is reaching its dangerous climax, the Prince knows that he must soon face his angry father and then take his place as a soldier. But before he assumes that more serious role he and Falstaff act out the parental scolding, first with Falstaff as King and the Prince as himself, and then with the roles reversed. It is one of the richest pieces of comic play in the literature of the theater. It is based on the primitive laughter of the Saturnalia, the momentary triumph of Misrule; but as played by the Prince and Falstaff it is full of the most sophisticated, ironic lights upon all three characters (King, Hal, and Falstaff) and even on the reverend crown itself. The Prince allows Falstaff the last word. Speaking as the Prince, Falstaff commends himself in words which have as much truth as poetry, as much insight as burlesque:

> But to say that I know more harm in him than in myself, were to say more than I know . . . banish plump Jack, and banish all the world.

The Prince must be off to war, yet he feels, and makes us feel, that Falstaff and all he stands for are not to be disowned even there.

If we have understood the Prince so far, we expect him to handle his father as well as he handled his disreputable companions in the tavern. He does not disappoint us. In the scene (Act III, scene 2) which is the climax and turning point of the play, Hal accepts the scolding with humility, allowing the King to get all of his anger and disappointment out of his system. He then gently but firmly reassures him:

> Percy is but my factor, good my lord,
> To engross up glorious deeds on my behalf.
> And I will call him to so strict account,
> That he shall render every glory up,
> Yea, even the slightest worship of his time.

The King is overjoyed: "A hundred thousand rebels die in this!" he cries. He had not realized that his son was perfectly well aware of his duties. Like a self-made man in our own country, he finds it hard to believe that Hal, brought up with all the "advantages," will ever have his own drive for success and "glory." The Prince thus reveals the King in a slightly comic light; but he turns now to his life-and-death duel with Hotspur as eagerly as Hotspur himself. And now we are to see how he deals with the chivalric theme of battle.

We follow the course of the ill-fated rebellion in a series of scenes in the rebel camp (Act IV, scenes 1, 2, and 3, and Act V, scene 2). Hotspur, strongly aided by Douglas, maintains the fighting spirit as one after another of his allies drop out. He is the same impatient young man whom we saw in so many comic lights during the first three acts, but the emergency shows him at his best: courageous, generous, and touching in his single-minded passion for honor and glory. He makes an exciting rival for the Prince.

But the Prince takes Falstaff to war too, and against that stirring background plump Jack appears in a new light—an ample representative of all the weaknesses of human flesh in war's dangerous confusion. He begins his military career by collecting bribes to release his conscripts, and then replacing them with "scarecrows" so ghastly that even he is ashamed to be seen with them. But when the Prince catches him in the act and tries to scold him, he has his usual unanswerable reply (Act IV, scene 2):

> Tut, tut, good enough to toss, food for powder, food for powder; they'll fill a pit as well as better; tush man, mortal men, mortal men.

On the eve of the fatal battle (Act V, scene 1) he confides to the Prince: "I would 'twere bedtime Hal, and all well," a line too deep for either blubbering or laughter. The Prince tries to tell him he "owes God a death," but that only inspires him to his famous meditation on that "honour" which Hal and Hotspur are pursuing with such fire:

> What is that honour? Air—a trim reckoning. Who hath it? He that died a Wednesday.

He returns to that wonderful thought (Act V, scene 4) when he encounters the dead hero, Sir Walter Blunt: "I like not such grinning honour as Sir Walter hath."

The battle scenes of Act V (scenes 3, 4, and 5) bring the story of the play to its triumphant conclusion with the defeat of the rebellion, the death of Hotspur, and the vindication of the Prince. But Falstaff is there too, larger than life, and what are we to make of him, as he cautiously steers his quaking belly through the melee?

When the two Harrys meet at last, Falstaff is on hand to cheer them on:

> Well said Hal, to it Hal. Nay you shall find no boy's play here I can tell you.

While the furious champions fight their duel, and Hotspur falls fatally wounded, Falstaff, attacked by Douglas, hastily tumbles down and plays dead. Hotspur packs all the pathos of his short, impatient life into his last words:

> O Harry, thou hast robbed me of my youth.
> I better brook the loss of brittle life
> Than those proud titles thou hast won of me;

They wound my thoughts worse than thy sword my flesh.
But thought's the slave of life, and life time's fool,
And time that takes survey of all the world
Must have a stop. O I could prophesy,
But that the earthy and cold hand of death
Lies on my tongue. No Percy, thou art dust,
And food for—

"For worms, brave Percy," says the Prince; "Fare thee well great heart./ Ill-weaved ambition, how much art thou shrunk." He bids his touching good-byes to the two grotesquely different bodies lying side by side, slender young Hotspur and mountainous Falstaff, and departs to finish the victory. And Falstaff (who listened to his own epitaph with mixed feelings) stabs dead Hotspur once more, to make sure, loads the trophy on his shoulders, and waddles off to claim his reward. The Prince, though momentarily appalled by such imperturbable shamelessness, accepts it—with the same laughter and pity, perhaps, as Shakespeare felt when he devised the scene:

Come bring your luggage nobly on your back;
For my part, if a lie may do thee grace,
I'll gild it with the happiest terms I have.

Falstaff marches off with the thin young corpse dangling over his big bulk, while the retreat is sounded, and the King and his generals gather for the majestic finale. He is literally "bearing honor from the field"—the same grinning honor he knew all along. And in this tableau the contrasting themes of Falstaff and Hotspur are visibly united.

Readers of the play who have fallen hopelessly in love with Falstaff or Hotspur or some of the other irresistible characters, often find it hard to accept the full effect of these last scenes. They are certainly a daring, even dismaying mixture of pathos and laughter. And when the Prince, at the center of the picture, lets huge Falstaff make off with his noble luggage, he may seem, with his enigmatic smile, hard to understand. It has been suggested that Shakespeare planned this scene in order to prepare for the final parting of Hal and Falstaff at the end of *Henry IV, Part 2;* and that may be true. But there is no need to think of the later play in order to understand the superb ending of this one.

The fact is that the whole form and meaning of *Henry IV, Part 1,* is closely akin to other masterpieces of Shakespeare's. Like *Hamlet,* for instance, it suggests a whole society, in which clowns and princes, fools, wise men, and heroes have their contrasted and conflicting lives. Some understand much, some little; but all have their places within the ideal order of the traditional monarchy, which the design of the play reflects. In *Hamlet* the conflicts have their tragic resolution as order is restored in the state and the design of the play is completed. But *Henry IV, Part 1,* throbs with the more joyous, fierce vitality of Shakespeare's youth and Elizabeth's thriving England. In the final scenes the insoluble paradoxes of folly and heroism, slovenly life and splendid death, are resolved in laughter as deep as that of tough old Aristophanes. The Prince turns from that celebration to the sober cares of rule. As for Falstaff, we have him always with us—though we know that he is mortal and that he eventually dies comfortably in his bed, just as he hoped he would: "bed-time Hal, and all well."

HENRY IV, PART 2

This play was written soon after *Part* v, in 1597 or 1598. The two plays make one story, and it is probable that Shakespeare planned them that way from the first. The comic and pathetic relationship of Falstaff, the Prince, and the King, which begins in *Part 1,* ends in this play with the death of Henry IV. But the two parts are different in tone, and may be read or performed separately. *Part 2* is sometimes thought to be disorganized, but a careful reading shows that it is, in fact, a subtle, sardonic, and consistent picture of England at the end of this king's troubled reign. And the Falstaff scenes have the magic of great comedy the moment they are put on the stage before a live audience, where they belong.

Shakespeare's main sources were the same as he used for *Part 1. Part 2* begins just after the battle that concludes *Part 1* when the rebels, misreading the signs of the times, are getting ready to try again. The "Induction" serves to remind the audience of the situation at that moment of history. By using "Rumor, painted full of tongues," for this purpose, Shakespeare suggests the faithless and deceptive atmosphere in England, which will last until the King's death.

In Act I, scene 1, we see the start of the new rebellion. Old Northumberland, that untrustworthy politician, receives Rumor's "false comfort," and then the bitter truth: that the battle is lost, and his son Hotspur killed. Pressed by Morton and Lord Bardolph, he decides to fight anyway: "In poison there is physic," he says; "let order die." Morton reports that the Archbishop of York (who will turn out to be the main strength of the rebellion) is in arms, "turns insurrection to religion," and so recruits a following among the discontented, who take his religious authority as their guide. This conspiracy has none of the foolish but generous drive of young Hotspur's rebellion in *Part 1;* we are made to feel that these older men are too late with their civil disturbance and should have known better.

In scene 2 the great Falstaff appears with his tiny page: "I do here walk before thee, like a sow that hath overwhelmed all her litter but one," he announces. Shakespeare's audience would presumably have greeted him with laughter and cheers, remembering him from *Part 1.* He is indeed the same wonderful monster, but like other people one knows he has grown older, more obvious, and more predictable. The Lord Chief Justice tries to scold him, but is obliged to let him off as a national hero and a privileged character. We learn that he is applying for an old soldier's pension, cheating his tailor, and slandering the Prince. Alone at the end of the scene, he reflects that the pox, the gout, and the infirmities of his age can all be made to fit his supposed role as the great old warrior: "I have the wars for my colour, and my pension shall seem the more reasonable. A good wit will make use of any thing: I will turn diseases to commodity."

By the end of this scene the play's two stories are begun, that of Falstaff and that of the rebels. Falstaff's plan to "turn diseases to commodity" reminds one of the Archbishop's turning insurrection to religion, and Northumberland's "in poison there is physic." The motives of the two stories are analogous: cynical in much the same way, though Falstaff's operations are broad farce, and the rebellion is presented in a sad light.

There is one all-important element in the design of the play which Shakespeare significantly reserves until Act II, scene 2: the Prince, the future King Henry V. The audience, remembering his brilliant role in *Part 1,* would presumably have been waiting eagerly for their hero's return, but when he appears at last his first line to Poins is, "Before God, I am exceeding weary." He explains:

PRINCE HENRY

But I tell thee, my heart bleeds inwardly that my father is so sick, and keeping such vile company as thou art hath in reason taken from me all ostentation of sorrow.

POINS

The reason?

PRINCE HENRY

What wouldst thou think of me if I should weep?

POINS

I would think thee a most princely hypocrite.

PRINCE HENRY

It would be every man's thought, and thou art a blessed fellow to think as every man thinks.

The Prince too is in a false position; while his father lingers on there is nothing he can do that would not be misinterpreted. In this mood of lonely detachment he and Poins plan to "see Falstaff bestow himself tonight in his true colors." In Act II, scene 4, they watch the end of the great tavern scene, when Falstaff indulges himself in drink, Doll Tearsheet's flattering caresses, and lying slander of the Prince. None of this is new to the Prince; he watches sadly, for lack of anything better to do. When Peto brings news of the King, the Prince feels "much to blame,/ So idly to profane the precious time," and abruptly takes his leave: "Falstaff, good night." But he will take no part in quelling the rebellion; he will find nothing to do until his father's death at the end of Act IV.

The rebellion unfolds as it has begun. In Act I, scene 3, the Archbishop of York, in a gloomy council of war with his allies, concludes that they have a chance of winning because the people are "sick" of Henry IV, and by nature fickle:

An habitation giddy and unsure
Hath he that buildeth on the vulgar heart.

The irony is that he is proposing to build on the vulgar heart himself. In Act II, scene 3, Hotspur's widow bitterly reproaches her father-in-law, Northumberland, for having deserted Hotspur at the battle of Shrewsbury. But then she and Lady Northumberland persuade the old man to flee to Scotland, thus deserting the rebels' cause once more.

We meet the ailing King for the first time in Act III, scene 1. This scene, a lyric or choral interlude, is filled with the feeling that the King's time has lasted too long. Frustrated and fretful, he is awake while his subjects sleep: "Uneasy lies the head that wears a crown." He tells Warwick that the "body of our kingdom is foul"; he sadly rehearses his own long career: his usurpation of the crown, the treachery of his former allies, the present rebellion. "Such things," Warwick replies, "become the hatch and brood of time": the Archbishop's rebellion might have been foreseen, it had to come. But its failure may be foreseen too, and he urges the King to stop worrying and go to sleep. The King, while he lives, is too uneasy to sleep; he returns to his improbable project of a crusade to unite the country and expiate his guilt. But we must agree with Warwick that he should relax; and this scene foreshadows scenes 4 and 5 of Act IV, when the rebellion is ending and the King, on his deathbed, is at last getting ready to sleep for good.

The rebellion, deluded though it is, must be ended, and that is accomplished in scenes 1 and 2 of Act IV. Prince John tricks the Archbishop into meeting peacefully with him between the two armies, whereupon the half-hearted rebel army goes home, and the Prince arrests the leaders. This episode is, of course, not designed as the turning point of a real struggle, but as a sardonic anticlimax. The folly of the rebellion has been clear all along, and its story, though ostensibly concerned with high politics, is plotted as a comedy.

The famous scenes at Henry IV's deathbed (Act IV, scenes 4 and 5) deal with the grave matter of the royal succession, but they too are plotted as a comedy of errors. The King, having been told that he is fated to die in Jerusalem, still plans a crusade, not realizing until the end that he is dying in the "Jerusalem Chamber." He gets the good news that the rebellion is over, but the happy shock proves to be the death of him. The Prince, as he watches his father's deep slumber, decides that he is dead already, and tries on the crown—the only occasion when he misreads the signs of the times. When the King wakes he too makes a mistake—his last: he thinks the Prince was too eager. But the Prince persuades him that he was only trying to get used to the terrible burden; and so the King can die happily, and the Prince can act without false pretenses to take charge of the drifting country.

The Falstaff scenes make a large proportion of the play, and in them the theme of false pretenses is presented with the verve and the exaggeration of farce. The Lord Chief Justice, honest and shrewd as he is, is baffled again and again by Falstaff's imperturbable pose as war hero and special friend of the Prince. As for Falstaff, he takes full advantage of everyone's delusions without sharing them. He has the wonderful ability to lie shamelessly and often cruelly without losing his "innocent" pleasure in vanity, lust and greed, wittily aware all the while of his own and everyone else's shabby motives. "Lord, lord, how subject we old men are to this vice of lying," he says, after making merry with Justice Shallow, and while planning to get his money (Act III, scene 1): "This same starved justice hath done nothing but prate to me of the wildness of his youth, and the feats he hath done about Turnbull Street, and every third word a lie." The only delusion he clings to himself is that the Prince will put up with him forever. The theme of the vanity of the old is laughable, but it is also the most poignant version of the theme of the play: Falstaff, like the King, is trying to pretend to life too long.

In Act V the Prince, now Henry V, quickly acts to set everything straight. He assures his brothers and the friends of the crown that he is no longer the playboy they knew, but will rule without fear or favor (scene 2). He relieves the Lord Chief Justice of his fears, thanks him for the severity which he himself had felt (in *Part 1*), and promises to back him up with the royal power. The arrest of Mistress Quickly and Doll Tearsheet, who had been involved in a murder, is a sign of the new order in England (scene 4).

Falstaff avoids facing the truth of his situation until the last scene of the play. He tries to interrupt the royal procession to reach his "sweet boy," and the King dismisses him as a "dream" from which he has recovered. It is a painful moment, and both Shakespeare and the King have been blamed for cutting off Falstaff. But this is the only possible end of the relationship, and one must remember that the audience, like the King, has been watching Falstaff "in his true colours" all evening. He gets his pension, but must deal with his mortally wounded vanity himself.

In the first four acts of this play, the Prince plays the important part of the one clear-eyed observer. Through his eyes we see both the sad futility of the old King's last days, and the laughable dishonesty of Falstaff's interminable mischief. But in the last act he plays the part of the long-lost rightful heir, the deus ex machina that traditional comic plots require to restore common sense and end the folly on a cheerful note. As the national hero, Henry V, he was perfectly suited to this task. Shakespeare seems to have counted on his long-awaited coronation to send his patriotic audience home in a good mood.

THE MERCHANT OF VENICE

The Merchant of Venice was written in about 1596, when Shakespeare was working at top speed to provide his acting company with plays that would please their large and growing audience. It is a romantic comedy and allegory, but it also contains the great and tragic figure of Shylock. Perhaps Shylock turned out to be more powerful than Shakespeare intended, for at that moment in his career he was not quite in control of the great characters that were taking possession of his imagination. The play has proved to be one of the most effective theater pieces ever written, but Shylock's role in it produces heated discussion in every generation.

The play is composed of several fables, or allegorical tales, which were popular at the time. The basic story of the pound of flesh is very old and had been retold in many versions. No less a dramatist than Marlowe had presented a persecuted Jew who fights his enemies and reveals their hypocrisy, in his high-spirited *The Jew of Malta.* The parable of the three caskets, the romance of Jessica's elopement, and the humorous anecdote of the rings were also "twice-told tales." But as one reads the play they all fit naturally and easily together to make one story. Everything depends on the bond which Antonio (the "merchant of Venice") gives Shylock, so that his friend Bassanio may woo Portia. The narrative, varied and ornamented as it is, unfolds with clarity and mounting excitement.

Part of the fun for the Elizabethan audience was in seeing the half-legendary characters of song and story "come alive" on the stage. In the performances of Shakespeare's actors, Portia, Jessica, and their friends, and (in a quite different way) Shylock, must have seemed to be the very people about whom the familiar stories were told. They are, in fact, so actable that we still discuss them as though they were real people. But the stories are, of course, improbable: who can believe Shylock's bond, or Portia's disguise, or the fairy-tale happy ending? The events of the play belong in the world of romantic comedy, like "Illyria," the country of *Twelfth Night,* and Shakespeare makes the characters of the comedy to fit there. Portia, for instance, with her wit, her wisdom, and her beauty, is the perfect fairy-tale heroine, but we must not expect her to wring our hearts with the weight of human experience. As in all of his romantic comedies, Shakespeare saves the more real and weighty aspects of life for the dark background of the fun, where the "villain" plots against the lovers; so he reminds us that love and music are not all of life. In this play Shylock provides the dark background. His world—in sharpest contrast with Portia's Belmont—is the Rialto, where the merchants of all Europe play their heartless game of money. But Belmont and the Rialto are both "golden Venice," and beneath all Venetian society are the mean facts of money.

In the first three scenes of Act I, Shakespeare evokes the Venetian setting in our imagination, gets the stories started, and sets the leisurely, fabulous tone of the romances to follow. In the opening speech Antonio playfully laments:

> In sooth I know not why I am so sad,
> It wearies me, you say it wearies you;
> But how I caught it, found it, or came by it . . .
> I am to learn.

His joking friends tell him he must either be worried about his wealth, now ventured in his ships on perilous seas, or else he must be in love; but we suspect he is simply bored with too much money. Bassanio comes to ask for Antonio's help in wooing the beautiful Portia, a "lady richly left," yet with a value beyond that of her gold or even her golden hair. So Antonio finds his motive: he will pledge all he has to help his penniless young friend.

In scene 2 we meet Portia in Belmont, and she too is bored: "By my troth, Nerissa," she tells her waiting-maid, "my little body is aweary of this great world." Nerissa accurately replies that she is simply suffering from too much money. They jokingly discuss the suitors who come from all over the world to take the test of the caskets. They also bore Portia, until Bassanio is mentioned, and then she suddenly livens. It is clear that her motive is the love of young Bassanio.

The story of Portia's wooing is played in Belmont, where the glamour of Venice, still the favorite setting for a light romance, is continually suggested. The difficulties the suitors face—finding the right casket and thus the right answer to love's requirements—are more symbolic than real. But good actors can make their efforts diverting, for Shakespeare uses the casket-test (a fairy-tale version of one of our "multiple choice" examinations) to show up the suitors' wrong thinking.

We are rooting for Bassanio and at the same time we are learning, in alternating scenes, how Antonio is faring in his attempts to get money from Shylock. Bassanio arrives (Act III, scene 2) and to the accompaniment of music chooses the right casket, the leaden one, whose inscription bids him "give and hazard all he hath." But at the very moment of success he hears that Antonio's bond is forfeit; and now he and Portia must "give and hazard" all for their friend. So the strands of the story come together to make the climax of the whole play.

The Shylock theme is introduced in Act I, scene 3, when Antonio goes to him for money. We feel at once that Shylock is a "real" human being, struggling with troubles which are not merely symbolical, like those at Belmont, but actual, stubbornly rooted in history, and painful even now. Shylock explains his difficulties with Antonio very clearly:

> I hate him for he is a Christian.
> But more, for that in low simplicity
> He lends out money gratis, and brings down
> The rate of usance ["usury" or interest] here with us in Venice.

In the oldest versions of the story the usurer is not a Jew. In Shakespeare's time money-lenders of whatever race were feared and hated, especially by peasants and artisans who had to borrow from them. Interest rates were not regulated by law, and money-lenders were therefore in a position to squeeze as much as they could out of their victims. The Christian philosophers of the Middle Ages had taught that it was unnatural and therefore immoral to take interest at all, because money itself produced nothing. They thought that only the labor of craftsman or farmer, and the natural growth and reproduction of crops and herds, could increase wealth. Taking interest they called "breeding money." This doctrine, which stresses the moral significance of work and the artificiality of money, is far from absurd in itself, and in Shakespeare's time there were still some who tried to live by it. But of course it cannot work in a capitalist society, and modern capitalism was already developing. Merchant cities like Venice or London needed the apparatus of credit and investment financing, devices for "putting money to work"; and lending money at interest was therefore practiced in spite of the religious theory against it. Such was the lawless and hypocritical world where Shylock and Antonio met as businessmen: the seamy side of "golden Venice."

Insofar as Antonio insists on lending money gratis, he has our sympathy, romantic though that may have been. But in the story Shakespeare seems to have used (*Il Pecorone,* by Ser Giovanni Fiorentino, 1378) the usurer is also a Jew. When Antonio loses his temper and expresses his anti-Jewish prejudice against Shylock, he sounds merely cruel and mean, and we see that the privileged Venetians of the romantic stories share the guilt of Shylock's cruelty. When Shylock utters his famous speech, "Hath not a Jew eyes?" (Act III, scene 1) he carries us with him. That speech establishes once and for all the humanity of the Jews and the inhumanity of the blind prejudices against them.

Though Shylock must play the savage money-game in order to survive in a hostile society, he is even less interested in money for its own sake than the weary Antonio or the weary Portia. When Antonio begs him for a loan, he sees a chance to secure "justice." He wants to make the hypocritical Christians recognize the wrongs they have done his race, and provide compensation for his own sufferings. Shylock, like the young people in Belmont, is seeking in his own way for the "right answer" to human problems in Venice. But under continual goading he comes to feel that only Antonio's death would be enough: "justice" is confused, in his rage, with vengeance. Like all of Shakespeare's tragic figures he is both sinned against and sinning. Behind the lightly handled romantic comedy, with its ancient allegorical themes, is Shylock's story —a variation in a different key, that of tragedy.

Jessica's elopement (Act II, scene 3) increases our sympathy for Shylock, grotesque though he appears in his grief. This tale seems to have been an amoral (or even immoral) romance from the first, and Shakespeare uses it as still another variation on the underlying motivation of the play. The love of Jessica and Lorenzo—the "right answer" for them—has the heedless selfishness of youthful love, but its glamour too. They run away on a night when Venice is filled with maskers, torches, and music; they celebrate their happiness (Act V, scene 1) in the famous duet, "In such a night as this . . ." It is very characteristic of Shakespeare to make us feel the sweetness of unregenerate human love, and at the same time the sadness of human guilt and folly.

After the climax of Act III, when the bond is forfeited, comes the great court scene (Act IV, scene 1). In this scene all of the interwoven stories are brought to their "happy ending," and at the same time the allegorical themes of the caskets, the rings, and the pound of flesh itself are harmoniously completed.

On the modern stage the court scene is primarily just the exciting denouement of the story. The Duke and the Magnificos appear in their gorgeous costumes; then Antonio, baring his breast for the sacrifice; then Shylock in his sober robes, with his long sharp knife. Already we impatiently expect Portia in her lawyer's disguise. Surely she will save

Antonio and her beloved Bassanio; but how? The whole situation is fabulous: an old, old fairy tale. But it is very easy to enter into the spirit of its make-believe, for it has all the natural suspense of the formal trial in which a human life is at stake. It is as effective in the theater as the climax of the latest whodunit. But Shakespeare also worked out its allegorical meaning with the greatest care, and one must learn to "read" the allegory in order to understand the philosophy of the play.

The scene is constructed as a discussion, and also a practical demonstration, of the necessity of *both* justice and mercy in human affairs. Shylock comes to demand justice, and everyone recognizes that the pound of flesh (fantastic though it be, as security for a loan) is legally and therefore justly his. They know that Venice, if it is to survive as a great merchant city, must recognize the sanctity of the formal contract at all costs. Behind this rather mercenary consideration is the moral authority of law itself, and behind that the rocklike majesty of Old Testament justice all the way back to Moses. Shylock is an awe-inspiring representative of that tradition, which Christians share with Jews. He and Portia understand each other very well on that point, for Portia "justifies" Shylock in his demand, and he calls her "A Daniel come to judgement": "O wise young judge," he says, "how I do honour thee." Portia makes it clear that Antonio and Bassanio are *justly* at Shylock's mercy, and she delays her final move so long that both of them prepare to die for justice. The point is that mercy has no meaning at all until justice has been fully recognized, and moreover that justice does not lead to mercy. Mercy is a different thing altogether.

When Portia asks Shylock for mercy, she recognizes that no one justly deserves mercy: "Consider this," she tells him, "That in the course of justice, none of us/ Should see salvation." She is giving him Christian doctrine, of course; but "mercy" also comes from the Old Testament. In using that word (instead of the Christian "love" or "charity") she is appealing to something as Jewish as justice itself; and when Shylock refuses mercy he is rejecting the authority of many an Old Testament prophet. Only then does Portia produce her famous trick. Having established justice in all its majesty, she demonstrates practically that it is not enough, i.e., Shylock himself cannot be content with literal justice, he too needs mercy.

The philosophy behind this scene echoes and sums up all of the allegorical themes of the play: the "right answer"—or the deepest answer—for the troubles of Venice is the undeserved, God-given quality of mercy, or "love" in its highest sense. Thus Bassanio in his wooing rejects the golden casket which stands for "what many men desire," money. He rejects the silver casket, which contains as much as its chooser "deserves," i.e., justice. He chooses the leaden casket, inscribed with the severe and forbidding requirement of love or mercy, that he give and hazard all. This ascending scale, money–justice–love, is repeated in the structure of the trial scene. Antonio gives and hazards all he has; and Portia and Bassanio give and hazard all *they* have, for him and for love. The fable of the rings is a humorous variation: Portia and Nerissa give the rings to their new husbands as a pledge of marital fidelity, but Portia as the "wise young judge" confiscates them, for at that moment she is not the jealous wife but the representative of the highest authority of all, mercy. Thus if one figures out the interrelated allegories, it is evident that the philosophy of the play is all in order. The great old concepts of justice and mercy are, of course, familiar in a way, being central in our whole Hebraic-Christian tradition. But one may see more in them by following Shakespeare's allegorical treatment of them. They are related in many subtle ways to the whole movement and texture of the play.

Thus, for example, the allegory is of a piece with Shakespeare's poetic vision of Venice, the city of glamour and money. The Venetian setting is (as always in Shakespeare) conveyed by the verse and its sensuous imagery. He uses music throughout to make us feel the beauty of Venice: musical metaphors, the melodious language of the young lovers, and real music, which we often hear in the play. In contrast, Shylock's language is harsh, and (excluded as he is, by prejudice, from Belmont and all it means) he is in no mood for music: it strikes him as "squealing." The symbol of "gold" also runs through the play, and it represents both aspects of Venice: the false glitter of money, and also the beauty of the world. Portia has gold, and *is* golden-haired, like the beautiful women in Venetian paintings; but in her case these visible delights are supposed to be signs of her spirit's "gold." In Act V, scene 1, when the painful complications are over, and the lovers are reunited in Belmont, Shakespeare brings together music and the imagery of gold as the beauty of the world and the spirit. Lorenzo murmurs to the beautiful Jessica:

> How sweet the moonlight sleeps upon this bank.
> Here will we sit, and let the sounds of music
> Creep in our ears. Soft stillness and the night
> Become the touches of sweet harmony.
> Sit Jessica. Look how the floor of heaven
> Is thick inlaid with patens of bright gold.

There's not the smallest orb which thou behold'st
But in his motion like an angel sings,
Still quiring to the young-eyed cherubins;
Such harmony is in immortal souls,
But whilst this muddy vesture of decay
Doth grossly close it in, we cannot hear it.
Enter MUSICIANS.
Come ho, and wake Diana with a hymn,
With sweetest touches pierce your mistress' ear,
And draw her home with music. *Music plays.*

If one reads *The Merchant of Venice* as romantic comedy, and as allegory with profound but lightly suggested meanings, all of the elements fall into place. The young lovers speak of wisdom far beyond anything they could have learned through experience. But by the time they are back in Belmont for the too-good-to-be-true happy ending, they have recognized in many ways that the harmony they enjoy is beyond anything they justly deserve—it is itself a "mercy." From the point of view of the allegory, even Shylock's story ends rightly: wronged as he has been, he has received both justice and mercy.

But many admirers of the play do not feel that Shylock is successfully related to the main movement of the comedy. They usually concentrate their criticisms on the transition from the court scene to the harmonious finale of Act V. They point out that poor Shylock is forced to become a Christian—which rubs us the wrong way, for we feel that a man's religion is his own business and that conversion by force is worse than useless. They cannot forget the strong, lonely old man who leaves the stage in silence; and with that figure haunting their imaginations, they cannot share the pleasure of Belmont. In our time these criticisms have special force, for we have seen the persecution of the Jews reach new depths of savagery. We do not like to be reminded of the Nazis' ovens just as we are opening the drinks and turning on the music for a carefree party of our own. Shylock's wrongs can hardly fail to remind us of the far greater wrongs of our enlightened epoch, and we transfer our feelings of remorse to Portia, Bassanio, Jessica, and Lorenzo. How can they be so happy when Shylock is so miserable?

Shakespeare seems to have had a much stronger stomach for the contradictions of human experience than we do. He puts scenes of farce in the midst of his deepest tragedies, and in all of his romantic comedies there are painful complications, which remind us of guilt and folly behind the music and fun. With his wonderfully supple stagecraft he can usually lead us smoothly from the harsh to the harmonious aspects of the story, and then reconcile them in a rich chord of feeling at the end. But in *The Merchant of Venice* this technical problem is very difficult, because playful allegory and tragedy must be read in quite different ways. In the fairy-tale world of the comedy we must not take the characters too seriously as people: the serious meaning of their story is in the language they speak, in the unfolding plot, and above all in the subtle interplay of "justice" and "mercy"—vast themes which dwarf the figures in the foreground. But when we meet Shylock it is his human reality and the depth of his actual problems which touch us. Allegory, as Shakespeare handles it, has its own beauty and fascination, but when it is too close to real tragedy it seems flimsy and insubstantial.

Shakespeare was to return, in later years, to some of the elements of *The Merchant of Venice,* and handle them with greater poetic and dramatic mastery. In *Much Ado About Nothing* the romantic comedy and its dark or sinister background are more deeply and poetically unified. In *The Tempest* he makes a far subtler and more endlessly suggestive use of allegory. In *Othello* he presents a much deeper picture of the seamy side of Venice, the merchant city, through the sharp and cynical eyes of Iago.

The Merchant of Venice does not have the depth or consistency of Shakespeare's greatest masterpieces. But it tells the great old story with incomparable theatrical verve. Like some huge Renaissance painting, it swarms with clowns and princes, contemporary portraits and figures of allegory and legend, each one full of his own stage-life. We cannot do without any of them: the brilliant Portia and the wronged and suffering Shylock alike are the permanent heritage of our theater.

A MIDSUMMER NIGHT'S DREAM

A Midsummer Night's Dream was written, most probably, no later than 1596, which makes it the first of Shakespeare's great romantic comedies. The title (like *As You Like It* and *Much Ado About Nothing*) accurately describes the heavenly mood of the play, in which nothing is to be taken too seriously. It has always been popular in the theater, but it seems to have been written originally as part of the entertainment at a wedding in a noble household. Wedding is the theme and motive of all its interwoven stories; and in its lavish use of lyric verse, pageantry, music, and dance, it suggests those elaborate masques which were often performed at court to entertain the Queen and her guests on some festive occasion.

Shakespeare took the stories, as usual, from that rich store of poetry and legend which most of his audience already knew. The main stories are those of Theseus, Duke of Athens, and his marriage to Hippolyta, Queen of the Amazons; the farcical troubles of the young lovers, Hermia, Lysander, Helena, and Demetrius; the jealous quarrels between Oberon, King of the Fairies, and his Queen Titania; and the Pyramus and Thisbe legend, the subject of Bottom's play. Bottom himself, his fellow actors, and their amateur theatricals are Shakespeare's invention. He knew the old stories in several versions, and he took elements from all his sources, changing and combining them at will, to make a show as marvelous, and at the same time as familiar, as a dream.

The wedding that gives all the characters, whether sprites or humans, their common motive, is announced by Theseus in the first line of the play:

> Now, fair Hippolyta, our nuptial hour
> Draws on apace. Four happy days bring in
> Another moon. But O, methinks, how slow
> This old moon wanes, she lingers my desires
> Like to a step-dame, or a dowager,
> Long withering out a young man's revenue.

And he asks Philostrate to start a general celebration, the proper prelude to marriage:

> Go Philostrate,
> Stir up the Athenian youth to merriments.

The Theseus of song and story was a legendary tyrant of Athens, who conquered the Amazons and their Queen, but in the play he probably represents the Elizabethan lord for whose wedding the play was written. It was the custom, in such entertainments, to flatter the noble patron by staging him as a mythic hero. Theseus is like a master of ceremonies, between the audience and the performance: he starts the proceedings and lends them his august approval.

Egeus appears with Hermia, Lysander, and Demetrius to present Theseus with the silly squabble which threatens the delights of the wedding festivities. Egeus' daughter, Hermia, and the youth Lysander are in love, but Egeus has chosen Demetrius for his daughter. Poor Demetrius loves Hermia, who loves Lysander, while Helena (the last of the procession) loves Demetrius. The reader may have some trouble at first in keeping these couples straight, for Shakespeare has characterized them very lightly, as though to say they are just any young people in love. We do not learn until the third act that Helena is short and peppery, while Hermia is tall and timid. But they are wonderfully actable, because their spats, delusions, and desperate changes of partner are, in fact, like those of any boys and girls when love first hits them, and Shakespeare puts them in a succession of brilliantly clear farcical situations. Before scene 1 is over they agree to resort to the woods, and so the main comic intrigue is under way: soon they will be chasing each other through moonlight and shadow, seeking the proper mates for *their* marriages.

Scene 2 introduces a farcical theme of a different kind: the creative labors of Quince, Snug, Bottom, Flute, Snout, and Starveling upon their "most lamentable comedy, and most cruel death of Pyramus and Thisby." The belly-laughs of countless audiences have proved that their rehearsals are farce—but farce as only Shakespeare can write it. The mechanicals are like old friends the moment we see them; we know their vanities, their artistic temperaments, even their physiques. When we laugh at them we laugh at all stagestruck or moonstruck humanity, including ourselves. To them the wedding is the most important thing in the world, for there they will star in their classic vehicle.

In the next scene (Act II, scene 1) the first Fairy and Puck appear "severally" to build, in our imaginations, the magic woodland where most of the play takes place:

> Over hill, over dale,
> Thorough bush, thorough brier,
> Over park, over pale,
> Thorough flood, thorough fire;
> I do wander everywhere,
> Swifter than the moon's sphere;
> And I serve the Fairy Queen,
> To dew her orbs upon the green.

Oberon and Titania appear: they have come to honor Theseus' wedding, but like the four young lovers and Theseus and Hippolyta (who first met in battle) they are bothered by their jealous quarreling, which interferes with love's delights. Their story is a variation of the main theme, and a crucial part of the plot. But Shakespeare lingers over this scene, far beyond the requirements of the story, in order to bring into his English woodland pretty pictures from classical legend. The reader should pause too, and listen to the fairy monarchs' melodious squabbling:

> How canst thou thus, for shame, Titania,
> Glance at my credit with Hippolyta,
> Knowing I know thy love to Theseus?
> Didst thou not lead him through the glimmering night
> From Perigenia, whom he ravished?
> And make him with fair Aegles break his faith,
> With Ariadne, and Antiopa?
>
> TITANIA
>
> These are the forgeries of jealousy.
> And never, since the middle of summer's spring,
> Met we on hill, in dale, forest, or mead,
> By paved fountain, or by rushy brook,
> Or in the beached margent of the sea,
> To dance our ringlets to the whistling wind,
> But with thy brawls thou hast disturbed our sport.

The reader (unless he remembers his classical mythology) will have to resort to the glossary to follow these adventures; but the pictures, like the dreamy little landscapes in the backgrounds of Renaissance paintings, are clear at once in the mind's eye. And the verse is as light, fluent, and melodious as the most miraculous "dinner-music." In the court masques such scenes were staged as elaborate spectacles accompanied by music; Shakespeare, thinking of such masques, produces his effects far more lightly and imaginatively by verse alone.

Demetrius, pursuing Hermia and pursued by the doleful but doting Helena, breaks into this moonlit realm, and now begins a complicated interplay of magic with young love's frustrations. The lovers' desperate flights and pursuits are as farcical as a chase in an old-fashioned Keystone Comedy, but the symmetrical changing of partners makes patterns as formal as dance-figures, and everything moves to the music of the verse. Bottom is the same broad-beamed, imperturbable citizen we met in Act I. But when he acquires his ass's head, the beautiful Titania winds him in her arms, and the most delicate sprites scratch his "fine, large ears," he too is at home in moonlight and magic. At the same time Oberon and Titania, moonshiny as they are, have their share of human foibles. Human puzzles, worries, and longings are mingled with the music and the beauty of the woods through Acts II and III, and the whole sequence is like a dream too good to be true; absurd and right, mocking and delightful at once. The comic climax is reached when the four lovers finally meet and start their desperate, bewildered squabbling. "Lord, what fools these mortals be!" says Puck, who is himself not a mortal. Instructed by Oberon, he darkens the night, and so saves the poor young people from themselves and from each other.

In Act IV Shakespeare winds up these complicated doings and leads us, through several delicately contrived effects, from the moonlit midnight woods back to daylight and Athens. The young lovers, exhausted by their frantic night, are innocently slumbering side by side, just where Puck left them. Titania, awake but enchanted, is caressing ass-headed Bottom, who cannot see himself as others see him; and Oberon and Puck are silently enjoying the foolish spectacle. They break the spell, restore the sleeping Bottom to his own shape, and wake Titania. She and Oberon are reconciled, but since fairies do not appear by day, they must vanish for the time being:

TITANIA
Come my lord, and in our flight,
Tell me how it came this night,
That I sleeping here was found,
With these mortals on the ground.
(*Exeunt. Wind horns.*)

The exciting sound of hunting horns, far off, marks night's end, the flight of all sprites and fairies, and the dawn of Theseus' longed-for wedding day. He and Hippolyta and Egeus and their train make their majestic entrance, dressed for the hunt no doubt; and we hear the baying of Theseus' hounds. Shakespeare himself must often have heard that beautiful sound, as a boy, on a summer morning:

never did I hear
Such gallant chiding. For besides the groves,
The skies, the fountains, every region near
Seem all one mutual cry. I never heard
So musical a discord, such sweet thunder.

When Theseus has had the lovers wakened with his hunting horns, he hears their stories, sorts them out properly, reconciles them with Egeus, and decrees that their marriages shall be celebrated that very day with his. Now everything is in order for that great event, the purpose of the whole play. Everything, that is, but the all-important production of *Pyramus and Thisby*. When Theseus and his glittering train depart, Bottom is left all alone onstage, to waken and wander off in bewilderment. In the next scene (Act IV, scene 2) we see Quince, Starveling, and the rest in a sad plight: having lost Bottom so strangely, how can the show go on? But then Bottom himself comes in; the lost is found again; the show is saved, and the artists hasten to join the procession to the wedding.

It is the strange events of Acts II and III, in woodland and summer moonlight, that give *A Midsummer Night's Dream* its name and its magical quality. In creating that sequence Shakespeare drew upon his memories of two age-old festivals of the summer season which must have been familiar, since childhood, to him and his audience: May Day and Midsummer Eve. The May Day games, when the young people ran through the woods all night to gather boughs and flowers for the maypole (a custom that scandalized the Puritans), suggest the nocturnal hide-and-seek of Hermia, Lysander, Helena, and Demetrius. Midsummer Eve, the summer solstice, was the time of "midsummer madness," and maidens were supposed to dream, that night, of their true loves—as Shakespeare's young people, and even his Bottom and Titania, do in their odd ways. The sprites and fairies who haunt the woods on summer nights, playing tricks on milkmaids and housewives like Puck, or leaving their dancing rings in the grass like Mustardseed and his troop, were familiar too, in many forms, in the superstitious popular lore of the time. But all of this is brought into the play as poetry, not folklore. Shakespeare uses it as playfully as he does the Greek tales told of Theseus and Hippolyta: to make poetry that, like a dream, feels both illusory and true.

In Act V, scene 1, we are reminded that the events of the night were not the main business of the play, but an interlude; to be marveled at, but not judged too literally. " 'Tis strange, my Theseus," says Hippolyta, "that these lovers speak of." And Theseus answers,

> More strange than true. I never may believe
> These antique fables, nor these fairy toys.

And he proceeds to make the famous speech on "the lunatic, the lover, and the poet," which is so often quoted as Shakespeare's own theory of poetry:

> And as imagination bodies forth
> The forms of things unknown, the poet's pen
> Turns them to shapes, and gives to airy nothing
> A local habitation, and a name.

Theseus' speech does seem to describe the work of Shakespeare's poetic imagination as it embodied the airy nothings of joy, love, and midsummer madness in verse that evokes the haunted woods. But we must remember that, at the same time, Shakespeare was constructing his ingenious plot as coolly as any engineer to lead at last to "true love" and daylight; that he was creating Theseus himself; and that at this moment in the play he feels, like any canny showman, the need to let the audience know that he knows—as well as any of them—the difference between imagination and reason. Shakespeare's reason is always alert, though hidden behind the scenes of the play: arranging and judging the wonderful things his imagination apprehends.

Theseus is in comand in Act V. The night of delicate lunacy is behind us; the three weddings have been celebrated; and now, as Theseus says, the question is,

> what masks, what dances shall we have,
> To wear away this long age of three hours,
> Between our after-supper and bed-time?

Not the splendid court masques proposed by Philostrate, but Bottom's homemade show:

> For never any thing can be amiss,
> When simpleness and duty tender it.

In staging Bottom's *Pyramus and Thisby* actors are often tempted to make it pure farce. They rely on the verse, a hilarious parody of old-fashioned conventions; on the wonderful foolishness of props and costumes, and on the humorous comments of Theseus and his guests. But Bottom and his friends should also have that "simpleness" Theseus speaks of—a capacity for total make-believe, like that of children. When Moonshine stalks on, with his bush and his dog, and announces, "This lanthorn doth the horned moon present," we should feel a touch of theater-magic if we could see the moon in the lanthorn as simply as the mechanicals do. After all, actors all need the audience's cooperation: "The best in this kind are but shadows," as Theseus tells Hippolyta; "and the worst are no worse, if imagination amend them." The mechanicals, helpless as they are, have their share of the poet's and lover's lunacy. Shakespeare is modestly suggesting that their moonshine differs from his (in Acts II and III) not in kind, but only in degree.

It was the custom in Shakespeare's time to end a show with apologies for its shortcomings, and compliments to the audience. Act V is full of such apologies and compliments, and Shakespeare has very cleverly given them all to Theseus, who represents the noble patron himself. Theseus gives the signal for the final dance, and announces the moment he has been so eagerly looking forward to since Act I:

Lovers to bed, 'tis almost fairy-time.
I fear we shall out-sleep the coming morn,
As much as we this night have overwatched.

And with that Theseus and Hippolyta, the young people, guests, entertainers, and attendants depart, leaving the stage empty and quiet.

It has been conjectured that in the play as we have it there are two epilogues after Theseus' departure, both being "fairy-time," and a blessing on the night. On this theory, Oberon, Titania, and their sprites performed a short masque, to end the wedding entertainment in the private household and playfully assure the noble patron that the midnight creatures were watching over him and his bride. Puck's epilogue, addressed directly to the audience, would have been written as an alternative ending for public performances. However that may be, it is clear that the performance must end with a *reprise*, however brief, of moonlight and magic, and a director who is aware of the imaginative opulence of the play may get the theatrical effects Shakespeare intended in many different ways. Here at the end—and indeed in the whole play—Shakespeare provides more food for the imagination than any director, designer, musician, or choreographer can use.

THE MERRY WIVES OF WINDSOR

Shakespeare is supposed to have written *The Merry Wives* in two weeks, at the command of Queen Elizabeth, who wished to see Falstaff in love. Falstaff makes his majestic debut in *Henry IV, Part 1,* and we learn in *Henry V* that he has died, "his nose as sharp as a pen." It is probable, therefore, that *The Merry Wives* was written between the two, about 1598.

There are many signs in this play that it was written (like *Henry V*) in fulfillment of some professional assignment. Critics usually find that Falstaff is less inspired here than he is in the Henry IV plays, and that the comedy as a whole lacks the imaginative distinction of Shakespeare's best work. But it has been popular on the stage in many free adaptations, and in a number of musical versions, including Verdi's famous opera. The last century found its local color, its rather complacent moralizing, and its good-natured high spirits very much to its taste: it is Shakespeare's most Victorian play, except for its bawdy humor, which can easily be cut.

There are two main stories in the play, Falstaff's misadventures with the wives, and the beauteous Anne Page's intrigue with her three suitors. In Shakespeare's time several stories like Falstaff's were known, in which a lover intent on adultery is tricked and mocked by unexpectedly faithful wives; and Anne's efforts to elude her parents' candidates in order to marry the man she wants remind one of other romantic and comic tales. No single source has been found for either plot, and it is probable that Shakespeare remembered several without following any of them closely. He added a number of incidents that have little relation to either of the main stories: Master William Page's Latin lesson; the absurd duel between Parson Evans and Doctor Caius, which the Host of the Garter Inn prevents by a trick; and the episode of the pretended German nobles who cheat the Host out of his post-horses. This last episode, which is very inadequately treated in the text we have, would have reminded Shakespeare's audience of Frederick Count Mompelgard, who visited England several times in the nineties, trying to get the Order of the Garter which the Queen had promised him. The topical allusion is of course meaningless now, and the episode is cut in production. The play ends with a masquerade based on the folklore of the Windsor region, Falstaff dressed as Herne the Hunter, and the citizens and their children as elves and goblins.

It was Shakespeare's custom to use materials of many different kinds in making his comedies, and *The Merry Wives* is like the rest in this respect. But in this play he makes no effort to fuse them imaginatively, as he usually does. Even the plots are clumsily woven together: the episodes of the two main stories alternate arbitrarily like the acts in an evening of vaudeville. Young Fenton's wooing of Anne is a romantic theme, but Shakespeare does not endow it with music, as he had the wooings of *A Midsummer Night's Dream.* Falstaff's intrigue with the wives suggests a farce of a Latin type, but Shakespeare does not give it the requisite pace and edge, though he had proved his mastery of that style in *The Comedy of Errors.*

Because of such consideration, it is often said that Shakespeare must indeed have written *The Merry Wives* in the two weeks' time the Queen is supposed to have allowed him. It does look more hasty, ill-digested, and unfinished than any of the other comedies. But I think that Shakespeare's modest intention was not to write a romantic comedy, nor a classical farce, but a more prosaic "middle-class" comedy in the spirit of Dekker's *Shoemaker's Holiday*. Probably he wrote it at the Queen's command, but he must have expected an audience of Windsor home-folks also, for the play (like *Abie's Irish Rose* or *Our Town*) appears to be aimed straight at the taste of the petty bourgeoisie. He shows them how the great Falstaff may be outwitted and chastized by the solid citizens. He offers them bawdy jokes, for manners were free then, but he carefully assures them that the moral of the tale is sound. He feels no need to worry about form, style, or poetic consistency, but he provides plenty of good-natured caricatures of the neighbors.

The large gallery of Dickensian local characters has something to satisfy any taste, though few, I think, would find all of them laughable. To enjoy Bardolph, Pistol, and Nym, who are carried over from the earlier Falstaff plays, one must be able to laugh at their hollow bullying and their laborious verbal flatulence. Caius, the French doctor, and Evans, the Welsh parson, are for those who find foreign accents amusing per se. The Host of the Garter is a professional glad-hander and backslapper, a type we recognize very easily, but usually without pleasure. Justice Shallow and his cousin Slender, the gentle mooncalf, are Shakespearean clowns of a good vintage. Mistress Quickly, another old associate of Falstaff's, is at her best in this play, shamelessly flattering all three of Anne's suitors and glibly betraying Falstaff to the wives. It is she who calls Mistress Page "as fartuous a civil modest wife . . . as any is in Windsor." This wonderfully evocative line must give Shakespeare's own uncensored picture of his buxom heroines, but except for that moment he is careful to present them in such a way as to enable the audience to identify itself with them in all their tussles with Falstaff. " I will consent to any villainy against him, that may not sully the chariness of our honesty," says Mistress Ford primly (Act II, scene 1); and Mistress Page is equally righteous (Act IV, scene 2):

> We'll leave a proof by that which we will do,
> Wives may be merry, and yet honest too.

The wives are not intended to be laughable, but to encourage the audience to laugh, with a good conscience, at Falstaff's undoing.

Falstaff is of course the chief raison d'être of the play. One can recognize the true Falstaff of the Henry IV plays in the first scene, when he flattens poor Shallow's and Slender's complaints of his bullying and deer-stealing, not by attempting any excuses or denials, but by the sheer weight of his insolence. He is himself again at the beginning of the final scene when the prospect of success and the costume of Herne inflate him once more; but in most of the play he is not at his best. There is no one like Prince Hal of *Henry IV, Part 1,* who scolds him half in fun and half in dismay, and so inspires him to build up, in self-defense, witty, lying, marvelous images of himself. There is no episode like the gallant death of Hotspur, which produces his appalling thoughts on death and honor, and serves as background to his ghoulish vanity, when he shoulders the young corpse and waddles off with it. Nothing happens in Windsor to bring out his more wonderful qualities, and the citizens are too moral, and too busy defending themselves, to relish the self-made myth of Falstaff, as Hal does in his contemplative or playful moments. The wives, when they first read his letters and learn that he proposes to seduce them both, briefly consider his physical bulk (Act II, scene 1):

MISTRESS FORD

What tempest, I trow, through this whale, with so many tuns of oil in his belly, ashore at Windsor?

MISTRESS PAGE

. . . he cares not what he puts into the press, when he would put us two. I had rather be a giantess, and lie under Mount Pelion.

But as soon as their plot gets started they are too busy, too self-righteously brisk, to enjoy one of the greatest comic creations of the theater. Their practical jokes do not reveal the true Falstaff to the audience either: it is hard to believe that he could have been fooled three times in the same way, and as for the slapstick, any fat man would do as a bundle of dirty laundry or an old woman with a full beard—Falstaff's unique talents are not required for that.

According to the tradition, Shakespeare wrote the play to show the Queen "Falstaff in love." He is, however, much less attached to the wives than he was to his whore, Doll Tearsheet, in *Henry IV, Part 2.* He explains his feelings to Nym and Pistol (Act I, scene 3): "O she did so course o'er my exteriors with such a greedy intention, that the appetite of her eye did seem to scorch me up like a burning-glass." The wives themselves tell each other that they eyed him, not with "amorous appetite" but with dismay, so it seems that Falstaff's infatuation is merely his vanity flattering his lust. He is, however, seriously interested in their money: "I will be cheaters to them both, and they shall be exchequers to me," he explains, to his disreputable companions.

The imaginative greatness of Falstaff is created less by anything he actually does than by what he inspires people to say about him, or what he says himself when the spirit moves him properly. In the beginning of the final scene, when he expects success at last, and appears appropriately costumed as Herne the Hunter, we can get a glimpse of his ability to generate comic myths of himself. Dr. Margaret Murray, in *The God of the Witches,* says, "Herne the Hunter, with horns on his head, was seen in Windsor Forest by the Earl of Surrey in the reign of Henry VIII." Herne was a local version of the wood-demon Robin Goodfellow who, in turn, was one of the descendants (according to Dr. Murray) of an ancient phallic deity, a horned god, whose cult was widespread in pre-Christian Europe. Shakespeare must have had some premonition of this bit of modern anthropological lore, for he has Falstaff, looming up in the moonlight with great stag's antlers on his head, play Herne as an erotic demon; and he associates himself with the amorous Jupiter of pagan antiquity:

> The Windsor bell hath struck twelve; the minute draws on. Now the hot-blooded gods assist me. Remember Jove, thou wast a bull for thy Europa, love set on thy horns. O powerful love, that in some respects makes a beast a man; in some other, a man a beast. You were also, Jupiter, a swan, for the love of Leda. O omnipotent love, how near the god drew to the complexion of a goose. A fault done first in the form of a beast—Jove, a beastly fault—and then another fault, in the semblance of a fowl, think on't, Jove, a foul fault. When gods have hot backs, what shall poor men do? For me, I am here a Windsor stag, and the fattest, I think, i' th' forest. Send me a cool rut-time, Jove, or who can blame me to piss my tallow? Who comes here? My doe?

Faced with both wives at once, he rises majestically to the occasion:

> Divide me like a bribed-buck, each a haunch. . . . my horns I bequeath your husbands. Am I a woodman, ha? Speak I like Herne the hunter?

But there is no one in Windsor to indulge him in such stupendous nonsense. His deflation follows quickly, and with singular thoroughness.

Shakespeare liked to place allegorical masque-like sequences near the ends of his romantic comedies, often mingling English elves with figures of classical legend, to celebrate the happy marriages and general harmony with which such comedies must end. He seems to have planted something similar here, with his nocturnal masquerade in fairy costumes, but it strikes one as rather artificial in a play of so prosaic a spirit. Mistress Page plans it, not because she enjoys the folklore of the woods, or sees any poetic or allegorical meaning in it, but simply as a device for trapping Falstaff again and showing him up publicly: "Well you know," she says (Act IV, scene 3), "the superstitious idle-headed eld/ Received, and did deliver to our age,/ This tale of Herne the hunter for a truth." She and Mistress Ford and Parson Evans marshal all the children in their homemade fairy dresses with all the efficiency of the entertainment committee of the PTA. And having caught Falstaff for all to see, they enforce the image, the small sad reality, which *they* can see:

FORD
What, a hodge-pudding? A bag of flax?
MISTRESS PAGE
A puffed man?
PAGE
Old, cold, withered, and of intolerable entrails?

After that the Pages accept Anne's secret marriage to her Fenton, and Falstaff is invited to dinner. But we do not feel in these patched-up reconciliations any of the heavenly harmony with which romantic comedies end. Probably no relation could be imagined, even by Shakespeare, between the spirit of Falstaff, that huge fake, and literal-minded Windsor. When the wives beat Falstaff they destroy him as Caesar does Antony: "Thou hast subdued his spirit too." It is true that in all the plays Falstaff is always being deflated and shown up, for Shakespeare knew all along, and much better than his infatuated audiences, that the greatness of Falstaff rose, like a daydream, out of a cowardly old liar. But there is no one in Windsor to appreciate this amoral mystery.

The Merry Wives has proved to be puzzling in many ways, and rather unsatisfying as a whole; it seems to be hastily built out of very diverse materials. But Shakespeare must have found these materials lying about in his workshop, and some of them, such as the local folklore and the vignettes of small-town life, are interesting in themselves and for what they can tell us about Shakespeare. Moreover it is so theatrically alive in all its parts—having been written by the master-showman—that no amount of cutting and adapting can kill it. It will continue to take the stage, in one form or another, as long as the language lasts.

MUCH ADO ABOUT NOTHING

Much Ado About Nothing, the second of Shakespeare's great romantic comedies, was written in 1598–1599. It has held the stage since it first appeared, chiefly, perhaps, because of those witty and reluctant lovers, Beatrice and Benedick, who seem "modern" to every generation. The play as a whole is closer to everyday life than *A Midsummer Night's Dream,* with magical woods, or *As You Like It,* with its fabulous Forest of Arden. But like the other great comedies, *Much Ado* is a holiday from the cares of the world; an entertainment in which humor of several kinds is delicately mingled with real music and the music of the verse.

The basis of the plot is hardly comic in itself: Don John's lying slander of young Hero, on the eve of her wedding to Claudio. That story ends happily when Don John's machinations are discovered; Claudio repents, Hero forgives him, and the marriage proceeds as planned. Shakespeare took the plot most directly from a novel by Bandello, but he also knew several other versions, including Ariosto's (in *Orlando Furioso*) and Spenser's (in *The Faerie Queene*). The play is much lighter than any of its sources: the characters are seen in a humorous light, and the intrigue is both quick and casual. Moreover Shakespeare wove into Bandello's plot two stories of his own invention, Benedick's wooing of the thorny Beatrice, which is high comedy, and Dogberry's dim-witted sleuthing, which may be described as poetic farce. In the play, the adventures of the two pairs of lovers are amusingly contrasted, and the audience, taking its ease, can smile with a certain detachment at the follies of all young love.

Shakespeare establishes this easy tone, as well as the scene and the chief characters, in the first scene of the play. Leonato learns from the Messenger that Don Pedro, after his victory in a jolly little war, is about to arrive for a long visit. He is bringing his bastard brother, Don John, and his two young followers, Claudio and Benedick. No one "of any note" has been killed, but Claudio has done "in the figure of a lamb, the feats of a lion," and Benedick has proved that he is "stuffed with all the honorable virtues." Leonato's household and the guests make a gay and cultivated company, such as Castiglione described in *The Book of the Courtier,* an idealized picture of society which the leisured classes in Shakespeare's England studied as a guide to "courtesy." The gentleman (according to Castiglione) must be skilled in sport and war; the ladies and gentlemen alike must be cultivated in languages and literature; and all must play the game of love with taste and sophistication which they had acquired from the poets, the allegorists, and the writers of romance. As soon as Leonato and Don Pedro have exchanged their majestic compliments, it is clear that the house party has nothing more serious in hand than the play of wit and sentiment leading (as in all good comedies) to the marriages of the young people.

Beatrice is the most impatient to begin. She makes fun of Benedick as soon as she hears he is coming, and when the warriors arrive she attacks him in the first pause in the conversation:

BEATRICE
I wonder that you will still be talking, Signior Benedick, nobody marks you.

BENEDICK
What my dear Lady Disdain! Are you yet living?

BEATRICE
Is it possible disdain should die, while she hath such meet food to feed it, as Signior Benedick? Courtesy itself must convert to disdain, if you come in her presence.

Disdain was a traditional figure of allegory, and Beatrice is half-jokingly identified with her, until (in Act III, scene 1) her friends trap her into confessing her love for Benedick—at which point she is converted to "courtesy." The word is derived from the medieval cult of courtly love, and in Shakespeare's time still meant the refinement of the heart, rather than mere manners. When Beatrice and Benedick are humbled by their love, we shall see them rather absurdly falling into some of the attitudes of the lady and the true knight; but at this point in the play they are interested only in their battle. Their wit is both learned and bawdy, and a modern reader must resort to the glossary to get the fine points. But the lovers themselves are brilliantly clear, whether one understands all their allusions or not. Beatrice, for all her learning and intelligence, reminds one of a little girl who can't resist sticking her tongue out at the boys; and Benedick, that bearded warrior and polished gentleman, is like a boy who expresses his interest in girls by pulling pigtails. When good actors play Beatrice and Benedick, they "throw away" the lines which would be hard for a modern audience, and bring out the love which is childishly frustrated by their poses of disdainful superiority.

As for Claudio and Hero, they are too bashful to say much in each other's presence. But when Claudio is left alone with his trusted friend and protector, Don Pedro, he tries to make up for lost time, and launches into an elaborate and melodious account of his feelings about Hero:

> But now I am returned, and that war-thoughts
> Have left their places vacant, in their rooms
> Come thronging soft and delicate desires,
> All prompting me how fair young Hero is,
> Saying I liked her ere I went to wars.

The Prince is a skilled lover himself, and has recognized the symptoms long ago. He gently chokes off the lyric flood:

> Thou wilt be like a lover presently,
> And tire the hearer with a book of words.

But he takes pity on poor innocent Claudio, and volunteers to woo Hero for him. So the main business of the evening is under way: two contrasting versions of young love's absurd and glamorous ordeal.

While Don John prowls around the edges of the fun and explains his envy of Claudio to Conrade and Borachio (Act I, scene 3), the rest are excitedly preparing for Leonato's masked ball, the first formal occasion of the house party. This festivity, with its graceful parade of masked couples, its music and its dance, provides an image of the action of the whole play. *Much Ado* is a comedy of mistaken identity, like so many others that Shakespeare wrote, from his early farce, *The Comedy of Errors,* to the more serious plays of the end of his career. In *Much Ado* the ancient plot-scheme is subtly handled, for the young lovers mistake each other only because they do not dare to trust themselves or each other. Everyone but Beatrice and Benedick can see that those two are moved by love, but they themselves are taken in by each other's scornful attitudes. Claudio is always losing Hero, when his own timidity makes her look strange—but his friends are not deluded, and they always straighten him out. Here in Act II, scene 1, when the drum gives the signal, and the maskers, two by two, play out their mocking and wistful flirtations, we can see how all are groping for "true love" behind its thin disguises.

Shakespeare gives this episode a shimmering quality by shifting between prose, verse, and music. The prose of the four masked couples (as beautiful as any of Shakespeare's prose) is designed to characterize each pair, and at the same time to provide a rhythmic anticipation of the dance music which soon follows. Shakespeare always controlled the all-important element of music with the greatest care, relating it to the spoken word and to the ceaseless movement of the story.

When the music stops, and the dancers depart, Don John lingers to whisper his poisonous suggestion to Claudio: that Don Pedro is wooing Hero for himself. Claudio instantly believes him, and expresses his needless despair in beautiful lyric verse:

> Friendship is constant in all other things,
> Save in the office and affairs of love.
> Therefore all hearts in love use their own tongues.
> Let every eye negotiate for itself,
> And trust no agent. For beauty is a witch,
> Against whose charms faith melteth into blood.

His speech sums up the glamorous party we have just seen, as well as Claudio's own bewilderment. And now we turn from the masked ball to the more urgent masquerade of the story.

Claudio's and Benedick's love stories are woven together, as the friends mock or help each other through the play. Before this long scene (Act II, scene 1) is over, Benedick, with Don Pedro and Leonato, rescues Claudio from Don John's first attempt. Leonato promises Claudio Hero's hand; and Claudio is instantly overcome with joy. Claudio, Don Pedro, and Leonato then plan to cure Benedick and Beatrice of their scornful attitudes by making them overhear some home truths. The men give Benedick this treatment in Act II, scene 3; and Hero, Margaret, and Ursula do as much for Beatrice in Act III, scene 1. These parallel scenes of elaborate fooling, frankly theatrical as they are, have much of the quality of the masked party. They are also full of insight into love's varied moods, from hearty bawdiness at one extreme to the wistfulness of song at the other. The monologues in which Benedick and then Beatrice repent are both comical and touching—virtuoso pieces for skilled actors.

Benedick's and Claudio's affairs both reach their climax and turning point in Act III, scene 2. Benedick accepts his friends' ribbing, and humbly departs to beg Leonato for Beatrice's hand. And then Don John upsets everything. He tells Claudio and Don Pedro of Hero's "unfaithfulness," and promises to show them his own masquerade that very night: Borachio's tryst with Margaret dressed up in Hero's clothes,

This time he deludes the Prince as well as Claudio; and now the whole house party will have to suffer from their painful mistake. It looks as though Claudio had lost a bride just as Benedick found one.

This moment, when the monster Slander darkens fair Hero's innocent image, is the crux of the romantic tale that Shakespeare took from Bandello. But in the play it is presented as another of poor Claudio's fond delusions, another figure in the dance-like movement of the plot. And in the next scene (Act III, scene 3) Don John's plot appears in the marvelously irrelevant context of farce, when Dogberry's watchmen apprehend the villains. It is night in idyllic Messina, when an "ancient and most quiet watchman," as Dogberry puts it, can count on getting his sleep. Dogberry's charge to the Watch is purest nonsense, but as orotund in tone as Leonato himself. With the aid of his instructions, and one small lantern, the ancient bumpkins are to make sure that no harm comes to Messina—their version of the action of the whole play, a fond but dim quest for the truth. The cream of the joke is that they actually do stumble upon Conrade and Borachio, and we see that Don John's subtle plan, which had overwhelmed both Claudio and the Prince, will be unmasked by the gentle yokels.

By making fun of Don John's efforts, and rendering them harmless in advance, Shakespeare softens the big scene in the church (Act IV, scene 1) when Claudio accuses Hero, and all must suffer the results of his mistake. Even so, this scene is often criticized as too painful for a comedy; and Claudio's heartfelt outburst, Hero's swoon, and Leonato's grief may be too strong on the stage unless the parts are very well acted. Shakespeare seems to have intended us to glimpse the real perils that lurk behind love's delusions, especially in a court-like society, where Slander is always busy. But if we have followed the play so far, this scene too may be viewed as both comic and touching. When the Friar leads them all solemnly in, Claudio, Don Pedro, and Don John playing their stiff parts and hiding their real feelings, the procession should recall the masquerade in Act II. Here again we shall see the witch, beauty, melt faith into blood, as Claudio put it when he received Don John's first malicious lie, and believed it. He himself feels the illusory effect very sharply:

> Is this the Prince? Is this the Prince's brother?
> Is this face Hero's? Are our eyes our own?

And Leonato echoes him:

> Are these things spoken, or do I but dream?

When Claudio parts from Hero, his final speech makes it clear that his love is sincere, though so easily wounded by appearances:

> farewell
> Thou pure impiety and impious purity.
> For thee I'll lock up all the gates of love,
> And on my eyelids shall conjecture hang,
> To turn all beauty into thoughts of harm,
> And never shall it more be gracious.

His lyric is so beautiful that it might make us blubber like Claudio himself, even as we smile at his exaggeration, and his gullibility. This mixture of feeling is very true to life, and very characteristic of Shakespeare's dramatic style.

Beatrice, Benedick, and the Friar, as they watch this scene, are ignorant of the facts that the audience knows, but they almost see the truth behind the false appearances created by Don John. When Don John, Don Pedro, and Claudio are gone, it is the Friar who points the way to clearing up "the strange misprision in the princes." He comforts Hero, and persuades the rest to conceal her and pretend that she has died. The semblance of death, he says, will restore Claudio's vision of his wronged bride:

> When he shall hear she died upon his words,
> Th' idea of her life shall sweetly creep,
> Into his study of imagination,
> And every lovely organ of her life,
> Shall come apparelled in more precious habit,
> More moving-delicate, and full of life,
> Into the eye and prospect of his soul,
> Than when she lived indeed.

As for Hero, "Come Lady," the Friar says to her, "die to live; this wedding-day/ Perhaps is but prolonged." His theme of suffering or "dying" in order to reach the truth of love is, of course, a very old one in our tradition. Shakespeare often presents it as issuing out of a tragic action, especially in his last plays. Here he touches it lightly, as the final movement in his comedy of masks. The Friar wants to substitute for Don John's lying masquerade a masquerade of his own, which, though literally false, will contain, and finally reveal, the truth.

Beatrice and Benedick are left alone to conclude the great scene. They are ahead of Claudio on the path to love; we have already seen them comically suffering for their pride and scorn. Now we can see that the crisis has brought them closer together, for there is a new tenderness in their words:

BENEDICK
I do love nothing in the world so well as you, is not that strange?
BEATRICE
As strange as the thing I know not. It were as possible for me to say I loved nothing so well as you. But believe me not; and yet I lie not. I confess nothing, nor I deny nothing. I am sorry for my cousin.

They are undeluded, and sure of each other, but the shadow of slander that makes Hero seem dead must keep them apart until it is dispelled. Beatrice, in her high-spirited way, demands that Benedick challenge Claudio, and Benedick, in the tradition of the courtly lover, somewhat ruefully accepts the ordeal his lady imposes on him. He will, if he must, slay the monster Slander in the person of his friend. Shall we smile at their high seriousness (which, we know, is really much ado about nothing) or shall we be touched by their generosity? We can only hope that Dogberry will manage to explain the truth in time.

The next scene (Act IV, scene 2) dissolves the high comedy of Beatrice and Benedick in joyful farce. Dogberry, with the Sexton and the Watch, examines Conrade and Borachio, and at last hurries off to report to Leonato. But in Act V, scene 1, we watch the painfully silly encounters between Claudio, Don Pedro, Benedick, Leonato, and Antonio, all ready to fight, all uncomfortably trying to act as they think they should. "What a pretty thing man is," says Don Pedro, "when he goes in his doublet and hose and leaves off his wit." Then Dogberry rescues them by revealing the real villains.

The transition from the comically deluded world of the play back to everyday reality, where real marriages are possible, is appropriately accomplished by Claudio and Don Pedro, who were partly to blame for the last big mistake. Their nocturnal visit to Hero's tomb is as formal as the masked ball or the wedding procession, and like those two ceremonious occasions, it is both true and false. For the Hero whom Claudio thought he knew is really dead, while the real Hero "lives in death with glorious fame," as his song says. Don Pedro's words mark the end of the little ceremony:

Good morrow masters, put your torches out.
The wolves have preyed, and look, the gentle day,
Before the wheels of Phœbus, round about
Dapples the drowsy east with spots of grey.

Now we are ready for the finale in broad daylight: the triumphant appearance of Hero alive; the pretty passages of wit and love; and the dance which concludes the entertainment.

When Shakespeare called this play *Much Ado About Nothing*, he plainly indicated that it was not to be taken too literally, like a modern "slice of life." The story is romantic, and highly improbable; but that is part of the fun. The elegant manners of Leonato's house party—the free and leisurely play of wit, the idealized, subtle code of love—are certainly remote from our experience; but Shakespeare himself presents these conventions of Renaissance society as part of the masquerade. When he writes comedy he is always in a holiday mood, always at play. Yet when he ends an evening of laughter and music we realize that much has been revealed about humanity and the forms its love may take.

HENRY V

This play is a celebration of the popular hero, "warlike Harry," and his famous victories in France. It has been severely criticized by devoted Shakespeareans, who object to the nationalistic pride which it expresses, and to the loose, fluent narrative style in which it is composed. But it has been a favorite in the theater, and some of its passages of high rhetoric have become as familiar as proverbs. The best way to enjoy it is to see it on the stage, before a popular audience.

Henry V, written in 1599, is a sequel to *Henry IV, Parts 1 and 2*. In those plays we meet Henry as young Prince Hal, frequenter of taverns and companion of the great Falstaff and his disreputable friends. We meet the Prince's father, Henry IV, who had usurped the crown by the murder of Richard II, and dreams of leading a crusade to the Holy Land to expiate that crime. The shadow of his father's regicide still hangs over Henry V, and perhaps his "holy war" against France was undertaken in order to unify his people, and to establish his own image as a religiously dedicated king. But *Henry V* is quite different from its predecessors. Henry had renounced the follies of his youth to assume the responsibilities of the crown, and in a famous scene in *Henry IV, Part 2*, he had disowned his old friend Falstaff. When this play opens,

Falstaff is dying offstage, and nothing matters but the conquest of France.

This focus upon the glories of war, unique in Shakespeare, makes *Henry* V quite unlike *Richard II* and the Henry IV plays. There is of course plenty of war, treachery, and private murder in them but that is never the point. The point is the quest for England's true welfare: peace, freedom, and order based on common loyalty to the crown. *Henry V* adds nothing to this great theme, and one must suppose that Shakespeare, the most popular playwright in London, was all but obliged to devote a play to the warrior-king. He promised it in *Henry IV, Part 2.* Henry V plays a stellar role in Shakespeare's two main sources, Holinshed's *Chronicles,* and *The Famous Victories of Henry the Fifth,* an earlier play by an unknown author. The old play and the chroniclers had made Henry and his victories into a familiar, exciting popular legend, and it is that figure, symbol of England's prowess, that Shakespeare re-creates for his own theater and acting company:

> O for a muse of fire, that would ascend
> The brightest heaven of invention:
> A kingdom for a stage, princes to act,
> And monarchs to behold the swelling scene.
> Then should the warlike Harry, like himself,
> Assume the port of Mars, and at his heels,
> Leashed in like hounds, should Famine, Sword, and Fire
> Crouch for employment.

We are gathered to celebrate once more Harry and his war, a patriotic ceremony; and the Chorus only hopes that the poet, his actors, and his stage will not disappoint the audience's expectations.

There is no difficulty in following the story of this play. Each act is based on a famous episode of Henry's career, and the Chorus with its superb verse-music maintains the martial mood and reminds us of the historic narrative that links the scenes. But in giving the audience the heroic legend that it demands, Shakespeare does not lose his own vision. He also presents a disillusioned picture of war itself, and that is why some critics think that his heart was not in this play. We can never know exactly what the play meant to Shakespeare or his audience; perhaps they relished it with more humor and irony than we usually give them credit for. But we can read it with an eye to the contrasting effects —stirring, comic, cruel—which it has on a modern reader. And we can see that it is all wonderfully well built to carry in the theater.

The first act is a prologue, for though the military motive is announced in the Chorus's very first words, we must go over the official "causes" of the war before the fighting can start. In scene 1 the Archbishop of Canterbury and the Bishop of Ely candidly explain that they are offering Henry a great deal of money for his French war in order to induce him—not to say "bribe" him—to defend the Church from a bill that threatens to deprive it of most of its revenues. When Henry appears (scene 2) he accepts the money, but also requires the Archbishop to justify his claim to the crown of France. The Archbishop obliges with a long, pedantic, legal argument straight from Holinshed. This scene can easily be played as comedy, and it is probable that Shakespeare intended it that way. No one could really follow the controversies about the Salic Law in the theater; everyone wants Henry to get started; and in that situation the Archbishop's long-winded rationalizing is bound to seem laughably irrelevant.

But the Archbishop then proceeds to find Biblical sanction for the English cause, thus quieting Henry's conscience, and making the attack on France appear as a kind of crusade. Henry's religious dedication was part of the legend, and it is stressed throughout the play. Moreover the Archbishop gives an eloquent picture of the ideal monarchy, in which the swarming diversity of human nature and purpose is united in obedience to the king:

> Therefore doth heaven divide
> The state of man in divers functions,
> Setting endeavour in continual motion;
> To which is fixed, as an aim or butt,
> Obedience: for so work the honey-bees,
> Creatures that by a rule in nature teach
> The act of order to a peopled kingdom.

The whole speech is a carefully written and richly metaphorical exposition of Shakespeare's own sense of order, both in human society and in the drama that reflects it. The effect of the speech is to relate this play to the theme of the histories, and to remind us that Henry, as king, is the symbol and custodian of England's moral well-being.

The act ends with a sharp turn from England's inner order to the simpler motive of foreign conquest: when Henry receives the Dauphin's insulting gift of tennis balls, and makes his spirited reply, we can yell "Hurrah for our side!" The Chorus, opening Act II, rejoices in this single-minded drive:

> Now all the youth of England are on fire,
> And silken dalliance in the wardrobe lies.

Now thrive the armourers, and honour's thought
Reigns solely in the breast of every man.

As the stage is peopled with characters of many kinds, in this act and the next, we see that they are all focused on the warlike "aim or butt," as the Archbishop put it: "So many a thousand actions once afoot,/ End in one purpose." The French, as we see them at various stages of the campaign, are perforce sucked into the same motivation: "honor" and obedience to *their* king.

There is one more famous episode to be dealt with before we embark: the conspiracy of Cambridge, Scroop, and Grey, who were bribed by the French, with their "pale policy," to murder King Henry. Shakespeare presents it swiftly in Act II, scene 2. The plot increases our sympathy for Henry and our war-fever; and when the conspirators repent on the way to their execution, the patriotic emotions acquire a new solemnity.

In Acts II, III, and IV the central story of Henry's invasion is accompanied by two contrasting themes, that of Falstaff's bedraggled old friends, and that of the British officers Gower, Fluellen, Macmorris, and Jamy, who represent respectively the English, Welsh, Irish, and Scottish soldiers that make up Henry's army.

Nym, Bardolph, Pistol, and Nell Quickly appear in Act II, scene 1, a sardonic contrast to the stirring Chorus that opens the act. Shakespeare's audience would have remembered them from *Henry IV*, the disreputable companions of Falstaff and of Henry himself, when he was young Prince Hal. But now they are older and sadder, and we learn from them that Falstaff, that sweet monster, is dying. Nell says, "The king hath killed his heart," thereby reminding us of the painful scene in *Henry IV, Part 2*, when Henry disowns his old friend. When they return in scene 3, Nell describes Falstaff's death in a speech which, with its mixture of pathos and humor, is worthy of Falstaff himself. This shameless crew is often thought of as comic relief, and they certainly do serve to deflate the pomposity of war with welcome laughter. Yet at the same time we see, through them, the meanest aspects of the army. Pistol's version of the war-motive (Act II, scene 3) is humorous, but the humor bites:

Let us to France, like horse-leeches my boys,
To suck, to suck, the very blood to suck.

As they appear throughout the play they always produce laughter with a somewhat bitter aftertaste.

Gower, Fluellen, Macmorris, and Jamy first appear in Act III, scene 2, where they serve to put Pistol and his confederates in their place, and counteract the impression they make. Shakespeare presents the racial types very much as popular fiction presents the racial types that make up our armies. He laughs affectionately at their accents and customs, while carefully demonstrating that they are all equally brave and equally loyal to the crown.

It is in the scenes in the French court and the French camp that we feel most strongly the jingoistic element in the play. We can only sympathize with King Charles when he receives Henry's impossible ultimatum (Act II, scene 4), and endeavors to rouse his countrymen. But thereafter the silly Dauphin becomes the chief representative of the French side. And the closer we come to the battle of Agincourt, the climax of the play (Act IV), the more broadly does Shakespeare caricature the fopperies and vanities of the French.

In representing the great battle, Shakespeare diverts attention, as much as possible, away from the actual fighting, which, as the Chorus says, could hardly be adequately staged. And he has nothing to say about the military reasons for the extraordinary English victory. Holinshed carefully explains that the French relied on their heavily armed cavalry, while the English relied on their yeomen foot-soldiers, armed with longbows. The English archers got behind sharpened poles, on which the French horses foundered, and then let loose their showers of arrows. This battle, like Crécy, still interests military historians, for it marks an important change in the composition of European armies: from the feudal knight to the yeoman foot-soldier. But in accounting for the English victory, Shakespeare focuses entirely on the contrasting attitudes in the two armies: the arrogant overconfidence of the French, and the pious fortitude of the vastly outnumbered English.

Henry is of course the heart and soul of his army, and Shakespeare gives us, in Act III, superb images of the conquering hero. But at the same time he offers us (if we care to see them) absurd or horrifying glimpses of military bravura. Consider, for example, the opening sequence of Act III. The Chorus paints its exhilarating picture of the English armada on its way:

> Hear the shrill whistle, which doth order give
> To sounds confused; behold the threaden sails,
> Borne with th' invisible and creeping wind,
> Draw the huge bottoms through the furrowed sea,

and so brings us, with "the celerity of thought," to besieged Harfleur:

and the nimble gunner
With linstock now the devilish cannon touches,
(*Alarum, and chambers go off within.*)
And down goes all before them.

Whereupon Henry himself rushes on to lead the charge, with that speech which countless actors, and countless reciters in schools and colleges, have made famous:

Once more unto the breach, dear friends, once more;
Or close the wall up with our English dead.

The effect can be electrifying in the theater; but if one reads Henry's speech quietly one may notice how technically he induces the proper spirit in his men:

Then imitate the action of the tiger;
Stiffen the sinews, conjure up the blood.

Modern soldiers are (or were) taught pugnacity in a similar way: they had to grunt savagely as they pushed their bayonets into the sandbags. When red-nosed Bardolph charges in at the head of his ragamuffins immediately after Henry's charge, yelling, "On, on, on, on, on, to the breach, to the breach, to the breach!" he can hardly fail to bring down the house. When we next see Henry (Act III, scene 3) he is forcing the citizens of Harfleur to open their gates, by reminding them of the fate of a sacked town:

What rein can hold licentious wickedness,
When down the hill he holds his fierce career?

We see him as a swift, relentless invader, who nevertheless offers mercy if the enemy will yield. But his speech also reminds us vividly of the mischief his war has let loose.

Shakespeare builds his most careful picture of Henry as the religiously dedicated warrior in Act IV, scene 1, the night before Agincourt. The Chorus sets the scene on the eve of battle:

Now entertain conjecture of a time,
When creeping murmur and the poring dark
Fills the wide vessel of the universe.
From camp to camp, through the foul womb of night
The hum of either army stilly sounds.

The French are waiting eagerly, in their thousands; the English are few and starving, but Henry restores their courage with "A little touch of Harry in the night":

> That every wretch, pining and pale before,
> Beholding him, plucks comfort from his looks.

Disguised as a soldier "under Sir Thomas Erpingham" Henry meets Bates, and Williams, who proves to be a tough-minded critic of the whole war. Williams wants to know how such slaughter can be justified; how he and other common soldiers can know whether the English cause is righteous or not; how the King can possibly take responsibility for so much suffering: just such questions as must torment any soldier as he waits for the carnage to begin. Henry tries to discuss these hard matters reasonably with Williams and they agree on the necessity of obedience to the commander, without which an army (or any common enterprise) is impossible. But Williams insists that the King has the best of it; and he and Henry both lose their tempers. They postpone their quarrel until after the battle, when we shall see it patched up as well as possible under the circumstances (Act IV, scenes 7 and 8).

Henry and Williams elude the question of the justice of their cause. We like to think that every soldier should know why he is fighting; but Henry and Williams seem to agree that a common soldier cannot be expected to know and correctly judge the causes of the war: they leave that to the King. We have seen that Henry as King had left it to the Archbishop of Canterbury (Act 1, scene 2). Thus, if we care to think about it, we may see King and soldier alike risking their lives in the faith, certified by the Church, that they are obeying the will of God. But at this point we are not given much time to think: the fatal night is near its end, Henry and all his men are in mortal peril. When Henry, left alone, meditates on the intolerable burden of rule, it is impossible not to sympathize with his human plight. And it seems natural, after he has bade old Erpingham good night, that he should resort to prayer (end of scene 1). Henry's religious faith is stressed again after the battle, when it is badly needed to explain (if not justify) the horrors of Agincourt. We have by that time seen Henry order his soldiers to murder their prisoners (scene 6). We have heard that the French slaughtered helpless English boys who were left with the baggage (scene 7). We have heard the amazing statistics of death and destruction (scene 8); but Henry attributes his almost incredible victory to God, and orders that prayers of thanksgiving be offered, and the dead properly buried.

Agincourt was Henry's most famous victory, but the war dragged on for years, and France was "lost" in the disastrous reign of Henry VI. The readers of the popular chronicles in Shakespeare's audience knew this very well, and the Chorus alludes to the facts before Act V and in the Epilogue; but only to dismiss them. The fifth act is based on Henry's betrothal to Princess Katharine, which triumphantly ends that phase of the war.

Act V has been sharply criticized by many authorities, including the great Dr. Johnson, who thought that Shakespeare had used up his material in Act IV, and was obliged to add the wooing scene to fiill out the evening. But we can see, I think, that the wooing of Katharine is the natural ending for the play as Shakespeare very knowingly planned it. Having seen our idol in action, winning against great odds, we want a glimpse of him after his victory, like a baseball player in the locker room after the big game, kissing his wife and bashfully accepting congratulations. We see Henry with Katharine in just such a relaxed and endearing mood, a surprisingly clumsy lover, a plainspoken, simple Englishman after all (scene 2). Like so much comedy, this scene plays far better than it reads; with an attractive and skillful Katharine, it may be charming in the theater. It makes us forget the bitterness of war, and like the traditional happy ending of comedy, sends us home content with the evening's entertainment.

It is evident that the Henry of this scene is not the subtle young man we know as Prince Hal in *Henry IV, Part 1.* It is a question whether he is consistent with Henry the conqueror, and Henry the pious king; whom we meet in the first parts of the play.

In constructing his play about warlike Harry for his popular audience, Shakespeare (being the poet he was) could not follow his predecessors very closely. He could not imitate the guileless style of *The Famous Victories of Henry V,* which resembles a boy's adventure story. He could not be content with the proud lyricism of conquest, as Marlowe was in his early *Tamburlaine*—though the Chorus' military verse-music may remind one of Marlowe's "mighty line." He had created the marvelously unwarlike Falstaff; he was probably already working on *Hamlet* (1600); and when he considered war, he saw a great deal besides the splendor of heroism. Nevertheless he made the play an evocation of the English fighting spirit which has served his countrymen as a sort of patriotic ceremony from that day to this, especially when (as in World War II) their country is in danger. His theater magic and his grasp of popular psychology is so sure in *Henry V* that a good production can move us too, in the theater, where the play belongs.

AS YOU LIKE IT

As You Like It was written, probably, in 1599, which would make it the next to the last of the great romantic comedies. As Shakespeare tells us in his title, he devised it to please his large and diversified popular audience. He put in something for every taste, from the subtle idealized love of Rosalind and Orlando to Touchstone's anti-romantic affair with his Audrey; and he devised the many amusing complications of the story, before the end which all good comedies must have: marriage for nearly everybody, with laughter and music. It is all warmed and lighted by Shakespeare's own holiday mood, which is both mocking and gentle; many readers think it the most perfect of his light, poetic entertainments.

He took the plot (as confectors of modern musical comedies so often do) from a popular novel, Lodge's *Rosalynde* (1590). He makes the story clearer and swifter than Lodge did, for he takes it much less seriously. Duke Frederick has usurped the dukedom of his elder brother ("Duke Senior"), who is living in exile with his loyal followers in the Forest of Arden. Frederick's daughter Celia and his brother's daughter Rosalind, childhood friends, are living at Frederick's court when the play opens. Sir Rowland de Boys' sons, Oliver the oldest and Orlando the youngest, are there too. The middle brother, Jaques (not to be confused with the "melancholy Jaques"), is away until the end of the play. Oliver and Orlando quarrel, and Orlando has to flee for his life, but not until he and Rosalind have fallen in love. Duke Frederick banishes Rosalind too, Celia follows her, and all join Duke Senior in the Forest of Arden. It is in that pretty realm that the main business of the play—flirtations and mocking laughter—takes place. The plot is wound up when Oliver and Duke Frederick repent their wickedness, Duke Senior is restored to his dukedom, and all the young people get married.

Lodge's novel is "pastoral romance": that is, a tale of somewhat Christianized shepherds and shepherdesses, nymphs and woodland gods, derived ultimately from Greek romances like those of Theocritus

—the whole set in a beautiful country suggesting both Eden and the classical Golden Age. Since Dante at the end of the thirteenth century saw Matelda in his earthly paradise, Europe had been fascinated with "pastoral." It is the basis of countless paintings, stories, early operas, masques, and ballets, and also of much love poetry. It is, of course, conventional and literary, but at its best it expresses the Renaissance delight in the world, and its idealized but sophisticated cult of human love. Lodge's story has some of the pastoral charm, and Shakespeare keeps it for his characters to play with, so to speak—especially Rosalind and Orlando, who use it in their flirting. But he mixes with Lodge's romance several comic themes of his own invention, notably those of Jaques, Touchstone, Audrey, and William the country bumpkin. The result is much livelier and much more comical than Lodge's (or anyone else's) purely pastoral narrative.

Lodge's characters are rather colorless, but *As You Like It* is filled with those figures that live for us both on the stage and in our imaginations. Shakespeare must have had English types in mind when he wrote the various roles, and also the actors who would play them: a particularly talented boy-actor for Rosalind, for instance. The part of Touchstone was apparently written for Robert Armin, a professional jester and well-known personality in London. Much of the life and meaning of the play is in the characters, and there is no difficulty in enjoying them, they throb with an unmistakable theatrical life. The modern producer does, however, have a problem with the Forest of Arden and its romantic conventions: how is one to make that setting visible and acceptable on the modern stage? The reader of course does not have to solve the technical problems of style, settings, and costumes. But the reader too must know a little about the manners, the poetic and theatrical conventions, and the popular ideas which Shakespeare used, if he is to enjoy the comedy and the poetry to the full. The characters are always making fun of their own romantic lovemaking; of the customs of the court; of the ideas current at the time. In their jokes and in their lyrics they build up the imagined scene, which is not to be taken too seriously, filled though it is with feeling.

The first act is a prologue, in which Shakespeare quickly sets forth the basis of the plot. The first scene moves like a simple adventure story: Orlando and Oliver have their fight, and Oliver engages Charles the Wrestler to finish off his younger brother. But in scene 2 we meet Rosalind and Celia, and their leisurely joking shows us what the main action of the play will be. "Let me see," says Rosalind, "what think you of falling in love?"

CELIA

Marry I prithee do, to make sport withal. But love no man in good earnest, nor no further in sport neither than with safety of a pure blush thou mayst in honour come off again.

That well describes Rosalind's delicate "sport" with Orlando, which will occupy her, in the Forest of Arden, till love overcomes her fears. But at this point she does not know Orlando, and Celia suggests the alternative pastime:

Let us sit and mock the good housewife Fortune from her wheel, that her gifts may henceforth be bestowed equally.

Since the Middle Ages Fortune had been personified as a goddess who turned her wheel, raising one man and lowering another, without regard to justice. She distributed the world's goods according to her whim, especially in cities, and in courts like Frederick's, where all were intriguing for power and money. Celia wants to blame Fortune for making honest women (among whom she counts herself, no doubt) "ill-favoredly"; but Rosalind says Nature is to blame for that. They continue the theme of Nature when Touchstone appears, calling him a "natural"—that is, a born idiot.

Everyone knew that Touchstone was played by Robert Armin, a very intelligent man; and everyone could see that Rosalind and Celia were both "honest" and "fair." The girls are only joking, like timid young people in any period; half-ironically blaming Fortune for a world they never made; half-secretly longing for love, and hoping that Nature has made them honest and fair enough for the right love—which, of course, would cure everything. But the notions of Love, Fortune, and Nature, which they start here, echo throughout the lyrics and the play of wit in the Forest of Arden. Soon the girls will flee there, abandoned by Fortune; and there they will find Nature, and test, in thir flirtations, their natures and those of their lovers.

The climax of Act I comes in scene 3, when Orlando throws the redoubtable Charles, knocking him out and breaking a few ribs in his enthusiasm. At the same time he and Rosalind (as they both remark) are "thrown" by each other's charms. Orlando's victory offends the Duke and makes him suspect Rosalind, who flees with Celia and Touchstone. So we are prepared for the main business of the evening: the play of love and wit which Fortune's exiles enjoy in the Forest of Arden.

The Forest of Arden is first described by Charles (Act I, scene 1) as the place where the exiled Duke lives with his followers "like old Robin Hood of England" and they all "fleet the time carelessly as they did in the golden world." Shakespeare wanted it to suggest the Golden Age of pastoral romance; but he does not hesitate to put the greenwood tree there, palms among the beeches, and a lion among the English sheep. He does not take any of these romantic settings too literally; he plays with them, in order to suggest a delightful state of mind, a vacation from the cares of the world. "Are not these woods/ More free from peril than the envious court?" says Duke Senior (Act II, scene 1). Even the winter winds, out here, are morally good for us: "counsellors that feelingly persuade me what I am." He has, of course, lost his dukedom through Fortune's whim, but "Sweet are the uses of adversity," for they leave us plenty of time to philosophize:

> And this our life, exempt from public haunt,
> Finds tongues in trees, books in the running brooks,
> Sermons in stones, and good in every thing.

Shakespeare expects us to smile at Duke Senior's middle-aged enthusiasms for the country (like that of a city man who has just moved to the suburbs); but we must agree with Amiens, who remarks,

> Happy is your Grace,
> That can translate the stubbornness of fortune
> Into so quiet and so sweet a style.

Duke Senior, in fact, shows us the Forest of Arden as it is for all his followers.

The "melancholy Jaques" is an even more tireless moralizer than Duke Senior, and soon (Act II, scene 7) he reports that he has found another kindred spirit in Touchstone:

> I met a fool,
> Who laid him down and basked him in the sun,
> And railed on Lady Fortune in good terms,
> In good set terms, and yet a motley fool.

These three characters, in their railing at Fortune, play many humorous and poetic variations on popular philosophic notions of the time. Thus Jaques, teased by Duke Senior (Act II, scene 7) gives a classic defense of the satirist's right to "speak his mind" and cleanse the world, provided he mentions no real individuals. When Orlando in the same scene breaks in on their picnic and demands food with his sword drawn, Duke Senior mildly remarks,

> Thou seest, we are not all alone unhappy.
> This wide and universal theatre

Presents more woeful pageants than the scene
Wherein we play in.

That starts Jaques off on his famous speech, "All the world's a stage." That idea is often heard in the Renaissance; Shakespeare himself touches upon it in several of his plays. Jaques combines it here with another familiar piece of popular wisdom, that of the Ages of Man. The result is that humorous and rueful little poem which everyone recognizes like an old tune. The philosophizing of Jaques is, in fact, closely akin to Amiens' beautiful songs: variations, touched with Shakespeare's genius, on old and standard themes. It is evident that Jaques enjoys his "melancholy" hugely. In our time only sophomores have enough leisure to enjoy their pessimistic "bull sessions," but for the Elizabethans mulling over ancient problems of man and Fortune seems to have been a favorite pastime. Duke Senior and his followers, too old for romantic love, are confirmed addicts of that more sedentary game.

But flirtation was more exciting than philosophy then, as it is now, and that sport begins when Rosalind, Celia, and Touchstone reach the Forest of Arden (Act II, scene 4). They are suitably dressed for the Golden Age: Touchstone in his motley, Celia as the "shepherdess" Aliena, and Rosalind as that pretty shepherd-boy Ganymede, who was Zeus' favorite in the old Greek story. The first people they meet are those very literary shepherds, Corin and Silvius. When Silvius utters the traditional complaint of the rejected lover and runs off crying "Phebe, Phebe, Phebe!" Rosalind and Touchstone both recognize their fates: to play once more the old game of pastoral romance:

ROSALIND
Jove, Jove, this shepherd's passion
Is much upon my fashion.
TOUCHSTONE
And mine, but it grows something stale with me.

Rosalind will put Orlando through all the paces; but Touchstone will tackle the problem of Audrey without a trace of romance, for he has long since passed the time of sighs and blushes.

In pastoral romance the lovers must always be kept apart as long as possible, for the point is not love's fulfillment, but the mysterious, painful, and Eden-like moment of love's first innocent revelation. Orlando and Rosalind-Ganymede, after their "fall" in Act I, do not meet again until Act III, scene 2. Even then Rosalind is miraculously insulated from Orlando by the thin disguise of her boy's costume. That disguise served Shakespeare the actor-manager well, for of course Rosalind was played by a boy-actor. And it serves Rosalind well, keeping Orlando at a distance, and at the same time (when she persuades him to practice his wooing on "Ganymede") enabling her to have the excitement without committing herself. It is the old game of flirtation, but Rosalind is not dishonest in this, for she suffers the pangs of love herself, and wearies Celia with her endless talk of Orlando. She is trying to make sure that Orlando loves her as much as he says he does, and as much as she loves him. She wants nothing less than the finest love of the Renaissance poets: innocent and free as Eden, but deep as faith. She makes poor Orlando, in his wooing, adopt (or pretend) all the attitudes of the desperate romantic lover; but she makes fun of these conventions even while she uses them. She never loses her balance, however, and is perfectly capable of enjoying a bawdy joke now and then. In short, she sees almost all the "angles" of love in the Forest of Arden.

The wooing of Rosalind and Orlando alternates with Silvius' wooing of Phebe, and Touchstone's businesslike arrangements with Audrey. At the same time the older characters continue to play witty variations on Fortune, Love, and Nature. Touchstone and old Corin, the court or city man and the country philosopher, slyly show up each other's delusions (Act III, scene 2). Corin reveals Touchstone's artificialities, and Touchstone makes clear, with plenty of gory details, just what a messy business the breeding of sheep really is. All are enjoying their vacations in the Forest of Arden—or the Golden Age—yet making fun of that poetic creation at the same time. The effect is like a country dance, in which people of many different "natures" keep time together: some young, some old, some glamorous, some laughable. Rosalind and Orlando are at the center of the kaleidoscope; Silvius and Phebe offer a burlesque of the literary and romantic aspects of their love, while Touchstone and Audrey keep us reminded of biology.

The enjoyment of love or wit in the leisure of Arden is the business of the play, but we do not expect that idyllic season to last forever. And Shakespeare keeps us reminded of the plot by means of very brief scenes in Frederick's court. When the repentant Oliver reaches the Forest (Act IV, scene 3) we realize that Fortune is turning her wheel again: she is smiling upon the exiles, and it is time for them to return, under these happy auspices, to the workaday world. The finale (Act V, scenes 2, 3, and 4) is elaborate, like that of a hit musical in our own theater; for each of the main characters has a few lines and takes a bow before the audience goes home.

Rosalind tells us that Oliver and Celia, the last of the lovers, have made up for lost time by a simultaneous case of love-at-first-sight: "They are in the very wrath of love, and they will together. Clubs cannot part them." As Ganymede, she takes charge of her affair with Orlando, and of Silvius' with Phebe. Each lover must affirm he is "made of sighs and tears," and also of "faith and service"; and each must promise to abide by Ganymede's commands. This passage (which defines the romantic commitment very carefully) is as ceremonious as a children's game, when all the players, blindfolded, march trustingly to claim their prizes when the magic word is spoken.

Touchstone and his bewildered Audrey have an interlude (scene 3) and the pages sing the beautiful song, "It was a lover and his lass," to remind us of real country-wooing in the fields. Then (scene 4) the rest of the cast begins to assemble, to hear Ganymede's mysterious decrees; and while "he" is offstage (to change his costume, no doubt) Jaques and Touchstone have a chance to make their final joking comments on the proceedings:

> JAQUES
>
> There is sure another flood toward, and these couples are coming to the ark. Here comes a pair of very strange beasts, which in all tongues are called fools.

Touchstone apparently agrees with him, for he describes his beast, Audrey, without flattery: "an ill-favored thing, sir, but mine own." He proceeds to his mock-pedantic account of "quarreling by the book," which must have amused Shakespeare's audience vastly, for fashionable dueling was a standard joke, and Touchstone is probably referring to an actual book on the subject (*Vincentio Saviolo his Practice*, 1595). Then, at last, music announces the ceremonious entrance of Hymen, attendants, and Rosalind in her proper female attire. Hymen was the Greek god of marriage, Apollo's son, who adorned many a splendid wedding masque in Shakespeare's time. He is the proper figure to preside over marriage in the Golden Age, with its mingling of classical and Christian feeling; and he takes the center of the stage long enough to sing of the ideal dream of marriage, "When earthly things made even/ Atone together"—that is, when they are made one in harmony.

Hardly has Hymen's moment ended in laughter at Touchstone and Audrey, when Jaques de Boys arrives to give the older exiles *their* prizes. Duke Frederick has turned from the world to religion, whither the melancholy Jaques will follow him; and Duke Senior is restored to his dukedom. It is melancholy Jaques who formally presents each one with his due, and then all "atone together" in the rhythm and harmony of the final dance. Rosalind, the most glamorous character, who has seen and enjoyed the most, speaks the epilogue.

Shakespeare, like Jaques, turned from this holiday entertainment to more sober concerns, for in the next six or seven years he wrote his great tragedies. He did not treat the pastoral themes again until his last plays, when that vision of innocence is part of a wider pattern which includes suffering and guilt. In *As You Like It* the Eden-like love of Rosalind and Orlando is seen in a purely comic context, that of the strange capers which all kinds of people fall into when love strikes them.

TWELFTH NIGHT

Twelfth Night, or What You Will, is the last in the series of romantic comedies which includes *A Midsummer Night's Dream, As You Like It,* and *Much Ado About Nothing.* It was written between 1598 and 1602, perhaps toward the end of 1600, that is, at the time when Shakespeare was writing *Julius Caesar* and *Hamlet,* his first tragedies. But it has none of the gloom and terror which Shakespeare is supposed to have felt at this time. It is as light in touch as anything he ever wrote; an evening of music and comic play. It is one of many signs that Shakespeare was a very conscious artist, in control of his own moods and the moods of his audience.

The main story is that of Duke Orsino and Viola in her boy's disguise; of the moody Lady Olivia, and of Viola's twin brother Sebastian. Shakespeare took this plot from Barnabie Riche's story, *Apolonius and Sila* (1581), and before Riche there are several Italian versions. The story was popular during the Renaissance, and Roman comedy is full of similar plots based on indistinguishable twins and the mistakes in identity which result. Shakespeare's predecessors treated it as worldly, often salacious farce; but Shakespeare fills the routine old scenario with new life, by endowing his four main characters with delicate and innocent feeling. And he adds a subplot of his own invention: the tipsy practical joking of Sir Toby Belch and his nocturnal companions, a farcical accompaniment to the romance and high comedy of the solemn young lovers.

Shakespeare's title, *Twelfth Night, or What You Will,* would have told his audience to expect an evening of play. Everyone knew that the twelfth night after Christmas, the Feast of Epiphany, was traditionally celebrated as a "Feast of Fools" when the order of the household was upset and everyone was free to do as he pleased. Some scholars think that a particular twelfth night was meant, January 6, 1601, and that the play was written for Queen Elizabeth as part of the "revels" with which her court celebrated Epiphany that year. This notion has not been proved, but certainly that occasion would have been right for the comedy as we have it. One can easily imagine Shakespeare and his actors, in a hall of the palace decked for the Christmas season, presenting the fond follies of the Lady Olivia's household to entertain the far grander household of the Queen herself.

At a good performance of the play, or on an early reading, the characters seem to be real people rather than the creations of the poet and his actors. And in fact Shakespeare does present the Italian story in a "real" English setting, with "real" English characters. The Lady Olivia's household, with her ne'er-do-well uncle, Sir Toby; sharp-tongued Maria, Sir Andrew the lingering house guest, would have seemed even more familiar then than they do now. Shakespeare may have been thinking of some ample, noble household near his native Stratford, or even of Elizabeth's court, which was, after all, only the greatest of such households.

It is no doubt the realistic life of the characters and their society that makes the play so clear and so actable. And yet *Twelfth Night* is also poetry, and it is the poetic impression which we remember, like a tune, long after we forget the realistic details. Miss Marianne Moore's famous definition of poetry, "an imaginary garden with real toads in it," fits *Twelfth Night* perfectly. The people are the kind we know, they have their share of vanity, greed, and foolishness. But by the music of his language, the make-believe of his actors, and the use of actual music, Shakespeare creates an "imaginary garden" for them, the poetic realm of Illyria. It is in that realm that we see them while the play lasts; and it is that realm we remember when the play is over.

He starts with music, to lead us into the romantic Illyria of Orsino and Olivia. Orsino speaks:

> If music be the food of love, play on,
> Give me excess of it; that, surfeiting,
> The appetite may sicken, and so die.

In this first speech Orsino is clear: he is in love with love, and indulging that mood with extravagant delicacy. He is comically solemn, but so melodious that we must share his fondness even as we smile at it. He thinks he is in love with Olivia, and Valentine reports that she will have none of him because she is mourning the death of her brother:

> The element itself, till seven years' heat,
> Shall not behold her face at ample view;
> But like a cloistress she will veiled walk,
> And water once a day her chamber round
> With eye-offering brine.

How silly of her to pamper the pose of grief; she must take herself terribly seriously. But as she denies the doting Orsino and the doting sky (the "element") a glimpse of her lovely face, piously moping about her room and "offending" her tender eyes with tears, she is laughable and beautiful at once.

In the next scene (Act I, scene 2) Viola appears in this realm of music and high comedy:

> VIOLA
> What country, friends, is this?
> CAPTAIN
> This is Illyria lady.
> VIOLA
> And what should I do in Illyria?

What indeed? For Viola, lost and shipwrecked though she is at the moment, is as sensible as anyone in the audience, many of whom must be wondering what *they* have to do in Illyria. Sane as she is, she now finds herself in the realm of romance. She was brought by a storm which must have wrecked her ship without wetting her garments, and like her brother Sebastian she was saved from an ornamental, storybook sea. The Captain gives us the picture, complete with a dolphin out of Ovid:

> I saw your brother,
> Most provident in peril, bind himself—
> Courage and hope both teaching him the practice—
> To a strong mast, that lived upon the sea;
> Where, like Arion on the dolphin's back,
> I saw him hold acquaintance with the waves,
> So long as I could see.

Much of the subtle comedy in Viola's role is in seeing so self-possessed a young woman trying to keep her wits about her in a land where only romance is real—Olivia's fond attachment to her, and, before long, her own secret infatuation with Orsino.

In the next scene (Act I, scene 3) Shakespeare creates in the colloquial prose of Sir Toby Belch and Maria a more earthy version of "What you will":

> SIR TOBY
> What a plague means my niece to take the death of her brother thus? I am sure care's an enemy to life.
>
> MARIA
> By my troth Sir Toby, you must come in earlier o' nights. Your cousin, my lady, takes great exceptions to your ill hours.

Soon they are joined by Sir Andrew Aguecheek, that foolish knight, and for him their high-jinks are as wonderful as a grown-up party to a child: "I am a fellow o' th' strangest mind i' th' world," he says; "I delight in masks and revels sometimes altogether." Shall we say that Sir Toby is a greedy and irresponsible tippler, Maria a mercenary minx with a rather cruel wit, and Sir Andrew a vain, gangling coward, cynically exploited by Sir Toby? We may say so, if we think about them in the light of morals and psychology, and Shakespeare of course knows all that. But as he shows them here, sneaking into the great house late at night, Sir Toby perhaps in stocking-feet—or later, when Feste joins them and sings his beautiful song, "O mistress mine" (Act II, scene 3)—we agree with Sir Toby: "Care's an enemy to life." Their particular parties are like a dream of what parties should be; we are made to feel that all of us, human beings of all kinds, can take part. So Shakespeare makes poetry out of farce, practical jokes, and the dimness of drink.

Malvolio, Lady Olivia's self-important steward, plays another variation on the theme of the play. He can't get the spirit either of romance or of jokes. Olivia comes out of her own daydream long enough to size him up exactly (Act I, scene 5): "O you are sick of self-love Malvolio, and taste with a distempered appetite." But he has great gusto in his peevishness. When he describes the beautiful Viola in her boy's costume as "a squash is before 'tis a peascod, or a codling when 'tis almost an apple" (Act I, scene 5), we laugh with him as well as at him. Anyone who has been waked up in the middle of the night by someone else's loud party will enjoy his description of Sir Toby's hearty bellowing (Act II, scene 3), "without any mitigation or remorse of voice." He is a perfect foil to the other characters; through his eyes we see the evening's foolishness from another, and necessary, angle. And at the end of the play, when he has been so devastatingly fooled, we agree with Olivia and Sir Toby that he has had enough, and must be brought back into the family.

Feste the Jester keeps his sanity better than any of the other characters, even Viola. It is Viola who tells us what to think of him (Act III, scene 1):

> This fellow is wise enough to play the fool,
> And to do that well, craves a kind of wit.
> He must observe their mood on whom he jests,
> The quality of persons, and the time.

Shakespeare wrote the part for Robert Armin, a professional jester who was then a member of Shakespeare's company. He was a famous personality in London, a goldsmith and a writer as well as an actor. As Feste, he moves through the play with a certain detachment, like a modern master of ceremonies, commenting on the characters with elaborate mockery, or charming everyone with his songs. Feste seems to be one of those characters who represent Shakespeare himself—in this case, Shakespeare the author of *Twelfth Night*, the professional entertainer, the master of moods, who can adjust his jokes to their objects, and vary his comedy, at just the right moment, with music. When Orsino dismisses Feste after his song, "Come away, come away death" (Act II, scene 4), Feste says, as he departs,

> Now the melancholy god protect thee, and the tailor make thy doublet of changeable taffeta, for thy mind is a very opal. I would have men of such constancy put to sea, that their business might be every thing, and their intent every where, for that's it that always makes a good voyage of nothing.

It is a beautiful description of Orsino, who knows his shifting moods, but not his mind. It might also be Shakespeare's description of his play: the "colors" of farce, of lyric, of high comedy alternate, and the entertainment seems to shimmer like an opal—all the more so because we know it is all based on the daydreams of the characters and the light make-believe of the actors—a good voyage, though made of "nothing."

Shakespeare ends his play as lightly as it began. By Act III the absurd tangles of mistaken identity and practical joking threaten to become serious. Poor Malvolio is in prison in disgrace; Olivia is in despair with her unrequited love for Viola's boyish appearance; Duke Orsino is ready to punish his supposed page for alienating Olivia's affections, and Viola herself is at her wit's end. In Act III, scene 4, these desperate situations are presented one after the other with great speed, as though the film were being run off at twice the natural pace. The effect is farcical; we feel that something must break soon. And then, in the nick of time, Sebastian at last arrives.

It is of course Sebastian in the old story who straightens out all the mistakes in identity, and unravels the absurd plot. Shakespeare uses him for that purpose, but he also makes use of the fact that Sebastian is new to Illyria in order to give us, through his eyes, a final impression of that never-never land and its fond inhabitants. So he completes the comic-poetic themes of the play as well as the story, and returns us gently to the everyday world.

When Sebastian first reaches Olivia's house (Act IV, scene 1) he is taken for his sister Viola by Feste, and then by Sir Andrew and Sir Toby. "Are all the people mad?" he asks, as he gives Toby and Andrew the good-natured beating they deserve. He is new to Illyria, as Viola was in Act I, when she asked, "What should I do in Illyria?" Like his sister, he expresses the feeling of the audience, for now we know the evening is nearly over, and all that we have seen was fooling.

But then the beautiful Olivia, in her turn, takes him for Viola, and endows him with her hand and her love. He decides that Illyria, mad or not, is the place for him:

> What relish is in this? How runs the stream?
> Or I am mad, or else this is a dream.
> Let fancy still my sense in Lethe steep;
> If it be thus to dream, still let me sleep.

Lethe was the stream in the classical world of the dead which was supposed to wash away all painful memories. Dante, in his pilgrimage through the other world, had to bathe in it and drink its waters before he could enter the part of Eden where human love is again made innocent and true. Sebastian means that he will gladly forget all he knows of the real world and its troubles, if only he can have the Eden-dream of Olivia's love. But we in the audience know that Sebastian is not dreaming: Olivia is real, and the real marriage follows fast. By the magic of the plot, Viola, Orsino, Toby, and Maria are provided with real marriages too. The whole comedy has been about the iridescent daydreams of youthful love, so wonderful and painful to the dreamer, so comical to the spectator. But now, as the play ends, Shakespeare plays another variation on that theme. Perhaps he wishes to suggest, through Sebastian's delicately managed shifts between reality and dream, that there was something real in the love that moved all the "mad" people in Illyria, however laughably they mistook its object.

He gives Feste the last word, ending the play, as it began, with music. Feste's song is as mysterious as a rhyme in a children's game: it can mean everything, or nothing. The first stanza may serve to remind us of the entertainment we have just seen:

When that I was and a little tiny boy,
with hey, ho, the wind and the rain:
A foolish thing was but a toy,
For the rain it raineth every day.

And the subsequent variations ("But when I came to man's estate") may remind us, humorously but poignantly, of experience. But it would be impertinent to analyze this song. It is feather-light; and, like the rest of the play, is to be enjoyed simply.

Twelfth Night may well be Shakespeare's most perfect comedy, for it combines the themes of his earlier work with unsurpassed sureness and delicacy. He had used a similar Latin plot in one of his earliest plays, the simpleminded and ingenious farce, *The Comedy of Errors.* In *Much Ado About Nothing* he had presented "real" English characters in a light at once comical and romantic. In *A Midsummer Night's Dream* he had created a whole imaginary realm—fairyland or dream—as the setting for the fun. But in *Twelfth Night* these elements, which had proved so popular with audiences, are fused to make a new piece of theater poetry. The characters are more natural, even, than those in *Much Ado;* their improbable doings are handled with more humorous sophistication. And Illyria seems to be not so much fairyland as the poetry of certain remembered moments in our common human life. The more one thinks over *Twelfth Night* in relation to the earlier comedies, the more one can relish the undeluded gentleness of its spirit, and the perfect control of its art. And one can begin to see how Shakespeare, with this control, could have written *Hamlet* about the same time. But the reader needs none of these reflections in order to enjoy the play.

PART THREE

1599–1608

The Many-Sided Tragic Vision of Shakespeare's Maturity

The eleven plays that Shakespeare wrote during the nine intense years at the summit of his career are more varied in theme, style, and genre than those he had written during all of the previous thirteen years. They include tragedies of three different kinds, and four unclassifiable works which I have placed together as "Sardonic Parable and 'Comicall Satyre.'" Such variety is bewildering; yet everything he wrote in this period has a somber tone in striking contrast to the sanguine plays of the preceding period. In the "comedies" as well as the tragedies of these years he is preoccupied with the hell, or loss of faith, or the "promised end" which always threatens the human scene, rather than the Edenic dream which beckons in the patriotic histories and smiling romances.

I suppose the events of Shakespeare's private life, if we knew enough about them, might help us to understand the genesis of this harder and darker vision; and the public troubles of the last years of Elizabeth's reign offered him fertile analogies to the sinister old stories he now chose to bring to life on his stage. All of his experience of life (and of books) was no doubt grist to his mill; but it would be a bad mistake to imagine that he was himself lost, like one of his tragic protagonists, at this time. He was not Hamlet, though romantic and Freudian critics often think so; nor was he Macbeth, or Iago, or Timon—unless one wishes to say that, with his actor's gift of sympathetic identification, he made himself each of these very different figures in rapid succession. His sympathy with the terror and pathos and evil of our experience represents a triumph of spirit, a heightened awareness; and the poetic power and virtuosity with which he projects it is even greater than before. The only way to understand what he saw is to become familiar with the plays themselves, and then seek, by comparing them, the underlying vision from which they all spring.

The Symbolic World of the Christian Monarchy

Hamlet, Macbeth, and *Lear* represent the culmination of the long series of history plays, and at the same time the transmutation of that genre into Shakespeare's full tragic form. Like the histories they depend for their theatrical life upon the familiar customs, conventions, symbols, and beliefs of the monarchy, which embodied the whole traditional view of man. As in the histories, the complex diversified motivation of the whole realm is all centered around the sacred crown, symbol of the common welfare both material and spiritual. Shakespeare assumes that his audience will understand that at once, and thus be able to interpret the meanings of the old, half-mythic stories of the Danish or Scottish or British crown by analogy with their own kingdom. But in these plays he is no longer tied to the well-known sequences of recent history, nor to the built-in happy ending of the Tudor epic, and his intention is no longer simply the patriotic one of rejoicing in the history of England. Now he quite consciously adopts a more serious, disinterested, contemplative aim: to reflect the recurrent tragedy of the political animal in the capacious mirror which his inherited wisdom provided.

It was near the beginning of this period that Shakespeare wrote Hamlet's charge to the players which I have already quoted as the basic formula of his drama: "to hold, as 'twere, the mirror up to nature; to show virtue her own feature, scorn her own image, and the very age and body of the time his form and pressure." In his mature view, mirroring human nature necessarily involved showing the universal aspects of moral and religious meaning; but if he can give the concrete persons and events of his stories such wide and timeless significance it is because the religious monarchy in which he and his audience actually lived represented all the traditional values symbolically. Shakespeare's monarchy is closely analogous to the ancient city-state which Sophocles uses so often as the basis of his tragic art: a community of human size under one monarch, with familial, political, and religious order based upon very old, even prehistoric, sanctions. The main elements of the human situation are concretely represented in such a society; and when Shakespeare recognized them in his own Christian country he rediscovered the root-drama of our whole tradition. That is one way to understand the fact that in *Hamlet, Macbeth,* and *Lear* he can so naturally employ mythic and iconographic materials from the childhood of the race, and at the same time make topical allusions for his alert, "modern" audience. What he is talking about in these plays is always relevant.

The tragic sequence of events is formally similar in all three plays. The de facto ruler, through evil or folly, creates a situation in his realm in which "God's truth" is lost to sight, and that is the basis of the tragic action. A series of blind struggles follows, which reaches a climax in the third act; and then, in Act IV, we are given visions of anarchy, or hell, i.e., a time when neither moral nor religious truths are publicly recognized: disorder in the body politic and in the individual soul. The end of the tragic action is brought about by a hidden, lonely act of faith on the part of one or more individuals. As the false ruler and his evil time are done away with, the human norm, the natural and divinely sanctioned order, can be seen once more—but one must hasten to add that this form is realized very differently in each play. In Shakespearean tragedy the individual characters and the particular temporal situations are so vivid that they seem (at first, anyway) to be *merely* unique, like the people and events we meet head-on in life.

I have indicated this form in my readings of each play, but one may understand it better by briefly comparing the three. In *Hamlet* the initial situation created by Claudius is so deeply hidden that only the Prince suspects it, until his father's dubious ghost comes to reveal it to him. It is this hidden quality of evil, sustained by the court's unwillingness to upset the status quo, that gives the tragic action of this play its special bitter, groping, seeking quality. Hamlet's quest leads to his curious act of faith in the "divinity that shapes our ends," and finally his providential martyrdom, which at last brings the truth to light. In *Macbeth* the tragic situation is created by Macbeth's murder of Duncan, which is at once the destruction of the true king and of trust itself; and the act of faith at the end is that of Malcolm, Macduff, and Ross, who learn, through a carefully built purgatorial sequence, to trust each other again. In *Lear* the impious division of the sacred crown produces the basic situation, and the tragic action which follows shows how "division" of every kind—familial, political, religious, or philosophical—multiplies in Britain. If the tragic conflicts can be ended, and the natural order of the family and the state be made publicly visible once more, it is because a few in Britain—Edgar especially—have lasted out the chaos in anonymity and in the "darkness of faith." In each play the action is a response to the unique situation created by the erring ruler, and accordingly the characterizations, rhythms, and imagery are different in each; but each one must be understood as an example of the full Shakespearean tragedy.

Shakespearean tragedy is analogous to Sophocles', but the religion from which it is derived is that of medieval Christianity. It is unthinkable without the Christian liturgical and symbolic order of society which it reflects; and the action of each play is best understood in the light of the medieval lore. Thus the "prison" of Denmark, as Hamlet feels it to be under Claudius; the hell into which Macbeth precipitates Scotland by "killing the bond of love," i.e., faith in the king; and the vision of the "promised end" of the world which hovers over the figure of the crazed Lear toward the end of that play, depend upon medieval conceptions of damnation, and are therefore akin to parts of the *Inferno*. The conception of poetry in Hamlet's formula is medieval; and Shakespeare is closer to Dante than to most of his contemporaries when he assumes that the poet, like the statesman, is obliged to lead his followers to the truth. *Measure for Measure*, written very near *Hamlet*, is based upon the analogies between the responsible ruler of the state and the responsible ruler of the theater; and in *The Tempest* Shakespeare returns to that fundamental theme, as part of his final apologia for his theatrical career.

But to recognize Shakespeare's dependence on medieval Christianity, as one must, does not require us to suppose that he was an orthodox believer. In the case of a theater artist it is very hard to tell the difference between belief and make-believe, and all we can say with certainty is that Shakespeare was using his inherited world-picture as a means of showing human action to his audience. For this purpose he sometimes even wished to de-emphasize the Christianity of his scheme. There is very little reference to the Church in *Hamlet* or *Macbeth*, and *Lear* is ostensibly set in pre-Christian Britain. In trying to understand what Shakespeare was up to one must never forget that his primary purpose is always to imitate an action: all else—setting, imagery, even the styles of characterization and language—is subsidiary to that end.

Moreover Shakespeare, as dramatic poet, was not limited for his settings to the "world" created by Christian belief, any more than Dante was. The realms of experience explored by Shakespeare correspond to those pictured by Dante from hell, through the world of nature and common sense where Greek moral and political wisdom can guide us, to Eden, that anomalous "figure" of earthly felicity where Christian faith appears for the first time—and even then in such "types," symbols, and ancient mythic "figures" as the mortal mind needs, in order to represent to itself "the evidence of things not seen." The symbolic world of the Christian monarchy provided Shakespeare with a framework capacious enough to include this whole earthly spectrum: everything but the supernatural beatific vision itself, which was supposed to be man's ultimate postmortem goal. But when he chose to do so he could picture human experience without Christian faith, as he did in the Roman plays, with their classical moral and political wisdom, and in the "Comical Satyres" and sardonic parables, where the human society he shows has lost both rational and religious guidance. *Hamlet, Macbeth,* and *Lear* represent the norm, the comprehensive scheme; but the other plays he wrote in this period are also parts of his many-sided but constant tragic vision.

Plutarch's Unredeemed Roman World

Shakespeare, like other men of the Renaissance, was aware of Rome from school days onward. His maiden efforts in the theater included Latinate farce and more or less Senecan horror; and in his maturity he used Plutarch's *Lives of the Noble Grecians and Romans,* in North's translations, to make *Julius Caesar, Antony and Cleopatra,* and *Coriolanus.* During the eight or nine years when he was preoccupied with tragedy, Plutarch's classical world represented a realm of human experience which he entered with confidence, and at will, apparently fully understanding just how it fitted into the more comprehensive medieval religious world-picture he was using at the same time in his tragedies of the monarchy.

Plutarch was a Greek who lived under the Roman Empire about 45–125 A.D. His importance has been explained as follows by Professor Moses Hadas: "If today a curious reader should ask for a single author who might communicate the fullest sense of the totality of classical culture, the answer would have to be Plutarch. . . . He . . . has been the greatest single channel for communicating to Europe a general sense of the men and manners of antiquity." [1] Plutarch's popularity was at its height when Shakespeare wrote, and so he could count on his audience's interest in the relentless wars of the Roman leaders, and in Plutarch's moral comments, which often applied to their own ambitious soldiers and statesmen. Shakespeare's Roman portraits often look very English, and he quite cheerfully disregards archaeological accuracy in putting "Rome" on his stage. But he carefully respects the pre-Christian beliefs implied in Roman society, in the motivations of the Roman characters, and in Plutarch's own philosophical comments.

Plutarch's classical philosophy had entered Europe long before he himself was rediscovered, notably in the thought of medieval theologians, by way of Aristotle, whose authority was regarded as second only to that of Scripture. I have mentioned the "classical component" in the standard theory of monarchy, the axiomatic diagram of the natural community. Plutarch represented this authority, that of reason and

[1] In *Ancilla to Classical Reading,* quoted in *Plutarch,* ed. by Edmund Fuller. New York: Laurel Classics, Dell Publishing Co. Inc., 1959.

common sense, and Shakespeare does not question the validity of his moral and political dicta. But at the same time Shakespeare sees the ancient world with the insight of his own Christian or post-Christian Europe, and represents it, therefore, with richer resonance than Plutarch himself.

Julius Caesar was written just as Shakespeare was turning from the English history play to tragedy, and it is "about" the welfare of Rome just as the histories are "about" the welfare of England. The problem is still to restore order, and the ideal order of the community is understood in the same way, with one crucial exception: in Plutarch's Rome there is no king sustained by faith, and in fact no notion whatever of a divinely sanctioned royal role. It is possible that Shakespeare himself was not unwilling to regard Rome as the providential ruler of the ancient world, for the Dantesque reverence for Rome was not extinct in Renaissance Europe, and it seems to be faintly echoed in two of Shakespeare's own plays, *Cymbeline* and *Troilus and Cressida.* However that may be, he respects Plutarch's world in which the state enjoys no Christian sanctions; but at the same time he sees the Roman political troubles in the light of his own knowledge of the religious monarchy and *its* troubles, which he had embodied in his nine histories.

Caesar is tempted to establish a crown, and Shakespeare suggests that he has natural authority—"that in thy countenance which I would fain call master," as Kent says of Lear—and the people, the soldiers, the Senators, even the conspirators, feel it, whether they love it or hate it. Caesar is confident of his own ability to rule with justice, and he even considers whether the gods, with their ambiguous omens, might have designated him for the job. But there is no precedent to guide him, no recognized royal role to fill; and in his efforts to act the unfamiliar part he adopts poses of superhuman infallibility that seem a bit absurd.

It is in Brutus that Shakespeare most poignantly concentrates the tragedy of the Roman situation. Brutus feels, more generously than anyone else, the love and loyalty that Caesar naturally commands, but he can find nothing in his philosophy, or in Rome, to justify it. In Rome there are no religious sanctions such as Caesar needs, and if Caesar cannot find a part in the liturgy of the state he can only be a man, and an overambitious one at that. Brutus cannot, on his rational, republican principles, justify making any man king, and so he nobly sacrifices his love for Caesar (and incidentally for Portia also) to the demands of his reason and his moral will. At the end of the play, when civil war has done its worst, Brutus realizes that by murdering what he loved he has accomplished nothing, but he does not really understand what went wrong. No one in the play really does, either; Shakespeare lets the Roman picture stand in all its hard, rational, and pathetic consistency.

Coriolanus assumes the same vision of the Roman world, and the action, with all its high-pitched conflicts, centers as before upon the welfare of the state. Wise but helpless old Menenius announces that familiar theme in scene 1, when he gives the parable of the belly and the members, the ancient organic metaphor for the proper order of society which Plutarch shared with the political theorists of Shakespeare's time. But in this play there is no Caesar, with his royal ambitions, and no Brutus, to warm the scene with his generous idealism. Rome looks hard and cold from the first, and we see that once "Rome and her rats are at the point of battle" there is no common loyalty which could prevent the relentless parts of the *Res Publica* from colliding like the parts of a machine gone wrong.

It is this faithlessness which accounts for the importance of the mob in both *Julius Caesar* and *Coriolanus*. When a mob appears at anarchic moments in the histories or in Claudius' Denmark, there is still the revered symbol, at least, of the crown; but when it appears in Rome it is because the disputes of the powerful have deprived the state of all common, significant entity. The formless mob threatens to supersede all public order, and each of the squabbling politicians must try, by means of his oratory, to give it the form his policy demands. That is why we hear so much of the resonance of classical rhetoric in the language of these plays (one may remember that Cicero, orator and statesman, thought that rhetoric was the very basis of the art of politics). The mob is swayed, now this way, now that, by the orator's emotional histrionics or plausible reasoning; but we never feel that oratory, however moving or however reasonable, could possibly transform the mob into a stable, responsible citizenry. Oratory is only the first phase of a struggle for power that moves inevitably toward naked violence.

I have pointed out that in the plays set in the world of the Christian monarchy the tragic action is ended by an act of faith, which ushers in a new and better time; but in the essentially unchanging world of Rome the end of the tragic action is not felt as bringing a new time. One general has proved stronger than the rest, and the end of the play merely celebrates his triumph and the pathos of the fallen hero. The warriors' Roman fortitude is reaffirmed, and the glory it achieved in death, but that is all. Of course Shakespeare celebrates the military virtues in the religious tragedies too, but never as the adequate basis for human life and human community. Hamlet envies Fortinbras his complete dedication to "honor," but his own course, based on his far wider awareness, is entirely different. In Plutarch's Rome Shakespeare sees no higher goal available than worldly power and glory, and no virtues beyond fortitude and the rational moral will. His tragedy of the high pagan world is thus closely akin to the neoclassic tragedy which would appear a generation after his time, in the age of rationalism.

Antony and Cleopatra (greatly admired by Dryden, with his neoclassic principles) also depends on Plutarch for the story and the moral framework of the tragedy, but Shakespeare's own sense of the limitations of reasoned morality is even clearer than in the other Roman plays. We have another struggle for power in Rome, but the interest is centered in Antony's passion, which threatens Roman virtue itself, the basis of empire: "Nay, but this dotage of our general's/O'erflows the measure," as the first line tells us. Following Plutarch, Shakespeare shows how, when Antony makes his passion "lord of his reason" he must lose everything, at last even his being as a man. But unlike Plutarch he also makes us feel how wonderful that may seem: "The nobleness of life," says Antony as he kisses Cleopatra, "is to do thus." And then the lovers open the world which their passion, like a religious revelation, seems to have unlocked for them:

CLEOPATRA
I'll set a bourn how far to be beloved.
ANTONY
Then must thou needs find out new heaven, new earth.

In Egypt, when the feelings are thus emancipated, moral Rome looks like a small dark spot at the other end of the Mediterranean, and its legions relentlessly creeping toward us are dwarfed by the vast world of nature.

The "nobleness" of the passion, with its visions of the world beyond the little human scene of struggle and rational scheming, plays little part in the story as Plutarch tells it. His Romans recognize the limits of their rational control in moments of frustration, and resort to oracles, dreams, and omens to divine the will of the gods. But even then their purpose is purely practical: they are never out of harness; and it does not occur to Plutarch to take the lovers' dreams and longings seriously. But Shakespeare, with his religiously informed imagination, shows us what Antony and Cleopatra see when love inspires them: when, for instance, Antony sees his own fond being as a thinning cloud, or Cleopatra gets her final cosmic vision of her lover in the sun, the moon, and the thunder.

The notion that human love and the dreams it generates may have significance beyond reason was alien to Plutarch's classical rationality, but it was a commonplace in Shakespeare's Christian Europe. For human love, according to the rich lore Shakespeare inherited, *naturally* demands what only the grace of God, and not unredeemed nature, can provide. That is the way he shows it in the romantic comedies, as well as in *Romeo and Juliet:* desperately dangerous when naive and uninstructed, supremely significant, a tiny analogue of "the love that moves the sun and the other stars," when guided by the proper faith. It is the painful paradox of love's exorbitant demands that enables Shakespeare to sympathize so deeply with Antony and Cleopatra when passion makes them disregard the hard truths of reason. But he does not either romanticize or Christianize their passion, he merely understands it by means of his own tradition: he sees it as Eros, rising out of the world of nature, and doomed to want more than it can find. "Think you there was, or might be, such a man/ As this I dream of?" Cleopatra asks (Act V, scene 2) when Antony is gone:

DOLABELLA
Gentle madam, no.
CLEOPATRA
You lie, up to the hearing of the gods.
But if there be, or ever were one such,
It's past the size of dreaming. Nature wants stuff
To vie strange forms with fancy, yet t'imagine
An Antony, were nature's piece 'gainst fancy,
Condemning shadows quite.

If her cosmic Antony existed he would be nature's answer to her natural need, but she almost knows that nature lacks the means to make such an answer, and the Antony of her vision is only what her fancy forms: a shadow that her passion projects upon the sky. The wonderful pathos of this effect comes from Shakespeare's own understanding of love, combined with his full acceptance of the world as it was before that religious understanding of love had appeared.

The Rome that Shakespeare pictures in these three plays is a well-defined part of the more comprehensive medieval vision of man, his society, and his history. He could enter that bleaker world of pagan antiquity in full awareness of what he was doing, like a good actor who can identify his being, for the moment, with that of another character in another setting. He could also enter the emptier world of *Othello,* and the more faithless worlds of the sardonic parables, in that way: in full sympathy but without losing his own bearings.

The Lonely World of Othello

Othello's world is even emptier of human understanding than that of Rome. The Venetian oligarchy that hires Othello to fight its wars lacks the moral grandeur of Rome, and neither Othello, nor Desdemona, a bored rich girl until she meets Othello, nor Iago, a Florentine and a mercenary like his master, finds anything in that city to love or admire. The motivation of the play is not centered in Venice, as the Roman plays are in Rome and the other tragedies in the sacred crown, but in the loved, hated, and envied Othello. The Roman *Res Publica,* as Shakespeare presents it, is less lovable than the sacred crown, and that is probably one reason why his Romans turn to each other with disproportionate intensity, seeking in their personal relationships what the public scene fails to provide. In the monarchical plays there is nothing quite like the painful bond that joins the emulous Brutus, Cassius, and Antony together, nor the love-hate relationship of Coriolanus and Aufidius, nor, of course, the passion of Antony and Cleopatra. In *Othello* the personal relationships are still more desperate, since there is nothing else: Othello, Desdemona, and Iago resemble the lost souls absurdly and helplessly knotted together that one meets from time to time in the *Inferno.* Shakespeare saw the three characters he took from Cinthio's novella as lost, and he expresses and partly accounts for their plight by carefully building for them a setting that offers them no understanding: one that owes its meaning precisely to the fact that it embodies neither moral nor religious values.

The monumental nobility of Othello makes him akin to the Roman warriors, and justifies us in thinking of the play as a tragedy. But the faithless human scene in which he looms so large is, from the beginning, like Denmark, or Scotland, or ancient Britain, when the tragic action has most completely demoralized the community. And it is, therefore, very much like the communities pictured in the sardonic parables.

"This False World": Sardonic Parable and "Comicall Satyre"

The plays in this group are notoriously hard to classify, but they represent, in various ways, one aspect of Shakespeare's tragic vision: the human scene when both rational moral order and religious faith have lost their public authority. This moment, when all seems lost, occurs in all the monarchical tragedies as part of their more comprehensive vision. Sometimes the scene looks terrifying, sometimes laughable, sometimes merely trivial, and Shakespeare defines it (and partly accounts for it) in a different way in each of these plays. But he does define it, though perhaps only through his mocking attitude; and thereby he invites his audience to accept it as limited: not the whole truth about human nature and destiny. In other words, he does not lose his sane and balanced perspective even when indulging in his most bitterly misanthropic portraiture.

If *Measure for Measure* belongs in this sardonic group it is because of the condition of Vienna before the Duke intervenes to enlighten the city: "Novelty is only in request," he says; ". . . there is scarce truth enough alive to make societies secure, but security enough to make fellowships accursed." He proceeds to arrest the course of events—which he can do by the terms of the make-believe of this play, for as ruler of Vienna he is a "figure" of God, and as a figure of the playwright he can arrange the plot to suit his purpose. His purpose is frankly didactic, "to unfold the properties of government," and that amounts to demonstrating the ideal moral-religious order that underlies all of Shakespeare's plays of this period, whether sardonic or tragic. *Measure for Measure* corresponds to *The Merchant of Venice,* which diagrams the moral-religious framework of the romantic motive; but now Shakespeare's eye is upon the community and its fallible leadership, instead of the loved woman.

In the first three acts Shakespeare "holds the mirror up to human nature" as it looks at that moment of history in corrupt old Vienna: a world of deceptive appearances in which that cynical liar, Lucio, is completely at home. Then the Duke-Shakespeare, in the carefully staged trial scene of Act V, slowly uncovers the true motives behind the disguises and confusions, and so shows "virtue her own feature, scorn her own image." Finally that all-powerful showman—figure of God, ruler of the state, and ruler of the theater—gives all the characters far more mercy than they deserve, and so enables his audience to see how the mischief and the delusions of Vienna, "the age and body of the time," appear in the ultimate perspective of religious faith. This play has displeased many critics with its disillusioned view of man combined with elaborate didacticism; but it is indispensable if one is trying to grasp Shakespeare's basic vision in his tragic period and the very self-conscious art whereby he was able to present it in so many ways.

The bright, worldly Paris of *All's Well That Ends Well* corresponds to corrupt Vienna; but this is the lightest and least bitter of the sardonic comedies. Its two narrative themes would seem to belong to romance: Helena's pursuit of her faithless lover Bertram, and her miraculous cure of the ailing old King; but both are presented in such a way as to make a mockery of the daydreamy romantic motive. Helena's motive is frankly worldly, she wants to get her handsome, well-connected man, for as a poor girl she has nothing else to hope for; and when she cures the King sharp-witted old Lafeu is on hand to suggest that it was her youthful good looks, rather than anything supernatural, that restored the old man's animal spirits. It is by means of the intelligent comments of various characters that Shakespeare defines the scene and lets us know how we are to take it. Parolles and Lavache (who are very much like Lucio in *Measure for Measure*) explain that in their Paris pleasure, snobbery, and time-serving define the endless game of life. Lafeu, the old Countess, and Helena, with their moral soundness and their clarity of perception, view that world with scorn, but they accept it as simply "the way the world is" in their time. "Full oft we see/ Cold wisdom waiting on superfluous folly," says Helena, as she prepares to enjoy Parolles' lecherous conversation and then pursue her fleeing Bertram. Such clarity gives the cynical scene a bracing, wintry quality, like that of classic high comedy, *Le Misanthrope,* for instance, or *The Way of the World.*

Timon of Athens is Shakespeare's version of the classic parable of misanthropy. It is much bitterer than *All's Well* because Timon, like Othello, has the strength to carry his disillusionment with mankind to its logical deathly conclusion, and also because the city of Athens is more completely lost than Paris. There is a king in Paris, and though nobody takes him seriously any more, he and the other old people suggest a decent past. But Athens, like the Venice of the merchant Shylock, and of Iago and Othello, is a strictly commercial city, i.e., one whose raison d'être is money. In one of the choruses of T. S. Eliot's *The Rock,* such a city is briefly defined:

> When the stranger says; "What is the meaning of this city?
> Do you huddle close together because you love each other?"
> What will you answer? "We dwell together
> To make money from each other?" or "This is a community?"

Shakespeare always saw the money-society as a sinister travesty of true community, and in *Timon* he plainly presents it that way in the opening scene, by means of the familiar parable of the goddess Fortune, who, as she turns her wheel, arbitrarily raises or lowers all whose motives are entirely fixed upon money. He assumed that this parable was familiar to his audience, and so could serve to define Athens, not as God's capacious world but as a small futile prison within it, like that part of hell where Dante sees the avaricious and the prodigal on their ceaseless round. The obviousness of the Fortune parable conveys Shakespeare's attitude not only to Athens but to Timon, its true son: he should know better than to stake his life on money, as though it could buy love itself.

Troilus and Cressida is Shakespeare's hugest, most complete and most carefully composed picture of man as lost. The situation of the play is not defined as that of a particular kind of society, like faithless Paris or money-worshipping Athens, nor does Shakespeare make use of explicit allegory to place the scene, as he does in *Measure for Measure* and in the parable of Fortune at the beginning of *Timon.* But he plainly places the human scene, nevertheless: it is that of the final phases of the war for whorish Helen, a war no one any longer believes in. The opening chorus puts it briefly: "The ravished Helen . . . With wanton Paris sleeps, and that's the quarrel . . . now good or bad, 'tis but the chance of war." After that, Ulysses with his chilly psychological accuracy, and Thersites, with his lewd and cruel pleasure in folly, are on hand to trace, with their comments, the swift process of degeneration as the war follows its inevitable course.

Shakespeare took care to show how *all* of the finest human qualities —those that he shows, in other plays, sustaining the true human community—are vitiated in this stale war-situation. Ulysses, as he preaches to the Greek soldiers, brings to bear all of the classical moral and political wisdom, as Shakespeare understood it; but reason itself proves helpless with those who are caught in the pointless struggle and its bristling animal motivations. On the Trojan side, Hector squanders his heroism along with his religious virtues of faith and loyalty upon the false cause of the war, and Troilus, analogously, "gives and hazards all" for his false Cressida. Because of the admirable qualities of some of the lost characters, the downward course of events is not only fascinating and laughable, but also pathetic and terrible at certain moments. I suppose the "sardonic" effect requires more sympathy than the lighter kinds of comedy, for it cuts deeper.

It is easy to see why many commentators see this play as proof of Shakespeare's utter pessimism when he wrote it. It certainly provides a very dreary image of the human animal. But Shakespeare did not offer that image as the whole, or the inevitable, human plight. The insights of Ulysses and of Hector, though they are unavailing at that stage of the war, serve to define the war itself as only a moment, a historic phase, which itself is attributed, at least in part, to human folly rather than hopeless depravity or pure fate. In this play, as in the tragedies, Shakespeare shows that man may get lost, totally lost; but he never sees that eventuality as the only possibility for us. In *Troilus* (as in the other plays of this group) he implies that his characters should know better, and that the audience can see quite clearly that they should. Hence the bleak, sometimes scornful, sometimes agonized and frightened smile with which he presents his varied versions of the faithless world.

The Plays in Chronological Order

JULIUS CAESAR

Julius Caesar was written in 1599, about a year before *Hamlet.* It is usually called the first of Shakespeare's tragedies, and "tragic" it certainly is, for it begins with the murder of Caesar and ends with the suicides of Brutus and Cassius. But in this play Shakespeare was not exploring the frontiers of human experience, and it does not have the terror and mystery we feel in *Hamlet.* The scene is warm and human; the story is that of the rivalries of vigorous men who know and love each other like brothers. It is exciting, bloody, and very touching, but even in its catastrophe it is full of the joy of life and battle. Perhaps that is why it has been popular ever since Shakespeare first produced it with his own fellow-actors.

Shakespeare had written *Titus Andronicus* at the beginning of his career, and plays on Roman themes were popular well before his *Julius Caesar.* There were no doubt plays about Caesar himself (now lost), for old Polonius had acted in one when he was at the university: "I did enact Julius Caesar," he tells Hamlet (Act III, scene 2); "I was killed i' th' Capitol; Brutus killed me." But the only certain source of the play is Plutarch's *Lives,* in North's translation. Shakespeare is faithful to the facts which Plutarch presents in his *Caesar, Brutus,* and *Antony,* and in several details he is close to North's actual language. But the theme and structure of the play are his own. He concentrates Plutarch's three rather leisurely narratives into one of the fastest and most exciting of his plays.

He starts the story at the end of Caesar's career, as that conqueror is returning in triumph to Rome, very shortly before the murder. At that moment in Roman history the virtuous old Roman Republic was in decline. Its august Senate, the guardian of law, had been bullied for years by a succession of victorious generals, who were bidding against each other for supreme power in the state. Caesar and Pompey were such generals. Shakespeare (who had read his history) knew that the Republic was doomed, and that Octavius Caesar would soon establish the

Empire. But some of the "noblest Romans," like Brutus and Cassius, were still loyal to the Republic and its ancient freedom under law; they were prepared to die rather than accept a monarchy. The common people, meanwhile, had lost faith in the Senators and the Tribunes, and they were ready for a strong man—Caesar or Pompey—who would promise to safeguard their interests. Shakespeare presents this situation in a few bold strokes in the first two scenes of Act I. The Roman crowd is veering from Pompey to Caesar; Caesar himself has the natural authority, the magic touch, of the born ruler. But the Tribunes in scene 1 and Brutus and Cassius in scene 2 share none of the popular enthusiasm for Caesar. They see in him a deadly threat to their own rights and privileges as citizens of the old Republic. By the end of scene 2 the action of the play is already in motion: a many-sided struggle to control Rome. Will the old Republican liberties be restored, or will Rome yield to the all-powerful spirit of Caesar and become a monarchy?

There is no difficulty whatever in following this struggle as Shakespeare presents it. Against a background of popular discontent, fear, and superstition, with sinister omens of trouble to come, Cassius and Brutus form their conspiracy, while Caesar tries to play his new role as head of state. The climax and turning point come (as usual in Shakespeare's plays) in the middle of Act III. Brutus and Cassius succeed, at that point, in murdering Caesar; but that is their last success. Antony in his famous funeral oration turns the crowd against the conspirators, and civil war follows at once between Antony and Octavius Caesar on one side and Brutus and Cassius on the other. Acts IV and V present that savage war, ending in Brutus' and Cassius' defeat at Philippi; and also the quarrels which develop between Antony and Octavius, and between Brutus and Cassius. In this chaos, where every man is against every other man, "Caesar's spirit" triumphs even in death.

Though the story of the play is clear and unmistakable, its meaning has been interpreted in various ways by readers who want to make one of the fighting Romans the "hero." In our time Brutus is the favorite, because of his republican principles. Thus some years ago, when Mussolini and Hitler were newly in power, Mr. Orson Welles made a very stimulating modern-dress production, in which Caesar was presented as a modern type of dictator, and Brutus as an embattled democrat or liberal. Shakespeare sees Brutus so sympathetically that he does make a good hero; but (as Mr. Welles's version showed) one cannot interpret the whole play that way without making drastic cuts, especially in Acts IV and V. There is really no "hero"; all the characters are sympathetically presented; and if one wants to grasp the play as Shakespeare wrote it one must learn to see the delicate "balance" he keeps between the main characters. The play is balanced upon the significant and mysterious figure of Caesar: all of the political issues, and the motives of all the characters, depend on Caesar the man and Caesar the symbol of Empire. What are we to make of him?

He is presented very briefly. His first appearance (Act I, scene 2) as he makes his way through the adoring crowd—controlled, shrewd, and detached—is impressive. But when we see him at home (Act II, scene 2) trying to decide whether to go to the Capitol in spite of the ill omens, he is indecisive. He is, however, not so much frightened as puzzled: he wants to find out what fate, or the gods, want him to do. In the Capitol (Act III, scene 1) when the conspirators try to make him revoke his banishment of Publius Cimber, he sounds pompous:

> I could be well moved, if I were as you;
> If I could pray to move, prayers would move me.
> But I am constant as the northern star,
> Of whose true-fixed and resting quality
> There is no fellow in the firmament.

We must remember that Shakespeare always sees his tragic characters with irony. When he gets ready to "carve them as a dish fit for the gods" he shows the pride or blindness which dooms them, as well as their greatness. Moreover, Caesar himself is consciously playing the role of supreme authority in Rome, trying to act, as well as *be,* the incorruptible ruler which the confusion of the times demands. The people recognize that authority in him, but there is no precedent for it in Rome; and Caesar finds the role rather new and strange.

The character of Caesar is interesting, but his significance is brought out by the other characters who love or hate him. Everyone in the play is deeply committed to the passionate game of politics, with Caesar in the center. As the game swirls around him the other characters show his meaning from their various points of view, and at the same time they reveal themselves completely in their relationships to him.

Cassius shows his motives at once (Act I, scene 2). According to Caesar, Cassius "thinks too much," and it is true that he is always brooding and contriving. But he does not think like a philosopher, to discover the truth, but passionately, to win the game. In the Roman free-for-all he cannot see why Caesar, whom he has known since school-days, should come out on top. He tells Brutus how he once beat Caesar in a race across the flooded Tiber:

> The torrent roared, and we did buffet it
> With lusty sinews, throwing it aside,
> And stemming it with hearts of controversy:

He tries to infect Brutus with this emulous spirit:

> I was born free as Caesar, so were you;
> We both have fed as well, and we can both
> Endure the winter's cold as well as he.

Cassius is sometimes led by his passions to play a dirty game, and, partly for this reason, he understands practical politics better than Brutus does. But he embodies the old republican independence, and in his impetuous courage he is likable and even admirable.

Brutus is also deeply worried by Caesar's sudden power; he too is a man of feeling, and a statesman rather than a thinker. But his temperament is the opposite of Cassius'. We cannot imagine him as "lean and hungry"; his moral weight must be embodied in a slower, solider frame. He is not interested in a personal contest with Caesar, and does not consent to head the conspiracy until Cassius makes him think it his duty as a Roman citizen. He is not revealed completely until Act II, scene 1, when Shakespeare draws a grave and touching portrait of him in his own garden on the night before the murder. He does not crave to destroy Caesar the man:

> For my part,
> I know no personal cause to spurn at him.

He instinctively feels that conspiracy itself is evil:

> O conspiracy,
> Sham'st thou to show thy dangerous brow by night,
> When evils are most free?

But like Macbeth hypnotized by the Witches, or Othello hypnotized by Iago, he feels the obsessive compulsion to murder:

> Since Cassius first did whet me against Caesar,
> I have not slept.
> Between the acting of a dreadful thing,
> And the first motion, all the interim is
> Like a phantasma, or a hideous dream.

The murder violates his habitual feeling of loyalty to his friend. When he yields to Cassius and the rest, he makes a pathetic attempt to rationalize his motive:

Let's be sacrificers, but not butchers, Caius.
We all stand up against the spirit of Caesar,
And in the spirit of men there is no blood.
O that we then could come by Caesar's spirit,
And not dismember Caesar! But alas,
Caesar must bleed for it. And gentle friends,
Let's kill him boldly, but not wrathfully;
Let's carve him as a dish fit for the gods,
Not hew him as a carcass fit for hounds.
And let our hearts, as subtle masters do,
Stir up their servants to an act of rage,
And after seem to chide 'em. This shall make
Our purpose necessary, and not envious;
Which so appearing to the common eyes,
We shall be called purgers, not murderers.

This speech, which is close to the central problem of the play, is a fine example of Shakespeare's pitying irony. Brutus has to think of the murder—and make the public think of it—as a just, even religious sacrifice. But in the staging of the murder, butchery is stressed; and when Antony comes he mocks the pretense of ceremony, and compares Caesar to a deer slaughtered by many hunters. The spirit of Caesar turns out to be stronger after the murder than before it. Brutus has little psychological insight; he is out of his depth in the situation which Cassius, and the course of Roman history, have forced upon him. But he is a strong, decent, simple man, and we know that he will take all the consequences of his decision without flinching.

It was a stroke of genius on Shakespeare's part to show us Brutus, on the night of his crucial decision, in his own household. In that setting he reminds one of the country-gentleman statesmen of our own early republic—Jefferson, say, or his friend Adams. Brutus' boy, Lucius, with whom he has such a gentle human relationship, is there to serve him. His wife Portia, awakened by the nocturnal comings and goings, fears that Brutus is lost to her; but, though she is "as dear to me as are the ruddy drops/ That visit my sad heart," Brutus cannot reassure her. The decision which separates him from Caesar also separates him from Portia and the love and loyalty which had joined them. This theme returns near the end of the play (Act IV, scene 3) when Brutus tells Cassius, after their quarrel, that Portia has committed suicide, and then, while the faithful Lucius sleeps, sees Caesar's ghost.

Antony is as clearly defined as Brutus and Cassius. While Caesar lives he serves him naturally and without envy, enjoying himself the while with military adventures and lots of late parties. But the moment

Caesar is murdered he sees that henceforth, in Rome, it will be every man for himself; and he proceeds to play that dangerous game in a style of his own. He has no principles to make him stiff and awkward, like Brutus; he does not burn with envy of other men, like Cassius; and so he proves more free and resourceful than either of them. He keeps his own counsel and improvises brilliantly. He takes advantage of Brutus' integrity to speak at the funeral, and then, subtly feeling his way with the moods of the crowd, rouses them suddenly against the conspirators. When the war starts he is ruthless: with the cold-blooded Octavius he slaughters every potential enemy he can lay hands on. He is a tough fighter, but full of warmth and charm, and when he gives his touching tribute to the dead Brutus at the end of the play we feel that his emotion is honest and generous.

With Caesar gone the struggle for Rome is far from ended, as Brutus had hoped it would be: it enters a more savage phase. In the power-vacuum after the funeral the leaders confront each other directly, all their mistrust of Caesar turned upon each other. The civil war quickly takes its murderous course (Acts IV and V) to its end at Philippi, but the struggles between the allied generals are even more significant. Octavius proves to have the drop on Antony, as he will again in *Antony and Cleopatra.* Cassius had succeeded in making Brutus head the conspiracy, but thereafter Brutus is stronger, and regularly overrules Cassius (a shrewder fighter) in the conduct of the war. They have it out in the great quarrel scene on the eve of Philippi (Act IV, scene 3). Cassius, with the insight of friendship, tells Brutus home-truths:

> Brutus, this sober form of yours hides wrongs.

But Brutus knows Cassius too, and in his anger and despair is determined to down his ally once and for all:

> By the gods,
> You shall digest the venom of your spleen,
> Though it do split you. For from this day forth,
> I'll use you for my mirth, yea for my laughter,
> When you are waspish.

Cassius yields in a characteristic burst of feeling:

> There is my dagger,
> And here my naked breast; within, a heart
> Dearer than Pluto's mine, richer than gold.
> If that thou beest a Roman, take it forth.
> I that denied thee gold, will give my heart.
> Strike as thou didst at Caesar. For I know,

When thou didst hate him worst, thou lovedst him better
Than ever thou lovedst Cassius.

This speech explains the motivation of the last two acts of the play. The fighting Romans are in a sense still loyal in feeling to Caesar; they are trying desperately to fill his place, but none of them can do it. In their failure and in the wider chaos of the war Caesar triumphs, as Brutus and Cassius both see after Philippi (Act V, scenes 3 and 5). By the end of the play all four leaders are somewhat tarnished, both physically and spiritually, by their violent battles; but when the pressure of fighting is removed, they recognize their errors and failures, as well as each other's gallantry. There is plenty of irony in the ending of the play, but no bitterness; and because the chief characters are so wonderfully and deeply human, their catastrophe is very touching.

If one thinks over the play in the light of Shakespeare's other work, one can understand the philosophy of history and politics which he built into it. He shared with the other men of his time a deep interest in Rome, especially Caesar, its legendary symbol. "How many ages hence," says Cassius after the murder, "Shall this our lofty scene be acted over,/ In state unborn and accent yet unknown." He unrolls before his audience's imagination a very wide Roman panorama: its frightened Senators, the soothsayers and their omens, the dangerous mobs, the distant provinces, pawns in the generals' wars. It is all very Roman; but Shakespeare interprets that turning point in Rome's history by analogy with the recent history of his own country. The theme of the play is like that of his English histories: the horrors of civil war, and the need for a strong central authority. Thus Antony prophesies over Caesar's corpse:

A curse shall light upon the limbs of men;
Domestic fury, and fierce civil strife,
Shall cumber all the parts of Italy.

. . .

And Caesar's spirit ranging for revenge,
With Ate by his side, come hot from hell,
Shall in these confines, with a monarch's voice,
Cry havoc, and let slip the dogs of war.

The Bishop of Carlisle (*Richard II,* Act IV, scene 1), just before the deposition of Richard which ushers in the Wars of the Roses, prophesies in the same way that the destruction of the monarch will bring chaos:

> The blood of English shall manure the ground,
> And future ages groan for this foul act.

Shakespeare certainly felt that Caesar was the right man to save Rome, and that Brutus and Cassius had failed to read Roman history correctly when they murdered him. He felt also that they were violating their own natural feelings for Caesar, refusing to obey the love and loyalty which would have made him the monarch that Rome needed. The theme of loyalty (family loyalty and loyalty to the king) runs through all of Shakespeare's plays about kings. Rome had no king, but Shakespeare shows the natural basis of monarchy, as he understood it, in the relationships of the people and the generals to Caesar.

For that reason it is not necessary to share Shakespeare's political philosophy, or his interpretation of history, in order to feel the power and pathos of the play. His Romans do not, like his Englishmen, have the traditional monarchy, with its religious sanctions, to worry about: they clash directly, recognizing no authority beyond themselves. Their story is clear in our age, or any age; and the language of the play is as simple and direct as the situation and the characters.

Some critics have complained that the language of the play lacks depth and subtlety. It certainly does not have such "overtones of meaning" as we hear in the verse of *Hamlet* or *Lear*. But it is wonderfully right for *this* play: it is the language of men of action, and it comes so naturally from their characters and their situations that we are hardly aware of it as poetry at all. But within its comparatively narrow range it is varied, with the greatest accuracy, to convey the essence of each character. Only Cassius could say this of Caesar:

> Why man, he doth bestride the narrow world
> Like a Colossus, and we petty men
> Walk under his huge legs, and peep about
> To find ourselves dishonourable graves.

The funeral orations of Brutus and Antony are both built on the serviceable principles of classical rhetoric, the natural forms of public speech-making which politicians still use instinctively to sway a crowd. But only the noble Brutus could say, with an air of unadorned sincerity,

> As Caesar loved me, I weep for him; as he was fortunate, I rejoice at it; as he was valiant, I honour him; but as he was ambitious, I slew him.

Only Antony, with his talent for acting, could use his own facile feelings to move the crowd to tears:

O judgement, thou art fled to brutish beasts,
And men have lost their reason. Bear with me;
My heart is in the coffin there with Caesar,
And I must pause till it come back to me.

These cadences are so right that there seems to be no "art" in them at all. Yet by means of such transparent language Shakespeare reveals the most intimate facets of character, the most delicate shifts in relationships.

We cannot tell how Shakespeare knew these men so well—that is the mystery of his genius. Even now they look familiar, as though we had known them and their rivalries in some fast game of our own, like poker, politics, or big-league baseball. They owe much to Plutarch, and no doubt to Shakespeare's knowledge of the political game in London. Against their Roman background, and with the splendor of their language, they are larger than life; yet they are visible, audible, almost tangible. Probably Shakespeare was thinking of the men in his own company, whom he knew and loved so well, when he created them. That would explain the vitality of productions which rely, not upon apparatus, but upon the actors and the characters and situations that Shakespeare wrote.

HAMLET

Shakespeare wrote *Hamlet* in 1600, when he was thirty-six years old. The turn of the century is also an important turning point in Shakespeare's own career. He was already a skilled and experienced playwright. He had been a member of his own highly trained acting company for six years, and they had just acquired the Globe Theatre, which Shakespeare had helped to plan. He seems suddenly to have seen new and greater possibilities in the theater art which he had mastered. *Hamlet* (with *Julius Caesar*) begins his "tragic period" when, in the space of six or seven years, he wrote his greatest plays.

Hamlet has proved to be the most popular, but also the most puzzling, of the great tragedies. Actors instantly recognize its superb theatricality, and other readers of every description—psychologists, moping poets, orators in search of quotable lines, comics seeking material to parody—also find in it just what they want. After three hundred and fifty years of stage life, the play still speaks with unique intimacy to everyone. But the lovers of *Hamlet* never agree. They have produced a vast literature devoted to its supposed problems, especially those of Hamlet's character.

The reader, however, need not be dismayed by the learned literature of Hamlet controversy. Some of the old problems have vanished, as scholars and theater men have taught us to understand Shakespeare's conventions, techniques, and theatrical intentions. Some of the problems are insoluble, being rooted in the deepest mysteries of human fate. Some real puzzles remain; but the play and its fascinating hero are clearer than they seemed fifty years ago, and closer to us than ever.

In making *Hamlet* Shakespeare started with an old and popular story which he might have known from several sources. There are references to a Hamlet play several years before Shakespeare's, but that play is lost, and we do not know who wrote it, or whether Shakespeare made any use of it. He must have read Belleforest's *Histoires Tragiques* (1576), which includes the story as told by Saxo Grammaticus, a twelfth-century Danish chronicler. It tells of a prince whose uncle has murdered his father and married his mother; who dedicates himself to vengeance; and who feigns madness to conceal his intentions from his uncle. That is the basis of Shakespeare's play, but the whole feeling is different: it looks like a good scenario for a typical Elizabethan "revenge play," like Kyd's *Spanish Tragedy*, which is often thought to be a forerunner of *Hamlet*. Shakespeare himself had written what is often called a revenge play, *Titus Andronicus*, at the very beginning of his career. But in dramatizing the tale for his own company and his own audience he brought the melodramatic plot, the Danish setting, and all the characters up to date. Hamlet has nothing in common with Saxo's primitive savage. With his doubts and his fears, he must have looked perfectly contemporary to the "super-subtle Elizabethans" of the worried days of the end of Elizabeth's reign. He still looks modern to us, in our time of troubles. And the other characters are also part of the familiar "modern" picture. Who has not met a good, old, boring Polonius, for instance, or a pair of sleek time-servers like Rosencrantz and Guildenstern?

In the imaginative process of embodying the old story in a modern setting, Shakespeare transformed the "revenge" motive, which is so simple in Saxo, into something much more significant. Sir Israel Gollancz has shown that the legendary figure of Hamlet (under various names) is to be found in Scandinavian tales and in the Roman myth of Brutus the Fool, who rid his country of the tyrannical Tarquins. Gilbert Murray thinks that the ultimate source is probably the same prehistoric rites of spring that gave rise to classic myths of the Orestes type. Murray points out many parallels between Orestes and Hamlet; and Hamlet is certainly more like Orestes than he is like Saxo's oafish chieftain. Orestes, like Hamlet, is a dispossessed king's son, whose father was murdered by his mother and her lover, and Orestes, like Hamlet, feels that it is up to him to set things right. His motive, as we see him in Greek tragedy, is more than simple revenge: he feels a religious obligation to restore order in his household and his community, and the Chorus, expressing the traditional beliefs of the people, accepts him as destined to purify the common moral life. He might have exclaimed, like Hamlet, "The time is out of joint; O cursed spite/ That ever I was born to set it right." Of course when Hamlet feels his destiny upon him, he is not thinking of Orestes. And there is no reason to suppose that Shakespeare was either, or that he had any notion of the ancient sources of the story. But in exploring the possibilities in Saxo's tale he seems to have found, once more, the classic theme, which is also a very modern theme.

However that may be, this theme of the illness of the state, and of the young prince who is "born" or destined to cure it, is clearly the basis of the play as a whole. Shakespeare came to it by way of the nine history plays which he had written before *Hamlet.* In the history plays, the central theme is always the welfare of the English monarchy, which is torn by the civil wars of Lancaster and York, struggling for the crown. England was "ill" with dissension until the Tudors cured it; that is the theme which commanded the passionate interest of his patriotic audiences. And in *Hamlet* he makes it clear, at the very beginning, that that play also is to be about Denmark's illness and its cure. In scene 1, the soldiers, on guard on the castle parapet, fear war or some other external danger. When the Ghost appears for the second time, they realize that the danger is closer to home and more troublesome: it "bodes some strange eruption to our state." That is before Hamlet, the unfortunate young man fated to clear up the malady, has appeared. When he does appear, in scene 2, he also expresses the dangerous decay of the state before the Ghost has told him the facts of his father's murder and given him his terrible assignment:

Fie on't, ah fie, 'tis an unweeded garden
That grows to seed, things rank and gross in nature
Possess it merely.

After the prologue scenes, the main conflict, that between Hamlet and his uncle, King Claudius, develops quickly. It is a dynastic struggle, like those in the history plays. But because the stakes are the crown, and therefore Denmark itself, all of the characters are involved in it. Laertes depends on the King for his conventional fling in Paris; Fortinbras, in Norway, has some claim to the throne. Gertrude and Ophelia are involved through Hamlet, Claudius, and Polonius, and at last destroyed by the conflicts between them. Polonius is a natural "pillar of society," the tool of anyone who is king. The cynical courtiers live off of Denmark; the Danish people, whom Laertes stirs to rebellion in Act IV, the grave-diggers in Act V, all suffer from and illustrate the Danish corruption. As soon as one realizes that the play is about Denmark and its hidden malady, all of the varied characters, the interwoven stories, and the contrasting effects of comedy, terror, and pathos which compose *Hamlet* fall naturally into place. It has been called a "Gothic tragedy," and, in fact, since it pictures a whole society, it is (like other great works of Renaissance art) composed on medieval principles. In its complex order, as in a Gothic cathedral, there is a place for heroes, for saints, and for gargoyles too.

King Claudius and Prince Hamlet fight for the central place in the state of Denmark. Claudius has deprived Hamlet of the crown, and also of his mother and (through Polonius) his beloved Ophelia. But the effects of his usurpation are supposed to extend far beyond the family circle. The Elizabethans regarded the monarch as a parental figure, of symbolic and even religious significance. More than the keystone of the social structure, the king set the tone for the life of the state: "woe to the nation that has a child for king." That is the way Claudius is taken in Denmark: as a "spirit, upon whose weal depends and rests/ The lives of many," as Rosencrantz puts it in Act III, scene 3. Claudius' secrecy, his smooth exterior which conceals corruption within, is reflected in the state of Danish society. The cynical courtiers take him at face value; honest old Polonius sees nothing wrong; and to them, and most of the rest, Denmark also looks normal enough. But Hamlet, who sees beneath the surface, knows that Claudius is a "smiling villain" and Denmark "a prison." Except for Horatio, who is probably not native to Elsinore, Hamlet is alone in his vision and his struggle. But the struggle is not so much for personal "honor" or "vengeance" as it is for the very soul or spirit of Denmark.

Shakespeare's first audiences might well have felt these issues in the play. The theme of the safety of the monarchy was familiar to them through many history plays, by Shakespeare and others. In 1600, Queen

Elizabeth was well beloved, but old, without an heir, and threatened by Essex' machinations at home and a ring of hostile powers abroad. There are enough topical allusions in the play—to drunkenness, to the situation in the theater—to suggest that Shakespeare expected the audience to take "Denmark" as a mirror of England and the times—or at least of what England might soon become.

If one listens to the music of the verse, with its interrelated images of darkness and disease, Shakespeare's imaginative picture of Denmark as it looks to Hamlet (or as it might look to any sensitive man living under a hidden tyranny) will emerge in all its suggestiveness. In the early parts of the play everything looks dark. The parapet scenes are nocturnal; Hamlet is dressed in his famous "nighted color"; monarchs and "out-stretched heroes" are the shadows of beggars. In the later scenes, after Hamlet has caught the King, many images of disease suggest the condition both of Denmark and of the individuals in it. Hamlet, inspired by the success of his play in showing up Claudius, tells his mother not to hide her guilt (Act III, scene 4): "It will but skin and film the ulcerous place,/ Whilst rank corruption mining all within/ Infects unseen." Claudius thinks of Hamlet as the disease: "for like the hectic in my blood he rages." Hamlet is indeed the "disease" of Claudius' regime; and in Act IV, scene 1, he decides he was wrong not to face that fact sooner: "We would not understand what was most fit/ But like the owner of a foul disease,/ To keep it from divulging, let it feed/ Even on the pith of life." On the eve of Laertes' rebellion he sees the malady in the whole state: "The people muddied,/ Thick and unwholesome in their thoughts and whispers."

Shakespeare presents Claudius' shadow over Denmark, the secrecy which is necessary to his tyranny, as an objective fact. It helps to explain Hamlet's famous uncertainties as expressed in such often-quoted lines as "sicklied o'er with the pale cast of thought," or "enterprises" that "lose the name of action," from the great monologue in Act III, scene 1. But the other characters also get lost in the dark. Polonius, who prides himself on his shrewdness, is always mistaken. Claudius himself, after Hamlet catches him, feels the imprisoning darkness and the paralysis of the will that goes with it. He gives a very Hamlet-like picture of the futility of human purpose to Laertes, in Act IV, scene 7:

> There lives within the very flame of love
> A kind of wick or snuff that will abate it,
> And nothing is at a like goodness still;
> For goodness growing to a plurisy
> Dies in his own too much.

The whole play, in fact, moves as though in the dark: there are long stretches of stalemate, when the antagonists, watching each other, are simply trying to see their way. When they do act, it is with violence, in response to some unforeseen event. The rhythm of *Hamlet,* which expresses its seeking and uncertain action, is entirely unlike that of a *Macbeth* or an *Othello,* where the conflict is clearly marked out and moves swiftly to the catastrophe.

The large structure of *Hamlet* is, however, planned on the same principles as the other tragedies. The first three acts show the treacherous struggle between Claudius, who tries to keep his guilt hidden, and Hamlet, who tries to bring it to light. Hamlet wins when he catches the conscience of the King with his play; and that is the climax and turning point. The plausible facade is cracked; the King and Gertrude must face their guilt; the "disease" begins to break out. When Hamlet accidentally kills Polonius, the destruction of that family, the timid Ophelia, the Ivy-League Laertes, is begun like that of the King on whom they had conventionally depended. The fourth act, during most of which Hamlet is in England, shows the sufferings in Denmark: Gertrude's, Claudius' as he tries to live with his guilt and still hide it; Ophelia's madness and death, and Laertes' impetuous rebellion which shakes the state. But the actual end is not yet. Shakespeare, as usual, reserves the final word of fate, which the characters fear but cannot clearly foresee, for the fifth act. Hamlet returns, and sees in the graveyard, in Ophelia's "maimed" funeral, and in the silly courtier Osric, the signs of the moral death of Claudius' Denmark. The sense of fate, or of his special destiny, is strong upon him, as he tells Horatio: "There's a divinity that shapes our ends/ Rough-hew them how we will." He does not know how the end will come, but is ready for it: "The readiness is all." It comes unexpectedly in the duel with Laertes. Claudius had planned it to corrupt Laertes and finish off Hamlet; Hamlet had intended it as a gesture of friendliness to Laertes; and here, as so often in the play, everyone's purposes are "mistook." But Hamlet's deepest purpose is achieved better than he could have planned it, though at the cost of his own life. The source of Denmark's hidden disease is revealed and destroyed at once; and with the arrival of Fortinbras the way is clear to a new and healthier life for Denmark.

The general course of the great story is clear, in the light of what is now known about it. Hamlet's "problem" in killing Claudius is like that of a modern conspirator under a Hitler or a Stalin, who wants to cure his country by getting rid of the tyrant, but hardly knows where to begin, or whom to trust. It is easier for us to understand his hesitations, his gloom, and his nervous outbursts than it was for the confident Victorians, who so self-righteously scolded him for cowardice and egg-headedness. That is because we are nearer than they were to social decay and tyranny in its various forms. As one thinks over the course of the play, the legendary figure of Hamlet, the sensitive young prince born, through no choice of his own, to set the time right, seems close to us and not too hard to understand.

There are, however, certain elements in the working out of the plot, and in the role of Hamlet, which puzzle careful readers, and actors and directors who must make every detail clear in performance. A few of the problems may be mentioned here; two of them are matters of staging.

There is, for instance, a dispute about Hamlet's exact motivation in the painful scene (Act III, scene 1) where he breaks with Ophelia. It is clear enough that his savage outburst is due to the fact that he thinks his beloved (like his mother) has betrayed him, sold out to the enemy, Claudius. But Hamlet always suspects more than he says, and it is hard to know just when, in this scene, he is sure of Ophelia's guilt. Has he overheard the plot of using her as a bait before the scene begins? Or does he catch a glimpse of Claudius and Polonius where they are hiding to watch him? Or does he simply guess the truth when he sees how constrained poor Ophelia is? The reader must decide for himself; and the actor or director, in making the decision, must keep in mind the necessity of staging the scene so as to make one interpretation clear to the audience.

There are more complicated problems in staging the Players' scene (Act III, scene 2). Hamlet's little play is itself far subtler than it looks at first. It does not literally present the facts of Claudius' murder of Hamlet I. It suggests murder in such a way as to catch any murderer in the audience, and it strongly hints at Hamlet's own desire to kill his uncle. The Player-King describes the sense of futility that bedevils Denmark, much as Claudius himself will express it to Laertes in the next act:

> Purpose is but the slave to memory,
> Of violent birth, but poor validity.

This scene gathers up much of the meaning of the play, and marks the climax; but how can it be staged clearly? When does Claudius take the bait? Why does he not guess during the dumb-show, when the murder is enacted in pantomime? Was the dumb-show itself interpolated by the actors, without Hamlet's consent? Such questions—

still hotly disputed—cannot be solved for good. But the producer may solve them for his audience by devising stage business which makes the moment of Claudius' entrapment clear. He may, for example, be conferring with Gertrude and Polonius during the dumb-show, and not see it at all. He goes to the show in the first place only to humor Hamlet, and is probably as bored as any tired businessman until he himself is plainly referred to.

There are many inconsistencies in the calendar of the play, but they should not bother the reader. How long does the whole action take? How much time is supposed to elapse between scenes? We can't tell—but neither could Shakespeare; and moreover he must have regarded such questions as irrelevant. He uses time and place, not, like the historian, for documentation, but to produce poetic effects, and to trace a certain sequence of motive and feeling. His time-scheme is geared to performance, and to understand it one must imagine the play unrolling on the bare stage, each scene imaginatively evoked in word and deed, never pausing for intermissions or changes of set. It is enough to know that it is "night," for that is the time to see a ghost. When the stage suddenly fills with gorgeously costumed figures for Claudius' court, or the Players' scene, or the duel, Shakespeare's audience would be reminded of one of Elizabeth's royal progresses through the streets of London. Such public ceremonies, focusing attention on the life of the state, meant a great deal then. When Hamlet, alone, in black, is left to comment savagely on the hollow glitter and pomp, we see what is really going on in Denmark; there is so much to take in, while the show moves before us, that we never think to ask ourselves what day of the week it is.

The most famous controversies center around Hamlet's own motives. And no wonder; for Hamlet is not only a "legend" but as we actually see him in the play, a character so lively and many-sided that we try to judge him as we do our flesh-and-blood friends. That is half the fun of the play, and it would be a pity to deprive the reader of his own opinion of Hamlet. But there is little danger of that; the effect of recent studies is not to solve Hamlet's problems, but to bring him, problems and all, closer to ourselves.

Hamlet's father's Ghost, who starts the Prince on his tragic course, has alienated some readers who object to ghosts on principle. There is no doubt that the Elizabethans, probably including Shakespeare himself, were readier than we are to believe in the possibility of ghosts. And it is certain that in Act I, scenes 1, 4, and 5, the Ghost must be taken as a "real" ghost, for Horatio, the soldiers, and Hamlet all see it.

But Shakespeare has taken care to make that apparition as anomalous as possible. Horatio refuses to believe it until he sees it. The soldiers speculate about it in different ways. Hamlet does not know whether it is a "spirit of health" or a "goblin damned," or even a vision due to his own "weakness and melancholy." Hamlet, in fact, takes the Ghost very much as a modern young man would, if he saw something that was at once so improbable and so suggestive. The Ghost confirms his worst suspicions; yet he refuses to credit what the Ghost says without further proof. That is why he is so paralyzed with terrifying doubts until he confirms the Ghost's information by catching the conscience of the King with his "mousetrap" play.

Hamlet's doubts are not hard to understand during the first three acts. But even after Claudius is caught, and he finds him helpless, in prayer, he hesitates again; and this scene (Act III, scene 3) has produced violent disputes. Hamlet himself says that he won't kill Claudius in prayer, for that would send him to heaven, and be no adequate vengeance for his father's murder. This rationalization sounds far-fetched, and few commentators accept it. Some think that Hamlet's delay proves that he is pathologically incapable of action. Others point out that we should hardly expect a fine, sensitive young man to stab the King in the back while he was praying. But few, if any, believe that Hamlet has given the real reason for his delay.

This raises, once more, the whole question of Hamlet's "revenge" motive. It is probable that the code of vengeance, and the melodramatic plays about it, were already beginning to look old-fashioned when Shakespeare wrote *Hamlet*. In dramatizing the old story Shakespeare seems to have asked himself how a modern young man of great intelligence would act if the old situation were suddenly repeated then and there. He shows us that Hamlet is obliged to recognize "vengeance" of some sort as his duty; and he hates Claudius enough to want to kill him. Yet the savage old code hardly covers the situation in Denmark as Hamlet sees it. He often wishes it did, and tries rather desperately to accept it. He does not want the larger task of curing his country's ills and "setting the time right," nor can he see how to do that. He envies Fortinbras (Act IV, scene 4) who for "honor" can risk his life and the lives of twenty thousand men "even for an egg-shell." He admires Laertes, who without thinking twice can start a revolution and lose his own soul to "avenge" his father Polonius. But he cannot act as those simpleminded young men-of-action do. He is obliged to feel his way, improvising in each new situation as he goes along. He does not want to be a martyr, but a gallant Prince, "the glass of fashion and the mold of form," as Ophelia puts it. Yet as he obeys his deepest feeling and his vision of Denmark's sad plight, it is a martyr, or witness, or scapegoat that he invariably becomes. He makes good his vision of Denmark: a society possessed by things "rank and gross in nature"; a plausible thug on the throne, the stupid content with the appearance of order, the nimble cynics content with their rackets. When he pays with his life, Shakespeare is careful to make his mysterious destiny feel right. Fortinbras majestically bids "Four captains/ Bear Hamlet like a soldier to the stage," and the military drums "speak loudly for him." Denmark is restored to health and trust; the Prince succeeds in death, and the soldierly code of honor and revenge is absorbed in the wider motive.

Hamlet is, even among great tragedies, one of the most mysterious of plays. It will remain so, no matter how many of its famous puzzles are solved. Everyone is held by the exciting story, the legendary figure of the Prince, and the music of the verse which touches one in so many ways and suggests so many insights. But just because it reaches us so intimately every reader will form his own opinion of Hamlet and his own notion of the meaning of the play as a whole.

ALL'S WELL THAT ENDS WELL

All's Well That Ends Well is usually dated about 1602; it is probably the revision of an earlier play. In 1602 Shakespeare was in possession of his mature style; *Hamlet* was behind him, and the other great tragedies were to follow in a very few years. But many of Shakespeare's admirers have found *All's Well* cynical and coarse, and they have been puzzled to know why the author of *Twelfth Night* (about 1600) should have written it. It certainly is a very unromantic comedy, appealing to the mind rather than the feelings, but the story is presented with Shakespeare's incomparable narrative skill, and the attentive reader will find it full of insights like those in *Measure for Measure* and

Troilus and Cressida, which were written in the same period. It represents only one aspect of Shakespeare's great vision, but he was aware of that, and he offers his play with a rather wintry smile.

He took the plot from Boccaccio's *Decameron* (Day III, Story 9), which he probably read in William Painter's *The Palace of Pleasure*. He follows Boccaccio's main plot with little change: that of the girl (Helena) who must perform a series of impossible feats in order to become the wife of the young man she loves (Bertram). Two very old themes are combined in Boccaccio's story, that of the cure and rejuvenation of the mortally ill old King by a young woman, and that of the tasks which the husband imposes on his wife—in this case conceiving a child by him during his absence and getting a ring which he swears will never leave his finger. Both themes are found in the popular fables of many countries. They have the dreamlike fascination, and perennial suggestiveness of true folktales, but Boccaccio is not interested in that quality of his old stories. He tells them with a straight face, as though they might have happened anywhere, any day; he focuses on the curious narrative itself.

One might have expected Shakespeare to bring out the allegorical and poetic quality in this story, as he did when he used similar tales to make his romantic comedies. In such plays as *Twelfth Night* and *As You Like It* he created a musical, dreamy scene to harmonize with the fable—Illyria or the Forest of Arden. But in dramatizing Boccaccio's story to make this play he adopts a far more realistic and deflated tone than Boccaccio's. There are no songs in the play, and no music beyond a few military flourishes. He seems to have had in mind a "modern" Continental, perhaps specifically French setting. Perhaps he would have associated Paris with wit and the relentlessly intelligent analysis of the feelings, as we do; the verse of this play has these qualities.

In the long first scene of the play he sets this tone, and quickly gets the story under way. Helena is the center of the whole scene, though she has little to say in the first part. The Countess and her friend, the "old lord" Lafeu, are bidding Bertram farewell as he starts for the King's court to make his fortune. All are in mourning for the Count—and so much black strikes one as an odd beginning for a comedy. But it dramatizes Helena's plight, an orphan now to be left alone with one old lady. Helena weeps when the Countess speaks of her and her father, but the moment the others leave she wryly admits to herself, "I think not on my father,/ And these great tears grace his remembrance more/ Than those I shed for him. My imagination/ Carries no favour in't but

Bertram's." She ruefully pictures her infatuation with the heedless Bertram:

'Twas pretty, though a plague,
To see him every hour, to sit and draw
His arched brows, his hawking eye, his curls,
In our heart's table.

And she plainly tells herself that her chance of getting him is slim: he is as far above her socially as a "bright particular star."

Her sad thoughts are interrupted by the arrival of Parolles, Bertram's follower and trusted friend. She analyzes him and her feelings about him without illusion:

I know him a notorious liar,
Think him a great way fool, solely a coward;
Yet these fixed evils sit so fit in him,
That they take place, when virtue's steely bones
Look bleak i' th' cold wind.

And she proceeds to engage in some very bawdy joking with Parolles on the subject of virginity—as a relief, no doubt, from the steely bones of her own clear, courageous mind. By the time Bertram leaves she is ready to try something on her own:

Our remedies oft in ourselves do lie;

And she hints that she will follow Bertram to Paris with the remedy which her father, a great physician, has left her:

The King's disease—my project may deceive me,
But my intents are fixed, and will not leave me.

So ends scene 1, with the main characters introduced and the story well begun.

Shakespeare has taken great care, here at the beginning, to make us trust Helena's candor and intelligence, for it is chiefly through her attitudes that he will show us what to make of the whole story. She presents her love for Bertram without romance: she thinks of his curls rather than his mind or spirit. She must have social position, but she does not delude herself about the accepted social values: Parolles with his shallow dishonesty is a sign of the tone of human intercourse in Paris and Rousillon. *All's Well* is a completely worldly comedy; all the characters accept the "world" just as it is, and try, according to their lights, to make the best of it. But Helena sees it all with perfect clarity, and plays the worldly game without bitterness.

It is of course Helena's pursuit of Bertram that makes the story. It has two main movements: her curing of the King, which results in her marriage to Bertram and his flight to the wars in Florence, and her final capture of him there by means of the notorious "bed-trick." Shakespeare presents the narrative very clearly, and with ceaseless movement, for he relies on the tried and true old plot to make the play go in the theater. But the characters are his own: he creates them with gusto, offering them to the thoughtful members of the audience, for whom the fabulous intrigue is not enough.

The Countess, Lafeu, and the King (like Helena) see the world with ironic clarity. "Love all, trust a few, do wrong to none," the Countess tells Bertram (Act I, scene 1), knowing, no doubt, that he is in no mood to accept such sober advice. The King's supposedly mortal illness gives him a certain sad, knowing detachment. When Bertram refuses Helena on the ground that she is beneath him, the King gives him a sermon on the folly of such snobbery: "From lowest place when virtuous things proceed,/ The place is dignified by th' doers' deed." When Bertram fails to get the point, the King makes the best of a bad job, and forces the marriage anyway.

When Helena, against all probability, actually cures the King, Shakespeare brings on Lafeu and Parolles, as his foil, to comment on that event (Act II, scene 3). Lafeu is delighted: "They say miracles are past, and we have our philosophical persons, to make modern and familiar, things supernatural and causeless. Hence it is that we make trifles of terrors, ensconscing ourselves into seeming knowledge, when we should submit ourselves to an unknown fear." And he wants to take the cure of the King as a miracle, even though he knows it would be against the prejudice of the times to do so: "A showing of a heavenly effect in an earthly actor." If it isn't a miracle, how could the King have grown so lively all of a sudden? "Why, your dolphin is not lustier. . . . Lustick, as the Dutchman says," he adds as he sees the King coming: "I'll like a maid the better whilst I have a tooth in my head."

I don't suppose Shakespeare would have expected the groundlings to appreciate Lafeu's ironies. They would have nodded wisely, like Parolles, who understands nothing, but wants to take credit for Lafeu's wit before he knows what Lafeu is trying to say: "So I say," he keeps repeating, "Why there 'tis, so say I too." But the judicious might see in Lafeu's remarks a clue to the curious dry tone of the whole play. In skeptical and self-consciously modern Paris, it is not possible to sense the "mystery of things" (Lear's phrase). We can't see anything "heavenly" in Helena's restoration of the King, but we can, and do, enjoy the signs of returning pep and potency in the old man.

Parolles and Lavache, both of them Shakespeare's additions to the cast of characters, are strictly creatures of the faithless little world pictured in this play. We accept them as the Countess and Helena do, for the sake of their lewd jibes. We let them live because we see that nothing will ever change them, as Lafeu does: "Though you are a fool and a knave," he tells Parolles (Act V, scene 2), "you shall eat." Parolles has been compared to Osric in *Hamlet,* and to Lucio in *Measure for Measure,* and he does in fact belong to their tribe of parasites. But he lacks their sinister quality: he is so shallow that even his ceaseless lying seems harmless. As for Lavache, he is just what the Countess calls him: "a foul-mouthed and calumnious knave," with none of the music and none of the insight that Shakespeare gave to jesters like Feste in *Twelfth Night.* In these two the worldly motivation of the play is presented at a farcically reduced level: they are time-servers who can imagine no human potentialities beyond the fashions of the moment.

Those who dislike *All's Well* object not only to the coarseness of Parolles' and Lavache's conversation, but to two important elements of structure, the bed-trick whereby Helena finally catches Bertram, and the character of the elusive Bertram himself.

The bed-trick, which Helena accomplishes with the aid of the Widow and her daughter Diana (Act III, scene 7, and Act IV, scene 2), is of course neither very probable nor very delicate. Shakespeare could hardly have avoided it once he had decided to dramatize Boccaccio's familiar story. It was a well-known plot device in the theater of the time, and we are told that audiences would not have thought it immoral, since the two are married; and Helena's deception is intended to keep her husband where he belongs. The Widow, a sober lady, approves when Helena explains the matter to her—though Shakespeare reminds us that she needs the money. He does not suggest that Helena's motive is either romantic or saintly. She has no illusions about Bertram's love for her, and she is not trying to save Bertram from himself, as Mariana in *Measure for Measure* is when she resorts to the same trick. In short, Shakespeare handles the episode dryly, which is in accord with Helena's tough-minded character and his own laconic way with the old story.

As for Bertram, Shakespeare certainly intends us to see him as a snobbish, spoiled, and lying boy. He makes him much less attractive than Boccaccio's Beltramo, introducing several episodes which reveal his worst traits. His reaction, when the King asks him to marry Helena, is natural enough: "I shall beseech your Highness,/ In such a business give me leave/ To use the help of mine own eyes." But when the King insists, he tries to wiggle out of his dilemma by going through with the ceremony and then running away to the wars, thus betraying the King (his benefactor) and Helena too. In the last scene of the play we are reminded of his deceptiveness again, when he tries to disown the ring which the King recognizes—an episode introduced by Shakespeare. He is completely taken in by Parolles, until his soldier friends laboriously show up that gentleman in the episode of the drum (Act III, scene 6, and Act IV, scene 1). One of Parolles' functions in the design of the play is to reflect Bertram's character. Bertram is not a physical coward, nor as silly as Parolles, but the two are unscrupulous time-servers together.

Shakespeare must have counted on a very attractive actor to play Bertram, so that the audience would understand Helena when she falls in love with "His arched brow, his hawking eye, his curls." He is a scalawag, but he ought to be an engaging one in the theater. After his Florentine soldiering, his affair with Diana (as he thinks), and the supposed death of Helena, he is ready to hurry back to Rousillon, and he sums up his adventures with a certain humorous verve (Act IV, scene 3): "I have tonight dispatched sixteen businesses, a month's length apiece, by an abstract of success. I have congied with the Duke, done my adieu with his nearest, buried a wife, mourned for her, writ to my lady mother I am returning, entertained my convoy, and between these main parcels of dispatch, effected many nicer needs." At such moments Bertram reminds one of the unheroic heroes of our own satirical fiction, O'Hara's Pal Joey, or Waugh's rogue Basil in *Black Mischief*.

Feckless as he is, Bertram is the focus of the action of the whole play. His worried mother, Lafeu, and the King all try to make something out of him, and he is of course Helena's object. But he eludes them all until the very end, when they at last surround him. Helena has no chance even to talk to him, except briefly in Act II when he sends her home. In this respect Helena's situation is quite unlike those of other heroines of Shakespeare's comedy. Rosalind (in *As You Like It*) has her Orlando, Beatrice (in *Much Ado*) has her Benedick, and those wonderful women, as they flirt with their lovers, can reveal a whole spectrum of love's forms. We may, if we like, give Helena credit for such knowledge of love, and some critics do so; but Shakespeare does not give her the opportunity to show it in this play. She can no more demonstrate the depths of love to the fleeing Bertram than Lafeu can explain the "heavenly effect" in the King's rejuvenation to Parolles.

Readers of modern fiction can hardly pretend to be much shocked by the lewdness and triviality of life in Paris and Rousillon, as some Victorian critics were. But the happy ending may strike us as out of key with all the rest. How can Helena and Bertram be expected to "live happily ever after"? Shakespeare makes no attempt to justify this psychologically, he simply lets us know that Helena has her man at last. He relies on his good old plot—"stirred to the tune of perpetual motion, and topped with the bread-sauce of the happy ending," as Henry James puts it—to send the theater crowd home in a good humor. But for the judicious in the audience he has a final word: the King, in the Epilogue, speaks to them for the author-actor-manager, Shakespeare himself:

> All is well ended, if this suit be won,
> That you express content.

He is directing our attention to the irony in the title: the story at least *ends* well, though the evening's doings may have been revealed in a far from romantic light. And the whole occasion will end well for the hard-working author if the audience thinks so.

Readers of this or any play must decide for themselves whether they like it or not. But one must understand it first, and it is essential to see this story through the eyes of the characters whom Shakespeare placed there for our guidance. The Countess, the King, Lafeu, and especially Helena herself, with her courage and sanity, see everything in unsparing light, but humorously and without bitterness.

TROILUS AND CRESSIDA

This play is supposed to have been written about 1602, shortly after *Hamlet.* It is apparently intended, not for Shakespeare's usual audience at the Globe Theatre, but for a sophisticated private audience, probably that of the Inns of Court. The two interwoven stories of the play, that of Troilus' infatuation for his false Cressida, and that of the Trojan War for "ravished Helen," are both bitter, and Shakespeare presents them in intricate and often bawdy language. The play could never be popular, and many of its critics, especially in the last century, find it too misanthropic for their taste, as well as faulty in structure. But in the last thirty or forty years we have seen that its picture of mankind demoralized by war applies with uncanny accuracy to our own time; the structure of the double plot has been better understood; and the best critics, connoisseurs of difficult modern poetry, have been fascinated by its subtleties of thought and language.

Shakespeare's main sources include Chaucer's *Troilus and Criseyde;* Homer's *Iliad* (by way of those parts of Chapman's translation which had appeared, and a French translation of the whole); and two Renaissance histories of Troy, Lydgate's and Caxton's. The story of Troilus and Cressida is not in Homer, it is Latin and medieval. And though Shakespeare takes a great deal from Homer's undeluded epic of "the wrath of Achilles," his treatment of that story also is Latin and medieval rather than Homeric. The Trojan Aeneas was the legendary founder of Rome, and later European nations (including the English) cherished the myth that they too were descended from Trojans. Thus Troy stood for filial piety, loyalty to home and ancestors, while the Greeks represented, rather, the intellect, which is so often dangerous and untrustworthy in its freedom. Perhaps the play is named after the Trojan Troilus because Shakespeare expected his audience to identify itself with Troy.

It is, however, the Trojan War that makes the basic situation of the play, and so determines the motivation of all the characters, and, at last, the outcome. The Prologue explains this at once:

> In Troy there lies the scene . . .
>
> The ravished Helen, Menelaus' queen,
> With wanton Paris sleeps, and that's the quarrel.
>
> Like, or find fault; do as your pleasures are;
> Now good, or bad, 'tis but the chance of war.

The Prologue suggests the cynical tone of the play also. Greeks and Trojans, fighters and lovers, all the characters in the big cast, try to win the war, or to cheat it; but the course of the play shows that such efforts are futile: "the chance of war" decides everything.

In the very beginning of the play Troilus, as he unarms, thinks that he is turning away from the war to his more urgent and doleful struggle to get Cressida: (Act I, scene 1):

> Why should I war without the walls of Troy,
> That find such cruel battle here within?

But when we next see him (Act II, scene 2) he and "wanton" Paris are insisting, against the better judgment of Priam, Hector, and Cassandra, that the war for ravished Helen must continue, no matter what the cost: his appetite for war and honor is just as romantically tyrannous as his passion for Cressida. And in spite of her desire for him (as hot as his, while they are together), and in spite of Pandarus' redundant pandering, the chance of war takes Cressida to the Greek camp and Diomedes, whom she finds attractive also. So poor Troilus' love for Cressida is turned into hate for Diomedes, and as he frantically seeks to kill him he perforce hands over everything to the chance of war.

In two great scenes (Act I, scene 3, and Act II, scene 2) Shakespeare presents the Greek and then the Trojan leaders attempting to make sense out of their involvement in a war whose aim no one believes in, and which neither side is able to win. These two scenes together show the basic situation of the play, and foretell the fatal course of its action.

In Act I, scene 3, Agamemnon and Nestor, in conference with the other Greek leaders, longwindedly maintain that their inability to destroy Troy simply means that the gods are testing their fortitude; but Ulysses offers a more rational explanation. Their frustration is due, not to Troy's strength, but to anarchy in the Greek army:

> And look how many Grecian tents do stand
> Hollow upon this plain, so many hollow factions.

Then follows his famous speech on "degree," in which the healthy human community, organized in obedience to its ruler, is compared to the orderly cosmos, with the sun "enthroned" as source of life, light, and lawful movement in the heavens and here below. Ulysses' vision of the ideal order or "degree" in nature and human affairs (ultimately derived from the moral-political philosophy of Plato and Aristotle) was often supposed to be what reason itself unmistakably reveals. Shakespeare presents it, with similar cosmic and organic metaphors, in many of his political plays. At this point we must take it that Ulysses represents the authority of reason: he has accurately diagnosed the Greek weakness, total lack of loyalty to their leaders. And he knows that Achilles, sulking in his tent with Patroclus, is a chief cause of this anarchy. When Aeneas interrupts the conference to bring Hector's chivalrous challenge to any Greek to single combat, Ulysses sees that as a way of getting Achilles into action. They will get the brainless Ajax, instead of Achilles, to accept the challenge, and that (as he explains to Nestor) will touch Achilles where he lives: in his fighter's vanity. This scheme again shows Ulysses' reason at work, but now he is more like the proverbial "Greek bearing gifts," who is not to be trusted, than the master of perennial wisdom. The course of the play will show that Ulysses' tricks with Ajax and Achilles, clever though they are, miscarry; Ulysses cannot after all give the Greeks loyalty and respect for order, but (like Menenius in *Coriolanus*) can only speak for the truth which is unavailing here.

The corresponding scene among the Trojans is Act II, scene 2. King Priam, his sons, Hector, Troilus, and Helenus (a priest), and his son-in-law, Paris, are met to discuss the Greek offer they have just received, to end the war if only they will give up Helen. All but Troilus and Paris would accept, on the ground that Helen could not possibly be worth all the lives she is costing. But Troilus' position is that having once taken Helen away from Menelaus, they cannot in honor give her back; the relative values of Helen and the slaughtered Trojans are irrelevant: "What's aught but as 'tis valued?" he asks. For Hector that is nonsense: "'Tis mad idolatry," he says, "To make the service greater than the god," and he adds that Paris and Troilus are like "young men, whom Aristotle thought/ Unfit to hear moral philosophy." They can only follow their feelings instead of heeding reason, the natural law, and the prophetic vision of their sister Cassandra, who interrupts the conference to cry that Troy is doomed. "Nay, if we talk of reason," says Troilus, "Let's shut our gates and sleep . . . reason and respect/ make livers pale and lustihood deject." We recognize in this hot rhetoric the passionate Troilus who will tell Cressida, when she asks him if he will be true (Act IV, scene 4), "Who, I? Alas it is my vice, my fault." It is the vice—or the virtue—of Troy: the Trojans cannot be untrue to their undertaking, however mad. Hector himself, at the end of the scene, decides for Troilus' romantically "honorable" Trojan values, in spite of his forebodings, his clear moral insight, and his respect for reason:

Hector's opinion
Is this in way of truth. Yet ne'ertheless,
My spritely brethren, I propend to you
In resolution to keep Helen still;
For 'tis a cause that hath no mean dependence
Upon our joint and several dignities.

So the Trojans, like the Greeks, find that they cannot escape, or change, their stale and foolish war.

Shakespeare seems to see this as a civil war, even a family quarrel, for it has the bitterness that only family relationships and intimacies can produce. The two sides are contrasted: the Trojans "true," hopelessly bound by their loyalties, the Greeks so free in mind as to be faithless and undependable. But reason and loyalty are two complementary values of the tradition, in a healthy society they must be combined, and Ulysses and Hector both recognize that. Both sides, however, are committed to the whorish Helen, a prize that makes mockery of both loyalty and reason, and so the wisdom of Ulysses and Hector can change nothing. The destructive course of the war is foretold on both sides, especially by Ulysses when he describes the inevitable degeneration of human motive when "degree"—loyalty and reason—is flouted (Act I, scene 3):

> Then every thing includes itself in power,
> Power into will, will into appetite,
> And appetite, an universal wolf,
> So doubly seconded with will and power,
> Must make perforce an universal prey,
> And last eat up himself.

By the time these two great scenes are over, the audience can watch the play with the ironic detachment one brings to comedy.

The actions of both stories take just the course Ulysses feared. Under the cruel chance of war the love of Troilus and Cressida is turned to sluttishness in her case, murderous hatred in his. The story of the war itself—which centers around Ulysses' efforts to mobilize the wrath of Achilles—is more elaborate, but it also ends in raw destructive "appetite." Ulysses' gambits are wise, witty, and full of insight (Act I, scene 3). They seem to have succeeded when he explains to Achilles that he will lose his fame if he continues to loll with Patroclus instead of fighting Hector, and Patroclus, like a wife who is careful of her husband's reputation, urges him to do as Ulysses advises (Act III, scene 3):

> Sweet, rouse yourself; and the weak wanton Cupid
> Shall from your neck unloose his amorous fold,
> And like a dewdrop from a lion's mane
> Be shook to air.

But the chance of war decrees, first, that Achilles shall change his mind again when Hecuba holds him to his oath not to fight Hector (Act V, scene 1), and then that the death of Patroclus change him for the last time—to an appetite for murder more black than Troilus'. He does kill Hector, treacherously, and drags the corpse around the field at his horse's tail; but the chance of war, not Ulysses, produced that result.

Shakespeare shows that the passions of "war and lechery" (as Thersites calls them) are practically interchangeable, when both are reduced to Ulysses' "universal wolf." This appears most clearly after the turning points in Act III, when Troilus gets and loses Cressida, and Achilles begins to turn toward Hector. Achilles tells Patroclus (Act III, scene 3):

I have a woman's longing,
An appetite that I am sick withal,
To see great Hector in his weeds of peace.

This theme is repeated when Diomedes comes to Troy to take Cressida and meets Aeneas (Act IV, scene 1):

AENEAS
By Venus' hand I swear,
No man alive can love in such a sort
The thing he means to kill, more excellently.
DIOMEDES
We sympathize.

Just after Troilus' and Cressida's parting, which is filled with premonitions of her falsity, the trumpet sounds to announce Hector's departure for the Greek camp to fight Ajax or Achilles, and Aeneas cries (Act IV, scene 4):

Yea, with a bridegroom's fresh alacrity,
Let us address to tend on Hector's heels.

The next scene (Act IV, scene 5) is the Greek camp, where all are awaiting Hector, and a trumpet is sounded for him. But instead of Hector, it is Cressida who appears. When she has kissed all the Greek leaders and departed with Diomedes, Ulysses sums up the impression: "sluttish spoil of opportunity," a phrase that might be applied, by this time in the play, to almost everyone. The effect of these touches, and many more like them, too numerous to quote, is to make the heroes' warlike, or romantic, or chivalrous pretensions look silly. By the time we reach the battles of Act V their motivation has nearly lost all human form; they are like dangerous animals working off a glandular discharge in the blood, except when, now and then, someone despairingly realizes their plight.

Troilus and Cressida is traditionally classified as a tragedy, but a number of recent critics think it is savage farce, or, as Professor O. J. Campbell would have it, "Comicall Satyre." I do not know how important it is to decide on a classification of the play, for it is never easy to assign Shakespeare's works to definite genres. But one must certainly see that the clarity and detachment with which the characters' deluded or dishonest actions are presented make for derisive laughter, as Professor Campbell says. And in the roles of Thersites and Pandarus, both of which are very important, Shakespeare gives his play a comic-satirical slant.

Thersites is often called the most unpleasant character in Shakespeare, a foul-mouthed hanger-on who is devoured by envy, but that must not prevent one from recognizing that he sees and describes the heroes with devastating accuracy. When he tells Ajax (Act II, scene 1), "thou art here but to thrash Trojans, and thou art bought and sold among those of any wit, like a barbarian slave," he sums up the "sodden-witted lord" exactly, and he does as much for Patroclus when he calls him Achilles' "male whore" (Act V, scene 1). As the final battle starts. Thersites hurries on to sharpen our impression of savage folly (Act V, scene 4): "Now they are clapper-clawing one another; I'll go look on." He catches sight of Troilus and Diomedes, then loses them as they disappear fighting: "What's become of the wenching rogues? I think they have swallowed one another. I would laugh at that miracle—yet in a sort, lechery eats itself. I'll seek them." In their fight he sees exactly what Ulysses had feared at the beginning of the play—appetite making a universal prey and eating up itself at last. He also points out that this result marks the failure of all Ulysses' schemes (Act V, scene 4):

> A th' t'other side, the policy of those crafty swearing rascals—that stale old mouse-eaten dry cheese Nestor; and that same dog-fox Ulysses—is not proved worth a blackberry. They set me up in policy that mongrel cur Ajax, against that dog of as bad a kind Achilles. And now is the cur Ajax prouder than the cur Achilles, and will not arm to-day; whereupon the Grecians begin to proclaim barbarism, and policy grows into an ill opinion.

Having seen that Ulysses' philosophy is powerless, though true, the Greeks turned to "policy," and now that that has failed they turn once more to the desperation of all-out strife; and it is Thersites who points that out to the audience, in his scornful way.

Pandarus lacks Thersites' intelligence sharpened by envy, his prurience being merely sentimental, but his role brings out much of the satiric meaning of the play. Pandarus' pandering to the lust of Troilus and Cressida is ironically parallel to Ulysses' pandering to Achilles' morose vanity; he and Ulysses both take satisfaction in the cleverness of their "policy," and both find at last that it fails, and earns "ill opinion." Probably that is one reason why Shakespeare gives Pandarus the last word in the play, just after the ungrateful Troilus has scornfully dismissed him (Act V, scene 10):

> O traders and bawds, how earnestly are you set awork, and how ill requited! Why should our endeavour be so loved, and the performance so loathed? . . .
>
> As many as be here of Pandar's hall,
> Your eyes, half out, weep out at Pandar's fall.

Pandarus' curtain-speech sounds very much like the "moral" we are expected to draw from the whole play.

The movement of the whole play is like that of comedy, and that is probably why Shakespeare did not end it with the death of Troilus and the fall of Troy. He has been criticized for leaving some of the stories unfinished—we do not even know what became of Cressida. But we know that the motives of all the characters are mocked and frustrated by their commitment to false Helen, and when that has been made abundantly clear it is appropriate to turn away from the fighting to hear Pandarus' ironic and bitter conclusion. But one must notice that the effect of this kind of comedy depends on our having sympathy for some of the characters at least. The romantic folly of Troilus and of Hector is as likable as that of Hotspur, or Fortinbras, or various other hot-blooded honor-seekers in Shakespeare, and so the murder of Hector (Act V, scene 7) when "ugly night comes breathing," is horrifying, not comical. We identify ourselves, in another way, with Ulysses, whenever he explains the action and its meaning, as he does when diagnosing the moral maladies of the Greek army and its heroes, Ajax and Achilles. The painful scene (Act V, scene 2) when Troilus watches Cressida betray him with Diomedes is reflected for us in Ulysses' clear intellect, and he holds a nice balance between scorn for the youth's stubborn infatuation and pity for his suffering. In these scenes Ulysses shows us how Shakespeare wished the audience to take the pathetic aspects of his theme.

Whether one laughs or cries at *Troilus and Cressida,* the picture of humanity that emerges from it is almost unrelievedly sardonic. Shakespeare offers it, however, as the way mankind appears at a stale and savage phase of the war—and not as the whole truth about us. Perhaps he was making oblique reference to that time in England, around the turn of the century, which many thought was "out of joint." But it was his custom to define the meaning of his serious stories not only in terms of the general truths of the human condition, but in terms also of the historic moment when they were supposed to occur. He had written, in

Hamlet, a year or two before, that the purpose of playing was not only to show the general and eternal truths of vice and virtue, but also "the very age and body of the *time* his form and pressure." One must be aware of this temporal, or historic aspect of *Troilus;* it adds greatly to its interest, and at the same time delimits the meaning Shakespeare attaches to it.

MEASURE FOR MEASURE

Measure for Measure was performed at the Court of James I in 1604. It was probably written to be played before the King (who was proud of his learning) rather than for the general public of the Globe Theatre, for which most of Shakespeare's plays were written. It is a sophisticated play in its intricate discussions of government, its bawdy humor, and its characters, who are seen without illusion, yet with sympathy. It is one of Shakespeare's plays which we have been learning to understand in recent years. It has been successfully produced here and in England, and the scholars have elucidated many matters which enable us to see what Shakespeare was doing far more clearly (as it seems to us) than our grandfathers did.

The main story of the play is that of Angelo, the strict magistrate left in charge of Vienna, who in his efforts to enforce the letter of the law condemns young Claudio to death for seducing his beloved Juliet before they were married; and of Isabella, Claudio's sister, who in pleading for her brother's life unintentionally awakens Angelo's lawless passion, and must then choose between yielding to him and letting her brother die. It is an old story, and various authors interested in Isabella's rather sensational moral dilemma had recounted it long before Shakespeare. He knew several versions, but his most direct source was an old play, *Promos and Cassandra,* by George Whetstone (1578). He created Whetstone's characters anew, endowing them with such passion and intelligence that the melodramatic situation comes intensely alive. Whetstone's farcical subplot becomes the story of Mistress Overdone and Pompey her bawd, who are among Shakespeare's most deeply comic portraits of incorrigible humanity.

Shakespeare's most basic change consisted in making Duke Vincentio of Vienna, instead of Angelo and Isabella, the central character in his play. It is the Duke who sets up the basic situation when he leaves the supposedly puritanical Angelo to rule the corrupt and pleasure-loving city. In his Friar's disguise he watches everyone, guiding Angelo's victims when he can, and secretly preventing the worst consequences of Angelo's tyranny. At the end he returns as Duke and restores order. He is thus both a character within the play and a figure quite outside it, like a stage director—or even a playwright who plans the situations of his plot in order to develop his characters, and explore the meaning of their actions. The audience thus watches the play in two ways: we follow the troubles of Angelo, Isabella, and the rest with sympathy and excitement, but at the same time with the disillusioned detachment of the Duke, who is conducting a practical and somewhat uncontrollable experiment in government.

A number of critics have disapproved of the Duke, on the ground that his ways are devious, but there are many reasons for thinking that Shakespeare saw him as a model prince. He may have had in mind the half-legendary Haroun al-Rashid, the wise Caliph who wandered among his people in disguise to study their ways. More probably, he was thinking of King James himself, who "loved the life removed," as the Duke says (Act I, scene 3). James explained the duties of a monarch to his son in an epistle called *Basilikon Doron,* in terms which the Duke would have approved: the ruler is responsible not only for the political and economic welfare of his people, but also for their education and spiritual welfare. Duke Vincentio is certainly trying to teach and lead his people through his experiment in government. As stage-director or showman, he is seeking to reveal the truth about human nature and government to the audience in the theater. The Duke (like Prospero in *The Tempest*) is one of Shakespeare's figures based on the analogy between the ruler of a city and the ruler of a theater: each is responsible for the "truth" in his own way. I like to think that Shakespeare himself may have played the Duke before the King. When the Duke says (in the first line of the play),

> Of government the properties to unfold,
> Would seem in me t'affect speech and discourse,

he sounds very much like an actor-manager flattering his royal patron, saying in effect that the play to follow will not show the King anything he does not know already about the properties of government.

The moment the Duke disappears, Angelo starts to enforce the law, and the bewildered Viennese are forced to share the Duke's motive:

they too must consider the "properties of government," and argue the eternal problems of law, justice, and "measure." There is no difficulty in following the stories of the play, the farcical adventure of Mistress Overdone and Pompey, the nearly tragic intrigue of Angelo, Isabella, and Claudio. But if we are to understand the play as Shakespeare intended it, we must notice that each episode is presented from the point of view of a character who is also a spectator; who "reflects" the action for us in a comic or pathetic light. The Duke is the most important character of this kind, but during the first two acts Lucio, and then old Escalus, perform this function.

In Act I, scene 2, Lucio, that witty and completely cynical man-about-town, shrewdly and lightly observes the first impact of Angelo's reform administration. He hears the distressing news from Mistress Overdone (whom he has patronized for years), and thus begins the farcical theme. The bewildered young Claudio appears on his way to prison, and through Lucio's eyes we see the beginning of the pathetic main story:

LUCIO
Why how now Claudio? Whence comes this restraint?
CLAUDIO
From too much liberty, my Lucio, liberty: . . .
Our natures do pursue
Like rats that ravin down their proper bane,
A thirsty evil, and when we drink, we die.

Claudio's lament is full of poetry, but Lucio's answer is joking: "If I could speak so wisely under restraint, I would send for certain of my creditors." Lucio is delighted to fetch Isabella from her convent to plead with Angelo for Claudio's life, for he sees an opportunity to make a mockery of all law.

The first scene between Angelo and Isabella (Act II, scene 2) is a discussion of the mystery with which the whole play is concerned: the relation between Justice and Mercy. The debate is subtle and interesting in itself, for Angelo is proud of his legal and philosophical learning, and Isabella (who likes to argue) is fresh from her formal religious instruction. But we are obliged to watch the scene through Lucio's sharp eyes, and for him the philosophical questions are quite unreal. He points out that Angelo's interest in the intellectually ardent young Isabella soon becomes more important than philosophy for him too. Isabella hardly knows what is happening, but Lucio coaches her, and (like a radio announcer at a prize fight) happily marks the stages of Angelo's collapse: "Ay to him, to him, wench. He will relent. He's coming, I perceive't."

Lucio is entirely Shakespeare's creation. He is admirably fitted to bring out the absurdities of Angelo's perfectionism in the early parts of the play. He has the will and the insight to undo Angelo and also Isabella, "a thing enskyed and sainted," as he ironically calls her (Act I, scene 4). When poor Angelo sees what has happened to him, he says (Act II, scene 2): "O cunning enemy, that to catch a saint,/ With saints dost bait thy hook." He refers to the devil, of course, but we have seen that it was only Lucio who baited the hook. And after that masterpiece of mischief, Lucio is out of his depth, for Angelo's course moves swiftly toward tragedy, and Shakespeare brings back the Duke, a clearer and deeper "reflector" of the action.

While Angelo secretly tries to force his will on Isabella, he insists on enforcing the letter of the law in public, and good old Escalus reflects that aspect of his tyranny. In Act II, scene 1, Escalus tries to soften Angelo, and then in a long comic sequence like a "family court" in one of our own big cities, he tries to sift the evidence of Pompey's crimes, and then to show him that he has done wrong. Through Escalus' eyes we see that Pompey will never learn or change. Angelo's legalism is reduced to absurdity when applied to Pompey and his likes; yet Pompey is human and must be accepted as part of the thorny problem of government.

In Act II, scene 3, the Duke, as Friar, visits poor pregnant Juliet; and from this point until the end of Act III we see the action from his point of view. He finds that Juliet has accepted her misfortunes with humility, that she and Claudio really love each other, and that, as Friar, he can do nothing more for her. In Act III, scene 1, he visits Claudio who is awaiting the sentence of death. In a most melodious speech he bids Claudio "Be absolute for death," and poor Claudio meekly agrees that "either death or life shall thereby be the sweeter." But when Isabella comes to tell Claudio of Angelo's ultimatum (while the Duke watches the brother and sister unseen) Claudio changes his mind and begs his sister for life.

The Claudio-Isabella scene often displeases modern readers, with its alternating effects of comedy and pathos. Claudio expresses his very natural, though wavering feelings in beautiful poetry:

> If I must die,
> I will encounter darkness as a bride,
> And hug it in my arms,

he cries, at one moment. But then he imagines death more sharply:

> This sensible warm motion to become
> A kneaded clod.

Isabella on the other hand is likely to strike us as a heartless prig when she screams,

> o dishonest wretch,
> Wilt thou be made a man out of my vice?

Her rhetoric is certainly laughable under the circumstances; but I think that, if properly staged, Isabella would appear at the same time just as pathetic as her brother.

We must remember that we have seen her, with the aid of Lucio, as totally inexperienced, with nothing to guide her but her convent lesson in morality. She comes to her brother confidently expecting him to defy Angelo as she had done and greet death with a romantic gesture. When he suddenly changes his mind she loses her head, becomes simply a lost, hysterical girl. She and Claudio are opposites in temperament, but equally young and bewildered. Moreover the Duke-Friar is there to remind us of the savage darkness of Angelo's Vienna, for which he is partly responsible. He sees that this boy and girl are out of their depth, and he intervenes to save them without letting Angelo know that he is being observed.

The famous "bed-trick" which the Friar persuades Isabella to use against Angelo often offends modern taste also. It was a common plot-device in Shakespeare's time, and he used it again in *All's Well That Ends Well.* The institution of marriage must have seemed more important to Shakespeare and his audience than a man's wandering erotic impulses; hence the trick is justified on the ground that it brings the husband back where he belongs. In this case the bed-trick, as the Friar explains, will benefit not only Angelo and Mariana, but Claudio, Isabella, and Juliet too.

The third act is the turning point of the play as a whole; Angelo's tyranny encounters the opposition that will bring it down. In Act III, scene 2, the Friar sees what is happening to Lucio, Pompey, and Mistress Overdone under Angelo's unavailing efforts to reform them. He sadly gives Escalus his impression of Vienna: "There is scarce truth enough alive to make societies secure, but security enough to make societies accursed. Much upon this riddle runs the wisdom of the world." He ends the act by addressing the audience directly, as showman or chorus, in an old-fashioned moralizing rhyme:

He who the sword of heaven will bear,
Should be as holy as severe.

The effect of this "choral" speech is to make us think of the swift events in Vienna which we have just seen, as an old story with a somewhat sardonic meaning. But the speech ends with a reminder that the desperate game with Angelo is not yet over:

So disguise shall by the disguised
Pay with falsehood false exacting,
And perform an old contracting.

And the Duke-showman resumes his Friar's role, to bring his plan to an end.

In the first three scenes of Act IV, the Friar appears not as chorus or stage-director, but as a character like all the rest, deeply involved in the treacherous game of deception. The act opens with the page's beautiful song, as night falls and Mariana awaits her deluded Angelo. It is a musical meditation on love's deceits:

Take, o take those lips away,
That so sweetly were forsworn . . .

Scenes 2 and 3 show us the prison, where the Friar puts in a busy night trying to forestall Angelo's last, worst, and most unexpected treachery: his order for Claudio's instant execution. There is wonderfully sardonic humor in these scenes, mostly at the Friar's expense; in spite of all of his careful plotting he is human and fallible after all. He manages to take Angelo's murderous order in his stride, but then he fails to persuade the gravel-hearted Barnardine to die properly. He is saved in the nick of time when the Provost substitutes Ragozine's head for Claudio's, "an accident that heaven provides." This line is certain to provoke a laugh in the theater, and Shakespeare stresses the absurd patness of the coincidence, like the happy ending of a comic plot. But it also reminds us that even the Duke, with all his power and foresight, depends upon a happy accident (or the unpredictable grace of God) for the success of his plans—a theme which recurs in many ways throughout the play.

In scene 4 Angelo and Escalus learn that the Duke is returning; in scene 5 the Duke gives Friar Peter his instructions, and in scene 6 Isabella and Mariana go over the roles which the Duke has assigned to them. So we are prepared for Act V, in which all the intrigues, all the philosophic themes, and all three roles of the Duke will be triumphantly concluded in the style of the traditional comic finale.

The fifth act is the Duke's masterpiece of playwrighting, a "courtroom drama" which demonstrates "The nature of our people,/ Our city's institutions, and the terms/ For common justice," as he put it in the first speech of the play. If we have understood the play up to this point, we can see how the true "nature" of each character is revealed behind his lies and disguises; how common justice is thereby achieved; and how justice itself turns out to be insufficient; we all need mercy too.

In the first movement or act, Isabella accuses Angelo of having violated her and murdered Claudio, and Angelo (who was prepared for this) discredits her with his dignified appearance and his reputation for gravity. The audience of course knows that he is false, and that Isabella is meeting his lie with a lie of her own: publicly accepting the "shame" she had so violently rejected in Act II. In the second short movement, when the Duke has left the stage, Lucio takes advantage of the false appearances to slander Isabella and the Friar, cynically enjoying the confusion and his own cleverness.

In the third movement the Duke, as Friar, is brought in to confront Lucio, opposing Lucio's probable lies with the improbable truth which only he (and the audience) know. Lucio carries the audience onstage (the people of Vienna) with him, until he goes too far, pulls off the Friar's hood, and so proves the truth of the adage he himself had quoted: *cucullus non facit monachum,* "the hood does not make the monk"; in other words, the appearance does not make the reality. This is the climax and turning point in the Duke's "courtroom drama": the lies and disguises have been removed, to reveal the true motives of the characters. Angelo sees that: "I perceive your Grace, like power divine,/ Hath looked upon my passes."

In the fourth movement the Duke administers justice in the light of the facts then available, and according to the letter of the law. Reason itself, at this point, demands an Angelo for a Claudio, "measure for measure" in the literal meaning of the phrase. Mariana pleads for Angelo, and Isabella forgives him, thus completing her own moral education. The charity she had had so much to say about in her debates with Angelo in Act II is now a reality for her, instead of a doctrine repeated by rote. But the Duke sticks to his verdict of death.

In the final movement the all-important fact known only to the Duke and the audience in the theater is brought to light: Angelo's murderous intention was forestalled by the Friar, acting like "grace divine" rather than "power divine"; and Claudio is alive. This enables the Duke to measure justice, as it had been revealed according to human motives and the fallible light of human knowledge and reason, with another scale of measurement: that of mercy or charity. Angelo gets the life he does not deserve, and Mariana, Claudio, Juliet, and Isabella receive more felicity than they could have achieved by their own efforts. The marriages are the conventional and traditional end of comedy, and in this case, as in most of Shakespeare's comedies, more or less dim human reflections of heavenly harmony.

The Duke's little play for the Viennese is similar in theme to the trial scene in *The Merchant of Venice,* in which Portia makes her famous demonstration of Justice and Mercy. *Measure for Measure* is among the most overtly Christian of Shakespeare's plays, as several scholars have shown recently. The Duke as Friar is using wisdom which is both classical and Christian when in Acts II and III he tries to make Juliet, Claudio, and Isabella accept their sufferings (as they then appear) in order to learn through them. The plot of the whole play, based as it is upon the Duke, is a dramatization of the relationships between human government and the unfathomable justice and mercy of God, according to the theology which Shakespeare had inherited from the Middle Ages. The Duke tries to represent God in Vienna: unseen himself, he endeavors to see all human motives in the light of truth; to forestall by his free "grace" those that are evil, and enlighten those that are only deluded; to render judgment in accord with reason itself, and then temper that absolute justice (which is too severe for human nature) with love or mercy. The characters represent different aspects of our ungovernable human nature. Angelo with his "absolute" temperament cannot accept his own imperfection: if he cannot be perfectly white he must be perfectly black. Claudio is the victim of his natural, innocent sensuality and his poetic imagination; Isabella has to unlearn her self-righteous intellectual pride the hard way. Lucio's cynical selfishness, and Pompey's sturdy stupidity, save them from the discomfort of learning at all. The more one knows of traditional theology the better one can understand the policies of the Duke, the follies of the characters, and the intricate turns of the plot, all of which embody the "allegorical" meaning.

But this is allegory of a type which is not very familiar to us: it is more like Dante's allegory than Bunyan's. The characters are not personifications of abstract concepts, but on the contrary are "real" as any of Shakespeare's personages, and the theological ideas, if we get them at all, emerge from varied experiences. Even the Duke, detached as he is, is not God but only a man trying to fulfill the duties of priest and monarch, who were supposed to represent God on earth. *Measure for*

Measure is addressed to the philosophical mind, but it is also dramatic poetry like Shakespeare's more popular plays.

It is, perhaps, most closely akin to *The Tempest.* Prospero, in that play, is analogous to the Duke of Vienna. In both, the problem of "appearance and reality" (which fascinated Shakespeare as it has Pirandello in our time) underlies much of the drama and poetry. Prospero expresses it in his famous line, "We are such stuff/ As dreams are made on; and our little life/ Is rounded with a sleep." In *Measure for Measure* we see it in Lucio's lies, in the Duke's disguises, in Angelo's reliance on his dignified reputation and appearance—"place and form"—to "tie the wiser souls to their false seeming." And the Duke-showman, like a Pirandello character, is always playing with make-believe and the treacherous magic of theatrical appearance.

Measure for Measure is not an easy play for the modern reader, but it repays any thought and study we may devote to it.

OTHELLO

Othello, written in 1604, is one of the masterpieces of Shakespeare's "tragic period." In splendor of language, and in the sheer power of the story, it belongs with the greatest. But some of its admirers find it too savage, or they complain that they do not understand the motivation, especially Iago's. The tragedy is, in fact, presented more simply, with less comment or explanation, than the tragedies of *Lear* or *Hamlet.* It has a desolate, laconic objectivity which makes it unique among Shakespeare's plays.

Shakespeare took the plot from a contemporary story (1565) by the Italian writer Giraldi Cinthio. Cinthio tells of a valiant Moor who marries a beautiful and virtuous Venetian lady, "Disdemona"; of a wicked Ensign who loves Disdemona in vain, deludes the Moor into thinking his wife has taken a certain Captain for her lover, and so persuades him to murder her. Cinthio relies on these sensational events, and the fascination of the Ensign's intrigues, to interest his readers; but he softens the impact at the end by drawing a prosy and self-righteous moral: well-brought-up young ladies should beware of marrying foreigners.

Shakespeare follows most of Cinthio's ingenious plot, but concentrates it all into a few days, and ends it more swiftly and simply. He omits none of Cinthio's sordidness and cruelty, and, moreover, he does not try to excuse it with moralizing at the end. And yet the effect of *Othello* is not like that of a newspaper scandal or a case history: the play has the scope and power of poetry. Larger-than-life characters——Othello, Desdemona, Iago—are caught in the painful tangle, and express their sufferings in the music and imagery of some of Shakespeare's most wonderful verse.

Because *Othello* has the high intensity of poetry, it makes very great demands upon its actors. The reader, however, is free of the practical problems of the modern theater. He may linger over the situations of the play, and allow his imagination to respond to the poetry. Shakespeare shows the action, now through Iago's eyes, now through Othello's or Desdemona's; and the reader, listening to them, can feel both the reality and the mysteriousness of the tragedy, much as one does in a painful experience of one's own.

Thus, for example, the very first scene is dominated by Iago, and we see it chiefly through his sharp eyes. It opens abruptly, in the midst of Iago's quarrel with his silly victim, Roderigo. The situation is soon clear: Iago is using Roderigo, who thinks he loves Desdemona, to make trouble between her father, Brabantio, and Othello, whom she has just married. On the surface, Iago is the tough-minded but "honest" soldier he always pretends to be. But listen to him the moment he has persuaded Roderigo to wake Brabantio with his yells:

IAGO
Do; with like timorous accent, and dire yell,
As when, by night and negligence, the fire
Is spied in populous cities.
RODERIGO
What ho! Brabantio, Signior Brabantio, ho!
IAGO
Awake! What ho, Brabantio! Thieves, thieves!
Look to your house, your daughter, and your bags!
. . .
Your heart is burst, you have lost half your soul;
Even now, now, very now, an old black ram
Is tupping your white ewe. Arise, arise,
Awake the snorting citizens with the bell,
Or else the devil will make a grandsire of you.

Iago is letting loose the wicked passion inside him, as he does from time to time throughout the play, when he slips his mask aside. At such moments he always resorts to this imagery of money-bags, treachery, and animal lust and violence. So he expresses his own faithless, envious spirit, and, by the same token, his vision of the populous city of Venice —Iago's "world," as it has been called. In this scene he stampedes Roderigo and Brabantio, hustles them, keeps them off balance, like a skilled bar-room brawler. So he makes Venice, at this midnight moment, appear to be just what he thinks it is. The whole scene moves in the agile, sudden rhythms of Iago's spirit.

In scene 2 we see the comings and goings of Brabantio, his followers, Othello, his followers, and the Duke's messengers who summon Othello to a council of war. And now Othello begins to take command; he seems to be entirely above Iago's excitement. "My parts, my title, and my perfect soul," he tells Iago, "shall manifest me rightly." And when Brabantio's followers threaten to attack his, he can quiet them all with a word: "Keep up your bright swords, for the dew will rust them." Even these few words dispel Iago's nightmare.

The full "Othello music" first resounds in the next scene (Act I, scene 3) when Othello tells the Duke how Desdemona fell in love when he told "my travel's history":

> Wherein of antres vast, and deserts idle,
> Rough quarries, rocks, and hills whose heads touch heaven,
> It was my hint to speak—such was the process;
> And of the Cannibals that each other eat,
> The Anthropophagi, and men whose heads
> Do grow beneath their shoulders.

It is our first sight of Othello's world: empty of human life as we know it, but filled with the sense of far-off, heroic adventure. We shall see it again, whenever Othello expresses his "perfect soul": rock, stars, danger, and triumph, in words that make sad but exhilarating music. It is the opposite of Iago's world; no wonder Iago described Othello's style so cynically to Roderigo (Act I, scene 1): "A bombast circumstance, horribly stuffed with epithets of war." Shakespeare expects us, perhaps, to see what Iago means; but he also intends to seduce us with Othello's words. The soldiers, the Duke, and the Senators yield to its melody; they all see, as we must, that Desdemona could not resist it. A sheltered rich girl, Desdemona must have felt that Othello had wakened her to life itself. "She wished," as Othello says, "that heaven had made her such a man." When Othello sums up their innocent infatuation, we must feel that he is more accurate than he knows:

She loved me for the dangers I had passed,
And I loved her that she did pity them.

Othello and Desdemona are so attractive that we tend to see them only as they see each other: the noble Moor, the pure white maiden. But Shakespeare shows their love, even here at the very beginning, as dreamy, utterly defenseless in a world that contains Iago.

He gives Iago the last word in Act I. Roderigo has been "washed out to sea" by Othello's story, like everyone else, and now wants "incontinently" to drown himself. Iago jolts him back to his own view: "Ere I would say, I would drown myself for the love of a guinea hen, I would change my humanity with a baboon." He then gives him a bracing sermon on the will and the reason, which make man more resourceful than the other brutes: "We have reason to cool our raging motion, our carnal stings, our unbitted lusts."

Iago himself certainly has plenty of reason. His picture of human motivation as essentially animal is like that of some kinds of disillusioned rationalists who were common in his time, as they are in ours. And he can control his own wicked passions when his reason tells him he must, in order to appear trustworthy. But that does not mean, as some of his critics have thought, that he lacks passion. On the contrary, in the "world" of his philosophy and his imagination, where his spirit lives, there is no cure for passion. He is, behind his mask, as restless as a cage of those cruel and lustful monkeys that he mentions so often. It has been pointed out that he has no intelligible plan for destroying Othello, and he never asks himself what good it will do him to ruin so many people. It is enough for him that he "hates" the Moor—he does not himself take seriously the rationalizations he makes, that Othello has not promoted him, or has seduced his wife. His satisfaction comes in the act of bringing down Othello; it is in that that he employs his sharp, relentless reason, brilliantly improvising his moves as the situations develop, tightening his ingenious nets with a comedian's verve and virtuosity. He is like a soul in Dante's *Inferno;* he has lost, not the intellect, but "the good of the intellect." His fine mind is tied to the service of the passion of hatred which drives him to the end.

Shakespeare always presents evil as a mystery that we can't quite solve. He does not attempt to tell us how Iago "got that way." But by the end of Act I he makes us feel that Iago and Othello are bound to have a life-and-death struggle. The very being of Othello reduces Iago to futility: he literally cannot bear to let him live.

The main conflict of the play is a strange one, for Othello cannot see his opponent until too late. But the audience sees with extraordinary clarity. In Act II Iago tricks Cassio into disgracing himself, and then takes advantage of the guileless affection between Cassio and Desdemona to create, for Othello, the appearance of evil. He explains this scheme to the audience, with mounting pleasure, as it develops; and by Act III he is ready to snare Othello himself.

Act III, scene 3, the turning point of the play, shows how Iago succeeds in subjugating Othello, a process which, in Cinthio's story, is supposed to take months. Yet Shakespeare shows more, in this terrible relationship, than Cinthio ever dreamed of. It is the best place in which to study both characters, and so to see the crux of the tragedy as Shakespeare presents it.

The beginning of this scene, when Othello sees Cassio pleading with Desdemona, and then, after Iago has hinted at his "suspicions," listens to Desdemona's insistent urging that he see Cassio, is one of the more painful sequences in the play. How can Desdemona insist, when every word puzzles and torments Othello? It shows her perfect trust, her pride in Othello's love for her; her blind faith in the Othello of her dreams. And when she leaves, Othello expresses the same faith, "perfect," but blind and helpless, in the Desdemona he loves:

Perdition catch my soul
But I do love thee; and when I love thee not,
Chaos is come again.

So we see what Iago has already explained, that Othello may be "had" through his dependence on Desdemona; and we are ready for the first round.

Iago starts very cautiously, wearing his most sympathetic mask. He reasonably and regretfully assembles all the false evidence, while warning Othello not to be troubled, or jump to conclusions. But when he feels that Othello is suffering, he permits himself the triumphant irony of his warning against jealousy:

O beware my lord of jealousy;
It is the green-eyed monster, which doth mock
The meat it feeds on.

He is of course gloating, but he too must feel the teeth of such a monster. He speaks as one who *knows* jealousy, or envy. Perhaps envy is the hidden passion which drives him to assault Othello and try to reduce him to his own level. Othello does not understand this, but he feels very sharply what his danger is:

Exchange me for a goat,
When I shall turn the business of my soul
To exsufflicate and blown surmises,
Matching thy inference.

He is in fact being exchanged for a goat; his soul is slowly being turned to Iago's world of animal lust and strife. This is the climax of the first round, and we can see already that Iago's spirit is forcing its vision upon Othello's spirit. But Iago, having gone so far, resumes his mask of reason. He contents himself with making Desdemona's adultery look probable: Venetian women are like that; Cassio is attractive; Othello is getting old, and he is a Moor. Poor Othello has had enough; he mutters, "Farewell, farewell," and Iago lets him go.

There follows the short interlude in which Desdemona drops her handkerchief while wiping Othello's brow, Emilia picks it up, and Iago gets it from her. This new piece of false evidence gives Iago another inspiration. When he sees Othello wandering back for the second round, he murmurs:

Look where he comes. Not poppy, nor mandragora,
Nor all the drowsy syrups of the world
Shall ever medicine thee to that sweet sleep
Which thou owedst yesterday.

The melody of these famous lines gives a wonderfully intimate sense of Othello's inner being. It is quite unlike Iago's usual harsh sounds and abrupt rhythms, as though, at the moment when the mastery passes to him, he were acquiring the magic of Othello's own music. Othello, when he sees Iago, instinctively wants to fight him: "Avaunt, be gone!" he cries. Perhaps he threatens him; but he can't throw off the evil vision Iago fastened on him, or see Iago as he really is. He sees his own world leaving him:

O now, for ever
Farewell the tranquil mind; farewell content;
Farewell the plumed troops and the big wars,
That makes ambition virtue. O farewell
. . . Othello's occupation's gone.

Now Iago feels that he is really inside Othello's defenses, and from this point onward he can more frankly surround his victim with his own hatred and lewdness:

Where's satisfaction?
It is impossible you should see this,

Were they as prime as goats, as hot as monkeys,
As salt as wolves in pride, and fools as gross
As ignorance made drunk.

So, as he wins, he hypnotizes Othello with the same nightmare as that with which he had startled old Brabantio in the first scene of the play.

Iago subjugates Othello with his illusions, but Iago himself is a victim of the same hellish sense of life. And when Othello dedicates himself to murder he shows, as before, bigger and stronger than Iago. "Like to the Pontic sea," says Othello,

Whose icy current and compulsive course
Never retiring ebbs, but keeps due on
To the Propontic, and the Hellespont;
Even so my bloody thoughts, with violent pace,
Shall ne'er look back, ne'er ebb to humble love.

Othello is one of those characters in Shakespeare, like Timon of Athens or Angelo in *Measure for Measure,* who cannot endure any self-doubt, remorse, or knowledge of their own failings. If Othello can't be "perfect" in his love, he will be perfect in vengeance; and now he starts for hell with the same exciting military music, and the same magnificent, cold, and far-away imagery with which he used to pursue ambition, love, and virtue. Iago is carried away, and as he falls on his knees with Othello, once more echoes the "Othello music":

Witness you ever-burning lights above,
You elements that clip us round about,
Witness that here Iago doth give up
The execution of his wit, hands, heart,
To wronged Othello's service.

When Iago says, "I am your own forever," he again reveals the truth more completely than he knows. He and Othello are, in fact, tied together in the blind passion of envy and hatred which can only destroy them. So Shakespeare ends the decisive struggle of the play.

In the fourth act we explore the results of Iago's strange victory. All he has to do, to keep control of Othello, is to show Cassio with the handkerchief, or laughing with his courtesan Bianca. He sees Othello at his feet, in "lethargy"; he can torment him at will. Iago seems to have the power, the satisfaction of his hatred or envy, which he wanted all along. Yet we know that the whole effect is based on delusion: Othello's, of course, but Iago's too, for the end is not yet. Othello has yet to act.

During Act IV Desdemona also acts the very part which Iago had devised for her. She insists yet again (Act IV, scene 1) that Othello pardon Cassio, which is "fire and brimstone" for Othello. Thus she blindly forces the Moor to see Iago's nightmare in her (Act IV, scene 2), "a cistern for foul toads," as Othello cries,

> there where I have garnered up my heart,
> Where either I must live, or bear no life,
> The fountain from which my current runs,
> Or else dries up.

She does not know what Othello thinks she has done, since he can't bear to name Cassio. She does not recognize the Othello she thought she knew, and she cannot imagine what has changed him. But she, like Othello, must live by their love, or "bear no life," and she feels that love is going. So, by the end of the act, she feels death coming, and welcomes it. The famous scene (Act IV, scene 3) when Emilia helps her prepare for bed, light, familiar, even joking as it is on the surface, is full of Desdemona's ghostly and unresisting sense of death—a triumph of Shakespeare's delicate theater-poetry.

Thus Act IV is filled (as always, in Shakespeare's tragedies) with the sufferings, and the partly deluded visions, which are the aftermath of the terrible conflict of Act III. But Act V quickly brings the denouement which none of the characters can quite foresee or control. Iago is carried down in the rush, for all his agility: he fails to get Cassio killed (Act V, scene 1), and Cassio knows his own and Desdemona's innocence. Soon Emilia, too, will see the truth.

Othello moves to kill Desdemona (Act V, scene 2) with that "icy current and compulsive course" which he had felt at the end of Act III, scene 3. We hear once more the music and the cold, magnificent images that express his perfect soul":

> Yet I'll not shed her blood,
> Nor scar that whiter skin or hers than snow,
> And smooth as monumental alabaster.

He tells himself that he is sacrificing Desdemona to "justice"; but we see how clumsily (like a great baby) he fumbles to get Desdemona smothered at the second try; how he roars and blubbers when it's over. When Emilia yells at him, "O gull! O dolt!" she only puts a name to what we have seen, even while the great Othello music was in our ears. Shakespeare does nothing to soften this discord; even Othello's last melodious speech, when he stabs himself, hardly wipes out the impression of grotesque horror.

Iago also does nothing to mitigate the starkness of the end. He lets the mischief he has accomplished express his vision of life, and the meaning of his motives:

> What you know, you know.
> From this time forth, I never will speak word.

Lodovico gives us a final image of Iago: "O Spartan dog,/ More fell than anguish, hunger, or the sea," but the mystery of Iago's evil, like the mystery of Othello's and Desdemona's helpless purity, is allowed to stand in all its bleakness.

It is easy to understand what those critics mean who speak of the intolerable cruelty of *Othello,* and point out that it expresses only part of Shakespeare's sense of human life. But it appears that Shakespeare wanted it that way; as usual, he knew what he was doing. One can see (thinking over the play) that it is extraordinarily consistent, both as psychology and as poetry.

Othello is at the center, the clue to everyone's motives. Venice relies on him as the state's greatest military servant. The innocent bystanders, soldiers, Senators, Cassio, even Roderigo, depend on his calm leadership. He is the center of Desdemona's life, and, for equal and opposite reasons, of Iago's. His large, noble spirit gives meaning to the lives around it, and to the movement of the play. But, if so, it is because there is little else in the scene which could command loyalty, love, or, for that matter, hatred. Cyprus is a barren military post which isolates the main characters, but as we see in the first act, they are isolated in Venice too. Othello and Iago are mercenary servants of the Venetian oligarchy, with little interest in what it stands for. Desdemona finds nothing to love there, either, until Othello appears. Shakespeare saw no nourishment for the spirit in the commercial republics which he used as settings: Athens, in *Timon,* and Venice, both in this play and in *The Merchant of Venice.* That is why Othello seems to have, there, an almost godlike manna. In this respect he is akin to Eilert Lövborg, the unstable genius in Ibsen's *Hedda Gabler:* the one vital character in sight, whom everyone loves or envies, and who is inevitably destroyed by those who try to get some of his magic to nourish themselves. Cinthio's modern story gave Shakespeare a modern theme, and he defines it partly by means of the setting, which feels so like a modern city. The characters in his Venice are as lonely as the faithless people in Ibsen's "drama of individualism," and their psychology, if one investigates it as realism, is similar.

But it is by means of poetry that Shakespeare reveals the deeper meanings he saw both in the motives and in the setting of his play. If one listens to the verse, one may see the play as a conflict between two views of the world, Iago's eternally restless city of goats and monkeys, and Othello's empty scene of stars and trumpets. In the early parts of the play the contrast between the two visions is unresolved. But after the intimate struggle in Act III, when Iago and Othello in their emotional utterances begin to echo each other, we begin to see how the two visions imply each other. In the foreground is the heartless game of the city, behind it the majestic machinery of Iago's "ever-burning lights," or Othello's "chaste stars." What is absent from this "scene" is human understanding, and the kind of love which can only come, take root, and grow through understanding.

If one remembers *Lear* or *Hamlet,* one can see how consciously Shakespeare defined the bleak scene of *Othello.* In both other plays there are characters who understand—or at least learn to understand—what is going on. In both of them the tragic action occurs in a traditional social order which, however shaken, does embody a sane view of human life. Both plays are full of symbols which command love and loyalty. But in order to make Cinthio's story understandable, and to bring out the meaning he saw in it, Shakespeare must show his people as lost. The brilliant but mysterious sharpness of the story, and the unrelieved blackness of the end, are consistent with the wonderful but heartless "scene" which the poetry builds; and all, together, define the meaning of the play.

KING LEAR

King Lear, which was written about 1605, is by common consent one of the very greatest of tragedies. It embodies the most comprehensive vision of human experience in its heights and depths that Shakespeare ever wrote. Its many characters live with intense, imaginative, and sharply individual life; and all is lifted to the level of poetry by the power of Shakespeare's language. During the last century many critics, bewildered by all this wealth, or seduced by the eloquence of some one character, have concluded that the play as a whole was a chaos. But now we have learned that Shakespeare, even in *Lear,* knew what he was doing both as poet and as practical man of the theater. It would be very hard to produce *Lear* properly under modern theatrical conditions; and the play has the inexhaustible meanings of all great works of art. But in itself it is beautifully composed both as poetry and as a play for the stage.

Shakespeare knew the story of Lear, King of ancient Britain, in several versions, including Holinshed's *Chronicles* and a play about "King Leir." The story of Gloucester and his sons is in Sidney's *Arcadia*. Both tales are legend rather than history, but Shakespeare, as usual, makes them exciting to the Londoners of his own time. He weaves the stories together with the skill of the master of plot, peoples them with characters of his own creation, and suggests to his patriotic and politically conscious audience that they may see, in the horrors which overtake Lear's ancient Britain, an image of dangers which may threaten their own society. Lear is of course the protagonist, but as rightful king he is also the central symbol of order, in individual, family, and community life. When he divides his crown, therefore, he divides his people, child against parent, man against man, even man against himself. All must suffer for his folly; and in the structure of the play as a whole, with its interwoven stories and swarming characters, the tragedy of Lear the man is only the center of the tragedy of all Britain at that legendary moment of its history.

Shakespeare presents, in scene 1, the fairy-tale-like dividing of the kingdom. He does not pause to argue the question, whether such an act is psychologically probable; he merely accepts it as the basis of the story to follow. But the life of the play is there already: in the stubborn arrogance of the old King; in the startled reactions of all who watch. Everyone knows that Lear's folly means anarchy to come; some, like Kent, see it with deepest grief; some, like Goneril and Regan, with stealthy delight.

In scene 2 Edmund, old Gloucester's bastard son, swiftly creates the analogous situation in his family, tricking his father and his legitimate brother Edgar into mutual mistrust and fear. "Thou, Nature, art my goddess; to thy law/ My services are bound," he says in his first monologue. He is thinking of "the lusty stealth of nature" that begat him, and of the "fierce quality" he feels in himself. All the law, loyalty, and love he knows is for his own proud animal vitality. He presumes upon it, much as Lear presumes upon his supposed "nature" as king and father.

These first two scenes make the prologue of the play. There are many subtle analogies between what Lear does to the royal family, and what Edmund does to his family; and the two together suggest the evil coming in all Britain. "Love cools, friendship falls off, brothers divide," says old Gloucester (scene 2); "We have seen the best of our time. Machinations, hollowness, treachery, and all ruinous disorders follow us disquietly to our graves." Edmund makes fun of his father's superstitious fatalism: "An admirable evasion of whoremaster man, to lay his goatish disposition to the charge of a star!" But he himself expresses a similar view when he orders Cordelia's murder (Act V, scene 3): "men/ Are as the time is." And there is no doubt that Shakespeare himself saw *Lear* as a picture of a time—one moment in the mysterious course of history, when, for unfathomable reasons, man loses his way. The history plays had taught him to recognize the reality of "the spirit of the times."

By Act I, scene 3, the action proper is under way. The traditional order of society and of the family having been lost or discredited, it is every man for himself. Each character begins to reveal what he believes in, what he really values; each one tries to get what he feels is rightfully his by "nature." Their feelings for human nature and human society reflect various currents of Renaissance thought. Kent clings to his modest loyalty to the King; Gloucester to his somewhat self-pitying fatalism; Edmund has a rationalistic individualism like Iago's, while Goneril and Regan pursue, faster and faster, their mirage of power. Shakespeare endows each one with his own poetry, and they all, therefore, express themselves with the brilliancy and virulence of creatures newly hatched. Much of the beauty and terror of the play reaches us directly, moment by moment, in the language itself.

But the form and meaning of the play as a whole is not to be found in the speeches of the characters, however profound and moving, but only in the relationships between them, and in the movement of the story. Shakespeare could identify himself with each character, yet at the same time move back, as it were, to see him objectively, and plan his role in the story. He was a master of "plot" in Aristotle's sense of the word: by the arrangement of the incidents he gives the action its embodiment, meaning, and form. He saw the fundamental action (or motive) of the play as an attempt, more or less conscious, more or less wise or wicked, to find the natural order in Lear's anarchic Britain. From the contrasting visions of the characters arise their terrible conflicts; and their conflicts (plus the incalculable element of chance) move the story to its conclusion. When some sort of common order is restored, the action is complete, and the play is over.

During the first three acts Britain and its inhabitants sink deeper and deeper into anarchy, as the savage struggles mount to their climaxes and turning points. In the center Lear fights off Goneril and Regan, endeavoring to hold his image of himself as "natural" king and father, while his daughters reduce him, bit by bit, to a helpless old animal, in accordance with their sense of human nature. A strange struggle, for Lear cannot see what his daughters are doing, without losing the battle and his sanity along with it (Act II, scene 2):

> O how this mother swells up toward my heart!
> Hysterica passio, down thou climbing sorrow,
> Thy element's below!

Kent tries to sustain him with his simple loyalty. The Fool offers him his love and insight, wrapped in bitter jests, to keep him sane. But in Act III, scene 6, his wits begin to turn; he succumbs to exhaustion, and is carried off into the darkness of the night to save what is left of life itself.

While Lear is losing his fight we have seen Gloucester striving, even more blindly, to sustain himself as loved and loving father. He has been frantically pursuing Edgar, to kill him, while Edmund, unseen, prepared his ruin. When the old man feebly tries to help Lear, Edmund betrays him to Goneril, Regan, and Cornwall. Only when they put out his eyes can he "see" his own folly—a turning point and recognition which is more sudden, clear, and savage, though less profound, than Lear's.

These two scenes (Act III, scenes 6 and 7) together constitute the turning point in the action of the play. They are tied together through Edmund's alliance with Goneril and Regan, and Gloucester's with Lear. Edgar (scene 6) points out the analogy between himself and Lear: "He childed as I fathered." Gloucester feels close to Lear because they are both old men. In both scenes Goneril and Regan are the victors, and their torture of Gloucester is, among other things, a physical image of their spiritual maiming of their father. Moreover, though they win, securing the power they have sought all along, the scene is a turning point for them too, for they throw off all pretense at last (Act III, scene 7):

> our power
> Shall do a court'sy to our wrath, which men
> May blame, but not control.

They do not see the implications of this change, though the audience should feel, if not understand them. Goneril and Regan are embarked on that course—"power into will, will into appetite"—which Ulysses in

Troilus and Cressida sets forth as the very essence of self-destructive anarchy.

After the cruel climax of Act III, we are left with many unanswered questions. Are Lear and Gloucester totally lost? Must the evil impulses in our nature triumph, when they are released? How, and whence, can any relief come? Shakespeare might have answered such questions by swiftly recounting the end of the story. Instead he shifts his focus (as he always does in the fourth act) from the narrative of events to the feelings, dreams, and groping thoughts of the characters, who nurse their wounds and try to see what is coming next. We hear of events offstage, the coming of the French army, quarrels between the Dukes, battles shaping up. But in the foreground, in a sort of hush before the final storm, we see the meaning of the struggles just past, now through the mind of one character, now through the mind of another.

Goneril and Regan see nothing outside their "appetite," which now focuses on Edmund. But *we* see through Albany, whose eyes have been opened. He tells Goneril (Act IV, scene 2):

> She that herself will sliver and disbranch
> From her material sap, perforce must wither,
> And come to deadly use.

He sees the hell she has let loose:

> It will come,
> Humanity must perforce prey on itself,
> Like monsters of the deep.

Old Gloucester would give up and die, if he were not sustained by Edgar:

> As flies to wanton boys, are we to the gods,
> They kill us for their sport.

Old Lear is much tougher. When he appears in scene 6, he is trying to meet his appalling experience head-on, and register it just as it is. The effect (as Edgar remarks) is "reason in madness," for he is seeing, with what reason he has, the madness opened up by his daughters beneath the hypocritical appearances of the human:

> But to the girdle do the gods inherit,
> Beneath is all the fiends';
> There's hell, there's darkness, there is the sulphurous pit.

He feels, in ironic despair, that his own moral being is in fragments, pulled this way and that by images of cruelty or lust:

> Fie, fie, fie; pah, pah! Give me an ounce of civet; good apothecary sweeten my imagination. There's money for thee.

Blind Gloucester feels in Lear himself the end of the world:

> O ruined piece of nature; this great world
> Shall so wear out to naught.

Kent and Edgar echo this thought (Act V, scene 3) when Lear appears with the dead Cordelia:

> Is this the promised end?
> Or image of that horror?

They are thinking of the "Dies Irae" when, according to the hymn, the world dissolves in sparks: *solvet saeculum in favilla.*

Shakespeare makes sure that the vision of hell or the world's end that we get through Lear shall be felt as utterly indigestible; an eternal pole of human experience opaque to reason. But through Albany, Edgar, and Cordelia, he reminds us that hell is not the only meaning of what we have seen and felt; there are other potentialities in human nature, other aspects of experience which are also true. In Act IV these three characters experience "hell," but not as Goneril and Regan do (as the one truth of human life); not as Lear does (in despair), but rather as a vision to be accepted in pain, for the sake of a better life ahead.

It is through Edgar, especially, that Shakespeare gradually reveals, behind the contrasting visions of the characters and the terrible events of the story, a possible order in human affairs. When Edgar is obliged to flee his deluded father (Act II, scene 3) he discards his own clothes to become

> the basest and most poorest shape
> That ever penury in contempt of man
> Brought near to beast.

He instinctively realizes that his standing as a man depended on a human order now lost to sight: "Edgar I nothing am." In the hovel (Act III, scene 6) he meets Lear, who has been reduced to a similar plight but can't accept it, or understand it as he himself does. The character Edgar creates, "poor Tom," reveals with poetic power the very dregs of society, and it is a premonition of the more appalling image of the world's end which we see later in Lear.

Edgar learns, when Lear's pathos is followed by that of his eyeless father (Act IV, scene 1) that hell is not to be plumbed by human eye: "O gods! Who is't can say 'I am at the worst'?" But his faithful acceptance of suffering reveals to him the ancient and traditional way to wisdom, and he uses it to help his father. The fantastic trick he plays on the old man—almost a practical joke—when he pretends that he has plunged over the cliff, is a demonstration that we must meet misfortune with some sort of faith, i.e., "die to live":

> Think that the clearest gods, who make them honours
> Of men's impossibilities, have preserved thee.

Through the whole sequence with Gloucester, Edgar opposes to the old man's feeble fatalism, his own maxim: "Bear free and patient thoughts."

From Gloucester's point of view Edgar (whom he cannot see) is an agent of the "clearest gods": he is like the grace of God in medieval theology, a mysterious help, neither earned nor deserved. Cordelia does as much for Lear, and in her role this theme of love or grace reaches its highest intensity. We hear of her coming (Act IV, scene 3) when the Gentleman tells Kent how she received the news of her father's plight: "her smiles and tears/ Were like a better way." In scene 4 we see her seeking her father; in scene 7 she finds him sleeping, and expresses her motive and its meaning:

> O you kind gods,
> Cure this great breach in his abused nature.
> The untuned and jarring senses, o, wind up
> Of this child-changed father.

When Lear wakes he puts it, with new humility, in another way:

> Thou art a soul in bliss, but I am bound
> Upon a wheel of fire, that mine own tears
> Do scald like molten lead.

Act IV is almost over, and we have been offered, through the eyes of one character after another, a great visionary scale of the potentialities in human nature, from blind hell, through the suffering of growth and change, to the enlightenment of a sort of "natural sanctity": our nature healed, and reconciled to the "clear" but unseen gods. But this vision is not realized in Britain; the hush is about to end, and the final battle, when Fate, or Chance, or Providence will make its pronouncement, must come soon. Shakespeare gives the last words in this act to sober Kent:

> My point and period will be thoroughly wrought,
> Or well, or ill, as this day's battle's fought.

So he prepares us for Act V, when the story ends, and all the themes are resolved in a "chord of feelings"—terror and pity—of almost intolerable power.

The end of the complicated story comes with great speed in Act V. The "bloody arbitrement" foretold in Act IV, the battle between the French army and the British, occurs offstage. But we see in the foreground the deathly struggle for power between Albany and Edmund; the sordid end of Goneril and Regan, consumed by their own lusts; and the duel between Edmund and Edgar, which is staged with ceremonious pomp. Edmund has a moment of clarity and repentance at the end, but it is too late to save himself or his victims. Edgar emerges from the ordeal of battle, and the longer ordeal of his nameless sufferings, to renewed life: he has at last fully found himself as Edgar.

Lear and Cordelia are at the center; in them is concentrated the greatest intensity of human experience. The vision of reconciliation and innocence they reached in Act IV is, in a sense, beyond earthly misfortunes. Their capture by Edmund does not destroy it: "For thee, oppressed King, I am cast down," says Cordelia; "myself could else outfrown false Fortune's frown." Lear answers with his most delicate music: we'll "take upon's the mystery of things,/ As if we were God's spies." After that, Cordelia's death, like that of a dog, a horse, a rat, savage reminder of mortality which brings man "near to beast," impresses many readers as intolerably cruel. Yet calamity was certainly "on the cards" for Lear; anything else would have rung false. Shakespeare does not soften it. Kent, now quite still and ghostly, speaks with the very voice of death:

> I have a journey sir, shortly to go.
> My master calls me, I must not say no.

Albany bids us accept it with awe:

> The weight of this sad time we must obey,
> Speak what we feel, not what we ought to say.
> The oldest hath borne most; we that are young
> Shall never see so much, nor live so long.

So ends the play. The oppression of Lear's time in Britain lifts; sanity is restored. But the "last things" we have seen, heights and depths of human experience, are not in time or history, and the sense of their reality is with us long after the play is done.

The sketch that I have attempted of the form and movement of the play as a whole is intended only as a preliminary map of the huge work. *Lear* has been studied from many other points of view. In recent years, for instance, the complex but consistent imagery has been carefully studied. Images of nakedness and clothing, stemming from the nakedness of Lear and Edgar, are woven through the whole play, and they embody some of the painful paradoxes of its tragic action. Is nakedness, which makes man defenseless and eliminates all distinctions of age, wealth, and status, the "natural" human state? The furred robes of corrupt magistrates, the prudish skirts of ancient bawds, are signs (in Act IV, scene 6) of deathly hypocrisy; yet the "bare forked animal" (Act III) is "near to beast." The animal images which start forth again and again—the "detested kite," the "soiled horse," the "monsters of the deep," give us the look of the depraved human. Countless variations are played upon the imagery of blindness, especially when old Gloucester's eyes—"vile jelly"—are plucked out (Act III); when eyeless Gloucester meets mad Lear (Act IV); and when Edgar (Act V) enlightens dying Edmund:

> The dark and vicious place where thee he got
> Cost him his eyes.

One must learn to hear the music of these and many other echoing images, as well as the music of the versification itself if one is to feel the true power of the play.

Those critics are right who say that Shakespeare has no "philosophy," if we mean by that a formal system of abstract concepts. But he had a consistent vision of our earthly life which he saw *within* the endless variety of human action, character, and fate. In most of his plays he presented a limited aspect of his whole vision. But in *Lear* he apparently wished to suggest its whole scope, by opening Lear's kingdom to all the conflicting motives hidden within it. The order he reveals behind the chaos is very much like what other great poets in our tradition have seen—especially Dante, in that part of *The Divine Comedy* which extends from the bottom of hell to the top of the purgatorial mountain, where human innocence and freedom on earth are briefly glimpsed. But in *Lear* nothing is presented in the terms of Christian theology. Ancient Britain is imagined as pre-Christian, pagan or "natural." Shakespeare's eye is upon our earthly life, and upon such experiences as may be recognized in every generation.

MACBETH

Macbeth was written in 1605–1606, very near *King Lear,* when Shakespeare was at the height of his power. Many critics regard it as the greatest of the tragedies. It is easy to agree with them while one is under its spell.

The story, the main characters, and the dark setting in eleventh-century Scotland, are derived from Holinshed's *Chronicles.* Shakespeare combined the story of Macbeth with that of Donwald's murder of King Duffe, to suit his poetic purpose. He was not trying to write a history, and he knew no doubt that Holinshed's account of that remote time was itself a mixture of fact and legend. But the story had a topical interest: James of Scotland, who had ascended the English throne in 1603, was supposed to be a descendant of the Banquo of the play. It is probable that Shakespeare wrote it for performance at James's court; certainly it would have had special interest for the King. As a young man, James had written his *Daemonologie,* an attempt to get at the truth in the popular superstitions about witches. As a learned amateur theologian, he would have appreciated the fine points in the philosophy of evil underlying the play. As a ruler, he would have watched the career of Macbeth, murderous usurper of the Scottish throne, with fascination. One can trace all of these elements in *Macbeth;* but for us, and for all ages, it lives as the most terrible murder story ever written, and as a poem which haunts the imagination like music.

It is the shortest and most concentrated of the tragedies, and Shakespeare gets it under way with more than his usual speed. The brief appearance of the Witches (Act I, scene 1) suggests that unnatural powers are abroad, seeking Macbeth; their childish doggerel, "Fair is foul, and foul is fair," tells us that things are not what they seem in Scotland. Good old King Duncan with his sons and attendants enters to meet the "bleeding Captain" who has news of a great battle (scene 2); and Duncan also finds that things are not what they seem. "Doubtful it stood," says the gasping Captain, of the battle, "as two spent swimmers, that do cling together,/ And choke their art." The battle is between the Scots under their generals Macbeth and Banquo, and the invading Norwegians allied with the Scottish traitor, the Thane of Cawdor. The Scots seem to be winning; then losing: "So from that spring, whence comfort seemed to come,/ Discomfort swells." The Captain faints before he can finish his story, but Ross appears to let us know that the Scots were victorious at last, mainly because of Macbeth's demoniac fighting, and that Cawdor is dead. King Duncan decides to reward Macbeth with the traitor's title—and that too sounds sinister and ambiguous, though poor old Duncan meant it so well.

The effect of these two scenes is to focus interest on Scotland, now threatened with mysterious dangers. As in all of Shakespeare's plays about kings, the fate of the monarchy underlies the action: *Macbeth* will not end until the monarchy is firmly established again. But in this play, more than in any other, Shakespeare is interested in evil itself: the way men feel its pull, the ways it may affect the individual and society. In these opening scenes he builds in our imagination the dark and deceptive atmosphere, the "world of the play," which affects all of the characters. He shows how their motives are hasty and irrational: even Duncan, who is so good, is caught in this drive. He overdoes his rewards to Macbeth; soon he will be racing to Macbeth's castle, supposedly to receive hospitality and honor, actually to meet his death.

But it is when we meet Macbeth (scene 3) that the action of the play begins to take on its full power. He and Banquo, leaving the field of battle, meet the Witches, who have been expecting them; and Macbeth's first line echoes the Witches' chant of scene 1: "So fair and foul a day I have not seen." Macbeth is not only the protagonist, he is also the character who sees most deeply into what is going on. It has often been pointed out that he is both a powerful and ambitious warrior, and a suffering poet and seer. Perhaps Shakespeare thought of him as one of the Celtic Scots, a distant cousin of the Welsh Glendower, who was also fighter, bard, and magician in one. It is Macbeth's subtle and fertile imagination that makes him so susceptible to temptation; but it also gives him his appalling insight into his own human passion and torment. In the sequence of his monologues in Act I we watch the murderous motivation grow; we can see how it looks from inside—in its own nightmarish light—and also in the sober light of Macbeth's reason.

When the Witches tell him (Act I, scene 3) that he will be Thane of Cawdor, and then King, they feed the secret dream he had shared only with his Lady. When Ross greets him as Thane of Cawdor, he is caught up—"rapt," as Banquo notices—in a vision of supreme power:

Two truths are told,
As happy prologues to the swelling act
Of the imperial theme.

But he knows, in a moment, that the Witches' truth is double-edged:

This supernatural soliciting
Cannot be ill, cannot be good.

And he sees, with dismay, that it has overpowered him:

. . . why do I yield to that suggestion,
Whose horrid image doth unfix my hair,
And make my seated heart knock at my ribs,
Against the use of nature?

He is alternating between his vision of murder as absolute power, and his vision of the same murder as reason and common-sense reveal it. In this paradoxical experience, he concludes, "Nothing is/ But what is not."

In the very next scene (scene 4) he learns that Duncan will spend the night at his castle; and now it seems all but certain that fate or hidden powers have decreed that he shall have the crown by murder. When he joins his lady, and she tells him (Act 1, scene 5):

Thy letters have transported me beyond
This ignorant present, and I feel now
The future in the instant

their dream of power seems more real to them than time itself, with its pedestrian facts. But Macbeth recovers even from that. In his great monologue on the brink (Act I, scene 7), the sense of reality, and time, is back; he is "on *this* bank and shoal of time," and cannot "jump the life to come." He sees exactly what Duncan's murder will mean:

He's here in double trust:
First, as I am his kinsman, and his subject,
Strong both against the deed; then, as his host,
Who should against the murderer shut the door,
Not bear the knife myself.

Worse than simple slaughter, the murder is treachery of the deepest kind, which Shakespeare (like Dante) regarded as the deathliest sin, for it cuts the root of all trust, without which no human relationship is possible. Macbeth sees that it will violate the feeling of all humanity: "Pity, like a naked newborn babe . . . Shall blow the horrid deed in every eye,/ That tears shall drown the wind." In this sober light, that of reason and experience, he sees the murder as the impossible stunt it is:

> I have no spur
> To prick the sides of my intent, but only
> Vaulting ambition, which o'erleaps itself,
> And falls on th'other—

But at that moment Lady Macbeth finds him.

Lady Macbeth lacks her husband's double vision, but she is an equally profound image of a human spirit in the grip of evil. When Lady Macbeth gets the news (Act I, scene 5) she is as "rapt" as Macbeth, and she too knows that what she wants to do is evil and will not bear the light of day and reason. But she is not appalled, perhaps because she will not perform the butchery directly, but through her husband. Moreover, she can protect herself from the physical horror by rationalizing the corpse as a mere "picture" or "painted devil." Her willful and doctrinaire heartlessness gives us our sharpest sense of human slaughter; but Lady Macbeth herself can repress all natural feeling until it returns, in the sleepwalking scene, to mock her.

Neither of the Macbeths could perform the murder alone. But they are united in a deep, if unregenerate, love; and as a team they feel omnipotent. "This night's great business," says Lady Macbeth, when her husband first joins her (Act I, scene 5), "shall to all our nights and days to come/ Give solely sovereign sway and masterdom." When Macbeth loses this power drive, she gives it to him again; and, sustained by her will, he can say,

> I am settled, and bend up
> Each corporal agent to this terrible feat.
> Away, and mock the time with fairest show.
> False face must hide what the false heart doth know.

Those lines sum up very briefly the themes of concealment, of trying to outwit or "mock" time, and of the murder as an unnatural tour de force. So ends Act I.

No one can miss the excitement of the offstage murder (Act II, scene 2) as reported first by Lady Macbeth, with her glassy self-command, and then by Macbeth, grotesquely helpless after his "feat." But the murder makes a crucial stage in the movement of the play. It is a good idea to pause a moment, to see how Shakespeare reveals this turning point from several points of view.

First there is the Porter who comes (Act II, scene 3) to answer the knocking that frightened the Macbeths. He is resentful at being waked up with a hangover, and he lets three imaginary sinners into hell before he opens the real door to the real knockers. His imaginary sinners were all familiar types. The farmer raises the price when crops are scarce, and absurdly hangs himself when they are abundant. The equivocator is one of the Jesuits who were intriguing against the government; they believed it right to equivocate in defense of their persecuted religion, i.e., "for God's sake." The tailor has stolen cloth from his customer's already tight French-style breeches. All three absurdly try to outwit evil by evil means, and are thus brothers-under-the-skin of Macbeth.

When the Porter at last lets in Macduff and Lennox he plays a final variation on his farcical theme. He makes them wait while he recounts his adventure with drink, "an equivocator with lechery." He had wrestled with drink, and after an even and dubious struggle, has "cast him." His drunkenness is grossly physical, but it reminds us of the Macbeths' more terrible inebriation and their even contest with it. Some readers, including even Coleridge, have found the Porter too coarse for their taste. But Shakespeare knew that a deep motive affects the whole being, including the body and its functions. Having shown the insane drive of evil in the high moral imagination of Macbeth, he now reveals it in the most homely, lewd, and farcical analogies. Moreover he wants his audience to recover, for a moment, from the excitement of the murder, and reflect that all Scotland is now entering the gates of hell.

The lords summoned by the clanging of the bell are at first too bewildered to think. But Macbeth, while they eye him, and while he maintains his pretense of innocence, is realizing his plight in all its hopelessness. Everything he says has a double meaning, which the audience can understand (Act II, scene 3):

> Had I but died an hour before this chance,
> I had lived a blessed time; for from this instant
> There's nothing serious in mortality.
> All is but toys.

That ostensibly expresses the grief of host, kinsman, and subject; but we hear in it his real despair. When Macduff asks him why he killed the grooms, instead of saving them for questioning, he replies:

> Th' expedition of my violent love
> Outrun the pauser, reason.

He is trying to say that the expedition (or hastiness) of his love for

Duncan got ahead of his reason, which would have told him to pause. But here again his insight betrays him: we know that it was the violent love of Lady Macbeth that outran his reason at the crucial moment. And we know that ever since the Witches tempted him with their equivocations he has been trying to outrun his own reason.

Anyone who has tried to wink at his own reason, when hurrying into some minor misdeed, can recognize the accuracy of this phrase, "to outrun the pauser, reason." Shakespeare knew all about this motive, in the commonest human experience; that is why Macbeth gets under our skin still. He understood it also in the light of the philosophy he had inherited from the Middle Ages. Reason was supposed to be God's gift to man, which, if obeyed, could reveal to him nature and nature's order, in the individual soul, in society, and even in the cosmos. Macbeth is therefore trying to violate his own nature, the basis of human society, and the divine order in the stars. He cannot succeed; his reason will be with him however fast he travels. At this moment in the play he senses the fact that this unwinnable race is all he has to look forward to.

When the lords recover from their first shock, they too begin to realize what Duncan's murder will mean to them. I have pointed out that during Act I everyone feels the deceptive and unnatural atmosphere in Scotland; and that though Duncan and his nobles do nothing criminal, they too find themselves hurrying like Macbeth, puzzled by the ambiguous meaning of events. Now they enter the hell created by Macbeth, as though Lady Macbeth's "blanket of the dark" covered the earth. Ross, in his talk with the Old Man (Act II, scene 4), builds the scene in our imaginations:

> Thou seest the heavens, as troubled with man's act,
> Threatens his bloody stage: by th' clock 'tis day,
> And yet dark night strangles the travelling lamp.
> Is't night's predominance, or the day's shame,
> That darkness does the face of earth entomb,
> When living light should kiss it?
>
> OLD MAN
>
> 'Tis unnatural,
> Even like the deed that's done.

This imagery of blood and darkness prevails until the end of Act IV, when Ross, Malcolm, and Macduff at last glimpse "living light" again. And the loss of natural time, which we know in the orderly sequence of day and night, is suggested in many ways. Scholars have pointed out that we cannot tell how long the action takes—months or years; they might have added that Shakespeare wanted precisely that effect.

Like Dante, he sees hell as outside time. The Macbeths feel that, in the phrases I have quoted above. We are made to feel it in many echoing images, and in the rhythm of the action, which sometimes seems lightning-swift, sometimes nightmare-slow, getting nowhere.

The experience of Macbeth and his Lady is, of course, the center of the play. But it is revealed to us in its wider meanings through two complementary themes, that of the Witches, who start the whole action, and that of Ross, Malcolm, and Macduff, who find their way out of the Scottish hell and end Macbeth's career.

The Witches as actually written by Shakespeare are only the three Weird Sisters; Hecate is a late addition by Middleton. With Hecate out of the way, the dramatic and poetic style of the Witch scenes is consistent. And in the light of recent studies we can understand how Shakespeare saw them as stage figures.

He found the Witches and their equivocal prophecies in Holinshed, but developed them according to the popular lore of the time. The Renaissance knew a bewildering variety of witches and magicians, creatures of Latin legend, Norse mythology, and the folklore of northern Europe. We cannot tell whether Shakespeare "believed" in any of this; but we can see that he used it in the play to make the Witches actable, and recognizable to his audience, and at the same time to suggest, behind them, further unseen powers of evil.

When the Witches first appear (Act I, scene 1) we gather that they have been summoned by their Familiars: "I come, Graymalkin"; "Paddock calls." Familiars were minor evil spirits who took possession of old women or other susceptible types, thus making them "witches." Witches had to obey their Familiars, but received in return some power to do mischief themselves, to travel by air, and to sail in sieves. Shakespeare apparently did not show the Familiars onstage, since they are not mentioned in the cast or in stage directions; their presence is indicated only by what the Witches say and by offstage cries and whines. According to folklore, Graymalkin is a cat, Paddock a toad, urchin, or "hedgepig," and Harpier an owl. Through their Familiars the Witches are associated with supernatural powers, the Norns (the Fates of Norse mythology), or Satan himself. But they are not themselves supernatural. They are old women, seduced and thwarted by the spirits they adore and serve.

As old women crazily inspired by evil, the Witches are extremely actable, and far more uncanny than they would be under gauze, with a spooky green light on them. Their appetite for mischief is infinite, but what they can accomplish in that line is limited. The first Witch yearns in vain (Act I, scene 3) to sink the homecoming Pilot's ship, but she can only torment him:

> Weary sev'nights, nine times nine,
> Shall he dwindle, peak, and pine.
> Though his bark cannot be lost,
> Yet it shall be tempest-tossed.

In these lines we hear the teasing whine of one who is herself teased. We hear it more piercingly in the half-truths with which the Witches tempt Macbeth. Unable to ruin him directly, they must tease him into ruining himself. They crave to subject him to the frustrations they suffer, much as Iago craves to subject Othello to the envy and hatred which possess him. There is humor in Shakespeare's conception of the Witches: with their mocking nursery-rhymes, they are queer childish images of Macbeth's terrible futility.

The Witches' charms and incantations are traditional magic. In their final scene (Act IV, scene 1) all that they do is significant at showing their bond with evil. They appear, as before, in response to the mew, the whine, and the cry of their Familiars; but thereafter they deal with their "masters"—probably more potent spirits. The apparitions they show Macbeth, in the form of bodies or parts of bodies, are "necromancy," supposedly the best kind of prophecy. They show in this scene the utmost their "art" can accomplish, stirring the cauldron, making their circles, and adding the ingredients according to the recipes of classical demonology.

They are treating Macbeth with new respect because they know that Macbeth himself now has status in hell. Like Faust, Macbeth has "mine eternal jewel/ Given to the common enemy of man." Moreover he has seen that he has probably sold his soul in vain, for Banquo rose from the dead to plague him (Act III, scene 4) and Banquo's son escaped for all his efforts. That point—the banquet scene and its aftermath—marks the climax and turning point in Macbeth's action. He has no hope of winning, nor can he turn back:

> I am in blood
> Stepped in so far, that should I wade no more,
> Returning were as tedious as go o'er—

the dreariest version of his nightmare race. Now (after the banquet scene), he is "bent to know/ By the worst means the worst," and he commands the Witches to show it to him even though "destruction sicken."

The Witches are his to command; yet they contrive to play with him a little longer. The apparitions are arranged in such a way as to make him hope, then despair, then hope again. Then they finish him off in triumph: "Show!/ Show!/ Show!/ Show his eyes, and grieve his heart./ Come like shadows, so depart."

The apparitions refer in their ambiguous way to Macbeth's fate as it actually overtakes him in Act V. They also suggest the nature of Macbeth's crimes, the judgment of God upon them, and the return of the pretty world once he is gone. They are announced by thunder, a sign of the voice of God since the most ancient times. Macbeth half understands that himself; he wants to "tell pale-hearted fear it lies;/ And sleep in spite of thunder." The Armed Head means Macbeth himself (whose head is cut off in the end) and Macduff, who kills him. The Bloody Child also means Macduff, of course; and it is a reminder of Lady Macbeth's babe (Act I, scene 7) whose boneless gums she is prepared to pluck from her nipple to dash its brains out; and Macbeth's "pity, like a naked, newborn babe" whom he was about to violate by murder. Shakespeare often uses children as the most touching and natural symbol of new life and hope; in this scene they suggest both what Macbeth was trying to kill, and his ultimate failure. The "Child, crowned, with a tree in his hand," carries all these meanings. He means Banquo's issue; the tree is the genealogical tree of the Scottish kings all the way down to James. The tree also means Birnam Wood, and as such gives Macbeth false hope. And the leafy tree is a symbol as old, and as universal, as thunder, for the springtime renewal of life itself. It occurs in countless primitive festivals which mark the death of Old Man Winter and the joyful birth of his successor. Shakespeare was familiar with it, as the Maypole, in the spring festivals all over England. It is still used in country districts.

These visions reveal what is going on in Macbeth's suffering, perceptive mind and spirit, and they are connected with the imagery of his monologues. In this respect they are like the premonitions of disaster that Shakespeare so often grants to his tragic protagonists in the fourth act of the tragedy. But by means of the Witches he gives them a kind of objective reality: behind them we can make out the whole ordered world of Shakespeare's tradition, violated by Macbeth, and now returning in triumph.

The Witches disappear as the endless procession of Kings begins, to the sound of hautboys, and we never see them again. Macbeth returns with a bump to present reality, and instantly hears "the galloping of horse," the windy sound of the losing race which is all he has to look forward to. We do not see him again until the final sequences in Dunsinane (Act V).

The rest of Act IV and much of Act V are dominated by Malcolm, Macduff, and Ross, who reverse the hellish course of events and end Macbeth's career. What Malcolm and his friends do is obviously essential to the whole plot, and equally important in revealing the meaning Shakespeare saw in the story. But the great scene in England (Act IV, scene 3), when they resolve to act, has puzzled some readers.

During the first three acts Macbeth's enemies have little to say for themselves; Macbeth is literally "getting away with murder." The darkness closes over them, and they are afraid to move. Ross sums up this situation when he tries (Act IV, scene 2) to explain to Lady Macduff why her husband has fled to England:

> I dare not speak much further,
> But cruel are the times, when we are traitors,
> And do not know ourselves; when we hold rumor
> From what we fear, yet know not what we fear,
> But float upon a wild and violent sea
> Each way and move.

When no man can trust himself, or anyone else, all are in a sense "traitors," no matter what they do. That is the plight of Malcolm and Macduff when we meet them in exile at the English court (Act IV, scene 3). The scene is in three movements: first, the painful dialogue between Malcolm and Macduff; second, the interlude with the English Doctor; and finally, the sequence with Ross, who brings the news of Lady Macduff's murder, after which they unite and take action.

The first movement of the scene, in which Malcolm and Macduff try in vain to find some basis for mutual trust, often seems too long, and is, therefore, usually cut in production. Malcolm's false confession, that he has more lust, avarice, and treachery than Macbeth himself, is taken from Holinshed. It is, of course, a piece of philosophizing about evil: lust is the lightest of sins, avarice more dangerous, but only treachery (Macbeth's sin) is beyond all remedy. The verse of this sequence lacks the visionary intensity of the rest of the play. The movement is slow, like that of careful, tentative thinking. And we are likely to feel that the classification of sins, when made so explicit, is rather stiff and old-fashioned. And yet Shakespeare had his dramatic intention in writing the scene in just this way. Malcolm and Macduff, in England, are free from the rush of immediate danger, but they do not "know themselves." They are in a kind of vacuum; time seems hardly to move at all; they resort to thought in their search for a way out. But they fail: Malcolm cannot trust Macduff, who left his wife and child, and Macduff, after Malcolm disavows his confession, sadly remarks, "Such welcome and unwelcome things at once/ 'Tis hard to reconcile," echoing the "fair is foul" theme with which the whole play started.

At that point the Doctor appears, and we learn that the English King, Edward the Confessor, is about to cure, by his touch, a disease which resists the Doctor's medical arts. According to an old legend the English kings inherited the miraculous gift of healing scrofula, "the King's evil," and James I, though skeptical, still "touched" for this disease. This scene also is often cut in production, and some critics think Shakespeare put it in at the last minute to flatter James. However that may be, it seems to be an essential part of Shakespeare's design. The Doctor foreshadows the Doctor (Act V, scene 1) who remarks of the sleepwalking Lady Macbeth, "More needs she the divine than the physician." King Edward may remind us of "the gracious Duncan," who glimpsed the clear evening sky just before entering Macbeth's dark castle. In this scene the interlude serves to remind us, not only that "sundry blessings hang about [Edward's] throne,/ That speak him full of grace," but also of the healthful world of nature which is still there, behind the nightmare. And it suggests that Malcolm and Macduff can never return to that reality by their own reason or their own efforts: some outside help is needed, some "grace of God."

The third movement of the scene, which begins with Ross's entrance, shows how the three exiles at last receive this grace. "Good God, betimes remove/ The means that makes us strangers," says Malcolm, when he recognizes Ross. His prayer defines the motive of all three exiles. But the prayer is not granted until they face the worst: the news of the slaughter of Lady Macduff and her children, which convicts them all of a share in Macbeth's guilt. Only then can they recognize themselves, and then each other, as they really are in the real world. Their way is clear at last; they find the faith to put their cause to the ordeal of battle; and in Malcolm's final words we already hear the healthy throb of military music:

> This tune goes manly.
> Come go we to the King, our power is ready,
> Our lack is nothing but our leave. Macbeth
> Is ripe for shaking, and the powers above
> Put on their instruments. Receive what cheer you may,
> The night is long that never finds the day.

Shakespeare apparently planned this scene (like so much of *Macbeth*) in accordance with medieval theories of evil and its cure through the grace of God. But he presents it all in terms of Malcolm's and Macduff's experience. They are lost, and they cannot think their way out. But when they accept that fact, the scene changes. The faith they get in each other and in their cause is, in the last analysis, as mysterious, as irrational, as Macbeth's evil drive; but such a suprarational act of faith is the only cure for the terrible uncertainty which has paralyzed them. The swift movement of the play starts again; the theme of striving beyond reason, now interpreted as an act of faith, resounds in a major key. Throughout the fifth act we are aware of the armies with their drums and trumpets converging on Dunsinane. When they triumph, all the ambiguous omens reveal their literal truth and their natural explanations; the nightmare dissolves, and the daylight world of reason and common sense comes back.

In the last act, however, the deepest images are those of Macbeth and his lady. Through the clear, but sympathetic, eyes of the Doctor and the Nurse we watch Lady Macbeth walking in her sleep. Is she fully human, or a puppet of her visions? As she reenacts the murder of Duncan, then of Banquo, she repeats her formulas for suppressing the horror, but now they no longer work. "Oh, oh, oh!" she sighs, smelling the blood: "The heart is sorely charged," says the Doctor. In her nightgown, alone, she would look less like the power-mad woman of Act I than like a little girl lost in the dark.

Macbeth has also become a kind of puppet, but a dangerous one. Caithness reports (Act V, scene 2):

> Some say he's mad; others, that lesser hate him,
> Do call it valiant fury, but for certain
> He cannot buckle his distempered cause
> Within the belt of rule.

As Macbeth tries in vain to rule his country and his fate, we see him as a mechanical monster: his pestered senses recoil; he is a dwarfish thief in a giant's robe: he sags with doubt or shakes with fear. At the end his head comes in on a pole, looking, I suppose, like Lady Macbeth's painted devil that scares the eye of childhood. But even here, in the last few hours, Macbeth's insight does not leave him. Out of the knowledge it gives him come some of the saddest melodies ever written:

> My way of life
> Is fallen into the sear, the yellow leaf,
> And that which should accompany old age,
> As honour, love, obedience, troops of friends,
> I must not look to have; but in their stead

> Curses, not loud but deep, mouth-honour, breath,
> Which the poor heart would feign deny, and dare not.

These lines express the same vision which Macbeth got just after Duncan's murder, that for him, henceforth, "there's nothing serious in mortality." *Macbeth* is the most unified of Shakespeare's tragedies; the whole meaning of the play resounds in all of the verse. If one listens to that music, there is little need for scholarly explanations.

ANTONY AND CLEOPATRA

Antony and Cleopatra, one of the world's greatest tales of human love, was written in 1606 or 1607. Like the other tragedies, it is filled with the immediate intensities of character and conflict, but at the same time it has that godlike breadth and clarity of vision—detachment combined with deepest feeling—which we associate with Shakespeare's final phase. Even he was never more completely the master of language, for the marvelous life of the play throbs in every word, from the first to the last.

Our first impression of *Antony and Cleopatra* comes directly from the music and imagery of the language; but the play is all of a piece, and one may learn to understand it also by considering Shakespeare's handling of the story itself, for that is poetry too. His starting point was Plutarch's *Life of Antony,* in North's fine translation. Plutarch, a shrewd and sober moralist, recounts Antony's important part in Roman history in order to draw the moral: the great Roman soldier was destroyed by his passion for Cleopatra. Shakespeare relies on Plutarch for the Roman history, and he appropriates many details which serve his purpose, and even a few passages, like the famous description of Cleopatra on her barge, which he transmutes from North's prose into his own music by a very few masterly adjustments. He does not contradict Plutarch's moral judgment of the "ne'er lust-wearied Antony," but he transcends it by making both Antony and the Queen large enough to know the whole scope of their passion. And he makes all the motivation of the play to center around that passion, which like a dream or the flickering light from a fire, dominates the Mediterranean world while the story lasts. So he gives the play the unity of action that poetic drama requires.

He starts the play near the end of Antony's career. After the murder of Julius Caesar and the civil wars that followed, the Empire was ruled by a triumvirate: Antony, Lepidus, and Octavius Caesar (who is usually called simply "Caesar" in this play). *Antony and Cleopatra* begins just as the triumvirate is beginning to crack apart. Antony, with Cleopatra in Egypt, has failed to keep order in the East; Caesar and Lepidus, in Rome, are defied by Fulvia, Antony's formidable wife, and by Sextus Pompeius who with his navy controls the sea. Caesar and Lepidus demand that Antony return to Rome and face his responsibilities; that is the "powerful mandate" he receives in Act I, scene 1. At first he scornfully rejects it:

> Let Rome in Tiber melt, and the wide arch
> Of the ranged empire fall. Here is my space.
> Kingdoms are clay. Our dungy earth alike
> Feeds beast as man. The nobleness of life
> Is to do thus [*kissing Cleopatra*]—when such a mutual pair
> And such a twain can do't.

But by scene 2 "a Roman thought hath struck him," as Cleopatra wryly notes; and by scene 3 he is pulling away, in body at least:

> Our separation so abides and flies,
> That thou residing here goes yet with me;
> And I hence fleeing here remain with thee.

By this time we already sense the depth of the passion that joins Antony and Cleopatra; its incommensurability with Rome and the cares of rule, and its mysterious property of filling the lovers now with exultation, now with mistrust and remorse.

After Act I, scene 3, the action moves away from Egypt and Cleopatra, as Antony engages in the treacherous contest with Caesar, Lepidus, and Pompey for the mastery of the world. But Antony's attachment to Cleopatra is always at the center of the wide panorama, for Antony is the clue to the balance of power, and his infatuation is the clue to his action. His rivals know that, and plan their moves according to the way they understand that passion from moment to moment, seeking always to take advantage of it for their own purposes.

First we see Caesar and Lepidus trying to estimate it (Act I, scene 4). Lepidus, an amiable mediocrity, wants to see Antony's weaknesses as "the spots of heaven,/ More fiery by night's blackness." Caesar rather primly replies,

> Let's grant it is not
> Amiss to tumble on the bed of Ptolemy. . . .

> yet must Antony
> No way excuse his foils, when we do bear
> So great weight in his lightness.

Caesar is the hardest and coldest of Antony's rivals. Contemptuous of his own feelings as he is of Antony's, he will try one way after another to control Antony through his love. As for Pompey (whom we meet in Act II, scene 1), he first guesses that Antony will never leave Cleopatra, and so thinks he can defy Caesar and Lepidus; but then he hears that Antony is already in Rome. He then guesses that Antony is free of Cleopatra, and decides that he must therefore compromise with the triumvirate. Both guesses are wrong, and Pompey is eliminated as a serious contender in the negotiations which conclude Act II (scenes 6 and 7).

During Act II we see the rival generals engaged in diplomacy—like poker, or the faithless international conferences of our own time. Caesar tries to tie down the amorous Antony by marrying him to his sister Octavia. This maneuver looks both cynical and unpromising to the friends of the triumvirs, who watch the game without illusion. Enobarbus sees everything with humorous but relentless clarity. He is one of those characters that Shakespeare often uses to reflect the action and its meaning. We soon learn to trust his insight, and he sees the masters of the world in a sardonic light: "If you borrow one another's love for the instant," he tells Antony and Caesar as their alliance is being arranged, "you may when you hear no more words of Pompey return it again." He and the other soldiers would much rather talk about Cleopatra than listen to the stale hypocrisies of their leaders. The moment the generals depart after their conference (Act II, scene 2) Enobarbus gives his glowing description of Cleopatra on her barge, as Maecenas murmurs, "O rare for Antony." His comment on the marriage to Octavia is brief: "He will to his Egyptian dish again." And the great banquet on Pompey's ship (Act II, scene 7)—the classic picture of the "stag party" of business, or military, or political rivals—looks to all the men except Caesar like an uninspired imitation of Antony's more glorious binges with Cleopatra in Alexandria.

Cleopatra herself plays no direct part in the power battle, but Shakespeare does not allow us to forget her. We see her three times in this sequence (Act I, scene 5, Act II, scene 5, and Act III, scene 3)—a piece of unfinished business so dangerous and alluring that the efforts of the generals to disregard her seem foolish. Even in her boredom and frustration she expresses every tiniest movement of feeling with freedom, style, and "infinite variety." No wonder that far-off soldiers at their cold toil of ruling "our dungy earth" dream of her as of the illicit promise of life itself.

Caesar, however, is immune to Cleopatra's magic, just as he is to the quality in Antony that makes him Cleopatra's lover. The painful relation between Caesar and Antony is near the heart of the play, and it is through their contrasted characters that Shakespeare expresses much of the tragic meaning of the action. The Egyptian Soothsayer warns Antony against Caesar (Act II, scene 3):

> Thy demon, that thy spirit which keeps thee, is
> Noble, courageous, high unmatchable,
> Where Ceasar's is not. But near him, thy angel
> Becomes a fear, as being o'erpowered: therefore
> Make space enough between you.

Antony bitterly confirms this: Caesar unaccountably wins all the games they play together. Antony can be himself among the soldiers, for they strongly respond to "the spirit that keeps him," a generous, daring spirit capable of giving itself completely to war, or to love, when Cleopatra makes him feel that therein lies "the nobleness of life." The charisma that makes him a great military leader, the idol of his followers, makes him also Cleopatra's passionate lover. But Caesar fights with reason, not passion, and when he meets Antony, forces him to contend in *his* way. When the two part, ostensibly allies and brothers-in-law (Act III, scene 2), we see how Antony instinctively tries to break the chilly paralysis: "Come sir, come," he cries as he throws his arms around Caesar, "I'll wrestle with you in my strength of love"—to which Caesar laconically replies, "Adieu; be happy." After that their struggle rapidly moves from diplomacy to war, and Caesar, taking advantage of Antony's "doting," administers a humiliating defeat at the battle of Actium (Act III, scene 10). Antony makes a last, absurd and desperate attempt to make Caesar fight his way, by challenging him to personal combat (Act III, scene 13). Caesar's reply (Act IV, scene 1) is a foregone conclusion: "let the old ruffian know/ I have many other ways to die; meantime/ Laugh at his challenge."

The story of the first three acts is mainly that of the Roman generals' contention for the world. But by making Antony's love the decisive factor, Shakespeare gives that struggle the same wavering rhythm as that of the passion itself. The lovers know both the towering flame of their passion, and its cold cinders; and the hard-bitten soldiers, as they try to get Antony in their power, follow a similar bewildering course. The verse expresses this fluctuation, both in its movement and in such images as "the vagabond flag upon the stream," for the inconstant loyalties of the Empire's polyglot populations; or "darkling stands/ The varying shore of the world," to suggest the shifting light and darkness of our earthly scene. The climax and turning point of the whole complex action comes in Act III, scene 13, when Antony has been stripped of his soldiership by his defeat at Actium, and his passion is left, with no defense but itself, to face the Roman power of Caesar. But that passion proves as unpredictable in its nakedness—an "old lion dying," in Enobarbus' words—as it was when we tried to define it from far away. Painful as it is, this scene (Act III, scene 13) gives off bewildering images and moves in a lightly varying rhythm.

Enobarbus watches it all, and his suffering but clear perception is always the center of the picture. He gives the clue at once, in the confusion after the naval defeat:

CLEOPATRA
Is Antony or we in fault for this?
ENOBARBUS
Antony only, that would make his will
Lord of his reason.

When Antony sends Caesar his wild challenge to fight "ourselves alone," Enobarbus bitterly notes, "Caesar thou hast subdued/ His judgement too." Enobarbus had founded his life's motive in his love for Antony, and now as he sees his leader falling to pieces he feels his own being torn apart too:

Mine honesty and I begin to square.
The loyalty well held to fools does make
Our faith mere folly. Yet he that can endure
To follow with allegiance a fallen lord
Does conquer him that did his master conquer,
And earns a place i' th' story.

He foresees the squalid tantrum that follows when Antony, thinking Cleopatra has betrayed him, has Caesar's emissary cruelly whipped, calls Cleopatra "a morsel cold upon dead Caesar's trencher," and so betrays Cleopatra, their love, and his own "noble" spirit. Enobarbus' Antony ends, or seems to end, here.

But Cleopatra recognizes him in his despair.

ANTONY
Cold-hearted toward me?
CLEOPATRA
Ah, dear, if I be so,

From my cold heart let heaven engender hail,
And poison it in the source.

From her infinite variety she draws yet another vision of love—love true till death, this time—and with it warms Antony back to life. As Antony leads her away for one more gaudy night, he can cry:

Come on, my Queen,
There's sap in't yet. The next time I do fight,
I'll make death love me; for I will contend
Even with his pestilent scythe.

It is one of the lovers' great moments; but Enobarbus, with his sad clarity, concludes the scene:

I see still
A diminution in our captain's brain
Restores his heart: when valour preys on reason,
It eats the sword it fights with. I will seek
Some way to leave him.

We shall hear the verse-melody of the last two lines again when Enobarbus dies in Act IV.

In all of Shakespeare's tragedies, the fourth act (which follows the climax and turning point of Act III) is focused, not on the swift course of events, but on the efforts of the characters to digest their victory or defeat. They get a new sense of the meaning of their action, and try to foretell its ultimate fate. In this play the battle that decides the mastery of the world occurs in Act IV; but it does not give Caesar control of the love of Antony and Cleopatra. We shall see him try to gain that in Act V, in his final struggle with Cleopatra. Shakespeare uses the changing fortunes of battle in Act IV, not to end the action, but to reveal in the deceptive lights of success and failure, and from the points of view of many characters, all the poignant strengths and weaknesses of the great passion, now all that Antony and Cleopatra have to call their own.

In scene 1 Caesar resumes Enobarbus' deathly tone: "Tomorrow the last of many battles/ We mean to fight," he says in his quiet way, and adds, "poor Antony." Enobarbus deepens this note in scene 2, as he watches Antony "make his followers weep" at their banquet on the eve of battle. He murmurs to Cleopatra, " 'Tis one of those odd tricks which sorrow shoots/ Out of the mind." And in scene 3 the night sentries in the Alexandrian streets hear music passing under the earth: "It signs well, does it not?—No.—Peace I say./ What should this mean?—

'Tis the god Hercules, whom Antony loved, now leaves him." But in scene 4 Antony, renewed and new-inspired after his night of revelry, can evoke the glamour of all early things:

> This morning, like the spirit of a youth
> That means to be of note, begins betimes,

And when he returns victorious from the first round of the battle, Cleopatra can respond with splendor:

> Lord of lords,
> O infinite virtue, com'st thou smiling from
> The world's great snare uncaught?

Their last affirmations of love are the more thrilling for their insubstantiality and the dark background against which they rise. For we know (from scene 7) that Caesar, though battered, is unshaken. And we know (from scene 6) that Enobarbus, whose desertion Antony had rewarded with wealth and messages of gratitude, is succumbing to the wound that his disloyalty makes in his moral being:

> I fight against thee? No, I will go seek
> Some ditch wherein to die.

The lovers' dreamlike moment of triumph is quickly followed by Enobarbus' death under the moon:

> O sovereign mistress of true melancholy,
> The poisonous damp of night disponge upon me,
> That life, a very rebel to my will,
> May hang no longer on me.

Upon which the listening sentries announce the final battle: "Hark the drums/ Demurely wake the sleepers"—and Antony's defeat is quickly indicated in scenes 10, 11, and 12.

The finale of Act IV is carried by Antony and Cleopatra. In the confusion and bitterness of defeat Antony thinks Cleopatra has betrayed him; he curses her, and she flees to her monument. And now Antony can see at last how his whole being had come to depend upon their love, weakening or strengthening just as it had seemed to do. He expresses this in the great speech to Eros, comparing himself to changing cloud-shapes: "Here I am Antony,/ Yet cannot hold this visible shape, my knave." This speech is the philosophical center of the play, and the basis of the wavering images and rhythms of its verse. When Antony hears Cleopatra's lying—or premature—message, that she has killed herself, he gives himself a mortal wound; and now their love appears against death, which we have felt coming through the whole act. The vision reaches a great height in Cleopatra's dirge:

> O see, my women,
> The crown o' th'earth doth melt. My lord!
> O withered is the garland of the war. . . .

And she foretells her own death,

> what's brave, what's noble,
> Let's do it after the high Roman fashion,
> And make death proud to take us,

just as we shall see it at the end of Act V.

Act IV is a masterpiece of poetry, whether one listens to the sound of the verse itself, or follows the varying tone and movement of the action from scene to scene. A lesser dramatist would have ended the play at this high point, if he could have reached it; but Shakespeare has more to say. While Cleopatra lives, her love for Antony—whatever that may be—remains, and we know that Caesar will try to seize her to complete his triumph, when he returns to Rome as undisputed master of the world.

During most of Act V Caesar seems to be winning the fight with Cleopatra just as he had won all of his fights with Antony. He plans (scene 1) to deceive Cleopatra with promises of honorable treatment, and so take her alive. She almost believes him, and, like Antony, loses her bearings as she tries to fight in Caesar's way. But as she talks to Dolabella (scene 2) her own cosmic vision of Antony and their love comes back:

> His legs bestrid the ocean; his reared arm
> Crested the world . . .
> In his livery
> Walked crowns and crownets; realms and islands were
> As plates dropped from his pocket.
>
> DOLABELLA
>
> Cleopatra—
>
> CLEOPATRA
>
> Think you there was, or might be, such a man
> As this I dream of?
>
> DOLABELLA
>
> Gentle madam, no.
>
> CLEOPATRA
>
> You lie, up to the hearing of the gods.
> But if there be, or ever were one such,
> It's past the size of dreaming.

When Caesar traps her, his cold vision prevails again; he catches her trying to filch some of the loot, and the game between the General and the Queen looks no better than the old, sordid wrangle between the invading soldier and the native whore. But Cleopatra secures the asp in spite of Caesar's vigilance, and as she applies it the inspiration of her love returns in all its vastness:

> Give me my robe, put on my crown, I have
> Immortal longings in me.

At that moment the love of Antony and Cleopatra seems to stand for mortal life itself, which warms its world with feeling, and fondly longs to be immortal.

As for Caesar, his appetite for power is appeased, first by the death of Antony (scene 1) and then by the death of Cleopatra. He is free at last to say "what he feels, not what he ought to say." He expresses generous and disinterested grief in the music that ends the play:

> No grave upon the earth shall clip in it
> A pair so famous. High events as these
> Strike those that make them; and their story is
> No less in pity than his glory which
> Brought them to be lamented.

In the course of this last act many of the painful discords, or insoluble paradoxes, in the lovers' passion, are resolved. Cleopatra can say with triumph, even after her life of whoring, "Husband, I come," and we assent. Caesar can welcome Antony back to the fold as a Roman after all; and in his phrase, "no less in pity than his glory," we feel that Rome and Egypt, war and love, reason and passion, are transcended and harmonized. But it takes death to make these "odds all even," and we remember the love of Antony and Cleopatra as we saw it in so many different lights, in the midst of life: as an ultimate mystery.

Antony and Cleopatra has baffled many modern producers, and now the most accomplished theater artists are afraid of it. They have reason to be; not that it is unplayable, for it is theater poetry of the most assured mastery, but because it requires more than a good director and a few good actors. It would require a highly trained ensemble to perform adequately all its subtle variations of tone and rhythm, and it would require an audience accustomed to poetry, for it to succeed. Let us hope that a theater of this kind will develop in our time. Meanwhile we can read the play, and allow the verse to build the ideal production in our imaginations.

TIMON OF ATHENS

The legendary figure of Timon, hater of all mankind, fascinated Shakespeare's contemporaries, and misanthropy has lost none of its appeal in our time. But the play as it has come down to us is puzzling, and many readers find it disappointing. It was not performed in Shakespeare's lifetime; it was left to a few famous actors to play the title role in adaptations of the play. It was not printed until 1623; the date of its composition is uncertain; and the text is so unsatisfactory that scholars have conjectured (plausibly, I think) that it was never finished. Yet the text we have is essentially Shakespeare's, and the question is, what did he mean by it, or (if it is unfinished) what was he planning to make of it?

Critics do not agree about how we are to take the play: is it comedy or tragedy? Is it consistent at all? We cannot be sure, if the text is corrupt or unfinished, what Shakespeare's intentions were. We can, however, consider his use of the Timon stories he inherited, and we can see how he handled certain themes, which are important in the rest of his work, in relation to his misanthropic hero.

The Timon legend was often recounted in Shakespeare's time. It appears briefly in North's translation of Plutarch, one of Shakespeare's favorite sources, in the *Lives* of Antony and Alcibiades. Lucian's witty dialogue, *Timon the Misanthrope,* written in Greek in the second century A.D., was available in Latin, French, and Italian translations, and Shakespeare must have known one of these, for his play owes a great deal to Lucian. There is an older Timon play, written at Oxford and also relying heavily on Lucian, that Shakespeare may or may not have known. In Painter's *Palace of Pleasure* it appears under the title, "Of the straunge and beastlie nature of Timon of Athens, enemie to all mankinde, with his death, buriall, and Epitaphe." Timon is usually presented as a marvelous monster, rather than a really tragic figure; and the sophisticated moralist Lucian treats his case very lightly indeed.

The plot of Shakespeare's play (except, perhaps, for Timon's part in Acts IV and V) seems to be inspired by Lucian: it has the ironic simplicity of classical comedy. It starts with Timon dispensing lavish gifts and hospitality to the Athenians, who crowd in with shameless flatteries to get what they can. Timon's steward, Flavius, tries to tell him that he is spending more than he has, and the cynic philosopher Apemantus tries to show him the hypocrisy of the Athenians. But Timon refuses to listen until one of his creditors, a Senator, calls in his loan, and so starts a disastrous run on Timon's vanishing resources. He finds that no one will help him, and the procession of Athenians beats a hasty retreat. His friend, the soldier Alcibiades, quarrels with Athens at about the same time, and they both curse the town for its greed and treachery and leave it, as they think, forever. Timon is now the full-fledged misanthrope, but as he curses all humanity on his empty beach and digs for roots to live on, he finds gold, and the Athenians instantly march back to him with flatteries more fulsome than before. We feel that that sordid game might go on forever in the same farcical form if it were not for Alcibiades, who chastens the Athenians with his avenging army, and makes them promise to do better. Alcibiades plays the part of the deus ex machina, who is often required to wind up the plot of classical comedies. But Timon dies, perhaps of a broken heart, and our final impression of his romantically bleak tomb washed forever by the sea, is not the traditional happy ending of comedy.

There are many problems of style and structure in this play, but there can be no doubt of its central motive. Everyone's motive is defined (in various different ways) by "gold," the only value recognized in Athens, and the point at issue in the quarrels between Timon and Athens, and between Alcibiades and Athens. Moreover "gold" in *Timon* —in contrast to "gold" in *The Merchant of Venice*—has only one simple meaning: money. In *The Merchant* Shakespeare exploits the sensuous qualities of gold, and makes it a symbol of a whole scale of values. It is only money for the merchants and usurers of the Rialto, but for Jessica and her Lorenzo it is associated with the glamour of love in golden Venice, and at last, in Belmont, it glitters in the night sky like the celestial harmony of charity itself. But in *Timon* there are no lovers, and no Portia to rescue us from the money-seekers. It has often been remarked that the language of the play, especially in the first three acts, lacks the sensuous richness and poetic resonance that we associate with Shakespeare. But such language is appropriate enough as an expression of the abstract money-motive, and it fits the simple mechanism of the plot: farcical if we consider the transparent intrigues of the Athenians, brutal if we consider the effect on Timon.

Shakespeare's treatment of setting and characterization in the first three acts also suggests this style. Athens is not the city of Pericles or of Plato, but the commercial city of any time and place: the scene of neoclassic comedy from Menander through the Latins and Italians to Shakespeare's contemporary, Ben Jonson. The Senators, merchants, and variegated hangers-on are not to be taken seriously as "real" people; they are rather caricatures of standard types like the masks of the commedia dell'arte. Good actors could play them with imagination and variety in such sequences as that of the three creditors in the first three scenes of Act III. But the point is always that their motives are identical—money—however different their hypocritical stratagems may be. And the farcical effect depends largely upon the mechanical figures of the plot: the procession of unctuous money-seekers descending upon Timon, and hastily departing when his money is gone; the same maneuver repeated, like clockwork, when he offers them his false banquet at the end of Act III, and again, more absurdly still, when he finds gold on the beach. Comedy of this kind is most effective in the theater, and because the play is so seldom staged we tend to underestimate its farcical verve.

The disillusioned laughter of neoclassic comedy, which assumes that all the world is venal, is, however, not the whole point, even in the first three acts. Flavius, Apemantus, Alcibiades, and the Strangers who watch Timon's cruel ruin, are detached from the Athenians' intrigues, and they serve to remind us that the money-motive is not necessarily all of life. And in the very first scene the Poet and the Painter discuss the Allegory of Fortune which applies exactly to this situation. Men work and connive for wealth, the Poet says, but the goddess Fortune, throned on a high hill, gives it or takes it away according to her whim. Timon has been raised high by Fortune, and the Athenians are clinging to him; but Fortune will surely drop him again, and then the Athenians, being in love not with him but with his money, will let him fall. This parable places Athens in the moral scheme of Shakespeare's tradition, and shows us that we are not to take it as the world, but as the particular man-made hell of getting and spending.

Shakespeare's audience would have known this parable in narratives and in "a thousand moral paintings," as the Painter says, and the philosophy behind it was a very ancient piece of traditional wisdom. Lucian presents it in his dialogue when Plutus (who signifies Gold) complains that the spendthrift Timon has treated him as badly as the misers: "My beau ideal," he says, "is the man who steers a middle course." Timon and the Athenians have opposite forms of the same vice: both have a disproportionate notion of gold, which in the last analysis is not theirs but Fortune's to command. Dante sees the avaricious and the prodigal in the same circle of hell, and learns that on earth their endless game is presided over by Fortuna, whose unpredictable intervention prevents any man, or city, or country from winning the money-game permanently.

Timon's disinterested friends see clearly that he is absurdly caught with the greedy Athenians, but they love him still. Flavius regards his irresponsible spending as a "noble" failing, and Alcibiades seems to feel, in Timon, a kind of magnanimity like his own. The story of Alcibiades looks like a typical Shakespearean sub-plot, but it is not handled with his usual skill. In Act III, scene 5, Alcibiades quarrels with the Senators about a "man"—never named—whom they have condemned to death, forgetting his heroic defense of their city. One has the impression, on a first reading, that the man is Timon; and when Alcibiades departs, cursing Athens for its hypocritical greed, he sounds too exactly like Timon. This is one of the parts of the play which is most awkward and confusing. It seems to need reworking; but we can see that Alcibiades was needed in the play. He has to conclude the intrigue at the end, and in Act III he serves, like Flavius, to show Timon (fatuous though he may be in thinking that his money buys true love) as honest enough to suffer. So we are prepared for his sudden conversion from general love of humanity to an equally general but more deeply felt hatred of the entire race.

In spite of this preparation, most critics feel that the turning point in the play and in Timon's character is not successfully handled. The plot, as I have pointed out, is coherent enough in the vein of sardonic comedy, but Timon himself has no heart for the game. His big tirades in Acts IV and V seem to express feelings too deep or too violent for the rest of the play, and their verse is supposed to be more "Shakespearean" than anything in the first three acts. It is often said that the play falls into two quite different parts, the last two acts being dominated by Timon in his misanthropic rage.

Several themes which are characteristic of Shakespeare's tragic poetry occur in Timon's tirades, but I do not think the total effect is "tragic" as Shakespeare's greatest plays teach us to understand the word. In Act IV, scene 1, "Without the wall of Athens," he cries,

Degrees, observances, customs, and laws,
Decline to your confounding contraries,
And yet confusion live.

This is Shakespeare's recipe for social anarchy, and one can find it, in various forms, just after the catastrophe in several of his tragedies. But Timon goes on to invoke all the other miseries he can think of, including sciatica for the reverend Senators, and then adds, for good measure,

And grant, as Timon grows, his hate may grow
To the whole race of mankind, high and low.
Amen.

Perhaps Shakespeare's audience would have been pleasurably shocked by this impious prayer, but Timon's multiplication of curses seems to me too helpless and too self-indulgent for a tragic, or even serious, effect. He often sees humans as sinister animals, "the black toad, and adder blue," and this has been likened to Lear's use of animal imagery. But Lear's visions express his own intimate remorse, and so move us to pity and terror, while Timon's, inspired by a kind of wholesale anger, are not touching in that way. We may marvel at his inspired hatred, but we do not identify ourselves with him. The appeal of his outbursts is like that of the arias of the cursing Queens in *Richard III:* overdone, but exhilarating: a letting-go which can be fun for both actor and audience.

There are, however, a number of carefully placed passages in Acts IV and V which are certainly intended to show Timon, not as the legendary prodigy of hatred, but as a suffering man. The faithful Flavius (Act IV, scene 2) gives us the clue:

Poor honest lord, brought low by his own heart,
Undone by goodness . . .

Alas, kind lord,
He's flung in rage from this ingrateful seat
Of monstrous friends.

And Timon himself, melted by Flavius' honest feeling, makes him the one exception to his universal hatred. When Apemantus visits him (Act IV, scene 3) their encounter is mostly in the style of high farce, as one might call it, a cursing-match between the two champion misanthropists. But Apemantus thoroughly enjoys himself, while Timon is wounded, and expresses a longing for death in seductive poetry:

I am sick of this false world, and will love naught
But even the mere necessities upon't.

> Then Timon presently prepare thy grave.
> Lie where the light foam of the sea may beat
> Thy gravestone daily.

Timon does not ever learn to understand the moral meaning of his own plight, for he thinks that gold is the root of *all* evil:

> [*To the gold.*] O thou sweet king-killer, and dear divorce
> 'Twixt natural son and sire, thou bright defiler
> Of Hymen's purest bed . . .

But his disgust with the money-seeking humanity he knows is genuine, and so is his death-wish. He expresses it in a famous melody (Act V, scene 1) just before his final exit:

> Come not to me again, but say to Athens,
> Timon hath made his everlasting mansion
> Upon the beached verge of the salt flood,
> Who once a day with his embossed froth
> The turbulent surge shall cover; thither come,
> And let my gravestone be your oracle.

One remembers this passage when his Epitaph—famous since antiquity—is quoted at the very end of the play.

Timon's plight is presented in these last two acts in two complementary perspectives, one comic and one pathetic. When he thinks about the Athenians, or is forced to deal with their tireless greed once more, he is overcome with helpless rage, and caught against his will in the classically laughable chase after money. He never learns enough to extricate himself from that; but when Flavius dissolves his anger, or he turns away from Athens, finding nothing but "nothing"—the void of death—to comfort him, he moves our pity. It is a strange and rather wry combination of feelings, but I think it possible that a fine actor, who understood Timon's rhythm as he turns and twists, might make the whole sequence understandable and effective in the theater. On this reading it would appear that Shakespeare does not take Timon's total misanthropy too seriously. He sees what fun it can be to damn the race; but at the same time accounts for Timon's hatred psychologically, as the result of placing a man of his type in greedy and cynical Athens.

From this point of view, the comparison of Timon to Othello is revealing. They are both very simple souls, "noble," but too innocent to understand themselves or their supposed friends. Timon is very much alone in money-worshipping Athens, as Othello is in Iago's Venice of ducats, money-bags, goats, and monkeys. Both are made vulnerable by their love, Othello's for Desdemona, Timon's for mankind; and neither can continue to love what seems to them to have any imperfection. When Othello loses faith in Desdemona, he must think her utterly foul, and when Timon loses faith in Athens' brotherly love, he must see all men as despicable. In both cases the action starts in the city, but is removed when it reaches its greatest intensity, as though the trivial human scene could not contain such passion. In both cases the commercial city is the counterpart of the heroes' large-spirited simplicity, enabling us to understand their mistakes and the bleakness of their ultimate fates.

Othello, of course, is a great tragedy, unified poetically and powerful in its total effect, while *Timon,* as we have seen, is comic and pathetic. Othello does love Desdemona, however blindly, and Iago intimately hates him, and these personal relations, in the moral void of Cyprus, can reach the ultimate intensity. Poor Timon, on the other hand, like some rather futile rich philanthropist in our time, has nothing more tangible to love or hate than humanity in general; hence the generalized, abstract quality of so much of the play, like that of classical comedy or the moralizing fable.

I do not think it is possible to see *Timon* as completely consistent. There are too many loose ends in it, too many elements which, by Shakespeare's usual standard, are thin and underdeveloped. But it is at the very least a significant sketch from his workshop. And a skilled performance might, I think, make an absorbing evening in the theater.

CORIOLANUS

Coriolanus, written about 1608, was probably the last of Shakespeare's tragedies. Its great power has been very generally recognized, but it has not been as popular as the other tragedies. Perhaps it is too cold and objective for a popular audience; but in the last thirty years it has been produced more and more frequently, for its theme, that of a gloomy military and political "strong man" against a background of war and revolution, is one that we can recognize all too easily. It is the closest of all Shakespeare's plays to our own public issues. When it was produced at the Comédie Française about 1932 there were riots between the partisans of the Right and the partisans of the Left.

Shakespeare took the story directly from North's famous translation of Plutarch's *Lives.* The real Coriolanus was a Roman general of the fifth century B.C., when Rome was a small city-state. Plutarch, writing in Greek more than five hundred years later, was less interested in that moment of history than he was in the permanent moral and political significance of Coriolanus' career. Shakespeare follows Plutarch in all essentials, and he even uses the language of North's translation in a few passages, with little change. But he sees more deeply than Plutarch into the motives of the main characters, and he sees the political dissensions of classical Rome from the point of view of Christian Europe, and in the light of his own lifelong meditations on politics.

The first long, tumultuous scene of the play introduces all the elements that are struggling to control Rome. The Citizens are starving and in revolt against the Patricians and the Senate, which (they believe) is holding the grain they must have to live on at too high a price. For this they blame Martius—who has not yet earned the title "Coriolanus"—for he is known to scorn the common people. Menenius, the only Patrician the Citizens trust, tries to reason with them, and tells them the humorous "parable of the belly"; but Martius himself arrives to revile the Citizens and upset Menenius' efforts for peace. He angrily reports that the Senate has granted the people two Tribunes, Sicinius and Brutus, to defend their interests, and predicts that this will mean the end of all order in Rome. At this heated moment a Messenger and then a delegation of Senators and Generals, with the two Tribunes, comes to Martius to tell him that the Volscians are in arms under Martius' old enemy, Aufidius; and they ask him to head the Roman forces. Martius is delighted; he looks forward eagerly to another fight with Aufidius; and now all Rome turns from its domestic squabbles to foreign war. The Tribunes, left alone onstage at the end of the scene, ruefully sum up the situation: as long as Rome is at war there will be no possibility of curbing Martius, that irresistible military hero.

Shakespeare placed wise old Menenius at the center of this angry scene in order to reveal, through his eyes, its significance for us in the audience. Menenius is the only character in the play with a disinterested love of Rome and a balanced vision of what the life of the community should be. In his parable of the belly and the members, the state is compared to an organism. Each element in the common life—productive workers, governing officials, soldiers—has its natural function which, like that of a bodily organ, serves the whole and, in turn, depends upon the whole. This conception of the ideal community was first explored in depth in the political philosophies of Plato and Aristotle; Shakespeare, like Plutarch, believed in its wisdom, for he presents it in many metaphors in his histories and his other tragedies. But one element, which Shakespeare seems to have thought essential, is missing in Menenius' philosophy: the figure of the king. Shakespeare's generation thought they had learned the hard way—through the long agony of the Wars of the Roses—that the crown was necessary to secure permanent order. The paternal figure of the king, with its religious sanction, its ultimate authority, its moral and familial meanings, was supposed to be above the squabbles between strong nobles, and the endless dissensions between the haves and the have-nots; a concrete symbol of the common life which might command the loyalty of all men. Menenius has no such visible figure to appeal to; nothing that incarnates the conception of the community. His wisdom, though "true," is too abstract, even in his parable, for the starving citizens, or the proud and hasty Martius, or the timid Senate, or the cynical Tribunes, to take seriously. The motive of the whole play—to control Rome for one's own interest—is clear in this first scene. It moves to the inevitable catastrophe in the same bleak, unchanging light. The style of *Coriolanus* reminds one of such clear-eyed and relentless historians of the classical world as Thucydides.

Coriolanus (as I shall call him henceforth) is the center of trouble, and the most radical example of Roman hardness. The next two scenes are devoted respectively to Aufidius and Volumnia, both of whom are important to Coriolanus and therefore to the unfolding story. In scene 2 Aufidius eagerly prepares for war, and we learn that he, like Coriolanus, is obsessed with their personal feud. In scene 3 Volumnia and Virgilia talk of Coriolanus, who is away at war. "Private faces in public places," Mr. W. H. Auden has written, "Are wiser and nicer/ Than public faces in private places." Poor Virgilia has only a private face, that of the worried wife, while Volumnia brings her grim public face, that of the ambitious Roman matron, into the home. A widow, she has made her son into an instrument of Roman power, and all her life is in him.

After this scene the many-sided struggle for Rome moves inevitably to its climax and turning point: the banishment of Coriolanus (Act III, scene 3). These acts are filled with the high-pitched excitement of battle and public controversy, but they have no passages of lyric meditation, no expressions of personal feeling, such as enrich the other tragedies. The focus of interest is upon public issues, the appeal is to the mind rather than the feelings. If one is to understand the fascination and the power of this part of the play, one must notice how objectively each element in Rome's public life is presented.

We have seen that everything starts with the starving and angry Citizens. Several of them are hasty and prejudiced; the Second Citizen tries very hard to be just; all are bewildered, and they cannot agree. When we meet them again as individuals as they try to talk to Coriolanus in his "gown of humility," in Act II, scene 3, they show the same variations in character and the same pathetic uncertainty. They are such citizens as we are, when we try to estimate our own leaders and their policies. But Rome is at a point of crisis, and we soon see that under the pressure of fear and anger the Citizens may lose all individual judgment and fuse into a passionate mob. The distinction between the Citizens as men, as individuals, and the "many-headed monster" is crucial, for the mob is felt throughout the play as a perpetual danger, and it appears in several forms. The Tribunes explain (at the end of Act II, scene 1) that Coriolanus has turned Rome into an adoring mob as he returns from war, the savior of Rome, the conquering hero. The Tribunes understand how to make a mob, and they need its blind power in their struggle with Coriolanus. In Act III, scene 3, they plan with the Aediles to use Coriolanus' ready anger to generate the mob passion, and then turn it against him. We then see how skillfully they stage the mob-scene of his banishment. It is like mob-scenes in German or Russian theater, or one of Hitler's great rallies in the period when he was building the Nazi crowd-passion.

Shakespeare shows why the office of Tribune was established in the first place: it was badly needed to safeguard the popular interest. Much of the Tribunes' oratory against Coriolanus is justified; but they never share Menenius' vision of the whole community. And because their own power depends upon the mob they inevitably become cynical demagogues, a type that always appears in times of social disorder.

The Patricians, Senators, and Generals seem almost as confused as the Citizens; certainly their policies are as "inconstant." They grant the people their Tribunes, when the mob frightens them, but when Aufidius frightens them they want Coriolanus.

Coriolanus alone is completely consistent until he collides with the Tribunes' mob, and is banished. But his vision of Rome is farthest of all from Menenius' wisdom: he wants it ruled as a military commander rules his forces in battle: without regard for the diversity of human functions and needs in a real community. When the mob, under the Tribunes' influence, revokes his election as Consul (Act III, scene 1) he gives a scornful and very strong picture of democratic vacillations:

This double worship,
Where one part does disdain with cause, the other
Insult without all reason; where gentry, title, wisdom,
Cannot conclude but by the yea and no
Of general ignorance, it must omit
Real necessities, and give way the while
To unstable slightness. Purpose so barred, it follows,
Nothing is done to purpose. Therefore beseech you,
. . .
at once pluck out
The multitudinous tongue, let them not lick
The sweet which is their poison.

We can, I think, easily feel the force of Coriolanus' strictures, for we know how clumsy and uncertain of purpose a democratic community, with its many tongues, may be. But it is clear that Coriolanus, with his romantic integrity, his gloomy pride, speaks only for himself—not even for a part of society, like the Tribunes or the Senators.

This play has been interpreted as a Fascist tract, and also as an anti-Fascist tract, but a careful reading of the first three acts shows that it is neither. Shakespeare shows that each partisan has a valid point which he can present with logic and rhetorical power, but without regard to other points of view. Menenius' voice of wisdom is lost in the angry yelling.

With the banishment of Coriolanus at the end of Act III, the fighting pauses, and Act IV shows that unstable peace as it looks in Rome, in Corioles, and between the two cities. It is there that the Roman traitor, Nicanor, meets the Volscian spy, Adrian (scene 3); their cynical conversation provides a humorous image of the prevailing mood. With Rome discredited and divided there is little left for anyone to be loyal to, and in that atmosphere of mistrust everyone is quietly trying to look out for himself.

It is in Corioles (scenes 4 and 5), where Coriolanus has gone to offer Aufidius his services against Rome, that the theme of this act is most fully explored. Coriolanus puts it with unrelieved clarity (scene 4):

O world, thy slippery turns! Friends now fast sworn,
Whose double bosoms seems to wear one heart,
Whose hours, whose bed, whose meal, and exercise,
Are still together; who twin, as 'twere, in love
Unseparable, shall within this hour,

On a dissension of a doit, break out
In bitterest enmity. So fellest foes,
Whose passions and whose plots have broke their sleep
To take the one the other, by some chance,
Some trick not worth an egg, shall grow dear friends
And interjoin their issues. So with me.

He and Aufidius then "interjoin their issues" (scene 5). This is a love scene, but the "love" in it, separated as it is from both reason and all loyalty, is as destructive as hate—only another form, in fact, of the same gloomy passion.

Shakespeare makes the momentary and faithless love of Coriolanus and Aufidius look both dreary and laughable, by reflecting it in the comments of the Servants who wait on them at their banquet. The Servants conclude their observations with rejoicing at the prospect of war, which, as they say, makes men need each other more than they do in peace. The Servants do not see the implications of their remarks—that is part of the deep irony of the whole scene—but their observations are sharp. We in the audience may see that the Servants, taking their cue from Coriolanus and Aufidius, are yielding to the passion of war, with its illusory sense of unity and common purpose, just as the Roman citizens did when they abandoned their own individual reason and fused into a mob.

By the end of the act we learn that Coriolanus is at the head of a conquering Volscian army, and the fate of Rome again depends upon him. Act V answers the question, what will he do with the power to destroy his country and family, now that he has it? We learn in scene 1 that he has refused to listen to his old comrade-in-arms, Cominius; in scene 2 we see how he humiliates good old Menenius, holding fast to his destructive drive. But in scene 3 a procession of women in mourning, led by Volumnia, Virgilia, and his young son, comes to him where he sits in glum conference with Aufidius and the Volscian Generals. Their familiar faces deflate his passion of hatred, and reason returns. In its sad light he sees that he has been playing an unnatural and impossible role, even as he tries to hold on to it by sheer willpower:

I melt, and am not
Of stronger earth than others. My mother bows,
As if Olympus to a molehill should
In supplication nod; and my young boy
Hath an aspect of intercession, which
Great nature cries, deny not. Let the Volsces
Plough Rome and harrow Italy! I'll never

Be such a gosling to obey instinct; but stand,
As if a man were author of himself,
And knew no other kin.

That last phrase defines the "part" which he has "forgot." He had tried in his whole career to deny the relationships of husband and wife, parent and child, which (in Shakespeare's often-expressed view) are the basis both of individual well-being and of the healthy community, bound together by loyalty. For the rest of the play he will try to recognize these realities of the human situation. At this moment he has a prophetic glimpse of what it will cost him to lose the role of "Coriolanus":

O my mother, mother! O!
You have won a happy victory to Rome,
But for your son, believe it, O believe it,
Most dangerously you have with him prevailed,
If not most mortal to him.

Aufidius, coldly watching, sees it too.

Volumnia, perhaps, does not realize how completely her son's life is identified with the role she had cast him for. But she has a grotesque and frightening image of her relation to him:

Thou hast never in thy life
Showed thy dear mother any courtesy,
When she, poor hen, fond of no second brood,
Has clucked thee to the wars, and safely home,
Loaden with honour.

Now she has clucked him home for the last time; but we can only guess what that victory means to her, for she says nothing as her black-robed procession moves off. In scenes 4 and 5 we get the rejoicing of the Romans whom she has reprieved: "Ne'er through an arch so hurried the blown tide/ As the recomforted through the gates." It is the last appearance of the inconstant mob, now hanging tearfully on Volumnia's skirts. But she keeps silence as her procession majestically crosses the stage.

The final scene, in Corioles, shows the end of Coriolanus the public figure, and also of Martius the suffering human being. Aufidius, inciting his soldiers to murder Coriolanus, points with savage triumph to the lost boy under the grim conqueror:

at his nurse's tears
He whined and roared away your victory,

That pages blushed at him, and men of heart
Looked wond'ring each at others.

CORIOLANUS

Hear'st thou, Mars?

AUFIDIUS

Name not the god, thou boy of tears.

Coriolanus, seeing the end, evokes the warrior-image as though it were already history or legend:

Cut me to pieces Volsces; men and lads,
Stain all your edges on me. Boy! False hound!
If you have writ your annals true, 'tis there,
That like an eagle in a dovecote I
Fluttered your Volscians in Corioles.
Alone I did it, boy!

It is at this point that we most deeply feel Coriolanus' terrible loneliness. Aufidius expresses the feeling of the audience when, having satisfied his ferocity by stepping on the corpse, he speaks the dirge:

My rage is gone,
And I am struck with sorrow. Take him up.
Help three a th' chiefest soldiers, I'll be one.
Beat thou the drum that it speak mournfully,
Trail your steel pikes. Though in this city he
Hath widowed and unchilded many a one,
Which to this hour bewail the injury,
Yet shall he have a noble memory.
Assist.

During most of the play we have watched with little sympathy as the contestants for control of Rome have repressed their feelings (except "rage") as one must in a power battle. We in the audience have been seeing in the cold light of reason, with Menenius, that none of them has the vision to rule Rome properly, logical though they may be on their narrow premises, and eloquent in their public orations. But now as the action ends, the deeper insights and emotions come to the surface, and we get the release of pity, which, as Joyce puts it, joins us with the human sufferer.

It has often been pointed out that Shakespeare had plenty of material in his own time and country for this play. In Essex he had an example of an impatient military hero with a dangerous appetite for power. There were corn riots in the Midlands about the time he wrote the play; and in his London (a city, by all accounts, very subject to rumor and therefore to popular unrest) he must have seen mobs form again and again. But the "world of the play" is not based (like his tragedies of monarchy) upon his own comparatively warm, intimate, monarchical England. It is based upon Plutarch's classical fable, and upon the large world of classical Rome as he saw it: the *Res Publica,* the "public thing" is seen as a rational but bleak and loveless power-structure. He thereby made a drama which speaks to our time even more, perhaps, than it did to his.

PART FOUR

1608–1616

The Final Retrospect: Faith and Make-Believe

Shakespeare's very last play, *Henry VIII,* was probably written on request, to celebrate the marriage of James I's daughter, Princess Elizabeth. It does not seem to emerge from Shakespeare's own interests, and like *The Merry Wives* and *Henry V* it is worth reading now mainly as an example of his perfect technical competence, which was at his command even when his usual inspiration was lacking. But the other four plays of the end of his career are very much his own. In them he plays over the themes that had held him all his life, but in the mood of the eve of his retirement, and with certain insights that came to him only at that late moment.

It is evident at once that *Pericles, Cymbeline, The Winter's Tale,* and *The Tempest* are sharply different in intention, and therefore in their dramaturgic style, from the masterpieces of Shakespeare's tragic period. Their stories, which always cover a whole generation instead of one brief, decisive crisis, are leisurely, episodic, and filled with frankly improbable situations, events, and fortunate coincidences. Their dramatis personae, though always easy to act, are as lightly characterized as the "good" or "bad" figures in fairy stories. These plays are rightly called "romances," and Shakespeare was probably influenced by the new vogue for such stories, for he was always responsive to the changing moods of the theater for which he wrote; but he certainly used the fashionable form for his own unique purposes. He fills it with the themes of his earlier comedies and tragedies, but sees all the familiar themes with the detachment of a man whose "every third thought shall be my grave," as Prospero puts it—when "death remembered should be like a mirror,/ Who tells us life's but breath, to trust it error," as Pericles says. In this rather ghostly frame of mind he does not take the struggles and complications of life very seriously: he is more interested in the peaceful visions which may (with luck) appear at the end. That is why these late romances are like the romantic comedies of his youth. Hippolyta's formula applies to their structure also: their lengthy plots are a tangle of "antique fables" and "fairy toys," but at the end something "of great constancy" appears. They differ from the early romances chiefly in covering a much longer span of time, which makes it possible for them to include, in their light, allusive way, many more of the perennial Shakespearean themes of innocence and experience, youth and age, love and rule.

In all of Shakespeare's serious drama the mysterious unfolding of time is recognized as an important and irreducible dimension of human experience; and, because it is mysterious, the only proper way to deal with it is by some sort of patient faith. In the English history plays, as I have mentioned, it is faith in the ultimate triumph of the Tudors that makes sense out of the endless battles and intrigues, and each of the history plays is felt as a moment in the temporal sequence of the "Tudor epic." In *Hamlet, Macbeth,* and *Lear* time is felt as "*the* time": i.e., a comparatively brief period created by the false or deluded monarch. The dramatist finds it significant because it opens frightening fissures in the symbolic structure of the body politic, and so "tries men's souls," revealing their virtues and vices. However, the tragic situation demands faith in what else time may bring, if the tragedy is to be ended and placed; and so these three tragedies, sharp and swift as they are, also appear against the background of history as faith makes it out. The histories and tragedies, in short, are defined and qualified by their moments in time, yet each one coincides with *one* time. But in these four late plays at least three quite different times are important: that of youthful innocence, that of evil or deluded experience, "the middle of the journey of life," and that unpredictable time near the end when the faith and hope of the early scene is restored in a new way, "the lost time found again," as Proust puts it.

Within this leisurely time-scheme Shakespeare can resume both the sanguine themes of his early romantic comedy and the tragic themes of his maturity, provided he plays them all over (as he does) very quickly and lightly. The basic theme of Shakespearean tragedy is treachery, and in these late plays it is treachery, or some milder form of faithlessness, that ends the time of innocence and brings experience of the world; a time of darkness, confusion, and painful conflict. Pericles is betrayed by the false King Antiochus, and again by Dionyza and Cleon. Cymbeline is betrayed by his second Queen, and her treachery darkens counsel in the whole realm. Leontes in *The Winter's Tale* makes sixteen bleak years for himself, his family, and his realm, when he groundlessly loses faith in his wife and acts faithlessly toward her. Prospero in *The Tempest* is betrayed by his brother, and that treachery nightmarishly reappears a generation later among the castaways on the magic isle. While the darkness produced by treachery prevails, no one can trust anyone else, or even "know himself": an effect which appears in all three monarchical tragedies just before the turning point. It appears also in the early romantic comedies, but in amusing ways: improbable disguises and far-fetched mistakes in identity, which are so often the basis of the comic plots. In these late plays the dark time when identity is lost is represented by separation, exile, and disguises even more improbable than those of the early comedies. We cannot take these intricate complications seriously in themselves, but in the fairy-story fables of these plays they stand well enough for "experience," the dark wood of the middle of the journey.

The counterpart of treachery is, of course, fidelity. In Shakespeare's histories and tragedies it is fidelity to the king, "figure of God's majesty"; in his romantic comedies, it is fidelity to a beautiful mistress, a "figure," or earthly analogue (if properly interpreted) of love itself. These are the two themes of his sanguine youth, as I have pointed out; in the late plays they are combined: and both symbols of rightly oriented faith are important. They are glimpsed in the time of innocence, lost to sight in the confused time of experience of the world, and reappear, near the end, to produce those final recognitions which correspond to the happy endings of the romantic comedies. In these plays, however, the finales are deeper in feeling, more resonant with meaning, and more ghostly than they are in the early comedies, since they represent a *return* of hope and innocence when those youthful modes of being are both rarer and more valuable. It is primarily a daughter, lost and now found again, rather than wife or mistress (except in *The Winter's Tale*), who is the bearer of this last revelation. Most critics, even when they object to the absurd plots of the late plays, agree that their final recognition scenes are filled with poetry of a kind unique in Shakespeare's work, but as beautiful in its own strange way as any he ever wrote.

The same sequence from innocence, to experience, to innocence regained underlies all four late plays. It resembles ancient parabolic representations of the course of human life, as a number of students of Shakespeare have pointed out in recent years: initiation ceremonies, rites of passage, myths of the religious quests and ordeals of "culture heroes"; Dante's *Purgatory*, in which so many versions of this "timeless theme" (as Colin Still called it) are combined. We do not know where Shakespeare got it; it is safest to say that it simply emerged from his own experience of life, of books, and of art. In any case, one can see that this root-parable of our life in time, neither comedy nor tragedy in itself, but with elements of both, was the predestined form that Shakespeare's detached meditations on the stages of his age and youth had to take.

Because of his detachment in this phase, and his awareness of the changes that time inevitably brings, Shakespeare is much more interested in faith as the clue to human motivation than he is in the conscious purposes of his characters. He shows us in these plays how in the course of a generation a man's rationalized purposes change, while he is driven by needs so basic that he himself does not understand them, and by a faith so deep that it resembles instinctive "animal faith" in life itself. Pericles expresses such a faith at the innocent outset of his career, as he prepares to obey his desire for Antiochus' dangerous daughter: "Nor ask advice of any other thought/ But faithfulness and courage," he says. After experience has deprived him of some of his innocence he realizes that his faith, more fearful but still courageous, must be faith in time itself:

> . . . I see that Time's the king of men,
> He's both their parent and he is their grave,
> And gives them what he will, not what they crave.

His faith in time is confirmed years later, and at last made visible in the form of his daughter, now miraculously re-found, with *her* youthful faith and hope; and he greets that vision with passionate amazement:

> Give me a gash, put me to present pain;
> Lest this great sea of joys rushing upon me
> O'erbear the shores of my mortality,
> And drown me with their sweetness.

His daughter is not only his own faith made visible for the first time, but a figure of faith itself, beyond his mortality.

Cymbeline and *The Winter's Tale* also present human action as determined primarily by a faith which must outlast "the masquerades which time resumes" in the course of a whole generation, before it is at last answered, and so clarified, in the new life of the new generation. There can be no doubt, I think, that Shakespeare knew just what he was doing when he turned his attention, in these late plays, to a lifetime's faith. He might have put it (following the medieval scheme) that he was now interested in the allegorical rather than the tropological meaning of the old stories he used. He must have known, in Hamlet's terms, that he was showing "the age and body of the time," rather than "virtue her own feature"; and in the language of his inherited theology he might have said that the unpredictable grace of God now seemed much more important to him than the efforts of the rational moral will. And it must have been in full technical awareness that he adjusted his dramaturgy to imitate action in this perspective—de-emphasizing individual characterization, relying upon long intricate narratives in his plot-making, and upon extended scenes of recognition and epiphany, with musical language, to conclude the stories. All of this requires a new attitude on the part of the showman, which the audiences must learn to share. Old Gower explains, at the beginning of *Pericles:*

> To sing a song that old was sung,
> From ashes ancient Gower is come,
> Assuming man's infirmities,
> To glad your ear, and please your eyes.
> It hath been sung at festivals,
> On ember-eves and holy-ales;
> And lords and ladies in their lives
> Have read it for restoratives.

Pericles must have faith in what time will bring; the showman-poet must have faith in the meaning of the improbable old tale he will retell, and we in the audience (like children listening to fairy stories) must *make* believe what we see onstage, if we are to get the intended pleasure, and the "restorative" effect at the end.

Shakespeare is playing with the suggestive analogies between faith and make-believe—or between life and the theater—in all four of the late romances, but especially in *The Tempest,* which is an epitome of its three predecessors. In *Pericles, Cymbeline,* and *The Winter's Tale* some dark instinctive faith of the protagonists carries us through the "mazes, forth-rights and meanders" of the plots to the final recognitions and epiphanies, where all is made clear; but *The Tempest* is *all* epiphany. Prospero's story is nearly done when the play begins; it only remains for him to bring to light the treacherous experiences of his past life for the old friends and enemies who are now magically in his power, and also for the still innocent Miranda and Ferdinand. By rehearsing, in the light of truth, the story of his generation, he evens old scores, provides what guidance he can, especially for the young, and so frees everyone, including himself, from the bonds of love and guilt that had tied them to each other and to life. But an important part of Prospero's final accounting is his very sophisticated apologia for the magic (that of his creator's theatrical imagination) whereby he holds his audience captive, until he dismantles its layers of make-believe at the end of the play.

I have pointed out in my remarks on *The Tempest,* below, that Prospero's control of Ariel represents Shakespeare's own control of his poetic imagination. As early as *A Midsummer Night's Dream* he had explained through Theseus and Hippolyta how the imagination alone, moved as it always is by emotion, is not to be taken seriously; but when subordinated to the responsible intentions of the poet who constructs the whole story it may lead to truth. That is what the images that Ariel creates in obedience to Prospero's plan do for the castaways on the magic isle. The storm that wets no one's garments; the pretty tune that leads Ferdinand to his love; the symbolic sights and sounds that show the stranded courtiers their true situation in the power of unseen Prospero, figure of God, are sensuously real in their own right, but, in their context, also signs of God's truth. The castaways, however, respond to the images that surround them according to their own habits and emotions, and if one pays close attention to their varied reactions one may learn to understand the manifold relations between character, the images of the imagination, and the reality which the human being continually seeks to apprehend or (for his own uncandid purposes) to distort or deny.

As the play draws to its end Prospero ceases to play the part of the magician, thereby freeing the castaways to act according to what they can see for themselves. And then the actor ceases to play the part of Prospero, thereby freeing us in the audience to see the whole dreamy evening's entertainment as the product of the showman's imagination. But (we are to suppose) if we have faithfully made believe it all, it has led us to what we may *really* believe. The dream-governed actions of the castaways accurately mirror human life, for according to Shakespeare's Aristotelian psychology all our knowledge and beliefs must start with what the senses offer, by way of the image-building power, to the mind. It is by way of the sensuously apprehended world that God speaks to us, as Dante is told in *Paradiso* IV:

> Needs must such speech address your faculty, which only from the sense-reported thing doth apprehend what it then proceedeth to make fit matter for the intellect.
>
> And therefore doth the Scripture condescend to your capacity, assigning foot and hand to God, with other meaning.
>
> (*Wicksteed translation*)

Prospero is a figure of the poet who created him, and the poet, if he is to discharge his function with full responsibility, should be, like the ruler of the state, a figure of the God who created *him,* and the world we see and hear around us. The poet endeavors to reflect God's world, both in its sensuous immediacy and variety and in the divine meanings it embodies; and that is what Shakespeare did all his life.

The Plays in Chronological Order

PERICLES

This play was written about 1607, the first of the final sequence that includes *Cymbeline, The Winter's Tale,* and *The Tempest.* It recounts the improbable story of Pericles' "painful adventures," which take the time of a whole generation and end joyfully when he finds his long-lost wife Thaisa and his daughter Marina, now a young woman. It is like the three other late plays, a "romance," a genre which had recently become popular in the theater; the Jacobean equivalent of our episodic and long-suffering radio and TV serials. This style is entirely unlike that of Shakespeare's maturity, and it is only in recent years that the late plays have been appreciated. *Pericles,* though popular in Shakespeare's time, has fared worse than the others, partly because the text is more than usually corrupt. But the lyric poets, notably T. S. Eliot and Professor Mark Van Doren, have rescued it for us, by calling attention to bits of strange and wonderful poetry which it contains, especially in the last three acts.

Shakespeare took the story, with little change, from the "Confessio Amantis" of John Gower, a contemporary of Chaucer, and from a prose version of the same story, "The Patterne of Painefull Adventures" by Laurence Twine, which was published in 1576. It is known in medieval Latin, and in French, Spanish, Italian, and English versions, and is thought to have been originally a Greek romance of Hellenistic times. Shakespeare prizes it for its very antiquity, as he tells us through the Chorus, Old Gower; and he carefully preserves the simple, fairy-tale manner of its telling.

Old Gower, who serves as narrator throughout, introduces the story (or "old song," as he puts it) in his old-fashioned eight-syllable rhyming couplets. It has given pleasure on many ember-eves, and moreover "lords and ladies in their lives/ Have read it for restoratives," i.e., to renew their morale. He explains the initial situation: Antiochus, King of Antioch, has an incestuous love affair with his daughter and endeavors to conceal and protect it by decreeing that any young man who wishes to woo the princess must either solve the riddle Antiochus proposes or forfeit his life: "So for her many a wight did die,/ As yon grim looks do testify." Scene 1, Act I, then shows us young Pericles as suitor, "inflamed with desire" for the young woman in whose beautiful face may be read "nothing but curious pleasures." Antiochus warns him of the risk, almost the certainty, of death, but he insists on hearing the riddle anyway, "For death remembered," he says, "should be like a mirror,/ Who tells us life's but breath, to trust it error." He professes the sturdy hopefulness that will carry him through the vicissitudes of the next twenty years: "Nor ask advice of any other thought/ But faithfulness and courage." But the moment he hears the riddle he needs all his virtue. He realizes that it means the incest of his beloved with her father; his desire suddenly cools, and he seizes the first chance to flee the court. Antiochus sees that Pericles has guessed right, and sends Thaliard after him to kill him. So begins the long series of his painful adventures.

If we are to take the old romance in the proper spirit, we must not demand probability, or any sort of realistic documentation, any more than one does when watching a ballet; and we must identify ourselves with Pericles as uncritically as a child might with the hero of a fairy tale. We must last out his trials as he does, never trusting completely to what life offers at the moment, but sustained by some sort of faith in what fate, or the gods, ultimately have in store: for old Gower, presiding over the evening's entertainment, has assured us that the story has "restorative" properties for its hearers, as Pericles' painful adventures ultimately prove to have for him. I do not know whether Shakespeare was responsible for all of the language of this opening sequence, but certain it is that it clearly establishes both the tone and the action of the play to follow. And the analogies between Pericles' pious motive in life and old Gower's in singing his song are characteristic of Shakespeare, especially toward the contemplative end of his life when he felt that poetry and remembered life were very close together.

In making the plot of the play Shakespeare followed the straightforward chronological order of Gower's and Twine's narratives. Acts I and II show how Pericles recovers from Antiochus' deathly daughter and finds his true wife at Pentapolis. He flees from Antioch to his own Tyre, and then on to Tharsus, where he relieves a famine with a gift of grain, and earns the gratitude of the people and their rulers, Cleon and

Dionyza. At Tharsus, however, he learns in a letter from home that Thaliard is still pursuing him, and he again flees by sea. A storm sinks his ship, but he is cast ashore at Pentapolis. There he is rescued by honest fishermen, who take him to the good King Simonides. A tourney is being held at court for the suitors of the King's daughter, and Pericles enters it as a "mean knight" whose crest is a withered branch green at the top, with the motto in *hoc spe vivo,* "in this hope I live." He wins the tourney, and soon marries the Princess Thaisa with Simonides' enthusiastic blessing (Act II, scene 5). His happiness momentarily seems complete when he learns (Chorus, Act III) that Antiochus and his daughter have been burned up by a bolt from heaven, and his life is therefore in no further danger from that quarter.

Shakespeare's authorship of these first two acts is questioned, as I have said, and it must be admitted that most of the language is pedestrian and marred in a number of places by clumsiness of syntax or versification. But Pericles' motive, formed by his faith, is still clearly the center, and from time to time we are explicitly reminded of it. His crest indicates it in the sign-language of a certain kind of allegory. And when, destitute and just rescued from the sea, he looks at the brilliant Simonides (Act II, scene 3), he gets a rich sense of the course of his life:

> Yon King's to me like to my father's picture,
> Which tells me in that glory once he was.

His father, I take it, is now in the ultimate darkness of death, and Pericles himself is (like Edgar in the first four acts of *Lear*) obscured by his anonymity and poverty; but rewarded with vision:

> Where now his son like a glowworm in the night,
> The which hath fire in darkness, none in light.
> Whereby I see that Time's the king of men,
> He's both their parent, and he is their grave,
> And gives them what he will, not what they crave.

The language is rather stiff, and Pericles' rhymes remind us of old Gower, but the complex interplay of the figures—the dead king-father and the live one; darkness and light; and Time as the all-powerful sire who lightens and darkens us with life and death, and to whom we owe filial faith and loyalty—strikes me as Shakespearean. It is a resonant formulation of the patient faith that gives the play its basic orientation.

With the beginning of Act III, Shakespeare's authorship is more evident in the language, but the naive, episodic plot continues to unroll as before. Pericles and his pregnant wife, at sea on their way back to Tyre, are caught in a storm, and Thaisa seems to die in giving birth to her daughter, whom Pericles names Marina. Thaisa is buried at sea in a sealed casket, but is washed ashore near Ephesus, and there Cerimon, a physician with quasi-magic powers, brings her back to life. Pericles continues to Tharsus, where he leaves the infant Marina to be cared for by his supposed friends, Cleon and Dionyza, and then returns to his kingdom of Tyre. When this eventful act ends, Thaisa is at Ephesus, in a temple, a votaress of the goddess Diana; Pericles at Tyre, and Marina at Tharsus. At this point, time must look like a "grave" to the family, divided and lost to each other; but the audience knows that they are all safe, and that time, therefore, may be pregnant with new life for all three. So ends the first major sequence of Pericles' life.

Gower appears as Chorus before Act IV to let us know that years have passed. Marina has grown into a beautiful and accomplished young woman at Tharsus; but Queen Dionyza finds her a threat to the prospects of her own plain daughter, Philoten. At the moment when the play resumes she is hiring Leonine to murder Marina.

The fourth act is devoted mostly to Marina's adventures. Leonine takes her to the seashore to kill her, but there she is seized by pirates, who sell her to a brothel in Mytilene. There, with a stubborn courage worthy of her father, she resolves to keep her virginity even at the cost of death. In Tharsus, meanwhile, Dionyza believes Marina dead, and she sets about concealing her crime by poisoning Leonine and persuading her husband Cleon to pretend that Marina had died of natural causes. They erect a monument to her, and when Pericles comes to Tharsus to fetch his daughter they deceive him. He goes back to Tyre in mourning, resolved never to cut his hair or beard again. Back in the brothel at Mytilene we see (to our surprise) that Marina is managing to hold at bay both her owners, the bawds, and their clients, the eager young men of the town. "I'll do anything now that is virtuous," says the First Gentleman (Act IV, scene 5) as he leaves the brothel utterly discouraged by the sermon Marina has just given him, "but I am out of the road of rutting for ever." At last the bawd himself, seeing his business ruined, cries out in despair (Act IV, scene 6), "Fie, fie upon her, she's able to freeze the god Priapus, and undo a whole generation." Shakespeare develops this situation more elaborately than either of his sources, and makes much more of its comical aspects. But we are not intended to lose sympathy for Marina: her "faithfulness and courage" are analogous to Pericles', and time rewards her when Lysimachus, governor of Mytilene, having visited the brothel and been converted by Marina, rescues her and sets her up in a respectable house as a teacher. By the end of Act IV all is ready for the turning points and recognition scenes of the last act, when Pericles, Marina, and Thaisa are finally reunited.

This long, improbable old romance may dismay one at first because it is so different from the stories Shakespeare used for his more familiar plays. But he must have known exactly what he was doing when he chose the story and dramatized it in the style he did: no one has ever understood better than he the properties and the meanings of narrative. He was the heir of a long tradition of allegorical interpretation of narratives, both Biblical and classical, and he assumed all his life that the stories he used had moral or religious meanings that might be revealed through the arts of the dramatist and his actors. The history plays, the tragedies, even the great comedies, are each based on a single, comparatively swift central action, with one climax and turning point. The action in these plays is always seen against the background of the unknown, where fate or Providence ultimately decides the issues, but Shakespeare's interest is in the human struggle in the foreground: the infinite variety of human character, the psychology of decision, intimate experiences of good and evil—all that constitutes the "moral" meaning of life and its reflection in history or legend. The story of *Pericles* on the other hand lasts twenty or thirty years, and has half a dozen climaxes and turning points, none of which therefore is crucial. Pericles can survive them because of his faith that "life's but breath, to trust it error," and Shakespeare evidently chose his story because his interest in the "moral" had waned, while his interest in the religious meaning, or "allegory" as it was called, had grown. The dramatis personae of the old tale have hardly more individual character or moral significance than the good guys and bad guys of our popular adventure stories, and Shakespeare leaves them as he found them. The episodic narrative has none of the psychological and ethical profundity that we associate with the tightly built histories and tragedies, and Shakespeare does not ask us to take the literal story seriously. But he makes it give off religious (or "allegorical") meanings, classical or Christian or both.

Gower's story has certain abstract symmetries of character and situation that strike a modern reader, with his Freudian habits of mind, as psychologically significant. Pericles in his amorous youth meets Antiochus and his daughter, with their depraved love, and then, after a sea-storm, Simonides and Thaisa, with their life-giving love, replace the deathly pair; and Simonides is also made to suggest (in the passage I have quoted) a reappearance of Pericles' own long-lost father. After two more storms on Neptune's ocean and about twenty troubled years, the filial and parental love between Marina and Pericles is realized, the mirror image of the attachment between Antiochus and his daughter: a parent-child relationship miraculously turned, not to lust and death, but to love and life. Shakespeare carefully keeps these analogies that mark the course of the old story, but he does not stress them, nor does he try to limit their suggestiveness to one psychological interpretation. In a similar way he keeps the pagan gods, especially Diana and Neptune: without emphasis, and without committing himself about the nature of their "reality." The effect is to convey a religious view of human experience, but whether classical, Christian, or post-Christian it would be hard to say. The realm of Providence or the gods, mysterious to us but somewhat responsive to faith and patience, is felt in all the play, but it is not mapped out according to any doctrine.

Pericles' religious "faith" is, I think, a faith in time itself as mediator between man and the unknown; and certain it is that time is essential to this kind of romantic story: there must be time to find, to lose, and to find again. It is time that shows us, if we have the patience, the allegorical meaning behind the literal events of the fairy tale: not in terms of a particular creed, but in the joyful circumstances of Pericles' life, at the end, which confirm and fulfill his faith. Gower, as Chorus, speaks the formal epilogue, a moralizing rhyme in the old-fashioned manner that Shakespeare preserves throughout:

> In Antiochus and his daughter you have heard
> Of monstrous lust the due and just reward:
> In Pericles, his Queen and daughter, seen,
> Although assailed with fortune fierce and keen,
> Virtue preserved from fell destruction's blast,
> Led on by heaven, and crowned with joy at last.

But it is in the recognition scenes of Act V that the implicit object of Pericles' faith—"substance of things hoped for"—is dramatically and musically embodied.

In Act V all the themes of the gods, of parent and child, and of time as bringer of life and death, are resumed and harmonized. The situation at Mytilene, when Lysimachus restores Marina to the mourning Pericles, is based on a number of utterly improbable coincidences, and (as I have mentioned) none of the dramatis personae has much individual character. Nevertheless the scene (Act V, scene 1) in which

Pericles slowly and humbly realizes that Marina is in fact alive before him is as touching as any recognition in Shakespeare, including Lear's of Cordelia. I suppose that is because the movement of Pericles' spirit from ignorance to knowledge, and from grief to "this great sea of joys rushing upon me," is so accurately realized in the verbal rhythms and imagery of the scene that it is almost irrelevant to consider the characters and the situation realistically. It is here that the lyrical or "musical" inspiration of the play is most evident. After that climax of feeling, the last scene, when Pericles, led by his dream-vision of Diana, finds his long-lost Thaisa again, can only be a quiet modulation into the peaceful end of the play.

CYMBELINE

Cymbeline was written, probably, in 1610, after *Pericles* and before *The Winter's Tale* and *The Tempest*—the second of Shakespeare's "late plays." It is one of his more puzzling and unsatisfying works, but it has proved fascinating for several different reasons. The absurdly complicated and improbable story—"and old-time story for a circle—not too critical—around the fire," as Henry James put it—is better in the theater than it is in the book, and actors interested in the roles of Imogen and Iachimo have kept it alive on the stage. The actual writing is so uneven that some scholars maintain that Shakespeare cannot be responsible for all of it; but some passages have all the magic and the music that we associate with Shakespeare's final phase. In spite of the play's imperfections, it is clear that Shakespeare had a definite intention in writing it, and that he worked out the plot with all of his usual care and skill. He chose to use two stories which seem, at first sight, to have little to do with each other: a tale from Boccaccio's *Decameron,* and the half-legendary story of "Kymbeline," King of England under the Roman Empire, which he found in Holinshed's *Chronicles.* He added, for good measure, Cymbeline's Queen, who is essentially the "wicked step-dame" of fairy tale, and another episode from Holinshed to make the battle in the last act. He was, of course, placing the play in that make-believe realm of Renaissance fable where characters from various times and places can mingle freely, and nothing is too improbable, provided that it makes a good story. But within this unrealistic convention he wove together his various sources, not only to make an elaborate adventure-story, but also to suggest allegorical meanings which echo themes from his earlier comedies and tragedies. In order to understand the play, therefore, one must first consider the form and movement that Shakespeare gave to the whole, for it is in that that his masterful hand is most evident.

King Cymbeline's story is the basis of the whole complicated intrigue. Cymbeline as a young king had lived in peace with Rome and with his Queen, who presented him with two sons, Guiderius and Arviragus, and a daughter, Imogen. His misfortunes began when he banished Belarius, who was falsely accused of treachery, and Belarius kidnapped his two sons. His Queen died, and he married the wicked Queen of the play. She persuades him to banish Posthumus, the poor but worthy gentleman whom Imogen has married, ostensibly because of his low birth, actually because she wants her oafish son Cloten to marry Imogen and so succeed to the throne. She then makes Cymbeline defy Rome, thus starting a war that nobody wants. Poor Cymbeline reaches the low point in his fortunes when his last child, Imogen, flees in search of Posthumus, and the Romans land an army in England. The play shows how these errors and deceits are finally cleared up, and Cymbeline can live at peace once more with his children and with Rome.

Most of the play is devoted to the story that Shakespeare took from Boccaccio, that of Imogen, Posthumus, Posthumus' loyal servant Pisanio, and the wicked Italian Iachimo, who, after the foolish wager on Imogen's chastity, deceives Posthumus into believing that he has seduced Imogen. This story is combined with that of Cloten, who is stupidly determined to have Imogen, and with the story of Belarius, Guiderius, and Arviragus, who have been living incognito as Welsh mountaineers. The intricate narrative is utterly improbable, but easy enough to follow as one reads the play, and I do not attempt to summarize it here. Suffice it to say that all the exiled characters, having lost the King's trust through error and deceit, have lost themselves and each other, and must live in disguise in order to live at all. Their efforts to find their way through so many mistaken identities sometimes seem romantic, somtimes comic, and sometimes merely silly.

Imogen's adventures in her disguise as the boy Fidele reach an end in Act IV, scene 2. This scene, which many readers object to because of its improbability and its mixture of comical, delicately musical, and absurdly gruesome effects, is a good example of the dreamlike quality of the play. Imogen has "by chance" joined Belarius and her brothers Guiderius and Arviragus, but they think her Fidele, and she thinks them wonderfully gentle mountaineers. The scene opens with a light pastoral sequence, almost a love scene between the sister and brothers, but love at a presexual level; the true nature and relationship of the three are almost felt through their countrified costumes. Fidele, tired and ill, decides to take the drug which the Queen had given to Pisanio, thinking it a deadly poison, and Pisanio had given to Imogen, thinking it a panacea. We, however, have been informed by the Queen's physician that it is only a sleeping potion that counterfeits death. While Imogen sleeps in the cave, Cloten, dressed in Posthumus' clothes and intent on raping Imogen, blunders in, and Guiderius, with his usual athletic good spirits, chops off his head. The boys then find Fidele, who seems to be dead, and give him (or her) a touching funeral, with the dirge which is one of Shakespeare's most beautiful songs:

> Fear no more the heat o' th' sun,
> Nor the furious winter's rages;
> Thou thy worldly task hast done,
> Home art gone, and ta'en thy wages.
> Golden lads and girls all must
> As chimney-sweepers come to dust.

They lay out Cloten's headless trunk beside the sleeping Imogen-Fidele, for Belarius points out that he is, after all, the Queen's son, and Guiderius adds,

> Thersites' body is as good as Ajax',
> When neither are alive.

When Fidele-Imogen wakes, she confirms this grisly thought, for she recognizes Posthumus' clothes, and thinks she recognizes his "martial thigh" also. Overcome with grief, she faints; and at that point the Roman General Lucius finds her, and rescues her as the boy Fidele. Lucius is supposed to be the invading enemy, but he will eventually restore Imogen to King Cymbeline; and with his intervention Imogen's story is complete, except for the happy ending in the last scene of the play. The scene as a whole, with its impossible mistakes and coincidences, and its boldly contrasting effects, is hard for us to accept. But there can be little doubt that Shakespeare devised it just that way, and the underlying vision of golden lads and girls groping for the true meaning of their love, with the falsity of court behind them and death a little way ahead, is very Shakespearean.

It is the Roman invasion that brings about the denouements of all the interwoven stories, for it forces the men to fight for England, and that act of faith or loyalty eventually reveals them as they truly are, cutting through all the deceits and delusions that had confused Cymbeline's kingdom. Pisanio is the first to take that course (Act IV, scene 3):

> These present wars shall find I love my country,
> Even to the note o' th' King, or I'll fall in them.
> All other doubts, by time let them be cleared;
> Fortune brings in some boats that are not steered.

He is followed (Act IV, scene 4) by Guiderius and Arviragus, whose "blood thinks scorn,/ Till it fly out, and show them princes born." And in the next scene Posthumus, who has returned to England as a Roman soldier, changes to the costume of an English peasant in order to "die for Imogen" and her country. The battle (Act V, scenes 2 and 3) is mostly in dumb-show, in accord with the unrealistic style of the play; and like so many battles near the end of Shakespeare's histories and tragedies, is felt as an "ordeal" that will reveal the gods' will. Cymbeline is captured, but with the miraculous intervention of Belarius, Guiderius, Arviragus, Pisanio, and Posthumus, he is rescued and Lucius is captured. Posthumus gets Iachimo down, but spares him, resumes his Roman disguise, and is led off to prison.

In prison Posthumus prays for death, for he thinks that Pisanio has carried out his orders and killed Imogen. He sleeps, and sees "as in an apparition," his dead father, mother, and brothers, who complain to Jupiter that he has sent Posthumus a great deal of undeserved suffering. Jupiter replies, "Whom best I love, I cross; to make my gift,/ The more delayed, delighted," and promises to make amends. Jupiter's explanation applies to all the characters in the play, from Cymbeline down; all have suffered more than they deserved, but, with patience, will see Jupiter's mercy at last—in the next scene in fact. The doggerel in which Jupiter and the ghosts speak offends many readers, but it is hardly "worse" than that of Hamlet's playlet, or Time's narrative in *The Winter's Tale*, or the rhymed couplets with which Shakespeare usually punctuates his plays. I think that he planned this scene just as it is, for it seems to be right for the "old-time story" he is telling. The clumsiness of the verse brings out the superannuated, helpless quality of the poor pleading ghosts, and at the same time reminds us that the whole play is old-fashioned, and must itself plead for our indulgence.

All of the tangled threads of the story are sorted out and neatly tied off in the final scene, which is rightly admired as an example of Shakespeare's dexterity in plot-construction. Cymbeline is at the center, both as the father who had lost his children and as the victorious king who must mete out justice and mercy as the truth is brought to light. The sequence of action in this final scene may be described as a joyful fugue of recognition, as the characters, one after another, penetrate the deceits and disguises that had separated them. The finale is reached when Posthumus, having found his true Imogen, and having been recognized himself as one of England's saviors in the battle, pardons Iachimo, and so inspires Cymbeline to pardon his prisoner Lucius, and then restore his country to the Roman Empire. Jupiter is to be thanked for this general reconciliation:

> Laud we the gods,
> And let our crooked smokes climb to their nostrils
> From our blessed altars.

This is one of the places, in *Cymbeline,* where the "inspiration" behind the play—the strange, timeless serenity of Shakespeare's final phase—may be felt directly in the language.

If one is to make sense out of *Cymbeline,* one must read it as one does the romantic comedies and the other late plays, with a continual "double take." The literal story is entertaining but silly, while the improbable course of events suggests Shakespeare's matured conception of the course of human life, and from that comes the poetic or visionary quality of the play. It is allegory, but reticent and lightly suggestive allegory, such as only Shakespeare could write.

Thus the story of Imogen, Posthumus, and Iachimo gives off meanings like some of those we feel in the romantic comedies. Imogen is very much like the other romantic heroines, whose patience and constancy at last clear up the mistrusts and delusions of young love. Like Rosalind in *As You Like It,* she moves between the "experience" of court intrigue and the pastoral or Eden-like "innocence" of the boys in their uncorrupted mountains.

Cymbeline's story is akin to that of Pericles, and also to those of Leontes in *The Winter's Tale* and Prospero in *The Tempest,* which Shakespeare would write next. These older men have passed the middle of the journey when the play opens, and through their stories the whole course of a human life that reaches its natural end is suggested. Cymbeline's story is analogous to that of the young people, for he too must lose his first innocence in experience, and sort out appearance and reality, but his story is longer, moves in a wider arc. And this wider focus deprives the events of the moment of some of their importance. The earlier plays are all based on significant conflict, and rise to a crucial climax in the third act, but *Cymbeline* like the other late plays moves more evenly to its conclusion. The theme of suffering as the road to truth and peace is important, but in this play it is less a matter of crime and repentance than it is a matter of time. Cymbeline, Imogen, and Posthumus are more sinned against than sinning, but they require time in order to digest their misfortunes, and time in which to see what the unaccountable "Jupiter" may have in store for them. The meaning of time in our experience is one of the major poetic themes in *Cymbeline,* as in the other late plays.

The theme of the relation between England and Rome, so important in *Cymbeline,* has (so far as I know) no parallel in any other play of Shakespeare's. He found it in the following passage in Holinshed:

> . . . by our writers it is reported, that Kymbeline being brought up in Rome, & knighted in the court of Augustus, euer shewed himselfe a friend to the Romans, & chieflie was loth to breake with them, because the youth of the Britaine nation should not be depriued of the benefit to be trained and brought vp among the Romans, whereby they might learne both to behaue themselues like ciuill men, and to attaine to the knowledge of feats of warre.

In Boccaccio's narrative of the wicked Iachimo we see a quite different Rome: Italy as it often appeared to Shakespeare's contemporaries—subtle, corrupt, and "Machiavellian." But this view is carefully related to the wider pattern. Iachimo, like the wicked English Queen, stands for "experience" as against the "innocence" of the blameless Posthumus; but from the first we also associate Rome with Posthumus' appropriately named benefactor, Philarmonus, and with the noble General Lucius, guardian of the universal Roman peace. Classical Rome was the schoolmaster of Shakespeare, and indeed of Renaissance Europe, and in the dreamy vision of peace at the end of the play harmony between Rome and England is as significant as harmony between man and woman, youth and age. One can think of various meanings that Shakespeare may have seen in this effect; a meditation on history and the westward course of empire; a "good European" view of the ideal relation between the central tradition and the new national cultures of the time; perhaps even a faint reference to the break between the English and the Roman Church. But it would be a mistake to seek too limited a meaning in these relationships.

Cymbeline is not a masterpiece by Shakespeare's own standards, for in *The Winter's Tale* and *The Tempest* he was able to do better almost everything he had attempted in this play. But it is full of interest, at various levels, in its own right, and it marks a significant stage in the growth of Shakespeare's final style.

THE WINTER'S TALE

The Winter's Tale was written in 1610 or 1611, between *Cymbeline* and *The Tempest.* These plays, the last that Shakespeare wrote, contain tragic, comic, and romantic elements, and they embody his final serene and mysterious vision of human life, from the cradle to the grave. They were not very well understood during most of the eighteenth and nineteenth centuries, and *The Winter's Tale* was supposed to be unstageable. It was performed from time to time by famous actors who were tempted by one of its great roles, but always in "adaptations," like the one by Garrick. In the last thirty or forty years, however, we have learned to understand Shakespeare's intentions in these last plays, and now *The Winter's Tale* appears as one of the masterpieces. It is staged as it was written, and its combination of tragedy, comedy, and unearthly poetry has proved very effective in the theater.

Shakespeare took the plot from a familiar story: *Pandosto: The Triumph of Time,* by Robert Greene (1588). He transformed Greene's colorless characters into intensely living figures, changed their names, and added several characters of his own. But the basic situation is Greene's: everything starts when Leontes, King of Sicilia, becomes violently (and mistakenly) jealous of his Queen, Hermione, and his childhood friend Polixenes, King of Bohemia. Leontes sends his baby daughter away, to be exposed to the elements, imprisons Hermione for adultery, and forces Polixenes to flee for his life. The story ends, sixteen years later, when Leontes' daughter, Perdita, marries Polixenes' son, Florizel; her identity is discovered, and the truth revealed. But Shakespeare changes the end of the story, and thereby its meaning. In Greene the Queen dies, and Leontes commits suicide when his crimes are revealed; the main story is the romance of Perdita and Florizel, with its routine happy ending. Greene's "triumph of time" merely reveals the facts. But Shakespeare has Leontes learn the facts from the

Oracle of Apollo as soon as the damage is done, and then spend the intervening sixteen years in repentance. Hermione does not die, but hides, and then reappears at the end. It was probably the theme of time—the time of a human generation—which attracted Shakespeare to Greene's story. But in his play time is "redeemed" through Hermione's patience and Leontes' fertile suffering; and time brings new life to the older generation too when the young lovers are found again.

The story of the play is clear enough, but the manner in which Shakespeare tells it may prove puzzling until one sees what he means by it. Leontes' jealousy is presented with tragic intensity; the Florizel-Perdita romance is both lyrical and comic. But the point of the play lies precisely in these contrasts between innocence and experience. The tale as Greene tells it is improbable, and Shakespeare makes it more improbable still by adding several intricate circumstances of his own invention. Nineteenth-century critics thought that Shakespeare had lost his art, or was simply careless, defying both good taste and common sense. But now we give him credit for knowing what he was doing: inviting his audience to smile at the familiar old story, as one does at a fairy tale, for the sake of its beauty and the meanings it suggests. The meanings of *The Winter's Tale* are so manifold that they will, no doubt, be discussed for generations to come; but at least we can now read the play with some understanding of its conscious style and its carefully managed shifting perspectives.

Leontes' jealousy runs its destructive course in the first three acts. After a brief scene between Camillo and Archidamus (Act I, scene 1), in which the idyllic friendship of the two Kings is described, we see Leontes, Hermione, and Polixenes together (scene 2). It is a picture of carefree and trusting merriment, but Leontes rips it to shreds. Shakespeare does not show the growth of Leontes' jealousy; he simply takes it as the fated starting point of the story. But he makes us feel all its bewildering pain: "Too hot, too hot," poor Leontes cries when he sees his wife and friend joking together:

> To mingle friendship far, is mingling bloods.
> I have tremor cordis on me; my heart dances,
> But not for joy, not joy.

When Leontes is left alone a moment with his beloved little son, Mamillius, he wonders whether Hermione really could deceive him with Polixenes. But he reflects that passion ("affection," as he calls it) is irrational, attached to its own dreams; and therefore if Hermione is passionate it is all the more credible that the real and attractive Polixenes might evoke her passion:

> Affection! Thy intention stabs the centre.
> Thou dost make possible things not so held,
> Communicat'st with dreams—how can this be?
> With what's unreal thou coactive art,
> And fellow'st nothing. Then 'tis very credent
> Thou may'st co-join with something—

that is, with Polixenes. His description of the movement of passion, which "intends" to pierce the center of things like the stab of a dagger, is wonderfully accurate. And he sees that passion generates beings, "fellows" which are illusory, "nothing." His own jealousy moves in exactly that way. By the time he tries to persuade old Camillo to murder Polixenes, he cannot believe that the dreams of his jealousy are unreal:

> Is whispering nothing?
> Is leaning cheek to cheek? Is meeting noses?

The verse in this long scene is difficult: full of nervous broken rhythms and contradictory flashes of insight. And it has its own cool, agile music, characteristic of Shakespeare's late style. It is worth the reader's careful attention, for it presents the assault of an evil passion as intense, and as clear, as that in *Othello* or *Macbeth.*

But Leontes' crazy drive looks quite different from Macbeth's, because we see it not only as it looks from the inside, to Leontes himself, but also as it looks to the sane and normal friends who surround him. Hermione, Polixenes, and Camillo, who love Leontes, find his growing violence hardly credible. When we hear of the two Kings' Arcadian childhood together,

> Two lads that thought there was no more behind,
> But such a day to-morrow, as to-day,
> And to be boy eternal,

we feel that what Leontes really wants is that innocence, which he thinks he has lost for good. When he plays with Mamillius he sees it again, as though he were peering through the prison of his passion to the real world outside. In short, Leontes' passion is seen, from the first, in a hard, objective, wintry light, which makes it seem all the more distressing, yet not without hope.

Once caught in his jealous dream, however, Leontes must rush on to the tragic catastrophe. During Act II we see how everything seems to confirm his nightmare. He takes Polixenes' flight with Camillo as proof. He cannot believe Paulina, who tells him that Hermione's newborn daughter is obviously his, and not Polixenes'; and he bullies Antigonus into taking it away into the wilderness (scene 3). Following the logic of his delusion, he summons the blameless Hermione to public trial for adultery.

The climax and turning point of the play come in Hermione's trial (Act III, scene 2), when all the evidence is brought to bear against Leontes' criminal folly. He holds out against Hermione herself, though her clear innocent spirit and the patient love she still has for her husband are beautifully embodied in her words. He even defies the Oracle of Apollo, whose message the Officer reads:

> Hermione is chaste, Polixenes blameless, Camillo a true subject, Leontes a jealous tyrant, his innocent babe truly begotten, and the King shall live without an heir, if that which is lost be not found.

But at that point Mamillius' death is reported, and Leontes breaks at last, his eyes are opened:

> Apollo's angry, and the heavens themselves
> Do strike at my injustice.

Hermione, overcome by Mamillius' death, is taken away by Paulina, who presently returns to report that she too has died. We do not learn that Paulina has hidden her, alive, until the very end of the play. Leontes is left, apparently bereaved of all his family, to devote himself to mourning and repentance.

The Oracle of Apollo is a central clue to the movement of the story, and also to its meaning. Cleomenes and Dion, as they talk over their experience at Delphi on their way back to the trial (Act III, scene 1), make the Oracle sound like truth and grace: mercy moving behind the scenes to rescue Leontes and his victims:

> The climate's delicate, the air most sweet,
> Fertile the isle, the temple much surpassing
> The common praise it bears. . . .
> And the ear-deaf'ning voice o' th' oracle,
> Kin to Jove's thunder, so surprised my sense,
> That I was nothing.

These sights and sounds are strangely similar to those in Sophocles' last play, *Oedipus at Colonus,* when in the sacred grove thunder summons the suffering old man to his mysterious destiny. A divinity behind nature is suggested in both passages; and when Apollo's word is heard in the trial, it is like truth itself, or grace—mercy moving to rescue Leontes and his victims. It confirms and completes the efforts which Leontes' friends had been making to save him; and it foreshadows the end of the story, sixteen years later, when what is lost here is found again.

Leontes' change of heart has been criticized as too sudden, and it does require careful acting and staging through the first three acts to make it work in the theater. But Shakespeare has prepared for it all along. He has shown Leontes suffering, as much as Hermione herself, from his jealousy, and candid enough, in his torment, to send to Delphi for Apollo's word of truth. And at this point we are to understand that Leontes, with the help he gets, meets his tragedy in the opposite way to Macbeth's, for instance. When Macbeth faces ruin (in Act III) he can only continue till death finishes him; the evil passion that drives him, like those in Dante's hell, has no issue, for Macbeth is completely committed to it. But Leontes is a more deeply divided soul, and when he realizes his guilt he can relive his own mistaken motives in the sad light of hindsight, like those figures that Dante meets in Purgatory. We leave him to visit the tombs of his wife and son every day, devoted to his grief and to the "passion that purges."

The gap of sixteen years which now follows in the action of the play has been criticized as awkward plotting, but it is appropriate enough for the romantic old story that Shakespeare is telling, for it wanders on for years, like one of our soap-operas. And time is essential to the meanings that Shakespeare wants to suggest in his fable.

He sketches the events quickly, and with a smiling emphasis on their fairy-tale improbability. Old Antigonus lands with baby Perdita (Act III, scene 3) upon "the seacoast of Bohemia," which Shakespeare must have known was not to be found in any map. The ship that brought them is destroyed in a sudden storm; Antigonus "exit pursued by a bear," and the bear, as we soon learn, "dines upon the gentleman." The old Shepherd arrives just in time to find the pretty babe and her "fairy gold." He and his son, country-bumpkins as they are, can only gape at the extraordinary events, and their incredible good fortune. Time, as Chorus, then takes up the story (Act IV, scene 1), explaining that while Leontes repents, Perdita is raised as a shepherdess, and Polixenes' son Florizel grows up too. Time speaks in a stiff, old-fashioned verse appropriate for a teller of old tales: "Impute it not a crime/ To me," he says, "or my swift passage, that I slide/ O'er sixteen years." And he bows out, leaving Polixenes and Camillo (Act IV, scene 2) to explain that Florizel, now a young man, is interested in a shepherdess; and they resolve to look into the matter.

Shakespeare seems to be saying that such marvelous coincidences occur only in old stories; but at the same time he suggests that they have a meaning which is marvelous in a different way. Antigonus' dream of Hermione, "like very sanctity," and the thunder of the storm that follows echo the Oracle of Apollo. When the old Shepherd tells his son, "Now bless thyself; thou met'st with things dying, I with things new-born," he refers to what has just happened, but his beautiful line also announces the theme of rebirth which is to be developed in what follows. And when Time as Chorus says,

> I that please some, try all; both joy and terror
> Of good, and bad; that makes, and unfolds error,
> Now take upon me,

he suggests that his story will try (or test) the audience, just as time, slowly sorting out joy and terror, good and bad, tests all of us. In the whole sequence one can see clearly how Shakespeare expects us to take the play: it hovers, so to speak, between playful make-believe and the reality of human experience.

In all of Shakespeare's tragedies, the climax and turning point comes in Act III, and Act IV is devoted largely to dreams and visions which ambiguously foretell the end. The Witches' shows, which Macbeth sees in Act IV, are such suggestive prophecies. *The Winter's Tale* is also built in this way, but the dreams and visions which follow Leontes' catastrophe and change of heart foretell, not damnation, but a renewal of his life and Hermione's. The new life appears most beautifully (after the hints which I have pointed out) in the sheep-shearing (Act IV, scene 4). The springtime festival is the scene of Florizel's and Perdita's delicate wooing, and those two young people are literally the new life which emerges from the old. The scene is a set-piece, like a masque; the story pauses, and we are invited to enjoy the music, the dances, and the poetry. Its interwoven themes of winter and spring, age and youth, guilt and innocence, pull together the imagery of the whole play.

But the scene is only a self-indulgent interlude, not the end of the story or of the play. Old Polixenes and Camillo, in their "disguises," watch it with a mixture of pleasure and dismay. Polixenes breaks the spell when he "discovers himself" (Act IV, scene 4). He threatens the lovers with dire consequences if they marry outside their proper stations, and departs in anger. The effect is very much like that in *The*

Tempest when old Prospero breaks off his daughter's wedding masque: it makes the pretty festival we have just seen look like a daydream which is, if not quite too good to be true, at least premature. And so we are returned to the story of Perdita and Florizel as only time can unroll it.

The Perdita-Florizel story, as Shakespeare found it in *Pandosto,* is a typical Arcadian romance. He handles it as he did a similar story in *As You Like It,* mingling the romantic love-intrigue with comedy which gently burlesques it. We are introduced to the idyllic countryside by Autolycus (Act IV, scene 3), who enters singing his wonderful song:

> When daffodils begin to peer,
> With hey, the doxy over the dale,
> Why then comes in the sweet o' the year;
> For the red blood reigns in the winter's pale.

Autolycus is a lusty rogue; he feels the "sweet o' the year" as keenly as Florizel, but for him the daffodils are no sweeter than the "doxy," a beggar's wench. While Florizel devotes himself to his chaste wooing, Autolycus is busy cheating the innocent countryfolk. When Polixenes departs and Camillo sets up his elaborate plot with disguises all around (Act IV, scene 4), Autolycus gets Florizel's finery in exchange for *his* clothes, while Perdita gets Florizel's hat. "I see," says Perdita, as though sharing the joke with the audience, "the play so lies/ That I must play a part," to which Camillo dryly replies, "No remedy." Camillo starts back to the court with Perdita and Florizel, on their romantic quest for love; and Autolycus starts for court too, gaily cheating and bullying the Shepherds as he goes. Shakespeare presents Autolycus and Florizel as two city-types, disporting themselves in the country under somewhat false pretenses, and now he drives the point home by having them actually disguise themselves as each other.

Before ending the story of Perdita and Florizel with the marriage which must conclude all good comedies, Shakespeare returns to the graver theme of Leontes and Hermione (Act V, scene 1). Leontes has done "more penitence than trespass," but grieves still for his son and for the wife and daughter he believes dead. Paulina is still severely reminding him of his guilt and his losses; and now she makes him a promise that he will marry again "when your first Queen's again in breath,/ Never till then," which must seem to poor Leontes, in the darkness of his ignorance, a bittersweet mockery. At that point Perdita and Florizel arrive to delight Leontes. But that happiness, too, proves insubstantial, for Perdita's identity is still unknown, and Polixenes' messenger comes to reveal Florizel's elaborate lies. Leontes must be patient a little longer.

Shakespeare planned the recognition of Hermione as the real end of the play, and for that reason, no doubt, he does not show us the recognition of Perdita. We hear about it (Act V, scene 2) from the humorous Gentlemen who describe it to the cynically grinning Autolycus:

> The oracle is fulfilled; the King's daughter is found; such a deal of wonder is broken out within this hour, that ballad-makers cannot be able to express it. . . . This news, which is called true, is so like an old tale, that the verity of it is in strong suspicion.

When the joyful "truth" about Perdita and Florizel comes to light, the scandalous truth about Autolycus is revealed too. Autolycus is at the Shepherds' mercy—which may suggest that the gods were less pleased with his false pretenses than they were with Florizel. But Autolycus shares in the general good fortune; the Shepherds relent, and Autolycus escapes with a whole skin after all.

The famous statue scene which concludes the play is as romantic in style as the rest of the story—and as filled with implicit meaning. It is prepared for from the very first scenes, in which we glimpse Leontes, Hermione, and Polixenes innocently enjoying their friendship; remembering the Kings' boyhood before they knew "the doctrine of ill-doing"; then losing that love and freedom of spirit when tragedy cuts them apart. The vision of such innocence—Eden or the Golden Age—hovers behind the whole play, and defines its action. Camillo, Paulina, Antigonus, and the other courtiers who struggle against the evil that seizes Leontes seem to feel that Eden is the norm in happy Sicilia. Perdita and Florizel embody that vision; even Autolycus, enviably free as he is from conscience, is innocent in his own engaging way. The guiding vision is obscured by time, or evil, or experience; but when Hermione, who seemed lost, is found again, everyone sees it once more, in a new and ghostly way. The statue that begins to live and breathe is a frankly, almost humorously theatrical device, but very touching in the theater, where it belongs. We would think Hermione was really a statue, when she is first unveiled, for her death has never been contradicted. As she begins to move, we would watch with both surprise and fascination. As she slowly melts and descends to embrace Leontes (to music and the music of Paulina's words) she would carry us with her, if the part were played by an actress with real feeling. Provided, that is, we could watch with a certain innocence of our own, moved by the marvels of make-believe and the greater marvel of the heart's desire finding, after years, and beyond all probability, the response it hardly hoped for.

We began to gain our present understanding of *The Winter's Tale* when it was realized that its theme of "death" or suffering and rebirth is very old. It is represented in many prehistoric vegetation ceremonies, which marked the seasonal turn from winter to spring. Perdita's sheep-shearing is a remote descendant of such festivals, whose purpose was to assure the renewal of animal and vegetable life, on which the physical survival of primitive agricultural communities depended. Shakespeare uses winter's withering and spring's new life to provide images of the death and rebirth of the human spirit as it loses and finds again its sense of freedom and innocence. He shows the process recurring through the changes of youth and age; and that is why the stirring of renewed life in Hermione, after her long petrifaction, rather than Perdita's tender and half understood wakening to love, is the vision he presents at the end. Serene though the play is, and full of the beauty of life, it is a winter's tale—and as T. S. Eliot writes, "Midwinter spring is its own season."

One may interpret the play (as many critics do) in Christian terms: "Dying to live." Certainly anyone who knows Dante's *Purgatory* with its conclusion in the earthly Paradise, must be struck by many similarities both in imagery and in structure; yet Shakespeare probably never read Dante. He never read Sophocles either, but the parallels between this play and Sophoclean tragedy (also derived from the primitive rites of spring) are striking too. Perhaps it is safest to say that Shakespeare rediscovered the old theme in his own experience, and in the Renaissance heritage of romance, philosophy, and religious allegory. The experience speaks to us directly, in Leontes' darkness and terror; in Perdita's delight. Because it is so universal, figures from various times and places are at home with it in this play: Apollo, the Italian sculptor Julio Romano, the Jacobean rogue Autolycus. Shakespeare presents the theme without limiting or defining its meanings too closely. And by means of his style—half-mockingly playing with the forms of his own earlier tragedies, comedies, and romances—he invites us to take it all as lightly or as seriously as we please.

THE TEMPEST

The Tempest (1610–1611) was Shakespeare's last play, except for the occasional piece, *Henry VIII*, and his share in *The Two Noble Kinsmen.* It is neither comedy, tragedy, nor romance, in the usual sense of those words; the dreamy sequence of its scenes is like a masque or pageant. Perhaps it should be called a fairy tale, for Prospero rules it all by magic. Perhaps Prospero represents Shakespeare himself as theater poet, and his renunciation of magic, at the end, Shakespeare's farewell to the theater. It is a mysterious play, but certain it is that it "enchants" its readers in every generation.

No direct source of the story has been found, but we know where Shakespeare got some of the details. The storm of Act I, scene 1, for instance, owes something to contemporary accounts of a wreck in the Bermudas. Gonzalo's wistful description of Utopia, Act II, scene 1, echoes a passage in Florio's translation of Montaigne. The main story seems to have been derived, by Shakespeare himself, from the stories of his other late plays, *Pericles, Cymbeline,* and *The Winter's Tale.* It recounts, not one great event, like the tragedies, but the course of a whole life. Prospero, like Pericles, Cymbeline, and Leontes, suffers defeats in the treacherous struggles of the world, but finds new life again as his career is ending, through a daughter who starts *her* life with trust and fresh hope. The plot of *The Tempest* is the simplest of all the late plays. We do not follow Prospero's history in chronological order, but begin at the end when his enemies are in his power and the painful events of his youth are only memories. Shakespeare took the essential theme of the late plays, and played it over like an old tune, as both memory and enchantment.

Most of Act I is prologue. The tone of the "twice-told tale" is set at once, for the storm of scene 1 is not a realistic storm, in spite of the thunder and lightning called for in the stage directions. It is Prospero's magic evocation of storm, and good actors can evoke it for us by *their* magic of make-believe, rhythmic effects, and properly spaced cries, better than the director can, if he gets too noisy and literal. After that we are ready for the sudden quiet of scene 2, when Prospero recounts to Miranda the "storm" of his own troubled youth and the remembered sea-storm that brought them to this isle in a leaky boat:

> There they hoist us,
> To cry to the sea, that roared to us; to sigh
> To the winds, whose pity sighing back again
> Did us but loving wrong.

Prospero insists on giving sleepy Miranda the facts of that distant time, and the reader also must get them straight if he is to understand the play to follow. Prospero is the rightful Duke of Milan; his treacherous brother Antonio with the help of Alonso, King of Naples, seized power and set Prospero and the infant Miranda adrift in a little boat. It was Gonzalo who gave them food, clothes, and Prospero's "book," the source of his magic. Those characters, with Alonso's son Ferdinand and a complement of sailors and courtiers, were wrecked in the storm, and are now safe and dry on the isle, though lost and (though they do not know it) in the power of Prospero's spells.

When Prospero's prologue is done, he dons his magic robes (Act I, scene 2) and summons Ariel and Caliban to start the action of the play. It is through the music and the visions created by Ariel that Prospero will lead the castaways—a sample of the all-too-human world—through the experiences he has planned for them. Part of his own past life, they are tied to Prospero still by blood-kinship, guilt, and suffering. He wants to even old scores, clear up misunderstandings; in short, free himself from the painful unresolved tangle of his youth. To do that he must free the castaways too. He must try to reveal the truth to them, give them a chance to repent and free themselves. "Freedom" in many different senses is the main motive of the play.

Ariel divides the lost travelers into three groups, each of which thinks the others drowned. Ferdinand, still uncorrupted by the ways of the world, is led straight to Miranda as he follows the enchanting sound of Ariel's songs. When the young people have "changed eyes" Prospero explains his plan for them at once (Act I, scene 2):

> They are both in either's powers. But this swift business
> I must uneasy make, lest too light winning
> Make the prize light—

and he sets Ferdinand to hauling logs while Miranda wails melodiously.

The second group is the court party, and Prospero at first (Act II, scene 1) shows them nothing. In the supposed solitude of the isle, each one feels free to express his deepest motive. Good old Gonzalo wants everyone to be happy, and half-playfully plans a Utopia for that temperate wilderness. Alonso despairs for his lost Ferdinand, fearing perhaps that he is receiving deserved retribution for his old crime. Antonio and Sebastian, courtiers who hate the outdoors, make bitter fun of old Gonzalo, and then, when Ariel lulls the rest to sleep with "solemn music," draw their rapiers to murder the King. We see as in a nightmare that the world is at its old tricks still, just as it was when Prospero was betrayed. But Ariel wakes the sleepers in time and the motley crowd wanders off after bereaved Alonso.

The third group consists of those comically trashy types, Stephano and Trinculo, and they are led to Caliban (Act II, scene 2). The three together feel strong enough to set up a rickety state with Stephano as king, thereby expressing *their* untrammeled dream of freedom:

CALIBAN
No more dams I'll make for fish,
Nor fetch in firing,
At requiring,
Nor scrape trenchering, nor wash dish.
'Ban 'Ban Ca-Caliban
Has a new master. Get a new man.
Freedom, high-day, high-day freedom, freedom high-day, freedom!

It is clear that Prospero's unwilling guests pose him a thorny problem.

In Act III Prospero's plans for the three groups begin to work. Ferdinand and Miranda continue to deepen their love by toil and separation (scene 1). Caliban and his new friends (scene 2), mocked and bewildered by Ariel, drunk on Stephano's liquor, are allowed to waver on toward the slaughter of Prospero, which would give them control of the isle. For the third group, Alonso and his followers, Prospero has more serious plans.

When we see them again (scene 3) Alonso and Gonzalo have had enough: "Here's a maze trod indeed," sighs Gonzalo, "through forthrights and meanders." But Antonio and Sebastian, sustained by their dream of power through murder, are as fresh as ever. While Prospero watches unseen, Ariel offers them music and a banquet served by strange "shapes." Alonso is appalled, for the strangeness of the apparition seems to touch his grief and guilt. Sebastian and Antonio eye the food with cynical greed. Gonzalo ruefully expresses the true quality of the "shapes":

. . . though they are of monstrous shape, yet note,
Their manners are more gentle-kind than of

Our human generation you shall find
Many, nay almost any.

The banquet vanishes with "a quaint device" the moment Sebastian and Antonio reach for the edibles, and Ariel in a melodious speech tells them and Alonso where they stand:

You are three men of sin, whom Destiny,
That hath to instrument this lower world
And what is in't, the never-surfeited sea
Hath caused to belch up you.

They are helpless here, he tells them, and their ancient crime is to be punished by "ling'ring perdition." To save themselves from that

is nothing but heart's sorrow,
And a clear life ensuing.

The audience hears Ariel's speech as an affirmation of Prospero's power and an explanation of his purposes. It marks the climax and turning point of the play. But the castaways, like restless dreamers, can understand it only in accordance with their own motives: Sebastian and Antonio as a challenge; Alonso (closer to the truth) as confirming his remorseful despair; Gonzalo, whose conscience is clear, with pity for Alonso. The King rushes off in a suicidal mood, and the rest follow.

In Act IV, scene 1, Prospero turns away from this painful sequence in order to "Bestow upon the eyes of this young couple /Some vanity of mine art." Miranda and Ferdinand are ending their time of trial; now they may plight their troth; and what Prospero bestows upon their eyes is an epithalamion, or wedding-song, in the form of a masque. Its mythical and pastoral figures, its music and delicate dance-like verse, present the most ancient themes of wedding: the hoped-for fertility safeguarded by purity; the impatient passions of the young subdued to stately rhythms as they move, too slowly, toward night, the marriage bed, and consummation. But this "ceremony of innocence" is broken off by the murderous approach of Stephano, Trinculo, and Caliban, whom Prospero had forgotten.

This drunken trio is inspired by *their* impatient passions (Act IV, scene 2), but unlike Ferdinand and Miranda they have been left to their own devices. They have blundered through scratching briers, struggled through a puddle in the backyard, and now "do smell all horse-piss." Prospero contemptuously sets out a sample of *their* goal: "glistering apparel," "trumpery in my house," "stale to catch these thieves"—the very opposite of the harmonious visions that lead Ferdinand and

Miranda on their way. Stephano and Trinculo, against poor Caliban's protests, gullibly take the bait, and are driven off by hunters and swift barking hounds.

In the center of Act IV, between the wedding masque and the trapping of the thieves, Prospero makes his famous comment upon human life:

> We are such stuff
> As dreams are made on; and our little life
> Is rounded with a sleep.

We have seen Ferdinand and Miranda "made on" their dreams of earthly felicity, Stephano and Trinculo made of gaudy trappings, and in the last act the court party defined by their more stubborn dreams of power, or guilt, or peace on earth. Prospero's speech has been rightly taken as the clue to much of the play. But Prospero himself is now ready to renounce both dreaming and the making of dreams.

In Act V we see how Prospero at last comes to terms with his subjects of the enchanted isle, and with the friends and enemies whom he has had in his power there. Everyone gets poetic justice plus forgiveness, in true fairy-story style. The old wounds are healed through the marriage of Ferdinand and Miranda; the ship and its mariners are restored as good as new; and all is ready for goodbye to the magic isle.

The literal story of *The Tempest* is easy enough, as I have tried to suggest in this short summary. But as one reads, the meditative sequence of scenes and the musing melody of the language give off more meanings than we can quite fathom. The best critics warn us not to try to "interpret" the play. They are right in one sense, for the play is not an allegory with a definite philosophical or theological key, but a revery with a power of suggestion like that of music. Yet one's enjoyment of this strange quality is enhanced when one learns to recognize some of the themes that Shakespeare was mulling over in *The Tempest:* themes from the long line of his own plays, and from the longer tradition of Europe, which he understood so deeply and skeptically at the end of his career.

Thus the double story of Prospero's betrayal by his brother Antonio and King Alonso's betrayal by his brother Sebastian echoes the theme of the usurpation of power which Shakespeare had found first in the histories and later and more deeply in *Hamlet, Lear,* and *Macbeth:* treachery rips the fabric of trust, and sleepless evil is revealed in the human scene. The smiling idyll of Miranda and her Ferdinand recalls the young lovers in *As You Like It, A Midsummer Night's Dream,* and

Twelfth Night. Miranda and Ferdinand fall in love at once, but Prospero imposes toil upon them to test and enlighten their naive infatuation. That is the principle upon which all the great comedies are plotted. The young lovers are kept apart by the absurd situations of the story, long enough to provide an evening's entertainment for the audience, and to teach the naive lovers a little of love's meaning. The sub-plot of Stephano and Trinculo is handled like the farcical strands in both the tragedies and comedies. It is analogous to the courtiers' scheme of getting political power through murder; at the same time it has a quality of simplemindedness (increased by drink) which relates it to Miranda's and Ferdinand's more lyrical and loving inebriation.

The Tempest reaffirms Shakespeare's complex vision of human life, but with a new detachment. The tragic or comic struggles are not realistically developed, but rather alluded to. Ferdinand's log-hauling is no full-scale lover's ordeal, but symbolic only. The nascent murder of the King, though it gives a sharp image of evil, is never completed. The events of the play occur with Prospero's permission, and are seen not only directly but also through his eyes; hence the dreamy "doubletake" that gives the play its unique quality.

Prospero, however, also has predecessors: those characters in Shakespeare's plays who are at the same time caught in the action and outside it, trying to watch and guide it. Hamlet tries something similar in the "mousetrap" play he shows to the Danish court; so does Edgar, in *Lear,* in his handling of his blinded father. Prospero's nearest relative is the Duke in *Measure for Measure.* Both are legitimate rulers whose power is for the moment unrecognized. Both, moving behind the scenes like an author-director, plot a series of significant situations in order to test and enlighten their subjects. They illustrate one of Shakespeare's favorite notions: that there is a close analogy between the little world of the theater, ruled by the poet-director, and the larger world of the human community under its king or duke.

The power of the Duke in *Measure for Measure* is that of the de facto ruler, whereas Prospero has only the power of his "magic." *Measure for Measure* is comparatively realistic in style, while *The Tempest* depends frankly on the enchantment of poetry. Caliban, associated with the "element" of earth, and Ariel associated with air, are creatures of the poetic imagination peculiar to this play; but they also embody insights which were the fruit of Shakespeare's long career. One can learn to understand some of their meanings by noticing the crucial parts they play in the development of the action.

We are told that Prospero's magic comes from his staff and his book, but Ariel is his agent. And Ariel enthralls the castaways as theater poetry does a willing audience: he frightens them with a sea-storm that does not wet their garments; holds them helplessly entranced, or leads them where he will, by the charm of his music. He acts very much like the poetic imagination as Shakespeare had learned to know it, long before, in his own experience. Like the poet's "eye" in *A Midsummer Night's Dream* he can glance with the speed of light "from heaven to earth, from earth to heaven." Obeying Prospero, he can show the worldlings images of the truth, but he cannot change their natures, and each one interprets his shows according to his own dubious moral insight. Ariel can take any form, as Shakespeare's imagination had done in the long gallery of his plays: embody "airy nothings" or monsters never seen; wake the long-dead "sleepers" of history or legend "from their graves." But he cannot "passion as they": he has no human feelings. He does not know or care what his songs and visions mean to people. He longs to be free of Prospero's human care, thought, and moral responsibility, and obey only the promptings of his own shimmering bodiless being.

Prospero controls Ariel with difficulty, and Caliban, Ariel's counterpart, is a darker and more stubborn problem for him. Caliban is as amoral as Ariel, and he too can never be changed. But in contrast to Ariel, poor Caliban helplessly suffers all the terrors, lusts, and deluding dreams of the flesh. It has been suggested that he represents the mob, as Shakespeare had pictured it in *Henry VI, Julius Caesar, Coriolanus.* Like the mob-man, Caliban cannot rule himself, and is therefore the natural prey of any demagogue. Stephano seduces him with a few drinks and tawdry daydreams. But Stephano and Trinculo are themselves more like Shakespeare's mobs than Caliban is. Their motives are cheap, variable, and superficial, while Caliban hardly knows what he wants; most of his dim bulk of feeling is far below the surface. From those depths emerge the oldest and most shameless human images: of murder, as when he whispers,

> Then thou mayst brain him,
> Having first seized his books. Or with a log
> Batter his skull, or paunch him with a stake,
> Or cut his wesand with thy knife.

Or of irresistible delight:

> Be not afeard, the isle is full of noises,
> Sounds, and sweet airs, that give delight and hurt not.
> Sometimes a thousand twangling instruments

Will hum about mine ears; and sometimes voices,
That if I then had waked after long sleep,
Will make me sleep again: and then in dreaming,
The clouds methought would open, and show riches
Ready to drop upon me, that when I waked
I cried to dream again.

Monster as he is, a tiny human spark lives, lost, somewhere in Caliban. Prospero speaks for us all when he says, at the end of the play,

This thing of darkness I
Acknowledge mine.

Ariel vanishes the moment Prospero releases him, light in his going as in his coming; but Caliban remains, heavy as earth; laughable, horrible, pathetic, and unreachable by reason or by love.

Prospero is often frustrated or dismayed in dealing with his "subjects," but like other Shakespearean rulers he feels deeply responsible for their welfare. He tries to *show* them, at least, how they ought to live: "Nothing but heart's sorrow/ And a clear life ensuing," in Ariel's beautiful words. That wisdom, or counsel of perfection, appears in many other plays of Shakespeare's, notably the great comedies and *The Winter's Tale.* And it had been expressed in many ways in the tradition of Europe. The Greeks put it as "Doing, Suffering, Learning." We know it in Christian writings in such phrases as "dying to live," and "losing your life to find it." Dante's *Purgatory,* which Shakespeare never read, is all built on that theme. The growing soul resuffers its mistaken or evil motives in the light of truth, in order to free itself from them. So Prospero tries (as I have pointed out) to free himself by freeing his subjects; but his power is limited; all he can do is *show* them, he cannot directly produce a change of heart in any of them.

That is why the situations which Prospero, as poet-director, "plots" for his subject-characters constitute not a drama, but rather a series of symbolic shows or ceremonies. It has been plausibly suggested that in composing *The Tempest* Shakespeare was influenced by the masques, allegorical pageants devised to celebrate some great occasion in a royal or noble household. Miranda's wedding song is staged like a masque. But students of folklore have found in this play traces of many other ancient rites representing the sufferings and ordeals through which the human must pass to reach true knowledge and freedom. The "mazes, forthrights, and meanders" through which Alonso and his followers are led remind the learned of the labyrinthine journeys of culture-heroes, and their symbolic reenactment in initiation rites like those of the Orphic cults. The banquet offered so mysteriously to Alonso and his followers suggests the sacred feasts in many primitive religions, and also the more familiar rites of Passover and Communion. It produces (as we saw) faith and hope in Gonzalo, despair in Alonso, and a sharper appetite for evil in Antonio and Sebastian: it avails only for those whose hearts are ready to receive it.

Prospero never seems to expect too much from his poetic-ceremonious shows. Stephano, Trinculo, and Caliban are presented, from the first, as laughably unteachable. We are never allowed to forget either Prospero's fallibility or the stubborn darkness in even those whom he loves best. When the fairy tale is ended, all the magic make-believe is gone too, and Prospero is revealed as the mere man he is. When he returns to speak the epilogue, the final illusory appearance is removed, and he speaks as the needy showman. He must have our applause if he is to depart in peace, and he appeals to what fellow-feeling we may have:

> As you from crimes would pardoned be,
> Let your indulgence set me free.

We are back in the real world where only "mercy" itself, not poetry or ceremony, however beautiful, can provide the freedom we need and seek through so many thorny ways. But there is no point in trying to gloss this final speech. It concludes the whole play, and partakes of its strange quality: full of deep feeling, but delicate, mocking, meaning all things to all men.

HENRY VIII

This play was almost certainly written in 1613, two years after *The Tempest*, which would make it the very last play Shakespeare wrote. Many critics during the last hundred years have questioned Shakespeare's authorship of it, rightly pointing out that its tone is different from the rest of his work. But Heminge and Condell, Shakespeare's lifelong associates and the publishers of the First Folio, attributed it all to him, and most experts are now inclined, for lack of any compelling evidence to the contrary, to accept their authority.

It was probably written on the occasion of the visit of the Elector Palatine, who was in England to celebrate his marriage to James I's daughter Elizabeth. This important state occasion, especially since it involved another Elizabeth, would explain why Shakespeare felt obliged to return to the theater after the "farewell" of *The Tempest.* It might also help one to understand the play's rather pedestrian quality—for it lacks the poetic inspiration, not only in the language but in characterization and the conception of the whole, which one expects in Shakespeare. It is not to be compared with the masterpieces; yet it is as competent and stageworthy as one would expect the work of an "old professional" like Shakespeare to be: he met his assignment "as our Roman actors do,/ With untired spirits and formal constancy" (*Julius Caesar,* Act I, scene 2).

For the events of Henry's reign pictured in the play, Shakespeare relied, as usual, upon the chroniclers, Holinshed and Hall, and (for Cranmer's story, the main matter of Act V) upon Foxe's *Booke of Martyrs.* He altered the chronology when it suited his purpose, but except for that he followed his sources very closely, often using their very language with only such slight changes as were required to turn the prose into blank verse. The events he chose to represent would have been familiar to his audience (who might have heard about them from their own fathers or grandfathers) and he calls attention to their authenticity in the Prologue: "Think ye see/ The very persons of our noble story,/ As they were living." Shakespeare's audience loved to see "the very persons" of legend or history walking and talking on the stage.

The play begins with an eyewitness account of the famous "Field of the Cloth of Gold" when Henry, as a young king, met the young King of France, François I, with a great display of emulous splendor; and it ends with the auspicious christening of the infant Elizabeth. It is hardly a play in the usual sense of the word, but rather a series of loosely interwoven stories of some of the strong personalities that rose and fell, in the ceaseless power-struggles of the court, during that part of Henry's reign. In the course of the first three acts we see Cardinal Wolsey reach the height of his power and prestige, and then fall in a moment when Henry discovers his secret correspondence with the Pope. Wolsey's machinations include his skillful ruin of his enemy, the Duke of Buckingham, and his careful promotion of Henry's divorce from his first wife, Katharine of Aragon. That divorce—Henry's first and most painful—enabled him to marry Anne Bullen, who was destined to become the mother of the great Elizabeth, as everyone in the audience knew. Ceremonious pageants and processions (staged as nearly as possible just as they had been originally) are a very important part of this play, and the fourth act consists entirely of two contrasting pageants: the elaborate procession celebrating Anne's coronation, and the pious death of Queen Katharine, with a ballet of white-robed figures that represent her vision of her reception into heaven. The fifth act is devoted largely to the rise of Cranmer, the Protestant churchman whom Henry made Archbishop of Canterbury after Wolsey's fall. Cranmer gives a prophetic eulogy of the infant Elizabeth at the christening ceremony that ends the play, and adds for good measure a prophecy of the felicitous reign of James I, who was of course on the throne when the play was first performed.

The stories of Wolsey and Buckingham, of Queen Katharine and Anne Bullen, and of Cranmer, as Henry protects him from his enemies and then makes him the head of the English Church, are fast-moving and easy to follow, but the meaning Shakespeare saw in them, and, in general, his purpose and attitude in writing this play, are still in dispute. *Henry VIII* superficially resembles the earlier history plays in its appeal to the audience's patriotism, and in its assumption that the national welfare depends upon the crown. But the crown is never in serious jeopardy, as it is in the plays about the Wars of the Roses, and there is no significant central conflict as there is in all the better histories and tragedies. It is true that Henry grows in personal freedom and power as he gets rid of the formidable Wolsey, divorces Katharine to marry young Anne, defies Rome, and makes his loyal servant Cranmer, Archbishop; but these successful moves, which cost the King very little, are hardly the result of a consistent or conscious policy on his part. His wives and his courtiers have clearer and stronger motives, and more interesting careers, than the King. We watch their rises and falls with the comfortable sense that the body politic is secure, much as we now cozily read about the careers of movie stars and the doings of the royal family.

It is often said that the play falls apart at Act IV, when Wolsey's story is over, and Cranmer's, which makes Act V, has not yet begun, and it is sometimes concluded, from this looseness of structure, that Shakespeare cannot have been responsible for the design of the play as a whole. But he employed an episodic structure in the late romances also, especially *Pericles* and *Cymbeline*, which also lack a single central conflict, with a clear climax and turning point. In such plays Shakespeare is less interested in the success or failure of conscious human effort than he is in the "divinity that shapes our ends,/

Rough-hew them how we will," as Hamlet puts it. The Prologue of *Henry VIII* calls our attention to the common mortal fate that inevitably overtakes Henry's famous courtiers:

> Think you see them great,
> And followed with the general throng and sweat
> Of thousand friends. Then, in a moment, see
> How soon this mightiness meets misery.

We are expected to watch the predestined course of events with detachment, and from that point of view above the battle—or subsequent to it—neither the moral qualities of individuals, nor the immediate political issues, seem very important.

That may be one reason why Shakespeare leaves unanswered a number of questions about the events of the play which seem important to us, if we are trying to judge the rights and wrongs of Henry's reign. What, for instance, was the king's real motive in divorcing Katharine? Was he really troubled, as he insists, about the legality of his marriage to his brother's widow? Or did he simply want to marry Anne? Or was he, like many another passionate man, "sincerely" deluding himself with his belated qualms of conscience (Act II, scenes 2 and 4)? Perhaps the whole matter was too awkward to handle frankly on the occasion of another royal marriage; but when a dramatist refrains from looking into his characters' hearts he forfeits the immediate sense of life. In the great plays the characters are vivid and convincing because Shakespeare has his eye on their true springs of action; in this play he shows little interest in motive in that intimate sense. The fact that Anne would give birth to the great Elizabeth was, from the point of view adopted in this play, much more significant than the actual cause of the cruel divorce that made the happy event possible.

Unresolved problems of motivation also surround the stories of Wolsey and Buckingham. Was Buckingham really guilty of treason, as the King seems to believe when he allows him to be executed? Or was he the straightforward, gruffly honest type he seems when we first meet him, an innocent victim of Wolsey's skillful machinations? We hear him protest his innocence and forgive everyone on his way to his execution, but the First and Second Gentlemen who discuss the case, though they like and pity him, seem unsure whether he is innocent or not. As for Cardinal Wolsey, we see unmistakably that he is cruel, ruthless, and unscrupulous as he destroys his enemies and builds his own wealth and power; but he too suddenly makes a pious end when the King cuts him down, assuring us that he repents his life of worldly greed and now craves only forgiveness all around and the peace of heaven. Of course there are plenty of characters in Shakespeare who are not what they seem, and plenty who have a change of heart when their battles are ended. What makes this play unusual is not the complex tangle of good and evil in the characters, but the fact that we see their contradictory acts only from a distance, just as the two Gentlemen do in their scene with Buckingham.

The portrait of Queen Katharine is strikingly different from that of the other important characters, for her motives, as she endeavors to surmount her unjust rejection with dignity, are perfectly clear. The majority of critics find Katharine the most credible and sympathetic character in the play. Perhaps that is because the personality of the real Katharine is so strongly felt in the chronicles which Shakespeare closely followed. She comes through as Spanish in her complete, dignified acceptance of the woman's role, no matter how meanly the King and his ecclesiastical advisers treat her. When she is robbed of her whole status as wife, mother, and Queen, instead of receiving the ceremonious respect traditionally accorded a Spanish matriarch, our sympathy is all with her, and our enthusiasm for Henry's marriage to Anne is correspondingly dampened. Thus the vitality of Katharine's role raises the question of how Shakespeare wanted us to feel about Henry's divorce and remarriage. Did he expect us to relish the irony of the story—the fact that such shabby dealing led to so happy a result, the birth of the miraculous Elizabeth herself? Was he showing us once more that God works in mysterious ways? Or did he assume that his audience, stimulated by the festivities of the royal marriage, and impatiently waiting for the birth of the great Queen, was in no mood to worry about moral problems?

I think one may find a clue to Shakespeare's own view of the ruthless game of court life in the scene (Act II, scene 3) between Anne Bullen and the Old Lady, which he must have devised himself without the help of his sources. They have just learned that Katharine is to be divorced; they agree that she does not deserve such treatment, and that in general it would be better to accept a lowly status than to fall from a high one:

OLD LADY

Alas poor lady,
She's a stranger now again.

ANNE

So much the more

Must pity drop upon her. Verily
I swear, 'tis better to be lowly born,
And range with humble livers in content,
Then to be perked up in a glistering grief,
And wear a golden sorrow.

OLD LADY

Our content
Is our best having.

But then Anne (who guesses Henry's infatuation with her) insists that she would not be a queen if she could, and the Old Lady, who has lived all her life at court, grows mocking:

'Tis strange; a threepence bowed would hire me,
Old as I am, to queen it. But I pray you,
What think you of a duchess? Have you limbs
To bear that load of title?

The Lord Chamberlain comes to announce to Anne that Henry has made her Marchioness of Pembroke, with an income of a thousand pounds a year, and the Old Lady is inspired to even more sardonic mirth:

By this time
I know your back will bear a duchess. Say,
Are you not stronger than you were?

The unjust ups and downs of life at court are seen with devastating clarity, but they are accepted as inevitable, greedy human nature being what it is. The Old Lady sees the worldly game, even while she is in it, with the objectivity that Buckingham and Wolsey reach only when they are ready to die. Old Lear, at the end of his life, has the same vision of the bitter struggles of ambitious men, but he expresses it in such poetry as is not to be found anywhere in this play:

So we'll live,
And pray, and sing, and tell old tales, and laugh
At gilded butterflies; and hear poor rogues
Talk of court news, and we'll talk with them too,
Who loses, and who wins, who's in, who's out;
And take upon's the mystery of things,
As if we were God's spies.

In *Henry VIII* we follow court news and learn who's in, who's out, but the deeper, more intense vision, "the mystery of things," is never reached.

If (as I believe) Shakespeare is responsible for this play, his masterful hand is to be recognized only in the sureness with which he fulfilled a modest professional assignment. His aim was to celebrate the marriage of Princess Elizabeth by reminding his audience of some of the great events that preceded the birth of the first and greatest Elizabeth. He wanted to put on his stage the "very persons" of history, and to reproduce as accurately as possible the pageantry of Katharine's trial, Anne's coronation, Elizabeth's christening, which must have moved the English of that time just as the wonderful pageantry of Churchill's funeral procession moved them in this century. Out of these ingredients he made a show which still holds us in the theater, and makes us forget all problems of psychology or ethics.

BIBLIOGRAPHICAL NOTES

INDEX

Bibliographical Notes

This short list is not intended as a guide to the Shakespeare literature, or even as an indication of my own indebtedness. The titles have been selected for their relevance to the theme of this book: an attempt to understand Shakespeare's basic theatrical aims in giving form and meaning to the old stories he used.

Bullough, Geoffrey (editor). *Narrative and Dramatic Sources of Shakespeare*. London and New York: 1957

Six volumes of this series have appeared (1968) and it is expected that the series will be completed within a very few years. It is now the only work of its kind, containing not only the chief sources and analogues, but very perceptive comments by the editor on Shakespeare's use of his sources.

PRELIMINARY CONSIDERATIONS

On Reading Shakespeare

Bryant, J. A., Jr. *Hippolyta's View. Some Christian Aspects of Shakespeare's Plays*. University of Kentucky: 1961

Curry, Walter Clyde. *Shakespeare's Philosophical Patterns*. Baton Rouge: 1937

Siegel, Paul N. *Shakespearean Tragedy and the Elizabethan Compromise*. New York: 1957

Tillyard, E. M. W. *The Elizabethan World-Picture*. London: 1943

The above four books are important recent studies of the classical-Christian "world-picture" that Shakespeare used in composing his plays.

Auerbach, Erich. *Mimesis*. Princeton: 1953

Auerbach, Erich. *Scenes from the Drama of European Literature*. New York: 1959

Fergusson, F. *Dante*. New York: 1966

Singleton, Charles S. *Dante Studies*, 1 and 2. Cambridge: 1958

The above books discuss, in various ways, the "religious realism" which first appears full-blown in Dante.

Aristotle's *Poetics*. With an Introductory Essay by Francis Fergusson. New York: 1961

Aristotle's theory of drama as the imitation of action is assumed in all the analyses of Shakespeare's plays in this book.

The Chronology of Shakespeare's Career

Bentley, Gerald Eades. *Shakespeare, a Biographical Handbook.* New Haven: 1961
A scholarly statement of the known facts, "with the strictest fidelity to the surviving documents," from many of which extensive quotations are offered.

Chute, Marchette. *Shakespeare of London.* New York: 1956
A very readable biography, containing the known facts without the usual uncertain speculations. Good on Shakespeare's Stratford and London.

Shakespeare's Theater

Hodges, C. Walter. *The Globe Restored.* New York: 1954
A short, readable account of the Globe Theatre, with many useful illustrations.

I. APPRENTICESHIP TO THE LONDON THEATER

Baker, Howard. *Induction to Tragedy.* Baton Rouge: 1939
This book is subtitled "A Study in a Development of Form in *Gorboduc, The Spanish Tragedy* and *Titus Andronicus.*" A useful study of the medieval and Senecan influences on Shakespeare in his youth.

Studies of Shakespeare, Milton and Donne. University of Michigan Publications. New York: 1925
Contains an important essay by O. J. Campbell on the influences of the *commedia dell'arte* on Shakespeare's early comedies.

Tillyard, E. M. W. *Shakespeare's History of Plays.* London: 1956
This is the standard account of Shakespeare's English history plays and their sources, especially the Chronicles.

II. MASTERY OF THE POPULAR THEATER: ROMANCE AND ENGLISH HISTORY

Barber, C. L. *Shakespeare's Festive Comedy. A Study of Dramatic Form and Its Relation to Social Custom.* Princeton: 1959

A most illuminating account of Shakespeare's use of folk festivals, rites and customs of various kinds, especially in his comedy.

The Book of the Courtier. By Baldassare Castiglione. Translated by Sir Thomas Hoby. Introduction by W. H. Rowse, with a note on Castiglione and English literature by W. B. Drayton Henderson. London and New York: 1956
This is the Elizabethan translation of the treatise on manners which is essential for understanding Shakespeare's romantic comedy.

De Rougemont, Denis. *Love in the Western World*. New York: 1957
An important if controversial study of the love-death theme in erotic literature from the troubadours to the present. There is a short chapter on *Romeo and Juliet*.

Empson, William, *Some Versions of Pastoral*. New York: 1961
An essay on the "double plot" in English drama, its moral and social meanings, and its theatrical utility; helpful in understanding the dramatic form which emerges clearly in Shakespeare's second phase.

Frye, Northrop. *A Natural Perspective. The Development of Shakespearean Comedy and Romance*. New York and London: 1965
A sophisticated and stimulating meditation on all of Shakespeare's plays that end happily, from *The Comedy of Errors* through *The Tempest*.

III. THE MANY-SIDED TRAGIC VISION OF SHAKESPEARE'S MATURITY

Bradley, A. C. *Shakespearean Tragedy*. New York: 1955
A standard work epitomizing the best nineteenth-century criticism of Shakespeare, which stresses the psychological analysis of his characters. This volume is concerned with *Hamlet, Othello, Lear*, and *Macbeth*.

Campbell, O. J. *Comicall Satyre and Shakespeare's Troilus and Cressida*. San Marino: 1959
A learned and perceptive account of "Comicall Satyre" as it had developed in England, and influenced not only *Troilus and Cressida* but other sardonic parables of Shakespeare.

Fergusson, F. *The Idea of a Theater*. Princeton: 1949
The chapter on *Hamlet* in this book endeavors to place that play in relation to other great forms of tragedy.

Knight, G. Wilson. *The Imperial Theme*. Oxford: 1931
Knight, G. Wilson. *The Wheel of Fire*. New York: 1957
These two books contain stimulating interpretations of Shakespeare's tragedies as religious poetry.

Lawrence, W. W. *Shakespeare's Problem Comedies.* New York: 1931
An influential (though now somewhat dated) study of *All's Well That Ends Well, Measure for Measure, Troilus and Cressida,* and *Cymbeline,* in the light of Shakespeare's medieval heritage.

MacCallum, M. W. *Shakespeare's Roman Plays and Their Background.* London: 1910
A standard work on the subject.

Murray, Gilbert. *The Classical Tradition in Poetry.* New York: 1957
Chapter VIII contains a useful summary of the evidence for the sources of *Hamlet* and a discussion of the many parallels between the legendary figures of Hamlet and Orestes.

Phillips, J. E. *The State in Shakespeare's Greek and Roman Plays.* New York: 1940
An account of the political philosophy of Shakespeare's time, and its influence on his plays about Rome or Greece.

IV. FINAL RETROSPECT: FAITH AND MAKE-BELIEVE

Still, Colin. *The Timeless Theme.* London: 1936
The thesis of this influential and suggestive book is that certain "permanent realities of human experience" are similarly represented in myth, ceremony, folklore, and art and literature. In the second part these ideas are used to interpret *The Tempest.*

Traversi, D. A. *Shakespeare, The Last Phase.* New York: 1953
One of the earliest and most important critical studies of the last group of plays, demonstrating their unique qualities and their importance in Shakespeare's work as a whole.

Index

THIS BOOK WAS SET IN
CALEDONIA AND BULMER TYPES BY
BROWN BROTHERS LINOTYPERS, INC.
IT WAS PRINTED AND BOUND BY
MONTAUK BOOK MFG. CO., INC.
IT WAS DESIGNED BY
LARRY KAMP AND JULIAN HAMER